Free but Regulated
Conflicting Traditions in Media Law

Free but Regulated

Conflicting Traditions in Media Law

(COLLECTED ESSAYS WITH COMMENTARY)

DANIEL L. BRENNER

AND

WILLIAM L. RIVERS

THE IOWA STATE UNIVERSITY PRESS / AMES

1 9 8 2

© 1982 The Iowa State University Press. All rights reserved

Composed and printed by The Iowa State University Press, Ames, Iowa 50010

First edition, 1982

Library of Congress Cataloging in Publication Data
Main entry under title:

Free but regulated.

Includes index.
1. Mass media—Law and legislation—United States—Addresses, essays, lectures. I. Brenner, Daniel L. 1951–   . II. Rivers, William L.

KF2750.A75F73	343.73′099	82–15362
ISBN 0–8138–0756–5	347.30399	AACR2

CONTENTS

PREFACE

OUR CHARACTERIZATION of mass media law as a "work in progress" has dictated the approach we have taken (as well as avoided) in this book. We have not attempted to collect a series of cases from the courts and administrative agencies dealing with communications law. Nor have we undertaken to provide a guidebook for practicing journalists as to the do's and don'ts of the law in this area.

What we have done is to collect a group of essays on several diverse legal topics that we believe belong under the rubric of mass media law. Some of the essays try to explain the concepts underlying the legal problems of the mass media; others review the course of the law and suggest future pathways. Often what is emphasized in the discussions of laws and cases are the issues that have not yet been decided by lawmakers or the courts. The gathered authors range from full-time academics to practicing journalists and attorneys, and the divergent professional outlooks often shape their expressions.

We follow each essay or group of essays with commentaries about what has been expressed. Readers may agree with the author or with the commentator or with only themselves. But they undoubtedly will experience reactions to the expression of ideas here. Because the rules are not already fixed, and so many subjective factors are involved, no two minds will always agree. By including the thoughts of one of the two commentators readers ought to become aware of the disagreements in the law and policies of mass media regulation.

The articles reprinted in full or in part represent a cross-section of periodicals, legal and general. The criterion for including an article was its pertinence to a media regulation trend that was consistent and yet undergoing redefinition in recent years by statute or case law.

A note or two about the ground rules for our abridgements is in order. Textual footnotes are deleted where not pertinent to the chapter topic, as are nonessential citation footnotes. United States Supreme Court decisions are cited to their location in *U.S. Reports,* regardless how they were cited in the original text. Deletion of material of less than a paragraph is indicated by three spaced ellipses; deletion of more than a paragraph is indicated by a full line of ellipses. Other changes appear within brackets; tables and references to tables are deleted without comment, as are corrections of minor typographic errors and solecisms. Citation to the original publication of each article appears on the opening page of the article.

This book takes a novel approach to the study of mass media law and, it is hoped, opens a new channel toward its understanding. We believe that it provides a rounded overview of the pertinent law surrounding the topics covered. As a course text, it can stand alone or be used in conjunction with judicial and administrative decisions selected by the instructor.

A final word about the collaborative process: happy it is when two individuals can work together over several years (as it turns out) to produce a finished work; happier still when they begin as apprentice and mentor and end as colleagues. For then, the student has learned and the teacher has taught.

This book is dedicated to our families, who provided the essential patience and encouragement for its completion.

DANIEL L. BRENNER
Washington, D.C.

WILLIAM L. RIVERS
Stanford, California

Free but Regulated

Conflicting Traditions in Media Law

1

Mass Media Law: An Overview

Daniel L. Brenner and William L. Rivers

In one sense, the development of mass media law has not differed significantly from the evolution of other bodies of American law. Like the growth of the law of contracts, property, or criminal procedure, legal doctrines pertaining to mass communications enterprises have matured as a consequence of other factors operating in society. Legal acts are the products of social forces: advances in technology, growing sophistication in describing and regulating economic relationships, and enhanced sensitivity to the interface between the individual and society, to mention three important ones. While not necessarily always in a cause-effect relationship with such forces, movement in another area of society often sets off a concomitant reaction in the law.

What separates the development of mass media law from other more established legal subjects is its special and unavoidable susceptibility to the mentioned factors of social change in the twentieth century.

While many fields of law have enjoyed slow, steady growth based on centuries of common understandings and commonsense applications of principles to often repeated human conduct, mass communications law has grown with celerity. Judicial output on the subject is better described by quantum jumps than by a smooth wave. Legal practitioners are more likely to find answers in looseleaf reporting services of recent cases or in technical developments newsletters than in bound treatises.

Growth of Technology

Prominent among the reasons for this hurried development is the seemingly never-ending advances in the technology of the media. Although media of expression have existed since humans first chose to communicate to their neighbors by a route that deviated from voice to ear, electronic message carrying has undergone a technological revolution in this century. Regulation of radio and television, the most influential of the message carriers today, is in an infant stage from the standpoint of Anglo-American legal history. Other electronic systems—cable television, in-home computer terminals, video discs, cassettes, games, and direct broadcast satellites—have yet to reach their full marketplace development. As they grow, they consume an important part of the law's attention.

Even today's newspaper industry, which can point to a tradition spanning 300 years, has become a different technological entity in the second half of this century. Ancestors of today's publishers would hardly recognize the modern aggregation of cold type printing systems carrying computer edited stories displayed on cathode ray tubes, and eventually published in competition with the electronic press, which usually bests it in a race to the buying public. By contrast, the centuries-old legal traditions surrounding most other forms of human conduct seem undynamic. They are not, of course; but activities addressed by other bodies of law, for example, transfer of a plot of land, a carrier's agreement to ship goods for a manufacturer, or breaking and entering a dwelling to commit larceny once inside—are by now familiar patterns of conduct, and the legal rules concerning them are fairly well established.

While the law in these areas continually undergoes refinements, the law of mass communications is continually overtaken by technological changes that confound those who attempt to contain its dimensions and consolidate its principles. Legal development usually is concerned with applying black-letter principles to novel fact situations; development in the media encounters first-run fact situations and must come up with novel principles at the same time.

SOPHISTICATION OF ECONOMIC RELATIONSHIPS

Economic relationships also affect the growth of communications law profoundly. Consider the cornerstone of mass media law, the First Amendment to the United States Constitution. It provides in unambiguous words (on the face) that "Congress shall make no law . . . abridging the freedom of speech, or of the press." During the three decades they served together on the United States Supreme Court, Justices Hugo Black and William O. Douglas argued that the First Amendment means literally what it says.

But the press of the Founding Fathers hardly resembles the mass media today. It is an unambiguous fact of contemporary life that control of many of the most powerful media voices (the contemporary "press" in First Amendment terms) primarily resides in corporations employing hundreds or thousands and owned by thousands of shareholders. Dozens of newspapers may belong to one chain, hundreds of television outlets are linked to the same program sources. Often, a company's media activities are one of many diverse enterprises spanning several industrial sectors. Total annual advertising revenues collected by the mass media in this country must be counted in billions of dollars. Television broadcasting, although organized around local stations, is heavily influenced by national network program service; daily newspapers rely on national press associations and worldwide feature syndicates.

Poised against this impressive array of power, talent, and capital are the First Amendment interests of individual readers, speakers, and listeners who rely on the editorial discretion of those in the media who have the responsibility for providing a proper flow of ideas and information. While the government surely is a potential censor of views and ideas—that disturbing possibility is, after all, the First Amendment's explicit concern—it is argued strenuously by some that those in control of large media operations also pose a significant threat to the ideal of free expression.

It is maintained that television networks especially are wary of alienating any substantial portion of their vast potential audience for their advertisers. This leads to two types of criticism. From the left side of the spectrum it is argued that networks steer away from offensive themes, unpopular ideas. From the right it is insisted that immorality is palmed off as the norm in order to attract audiences. By limiting the level of entertainment programming to the lowest common denominator, television maintains high returns from advertising even though it is done at the expense of the diversity contemplated by the First Amendment. Similarly, mass market motion picture distributors and publishers avoid coverage of the unpopular or unknown in order to maximize circulation of the products they provide.

Whatever the occasional merit of these arguments, the media are shielded by the First Amendment from attempts to use the government to force greater access for particular ideas. This is as it should be, for governmental dictation over what the media carry poses a far more sinister threat to the aims of freedom of speech and press than do the excesses that media critics identify from time to time.

Part of the assault on the media stems from the size of television networks and other conglomerate enterprises. Yet the actual impact of large corporate ownership of important media outlets may have little to do with the resulting product; output may be more a matter of the mass audience served than who does the serving. And greater diversity may result by increasing the number of outlets and the demographics of their owners rather than by trying to tinker with the operation of existing owners. Still, changing patterns of media ownership keep the laws regulating these industries from firming up into a comprehensive, orderly scheme.

THE INDIVIDUAL AND SOCIETY

In ways that more doctrinally established laws do not, communications law seems to be affected by the growing concern for the individual in society. As citizens become increasingly devoted to leisure-time activity and as information processing enlarges in social significance, the media cannot avoid influencing each of us. Again, television provides a preeminent example of a medium caught up in these changes and significantly influencing our thought and our behavior.

Today, television is present in 98 percent of American homes and on average is turned on from six to seven hours each day. In public opinion surveys of Americans it consistently ranks as the most popular free-time activity. This ever-mounting interaction with television programming and advertising has triggered increasing concern about possible consequences on child development, especially in the areas of sex and violence, as well as on the cultivation of community values and individual self-image. As the child experiences more and more of life vicariously through television, role models and value choices become increasingly influenced by the medium's view of life. As with other media, television does not simply reflect society but becomes integrated into social processes and effects on individuals.

As carriers of advertising, the mass media, serving as an industry peripheral to others, possess an impact that, though seldom as baleful as some claim, is more pervasive than any other social institution. Nor can their effectiveness in generating new wants and desires for products and services be denied. Psychologists have only dimly explained the interaction of the mass media with individual choice; yet the significant extent of that interaction is evident, even if measured only by the time spent attending to television, radio, newspapers, and magazines.

Moreover, as concern for self-understanding increases, we set increasing store by the media's ability to provide a mirror and model for ourselves. We want programs and periodicals that make us think more and react more, and that heighten our sense of self and environment, both physical and spiritual. Yet, historically speaking, the legal mandate for such challenging expression, the First Amendment, was fashioned in a world where exploration into the human mind and soul did not act as a spur to its adoption. Its framers' rather narrow objective, it seems, was to incorporate into American law the English doctrine that forbade prior restraint of the press for publishing seditious libel. As Leonard Levy in *Freedom of Speech and Press in Early American History* (1963) explained: "The persistent image of colonial America as a society in which freedom of expression was cherished is an hallucination of sentiment that ignores history."

In fact, the concept that the First Amendment supplies a legal foundation for protecting expression to enrich the individual no matter how objectionable it may be to the authorities appears for the first time in court opinions in the twentieth century and is yet to receive extensive approval in the Supreme Court. Case law supporting wide-ranging opportunity for free expression as a constitutionally sanctioned route to greater understanding of humankind and society has simply not kept pace with our proclivity for self-knowledge and personal and social experimentation.

What is significant here about the three dynamic social forces of technology, economics, and personal discovery is that each has operated so rapidly as to outpace the ability of mass media law to account adequately for them. Courts and legislatures have been incapable of providing a steady framework in which to balance these forces as they apply to the media. Instead, the case law development has been interstitial, that is, directed to particular fact situations with particular solutions, leaving little guidance as to the broad strokes of this new body of law.

With so dynamic and unfinished a field, piece by piece development is natural. And since the time a majority of the Supreme Court declined to follow Black's and Douglas's absolutists' views of the First Amendment, communications law has been beset by the tension implicit in keeping as small as possible the distance between the literal words of the First Amendment and its judicial interpretation. This healthy tension produces the tentativeness that characterizes media law today: media that are free but regulated—a complicated, often entertaining balancing act, featuring myriad competing significant interests, each of which must be considered if the outcome is to be sensible.

THE ISSUES COVERED

Despite the erratic growth of mass media jurisprudence, certain principles underlying each area have remained fairly steady. These principles constitute the core Law behind each body of laws. Looking sequentially at the subjects addressed by the essays and commentaries that follow, we can in a general way summarize the common understandings underpinning the law in each area. While hardly exhaustive, this synopsis can be kept in mind as these diverse opinions are examined.

FREEDOM OF EXPRESSION: THE FIRST AMENDMENT SPEECH AND PRESS GUARANTEES. The grant of a free press in the Bill of Rights provides a constitutional footing for individuals and organizations to go about publishing what they desire without fear that the government will stop them before they distribute their expression or that they will be punished afterward for having done so. The "law" of the First Amendment is somewhat idiosyncratic; while we may all agree on broad principles, unless you share the position, as Justices Black and Douglas urged, that no line may be permissibly drawn between protected and unprotected speech, then you will draw it closer or farther away from the line of absolute protection than will the next person. It is here that the subjectivity in First Amendment law arises initially.

Freedom of the press, and, more generally, freedom of speech, spring primarily from the libertarian philosophy on which this country was founded: everyone should be free to speak and write his or her own thoughts. The clash of conflicting ideas, the Founding Fathers believed, would produce something called Truth. And even if Truth did not emerge right away, the evil of censorship outweighed the benefits that prior censorship might bring.

But this interpretation reflects the lofty *philosophy* of freedom. However ringingly a nation's constitution states a belief in freedom, in practice every society restricts free expression.

As an integral part of the "Supreme Law of the Land," the free speech and free press guarantees of the First Amendment have become the fount from which all laws protective of the press flow. It is language to which journalists ultimately can turn to anchor their claim of protection against government interference in the reporting functions of gathering and distributing information. As you examine the issues covered by this book, you should consider how the First Amendment operates as an independent objective to be served by the established legal doctrines.

DIFFERENT MEDIA, DIFFERING TREATMENT? The Supreme Court observed in the 1952 decision *Joseph Burstyn, Inc.* v. *Wilson* that each method of expression "tends to present its own peculiar problems" when it comes to the First Amendment. But how different should the First Amendment treatment of print and electronic journalism be? The justifications that sanctioned a licensing scheme for broadcasting wane in the world of channel plenty promised by cable and other modes of video delivery. The providing of First Amendment parity for all media may be desirable for many reasons but what do broadcasters lose when they abandon the more than half a century of licensing? Still, what can justify a content related approach to one segment of mass media that would be intolerable if applied to another?

ACCESS TO INFORMATION: PROTECTING THE GATHERER. Whether it is print or electronic, every mass medium obtains some protection from governmental intrusion as it undertakes to gather, analyze, and distribute information. Each of these sequential functions has legal principles attached that restrict or protect them. When it comes to obtaining access to information, reporters must be able to gain the trust of confidential informants and they must not be viewed as conduits to the police. An important issue is whether reporters may be permitted to remain silent as to the names of confidants, even when the identity of news sources would be helpful to law enforcement officials. The competing public policy interests of first, obtaining every person's evidence for use in investigations and trials, and second, maintaining a free press by protecting reporters' ability to remain silent about sources, produce a conflict in our law. This conflict becomes especially acute when the need for the source's identity is critical in the eyes of the general public and the injury to the reporter's continued access to information appears to be slight.

ACCESS TO INFORMATION: WHAT SHOULD BE AVAILABLE? The purpose behind privacy laws, both common law and statutory, is to enforce "the right to be let alone," that is, to be free from unwarranted publicity. To a reporter bent on disclosing an item of information hitherto uncirculated and within his or her self-styled scope of what is newsworthy, the ends served by a vigorously enforced right to privacy seem at odds with the purposes of the First Amendment. It is the clash between these two rights—the public's right to know and the individual's right to be left alone—that makes hazardous any absolute judgments regarding the enforceability of the right to privacy.

DISTRIBUTING INFORMATION: WHEN THE EXECUTIVE TRIES TO STOP RELEASE. If any purpose is served by allowing the government to be able to prevent the publication of information, it would rest on the reasoning that on balance the harm visited upon the public interest by publication outweighs the offense to the First Amendment's guarantees against restraining speech prior to distribution. During time of war, when release of sensitive information could lead to death of United States soldiers or defeat of our military, the doctrine of prior restraints becomes more reasonable. In such circumstances the doctrine constitutes part of society's self-defense against destruction by its own liberality. Other than in these limited situations, however, the application of prior restraint has been disfavored.

DISTRIBUTING INFORMATION: WHEN COURTS TRY TO STOP RELEASE. While the guarantee of a free and unbridled press holds a high place in our constitutional regime, it must also be recognized that exercise of that guarantee can harm the orderly administration of justice. More particularly, the right of an accused individual to a fair trial can be abridged by excessive publicity that may make selection of an unbiased jury extremely difficult or may leave the impression of guilt in the minds of the public even though the individual is ultimately judged to be not guilty. The right to a fair trial based on evidence presented in the courtroom instead of a trial by headline is the essence of a constitutional democracy. Determining a fair press law for the courtroom, in which the rights of both the defendant and the public (as put forward by the reporter) are fairly balanced, eludes a simple, one-rule answer.

"UNPROTECTED" EXPRESSION: OBSCENITY. The purpose of obscenity laws has, at least on the surface, been clear: to deny to sexually oriented material so lewd as to exceed the limits of acceptability of the individual receiving it the constitutional protection generally accorded to all other expression. More than any other subpart of mass media law discussed in this book, the enforcement of obscenity laws draws impetus from a perceived moral tone of the society in which such expression seeks to survive and thrive. Obscenity laws inquire into how disgusting expression can become before the shield of the First Amendment must be withdrawn in order to preserve a particular level of public civility. As a result of this deference shown to the heterogeneous animal known as "contemporary society," the questions of what obscenity is, and, more important, who should be passing judgment on expression alleged to be obscene, have remain unsolved mysteries. In light of the widespread proliferation of and definitional ambiguity surrounding scatological words and pictures, it has become questionable whether continued prosecutions under obscenity laws make practical or moral sense.

"UNPROTECTED" EXPRESSION: OFFENSIVE SPEECH. While obscenity, once recognized, has been held to be unprotected speech, nonobscene expression—for example, violence on television and in motion pictures; distribution of indecent (but not obscene) material; offensive or grotesque depictions; or sick or indisputable lowbrow entertainment—is assumably protected by the First Amendment. Yet it is clear that such expression offends many people, which explains why efforts to censor such work often enjoy popular support. Many persons believe that the First Amendment should protect the interests of people who do *not* wish to receive expression they consider offensive. The ensuing battle between the would-haves and the would-have-nots of offensive expression often ends with no clear victor.

"UNPROTECTED" EXPRESSION: ONE-SIDED, DECEPTIVE, UNFAIR SPEECH. The purposes traditionally ascribed to advertising regulations include driving from the marketplace deceptive and false claims for goods and services and controlling the distribution of dangerous products, or at least affecting their use. While the obvious dangers of advertising excesses, such as cash swindles or snake-oil poisoning, make regulation of advertising not wholly repugnant to civil libertarians, the limits of the power of government to regulate advertising under the First Amendment have only begun to be tested. And the trend suggests that much government interference with advertising, as with editorial content, cannot withstand First Amendment scrutiny.

When it comes to television, "fairness" is supposedly assured by the Federal Communications Commission's fairness doctrine, which requires radio and television licensees to provide contrasting viewpoints of controversial issues of public importance. The issue presented by continued enforcement of the doctrine is not whether the presentation of diverse viewpoints is a good idea. Nearly everyone assumes it is. Rather, the debate concerns who should determine when the proper balance of viewpoints has been struck: the government or the press?

"UNPROTECTED" EXPRESSION: SPEECH THAT INJURES REPUTATION OR ECONOMIC INTERESTS. In one sense defamation (libel and slander) constitutes the oldest branch of mass media regulation. It is the centuries-old legal recognition that the state must permit an individual to recover for injury to reputation by the written or spoken word of another. In a different sense, however, defamation by the mass media became a new issue when the Supreme Court in 1964 in *New York Times Co.* v. *Sullivan* indicated that the First Amendment provided a limited immunity for the press from liability for defamatory publication. The decision relied upon the assumption that in the absence of a constitutionally provided "breathing space," the press would be reluctant to publish information that would be useful to discussion of issues of public importance but possibly also injurious to reputation. To encourage free expression in such sensitive areas, the Supreme Court created a region of constitutional privilege for defamatory statements published by the press. The end zones of that region are being probed by the courts.

Copyright is a further economic interest that ties together the individual with the creative possibilities in a society possessing a First Amendment. By protecting an author's economic interest in original work by punishing unauthorized copying, copyright law creates an incentive in the marketplace to spur artistic expression. This result is also consistent with the First Amendment's hospitality toward diverse, original ideas.

Not only can intellectual invention be rewarded by the copyright law grant of a copying monopoly; reward may also be had by planned exploitation of one's name and likeness for whatever it may fetch in the marketplace, from product endorsements to appearances on television talk shows. The right of a celebrity to control and profit from public exposure—the right of publicity—is another economic interest over which the individual and the media interact. It lacks the assumption of the right of privacy for the celebrity does not expect to be let alone. Yet it is akin to privacy for it protects the individual's right to determine the timing and terms of exposure.

ESPECIALLY PROTECTED SPEECH: RIGHTS OF ACCESS TO THE MEDIA. "Media access" suggests a broad range of concepts: access to particular ideas or speakers, access to television channels, access to decision makers in the newsroom or in the front office. Our concern here is with the availability of access for the individual speaker, particularly with respect to television or radio. Just as the soapbox of the nineteenth century provided a would-be orator with a platform (literally) from which to exercise his or her freedom of expression, so today the television or radio channel has become an electronic soapbox for those privileged to enjoy access to it. Access therefore involves more than the fairness doctrine, for it relates not only to what ideas will be heard, but who will be entitled to express them, and who will control how they will be expressed.

TOWARD A TRUE MARKETPLACE FOR THE MARKETPLACE OF IDEAS. The initial motivation for treating broadcast speech differently from other communication was that radio frequencies were considered so scarce that those permitted to hold licenses were to act as proxies for those not so privileged. This decision, implemented by the active involvement of government regulators, would assure wider diversity of expression in a medium where all who wished to speak could not practically do so.

Difficulties arose under this assumption in light of the First Amendment's abhorrence of official tinkering with private expression. Abolition of the fairness doctrine, even of the licensing scheme itself with its "public interest" test, has been advocated.

While the need to safeguard the First Amendment rights of non-licensees is no less significant today than when federal regulation was first introduced in 1927, doubt has been cast on the continuing wisdom of comprehensive broadcast regulation based on electromagnetic spectrum scarcity.

Meanwhile cable television sidesteps the spectrum question by transmitting by wires instead of over the air. Its pay cable service, which permits viewers to pay directly for programs they like rather than allowing advertiser supported television stations to preselect programming, has become the most significant threat and alternative to over-the-air television. And, as cable burrows beneath our neighborhoods, satellites with direct-to-home transmissions present another video delivery system that will compete with existing distribution channels.

The topics examined by means of essays and commentaries do not represent the entire range of legal problems that confronts journalists and media operators. Like all industries, the communications industry has developed its own special customs and practices in such fields as labor law, contracts, and taxation; and antitrust litigation involving communications entities has been particularly active, with scores of media defendants. The topics we have chosen deal particularly with interpreting the First Amendment in the light of competing public policy interests. Together they suggest the degree to which all journalists are involved in the legal process and all lawyers in the information gathering and distribution process.

Reporters need not be attorneys, but they must always be students of communications law. Otherwise they may bring down suits on their employers (and their employers' wrath on themselves); or, recognizing their own ignorance, they will be timid in carrying out their functions as stewards of the public's right to know. Neither result bodes well for the First Amendment.

Likewise lawyers must be aware that the body of law dealing with the mass media includes a heavy public policy component as a result of its grounding in the First Amendment. Consequently the issues that arise often are not decided on purely legal considerations, but involve decisions based on an articulation and weighing of competing public policies present in a particular set of facts. In fashioning advice to a communications client, lawyer sensitivity to the way in which the press collects, produces, and distributes its product contributes much to competent representation.

If it has not already been made apparent by now, neither our essayists nor we possess any monopoly on the right answers here. Beginning from the working principles described above, each mass media law topic lends itself to varying shades of refinement, based pretty much on how literally the decision maker believes that the command of the First Amendment should be taken. The greater its application, the less the government should be involved with the media, and the less compelling the rationales behind laws permitting government intervention become.

The excitement and appeal of the study of mass media law lies in the subjective evaluation of the First Amendment. The authors, as students of the media and the First Amendment, have found the questions posed by the essays in this book to be highly challenging and we hope readers, in thinking critically about the logic they offer, will find them equally so.

2

Freedom of Expression: The First Amendment Speech and Press Guarantees

THE AUTHORS

JUSTICE POTTER STEWART served as an associate justice of the United States Supreme Court from 1958 to 1981 and of course had a full, close view of the many cases involving the press that came before the Court. Long considered a "swing vote" on both the Warren and Burger courts, Justice Stewart defied classification in his voting as being predominantly liberal or conservative. He was graduated cum laude from Yale, then was graduated cum laude from Yale Law School.

When a justice of the Supreme Court speaks, those who are not lawyers listen with respect. So, too, do scholarly lawyers but often with a more critical ear.

MELVILLE B. NIMMER, professor of law at the University of California, Los Angeles, attacks the problem of freedom of the press from a somewhat different stance. Nimmer earned the B.A. degree at the University of California, Berkeley, then a law degree from Harvard, which he completed in 1950. Author of a leading treatise on United States copyright law, he has been a professor of law since 1963; he serves also as counsel to a leading motion picture law firm in Los Angeles.

"Or of the Press"

POTTER STEWART

I TURN this morning to an inquiry into an aspect of constitutional law that has only recently begun to engage the attention of the Supreme Court. Specifically, I shall discuss the role of the organized press—of the daily newspapers and other established news media—in the system of government created by our Constitution.

It was less than a decade ago—during the Vietnam years—that the people of our country began to become aware of the twin phenomena on a national scale of so-called investigative reporting and an adversary press—that is, a press adversary to the Executive Branch of the Federal Government. And only in the two short years that culminated last summer in the resignation of a President did we fully realize the enormous power that an investigative and adversary press can exert.

The public opinion polls that I have seen indicate that some Americans firmly believe that the former Vice President and former President of the United States were hounded out of office by an arrogant and irresponsible press that had outrageously usurped dictatorial power. And it

Excerpted from an address on November 2, 1974, at the Yale Law School Sesquicentennial Convocation, New Haven, Connecticut.
Reprinted from *Hastings Law Journal* 26(1975):632–37. Courtesy, Justice Potter Stewart.

seems clear that many more Americans, while appreciating and even applauding the service performed by the press in exposing official wrongdoing at the highest levels of our national government, are nonetheless deeply disturbed by what they consider to be the illegitimate power of the organized press in the political structure of our society. It is my thesis this morning that, on the contrary, the established American press in the past ten years, and particularly in the past two years, has performed precisely the function it was intended to perform by those who wrote the First Amendment of our Constitution. I further submit that this thesis is supported by the relevant decisions of the Supreme Court.

Surprisingly, despite the importance of newspapers in the political and social life of our country the Supreme Court has not until very recently been called upon to delineate their constitutional role in our structure of government.

Our history is filled with struggles over the rights and prerogatives of the press, but these disputes rarely found their way to the Supreme Court. The early years of the Republic witnessed controversy over the constitutional validity of the short-lived Alien and Sedition Act, but the controversy never reached the Court. In the next half century there was nationwide turmoil over the right of the organized press to advocate the then subversive view that slavery should be abolished. In Illinois a publisher was killed for publishing abolitionist views. But none of this history made First Amendment law because the Court had earlier held that the Bill of Rights applied only against the Federal Government, not against the individual states.

With the passage of the Fourteenth Amendment, the constitutional framework was modified, and by the 1920's the Court had established that the protections of the First Amendment extend against all government—federal, state, and local.

The next fifty years witnessed a great outpouring of First Amendment litigation, all of which inspired books and articles beyond number. But, with few exceptions, neither these First Amendment cases nor their commentators squarely considered the Constitution's guarantee of a Free Press. Instead, the focus was on its guarantee of free speech. The Court's decisions dealt with the rights of isolated individuals, or of unpopular minority groups, to stand up against governmental power representing an angry or frightened majority. The cases that came to the Court during those years involved the rights of the soapbox orator, the nonconformist pamphleteer, the religious evangelist. The Court was seldom asked to define the rights and privileges, or the responsibilities, of the organized press.

In very recent years cases involving the established press finally have begun to reach the Supreme Court, and they have presented a variety of problems, sometimes arising in complicated factual settings.

In a series of cases, the Court has been called upon to consider the limits imposed by the free press guarantee upon a state's common or statutory law of libel. As a result of those cases, a public figure cannot successfully sue a publisher for libel unless he can show that the publisher maliciously printed a damaging untruth.

The Court has also been called upon to decide whether a newspaper reporter has a First Amendment privilege to refuse to disclose his confidential sources to a grand jury. By a divided vote, the Court found no such privilege to exist in the circumstances of the cases before it.[1]

In another noteworthy case, the Court was asked by the Justice Department to restrain publication by the *New York Times* and other newspapers of the so-called Pentagon Papers. The Court declined to do so.[2]

In yet another case, the question to be decided was whether political groups have a First Amendment or statutory right of access to the federally regulated broadcast channels of radio and television. The Court held there was no such right of access.[3]

Last Term the Court confronted a Florida statute that required newspapers to grant a "right of reply" to political candidates they had criticized. The Court unanimously held this statute to be inconsistent with the guarantees of a free press.[4]

It seems to me that the Court's approach to all these cases has uniformly reflected its understanding that the Free Press guarantee is, in essence, a *structural* provision of the Constitution. Most of the other provisions in the Bill of Rights protect specific liberties or specific rights of individuals: freedom of speech, freedom of worship, the right to counsel, the privilege against compulsory self-incrimination, to name a few. In contrast, the Free Press Clause extends protection to an institution. The publishing business is, in short, the only organized private business that is given explicit constitutional protection.

This basic understanding is essential, I think, to avoid an elementary error of constitutional law. It is tempting to suggest that freedom of the press means only that newspaper publishers are guaranteed freedom of expression. They *are* guaranteed that freedom, to be sure, but so are we all, because of the Free Speech Clause. If the Free Press guarantee meant no more than freedom of expression, it would be a constitutional redundancy. Between 1776 and the drafting of our Constitution, many of the state constitutions contained clauses protecting freedom of the press while at the same time recognizing no general freedom of speech. By including both guarantees in the First Amendment, the Founders quite clearly recognized the distinction between the two.

It is also a mistake to suppose that the only purpose of the constitutional guarantee of a free press is to insure that a newspaper will serve as a neutral forum for debate, a "market place for ideas," a kind of Hyde Park corner for the community. A related theory sees the press as a neutral conduit of information between the people and their elected

1. Branzburg v. Hayes, 408 U.S. 665 (1972).
2. New York Times Co. v. United States, 403 U.S. 713 (1971).
3. Columbia Broadcasting Sys., Inc. v. Democratic Nat'l Comm., 412 U.S. 94 (1973).
4. Miami Herald Publ. Co. v. Tornillo, 418 U.S. 241 (1974).

leaders. These theories, in my view, again give insufficient weight to the institutional autonomy of the press that it was the purpose of the Constitution to guarantee.

In setting up the three branches of the Federal Government, the Founders deliberately created an internally competitive system. As Mr. Justice Brandeis once wrote:[5]

> The [Founders'] purpose was, not to avoid friction, but, by means of the inevitable friction incident to the distribution of the governmental powers among three departments, to save the people from autocracy.

The primary purpose of the constitutional guarantee of a free press was a similar one: to create a fourth institution outside the Government as an additional check on the three official branches. Consider the opening words of the Free Press Clause of the Massachusetts Constitution, drafted by John Adams:

> The liberty of the press is essential to the security of the state.

The relevant metaphor, I think, is the metaphor of the Fourth Estate. What Thomas Carlyle wrote about the British Government a century ago has a curiously contemporary ring:

> Burke said there were Three Estates in parliament; but, in the Reporters' Gallery yonder, there sat a Fourth Estate more important far than they all. It is not a figure of speech or witty saying; it is a literal fact—very momentous to us in these times.

For centuries before our Revolution, the press in England had been licensed, censored, and bedeviled by prosecutions for seditious libel. The British Crown knew that a free press was not just a neutral vehicle for the balanced discussion of diverse ideas. Instead, the free press meant organized, expert scrutiny of government. The press was a conspiracy of the intellect, with the courage of numbers. This formidable check on official power was what the British Crown had feared—and what the American Founders decided to risk.

It is this constitutional understanding, I think, that provides the unifying principle underlying the Supreme Court's recent decisions dealing with the organized press.

Consider first the libel cases. Officials within the three governmental branches are, for all practical purposes, immune from libel and slander suits for statements that they make in the line of duty.[6] This immunity, which has both constitutional and common law origins, aims to insure bold and vigorous prosecution of the public's business. The same basic reasoning applies to the press. By contrast, the court has never suggested

---

5. Myers v. United States, 272 U.S. 52, 293 (1926) (dissenting opinion).
6. *See* Barr v. Matteo, 360 U.S. 564 (1959).

that the constitutional right of free *speech* gives an *individual* any immunity from liability for either libel or slander.

In the cases involving the newspaper reporters' claims that they had a constitutional privilege not to disclose their confidential news sources to a grand jury, the Court rejected the claims by a vote of five to four, or, considering Mr. Justice Powell's concurring opinion, perhaps by a vote of four and a half to four and a half. But if freedom of the press means simply freedom of speech for reporters, this question of a reporter's asserted right to withhold information would have answered itself. None of us—as individuals—has a "free speech" right to refuse to tell a grand jury the identity of someone who has given us information relevant to the grand jury's legitimate inquiry. Only if a reporter is a representative of a protected *institution* does the question become a different one. The members of the Court disagreed in answering the question, but the question did not answer itself.

The cases involving the so-called "right of access" to the press raised the issue whether the First Amendment allows government, or indeed *requires* government, to regulate the press so as to make it a genuinely fair and open "market place for ideas." The Court's answer was "no" to both questions. If a newspaper wants to serve as a neutral market place for debate, that is an objective which it is free to choose. And, within limits, that choice is probably necessary to commercially successful journalism. But it is a choice that government cannot constitutionally impose.

Finally the Pentagon Papers case involved the line between secrecy and openness in the affairs of Government. The question, or at least one question, was whether that line is drawn by the Constitution itself. The Justice Department asked the Court to find in the Constitution a basis for prohibiting the publication of allegedly stolen government documents. The Court could find no such prohibition. So far as the Constitution goes, the autonomous press may publish what it knows, and may seek to learn what it can.

But this autonomy cuts both ways. The press is free to do battle against secrecy and deception in government. But the press cannot expect from the Constitution any guarantee that it will succeed. There is no constitutional right to have access to particular government information, or to require openness from the bureaucracy.[7] The public's interest in knowing about its government is protected by the guarantee of a Free Press, but the protection is indirect. The Constitution itself is neither a Freedom of Information Act nor an Official Secrets Act.

The Constitution, in other words, establishes the contest, not its resolution. Congress may provide a resolution, at least in some instances, through carefully drawn legislation. For the rest, we must rely, as so often in our system we must, on the tug and pull of the political forces in American society.

Newspapers, television networks, and magazines have sometimes been outrageously abusive, untruthful, arrogant, and hypocritical. But it

---

7. *Cf.* Pell v. Procunier, 417 U.S. 817 (1974); Saxbe v. Washington Post Co., 417 U.S. 843 (1974).

hardly follows that elimination of a strong and independent press is the way to eliminate abusiveness, untruth, arrogance, or hypocrisy from government itself.

It is quite possible to conceive of the survival of our Republic without an autonomous press. For openness and honesty in government, for an adequate flow of information between the people and their representatives, for a sufficient check on autocracy and despotism, the traditional competition between the three branches of government, supplemented by vigorous political activity, might be enough.

The press could be relegated to the status of a public utility. The guarantee of free speech would presumably put some limitation on the regulation to which the press could be subjected. But if there were no guarantee of a free press, government could convert the communications media into a neutral "market place of ideas." Newspapers and television networks could then be required to promote contemporary government policy or current notions of social justice.[8]

Such a constitution is possible; it might work reasonably well. But it is not the Constitution the Founders wrote. It is not the Constitution that has carried us through nearly two centuries of national life. Perhaps our liberties might survive without an independent established press. But the Founders doubted it, and, in the year 1974, I think we can all be thankful for their doubts.

---

8. *Cf.* Pittsburgh Press Co. v. Pittsburgh Comm'n on Human Relations, 413 U.S. 376 (1973).

Is Freedom of the Press a Redundancy: What Does It Add to Freedom of Speech?

MELVILLE B. NIMMER

. . . In the voluminous discussions, judicial and otherwise, of the rights of the media, one issue appears to have been virtually ignored. That the First Amendment guarantee of freedom of expression, whatever its scope, may be claimed not just for newspapers and other printed publications, but also for motion pictures[1] and radio and television broadcasts,[2] is clear enough. Freedom of the press amounts to freedom of "the media."[3] But the constitutional text protects against "abridging the freedom of speech, or of the press." Why this duality? Is any freedom conferred upon

---

© 1975 by Melville B. Nimmer. Reprinted by permission from *Hastings Law Journal* 26 (1975):639–58.
1. Joseph Burstyn, Inc. v. Wilson, 343 U.S. 495 (1952).
2. Columbia Broadcasting Sys., Inc. v. Democratic Nat'l Commn., 412 U.S. 94 (1973).
3. *See* Gertz v. Robert Welch, Inc., 418 U.S. 323 (1974); United States v. Paramount Pictures, Inc., 334 U.S. 131, 166 (1948).

"the press" by the freedom of the press clause which would not be available to it (as well as to nonmedia speakers) by the freedom of speech clause? Alternatively, may it be argued that a separate press clause implies that speech via the press is subject to some restraints that would not be applicable to other speech? If each of these inquiries is to be answered in the negative, does this mean that "freedom of the press" is a meaningless appendage to the speech clause?

As nature abhors a vacuum, the law cannot abide a redundancy. The presumption is strong that language used in a legal instrument, be it a constitution, a statute, or a contract, has meaning, else it would not have been employed. In the real world we know that even lawyers sometimes employ unnecessary phrases. But the legal presumption against futile verbiage is itself a part of the real world, and must be taken into account. Apart from the force of the canons of construction, we are beginning to observe a tension between the rights of the press and of those who would speak although they do not command the press. It may well be, then, that the courts will ultimately reach for some independent meaning in the freedom of the press clause. It is the purpose of this introduction preliminarily to explore that issue.

History casts little light on the question here posed. The foremost historian of the First Amendment tells us that prior to and contemporaneous with its adoption "[m]ost writers, including Addison, Cato, and Alexander, who employed the term 'freedom of speech' with great frequency, used it synonymously with freedom of the press."[4] Insofar as a few writers did distinguish the two concepts, it was based upon the now discarded theory that for purposes of defamation "speech was free so long as it was truthful, while truth was not a defense to a charge of libelous publication."[5] Nothing in the fragmentary records of debate attending the adoption of the First Amendment suggests that the Founding Fathers had this, or, indeed, any other distinction in mind, when they chose to protect both freedom of speech and of the press against abridgment. It may be surmised that to some this duality was deemed necessary because the reference to "speech" might be construed to protect only oral expression, so that the reference to "the press" was added in order explicitly to protect written expression.

This rationale is somewhat remotely suggested by the language of Pennsylvania's first constitution, adopted in 1776. It provided: "That the people have a right to freedom of speech, and of writing, and publishing their sentiments; therefore the freedom of the press ought not to be restrained." But only the state constitutions of Pennsylvania and Vermont at the time of the adoption of the First Amendment purported to protect freedom of speech as such, while all but four of the states at that time expressly provided constitutional protection for freedom of the press.[6] This fact, when combined with the prevailing rhetoric in the post-Revolutionary period recognizing freedom of speech, tends to support

---

4. L. Levy, Legacy of Suppression 174 (1960).
5. *Id.*
6. *Id.* 183–85.

Professor Levy's conclusion that freedom of speech and of the press were at that time thought of as interchangeable.

But as we have seen in other constitutional contexts, the original understanding of the Founders is not necessarily controlling. It is what they said, and not necessarily what they meant, that in the last analysis may be determinative. This is particularly true when constitutional language is subjected to tensions not anticipated when the text was written. During the [1973–1974] term of the Supreme Court, several cases were decided which suggest that just such a tension is building between the rights of speech and of the press.

THE PRISON VISITATION CASES

There are, for example, the prison visitation cases, *Pell v. Procunier*[7] and *Saxbe v. Washington Post Co.*,[8] which, although not articulated as such, may be said to pose the issue of whether those who assert claims under the freedom of the press clause are entitled to greater rights than those who claim under the freedom of speech clause. In both of the cases members of the press challenged prison regulations which forbade press and other media interviews with specific individual inmates.[9] In each instance the challenge was based upon the freedom of the press clause. In *Pell* there was a companion case in which the same regulations were challenged by a group of prisoners, relying upon the freedom of speech clause.

The Court first disposed of the freedom of speech issue. Proceeding upon "the hypothesis that under some circumstances the right of free speech includes a right to communicate a person's views to any willing listener, including a willing representative of the press for the purpose of publication by a willing publisher," the Court nevertheless denied the free speech claim. It found that the applicable countervailing interests, especially that of internal security within the corrections facilities, outweighed any speech interests asserted by the prisoners, particularly in view of the alternative modes of communications open to prisoners.[10]

The media representatives asserted a freedom of the press claim that markedly differed from the free speech position of the prisoners. They argued that freedom of the press includes a right of access to the sources of newsworthy information. The Court, borrowing from its opinion in the reporter privilege case, *Branzburg v. Hayes,* acknowledged that " 'news gathering is not without its First Amendment protections' . . . for 'without some protection for seeking out the news, freedom of the press could be eviscerated.' " By this concession, the Court appeared to recognize a right under freedom of the press not available under freedom

---

7. 417 U.S. 817 (1974).
8. 417 U.S. 843 (1974).
9. Visitation with prisoners was limited to the inmate's family, friends, attorneys and clergy.
10. These were found to include communications by mail, and via those persons who were permitted visitation rights.

of speech. But the concession was quickly withdrawn by the further statement that "[t]he Constitution does not, however, require government to accord the press special access to information not shared by members of the public generally."Since members of the public were denied visitation rights, the Court denied such rights to the press. The proposition that the press may claim greater rights than the public generally, said the Court, "finds no support in the words of the Constitution or in any decision of this Court."

This is as clear a statement as has thus far emerged from any decision of the Court that those words in the Constitution which speak of "freedom of the press" do not carry any meaning beyond that contained in the reference to "freedom of speech." Yet, the Court's reasoning in the *Pell* and *Saxbe* opinions raises doubts that are not entirely set at rest by the decisions. The Court reacknowledged that "without some protection for seeking out the news, freedom of the press could be eviscerated." Can it be said, in the same sense, that without some protection for seeking out the news, freedom of speech could be eviscerated?[11] Even the restrictive prison regulations challenged in both *Pell* and *Saxbe* accorded greater visitation rights to the press than to members of the public. For example, the California prison regulations involved in *Pell* permit newsmen (but not general members of the public) to enter prisons to interview inmates selected at random by the corrections officials from the prison population. They also permit newsmen to sit in on group meetings in connection with prison programs, and to interview inmate participants. In the federal system, the subject of *Saxbe,* newsmen (but not members of the public) are permitted to tour the premises, to photograph prison facilities, and to interview inmates who may be encountered in such a tour. The Court made a point of noting these greater rights for the press, but apparently found them of no constitutional significance.

One may wonder, however, had the prison regulations in fact granted no greater rights to the press than to members of the public, whether the Court would as easily have concluded that freedom of the press confers no rights beyond those of freedom of speech. The question is particularly pertinent since even where the press enjoyed greater de facto rights than

---

11. *Compare* Zemel v. Rusk, 381 U.S. 1 (1965), *with* Branzburg v. Hayes, 408 U.S. 665 (1972). In *Zemel* the Court affirmed denial of a passport to Cuba where the claimant's stated purpose was " 'to satisfy my curiosity about the state of affairs in Cuba and to make me a better informed citizen.' " In denying Zemel's First Amendment claim, the Court stated: "The right to speak and publish does not carry with it the unrestrained right to gather information." But Zemel did not allege a purpose to publish, only to gather information for himself. This is, then, at most, a "speech" and not a "press" claim. . . .
   Contrast this with *Branzburg,* where the reporters asserted a right to gather information for press purposes. Although a majority of the Court denied this claim as well (insofar as it impliedly granted a privilege against disclosure of sources), four of the Justices dissented on First Amendment grounds. . . .
   Taking *Zemel* and *Branzburg* together, it is arguable that a majority of the Justices would find no "speech" right to seek out information, but that, at least in some circumstances, there is a "press" right to seek out news. The quoted passage from *Zemel,* particularly with the gloss cast by *Branzburg,* suggests by "necessary implication" that the right to "speak *and* publish [provided both functions are involved] does carry with it a "restrained" right to gather information. . . .

the general public, as in *Pell* and *Saxbe,* only five justices were prepared to deny the press still greater constitutional rights and to concur in the stated equating of press and speech rights. In a case involving the reporting of news where press and public are in fact equally restricted, it is not difficult to envisage at least one member of the *Pell-Saxbe* majority shifting sides so as to produce a constitutionally cognizable freedom of the press that goes beyond freedom of speech.

THE RIGHT OF ACCESS CASES

Pell and *Saxbe* were cases in which both freedom of the press and freedom of speech were invoked in support of the same objective. What of a case where the freedoms of press and speech may be said to be in conflict? What is to prevail?

The day after the decisions in *Pell* and *Saxbe* the Supreme Court handed down a decision which may be viewed as just such a case. In *Miami Herald Publishing Co. v. Tornillo*[12] the validity of a Florida right of reply statute was put in issue. The *Miami Herald* argued that the statute, by requiring a newspaper to grant political candidates a right to equal space in order to answer such newspaper's criticism, violated the freedom of the press guarantee. The Florida circuit court upheld the *Herald*'s position, expressly holding the statute unconstitutional under the freedom of the press clause. On direct appeal, the Florida Supreme Court reversed, ruling that "free speech" was enhanced rather than abridged by the right of reply statute. It may be said that both of the Florida courts were correct in their conclusions, but each ignored the competing right involved. The circuit court properly concluded that the operation of the right of reply statute served to limit freedom of the press, while the Florida Supreme Court was equally correct in deciding that the same statute enhanced the public's freedom of speech. The largely unarticulated but crucial issue presented to the United States Supreme Court was as to which of these rights is to prevail when they are in conflict.

Chief Justice Burger, speaking for the Court, stated that "[c]ompelling editors or publishers to publish that which 'reason' tells them should not be published is what is at issue in this case." With the issue thus characterized, the Court had no difficulty in concluding that the right of reply statute was violative of the freedom of the press guarantee.[13]

---

12. 418 U.S. 241 (1974).

13. *Cf.* Pittsburgh Press Co. v. Pittsburgh Comm'n on Human Relations, 413 U.S. 376 (1973). In *Pittsburgh Press* the freedom of a newspaper to determine the content of its publication was held to be subordinate to a city ordinance which forbade sex-designated columns in help-wanted advertisements. The Court emphasized the commercial nature of the advertisements, and made the point that its decision did not "authorize any restriction whatever, whether of content or layout, on stories or commentary originated by Pittsburgh Press, its columnists, or its contributors." *Id.* at 391. The same might be said of material appearing in a newspaper pursuant to a right of reply statute, yet the Court in *Tornillo* concluded that freedom of the press precluded injection of material not originated or consented to by the newspaper. Is it significant that in *Pittsburgh Press* the interest competing with freedom of the press was not freedom of speech, but rather sex equality in employment practices?

Nowhere does the *Tornillo* opinion explicitly acknowledge a confrontation between the rights of speech and press, but implicit recognition of the speech interest may be found in the Court's reference to the "access advocates'" argument that, given the present semimonopolistic posture of the press, speech can be effective and therefore free only if enhanced by devices such as a right of reply statute. The Court in accepting the press clause argument in effect necessarily found it to be superior to any competing speech clause claims.

Still, the appellee in *Tornillo* did not assert that a right of access was required by the freedom of speech clause, but only that the Florida statute which provided such a right was not a violation of the freedom of press clause. Without such a statute it would have been necessary to invoke the speech clause as a sword against the shield of the press clause. That was precisely the nature of the claim in *Columbia Broadcasting System, Inc. v. Democratic National Committee.*[14] In that case the complainants argued that they had a First Amendment right to purchase television advertising time in order to comment on public issues without regard to whether the broadcaster had complied with the Federal Communications Commission's "fairness doctrine."

Since both the speech and press clauses of the First Amendment only protect against governmental abridgment, *i.e.,* "state action," an issue not posed in *Tornillo* was presented in *Democratic National Committee.* In *Tornillo* the right of reply statute both constituted state action with respect to the newspaper's defense under the press clause and at the same time obviated any need for the plaintiff to establish state action as a basis of claim under the speech clause. The complainants' reliance in *Democratic National Committee* upon the speech clause as the source of a right of access apart from the commands of any statute required a showing that the broadcaster's refusal to accord such access constituted state action. A majority of the Court in denying the public such right of access to television nevertheless assumed that the network's refusal of access constituted state action. This decision then may be said to be predicated, like *Tornillo,* upon a determination that the rights of the media, under the press clause, outweigh the speech clause rights of those who do not control the media.

In reaching its decision, the Court in *Democratic National Committee* recognized that it was "[b]alancing the various First Amendment interests involved in the broadcast media and determining what best serves the public's right to be informed." What was *not* acknowledged was that it was the press clause which was being weighed against the speech clause. In essence, however, the Court's decision may be seen as drawing just such a balance, and finding in favor of "the press."[15]

---

14. 412 U.S. 94 (1973).

15. The *Democratic National Committee* opinion does suggest that a statute might constitutionally provide for a right of access to broadcasting, but this option may have been removed by the subsequent decision in *Tornillo,* unless broadcasting is to be distinguished from newspapers in this respect.

THE DEFAMATION CASES

Nowhere has the Supreme Court's failure to discern or articulate a distinction between the freedoms of speech and the press been more evident than in the libel cases. In its latest venture into this field, *Gertz v. Robert Welch, Inc.*,[16] the Court both limited and extended the application of *New York Times v. Sullivan*.[17] *Times* had enunciated a standard whereby defamatory statements against public officials were protected by the First Amendment provided such statements were neither knowingly false nor made with reckless disregard of their truth. That rule was subsequently extended to defamatory statements made against public figures as well as public officials. In *Rosenbloom v. Metromedia, Inc.*[18] a plurality opinion extended the doctrine still further by invoking First Amendment immunity for defamatory statements relating to matters "of public or general interest."

The majority opinion in *Gertz* retreated from the farthest reaches of *Rosenbloom* by restricting application of the *Times* doctrine to statements against public officials or figures. But while limiting the First Amendment impact upon the law of defamation in this respect, in another respect it greatly increased that impact. The Court in *Gertz* for the first time formulated, as a constitutional matter, rules governing recoverable damages even for defamatory utterances against private individuals.[19] These constitute sweeping changes in the law of defamation, and much can be said both for and against the Court's new rules. Such is not the intent of this commentary. What should be here pointed out is the ambiguity in the sweep of the *Gertz* damage rules resulting from the Court's failure to acknowledge that speech and press represent two separable interests.

Mr. Justice Powell, at the beginning of the Court's opinion in *Gertz*, spoke of the need to accommodate "the law of defamation" on the one hand, and "the freedoms of speech and press" on the other. From this it might appear that no distinction was intended as between speech and press in the application of the doctrine which was to follow. Later, however, the court stated that "[t]he principal issue in this case is whether a *newspaper or broadcaster* that publishes defamatory falsehoods about an individual who is neither a public official nor a public figure may claim a constitutional privilege against liability for the injury inflicted by those statements." Since for constitutional purposes a broadcaster is no less a part of "the press" than is a newspaper, the above statement of "the principal issue" seems to relate exclusively to freedom of the press. Further, the opinion stated "that a rule of strict liability that compels a

---

16. 418 U.S. 323 (1974).
17. 376 U.S. 254 (1964).
18. 403 U.S. 29 (1971).
19. The rules set out by the Court may be summarized as follows: No longer may there be any recovery without fault in defamation actions; the plaintiff must at least offer proof of negligence by the defendant. Further, the damage award must be limited to compensation for actual injury in such cases; there is to be no recovery of presumed or punitive damages, at least in the absence of a showing of knowing falsity or reckless disregard of the truth.

publisher or broadcaster to guarantee the accuracy of his factual assertions may lead to intolerable self-censorship."

That the term "publisher" was not here used in the broad sense of anyone who causes a "publication" within the meaning of the law of defamation is evident from the sentence which immediately followed: "Allowing *the media* to avoid liability only by proving the truth of all injurious statements does not accord adequate protection to First Amendment liberties." Later the Court apparently spoke interchangeably of the needs of "the press" and of "the communications media." In enunciating the new damage limitations, the Court stated: "We hold that, so long as they do not impose liability without fault, the States may define for themselves the appropriate standard of liability for a *publisher or broadcaster* of defamatory falsehood injurious to a private individual," adding that it thus "shields the *press and broadcast media* from the rigors of strict liability for defamation." At one point Justice Powell restated the balance referred to at the beginning of the opinion, but this time characterized it as "the balance between the needs of *the press* and the individual's claim to compensation for wrongful injury."

It seems fair, then, to conclude that the *Gertz* opinion formulates doctrine applicable only to defamatory statements made by newspapers and broadcasters, *i.e.,* "the media." If the Court's opinion is thus to be read literally, it leaves untouched a significant area of defamation involving written and spoken statements *not* uttered via the media. Yet, one is left with the uneasy feeling that the Court's application of the new doctrine to what may be regarded as the freedom of the press arena, and its unarticulated exclusion of other "speech," may have been inadvertent, and that, further, the inadvertence was due precisely to the failure of the Court to recognize that the freedoms of speech and press are not necessarily coextensive. This failure to distinguish between the two concepts may be even more evident in Mr. Justice White's dissent in *Gertz*. He there characterized the majority opinion as applicable to "each and every defamation action," and "to all defamation actions," thus seeming to ignore the majority's repeated and apparently limiting references to defamations by newspapers and broadcasters.

The point here made is not that the majority and Justice White were necessarily in disagreement as to the scope of the majority opinion. It is rather that neither appears to have been aware that there is a contradiction between the Court's stated scope of its opinion and the description of that scope in the White dissent. The majority assumed without explanation that only "the press" was implicated in its holding, while Justice White, equally without discussion, asserted that all defamatory "speech" was involved.

Other areas of actual or potential tension between speech and press could be noted. Enough has been said, perhaps, to point up the need to articulate unstated and perhaps unconscious premises as to the relationship between these two forms of expression. When such premises are made explicit it may be that the Court will decide to treat freedom of speech and freedom of the press as coextensive and as merely alternative descriptions of a unitary concept. But this need not be the conclusion to be drawn. It may be that for some purposes freedom of the press should confer greater rights than does freedom of speech, and for other purposes lesser rights.

"THE PRESS": DEFINING THE PHYSICAL SCOPE

A first step in making this determination must be a clarification as to what physical acts are referred to under the concept of freedom of the press, and how, if at all, these differ from the acts encompassed under freedom of speech. These First Amendment principles are not self-defining, so that it is open to the Court to supply definitions. If "speech" is held to refer to all forms of expression, it would include speech by newspapers and other segments of "the press," and freedom of the press would be a meaningless redundancy. At the other polar extreme "speech" could be held to be limited to spoken, and perhaps symbolic, expression, leaving the protection of written expression to the freedom of the press clause. Such a construction might find some support in early First Amendment history.

But such a definition of "the press" would be odd because it is both too narrow and too broad. It is too narrow in that it would exclude from "the press" those components of the media which deal in spoken rather than written expression. Television and motion pictures consist in large part, and radio in its entirety, in spoken rather than visual expression. If any substantive distinction is to be made between the rights of speech and press, in most contexts it would make little sense to vary the rights to be accorded various components of the media depending upon whether they deal in the spoken or the written word. This conclusion is implicit in the Supreme Court's acknowledgment that broadcasters in particular, and "the media" in general, are entitled to claim freedom of "the press."

But to regard "the press" as relating to all written expression would also constitute an unduly broad definition. It is true that the Supreme Court has said that "[t]he liberty of the press is not confined to newspapers and periodicals. It necessarily embraces pamphlets and leaflets. . . . The press in its historic connotation comprehends every sort of publication which affords a vehicle of information and opinion,"[20] and, further, that it includes "the right of the lonely pamphleteer who uses carbon paper or a mimeograph as much as of the large metropolitan publisher who utilizes the latest photocomposition methods."[21] Flexible as this concept may be in terms of sophistication of equipment and production cost, it would seem that something more is called for than the mere act of applying words to paper, even if followed by a transfer of the paper to a

---

20. Lovell v. City of Griffin, 303 U.S. 444, 452 (1938).
21. Branzburg v. Hayes, 408 U.S. 665, 704 (1972).

given individual. As the above quoted passage suggests, at the very least in order to qualify as a part of "the press" there must be a "publication." That is, there must be an act of publishing in the copyright sense, *i.e.,* copies of the work must be made available to members of the public.

One who duplicates a document and then passes it on to an agent of a foreign government is in a sense engaged in an act of "speech" (whether or not protected by "freedom of speech"), but it would be strange indeed to regard the actor as performing a function of "the press." If the actor turns the same document over to the representative of a newspaper, which proceeds to publish it, we may well then regard the entire process as within the sphere of "press" activities. This distinction does not in itself tell us whether either the former or the latter act should be regarded as constitutionally protected, although I will argue below that at least in some circumstances the latter act should be protected when the former is not. The point here to be made is that we both forego the possibility of analytical distinctions and do violence to the plain meaning of language if we indiscriminately regard any dissemination of printed material as an activity of "the press." Whether the distinction is to turn on the copyright definition of publication or on some other standard, it is clear that accepted usage already distinguishes between visual materials which comprise a part of press activities and those which are speech but not press.

THE FUNCTIONS OF SPEECH AND PRESS

Having concluded that it is possible to distinguish between press and speech activities, the question remains as to whether the "freedom" of the press should differ substantively from that accorded to speech. This introduction is intended only as the beginning of that inquiry. No more will be attempted here than to suggest certain guidelines and directions that may be helpful in delineating the constitutional relationship between press and speech.

An understanding of the press-speech relationship must begin with a brief review of the reasons why freedom of speech is important, in order to determine whether those reasons are equally applicable to freedom of the press. Mr. Justice Brandeis, in his concurring opinion in *Whitney v. California,*[22] summed up the three major justifications for freedom of speech. First, free speech is a necessary concomitant of a democratic society. We cannot intelligently make decisions required of a self-governing people unless we are permitted to hear all possible views bearing upon such decisions. This is sometimes called the democratic dialogue function. Second, quite apart from its utility in the democratic process, freedom of expression is an end in itself. Self-expression is a part of self-fulfillment, or as Justice Brandeis suggested, liberty is "the secret of happiness." Third, freedom of speech is a necessary safety valve. Those who

---

22. 274 U.S. 357, 372 (1927).

are not permitted to express themselves in words are more likely to seek expression in violent deeds. There may be other justifications for freedom of speech but these are sufficient for our purposes.

Are these purposes equally applicable to freedom of the press? Speech on a one-to-one basis between friends, neighbors and fellow workers may sometimes prove more significant than the media in the shaping of public opinion. This is occasionally the case in a political context, and somewhat more frequently in other contexts, as with respect to critical reviews of books and films. The *succèss d'estime* is a phenomenon sufficiently familiar to have been given a name. Still, these are the exception. The democratic dialogue rationale is eminently applicable to the press. The informing and opinion-shaping function of the press is unquestioned. Most would agree that generally speech via the press is much more significant as a contribution to the democratic dialogue than is speech through nonmedia channels.

The self-fulfillment function of speech finds little counterpart in relation to the press. To be sure, the individual contributor to the press may experience self-fulfillment by the publication of his work. But for the press *qua* press, apart from the individual pamphleteer, it is unlikely that this is a significant factor. Even less relevant to the press is the safety valve aspect of speech.

In evaluating the significance of the differences between the speech and press functions, it is helpful to consider separately those situations in which the forces of speech and press pull in the same direction, and those in which they are antithetical. The prison visitation and defamation cases and, indeed, most First Amendment issues, fall in the former category. The access cases are an example of the latter. In *Pell* and *Saxbe* both the prisoners' speech claim and the media's press claim sought the same result, *i.e.,* prisoner interviews by the media. Moreover, the speech claim was not asserted independently of the press claim; both the prisoners and the media wanted the prisoners' speech to be disseminated via the press. In such circumstances the substantial democratic dialogue function of the press is combined with the prisoners' self-fulfillment and safety valve functions, as well as their own contribution to the democratic dialogue. The combined weight of the speech-press interests is considerable.

Against this the Court weighed the interests in prison administration, and found in particular that "security considerations" outweighed the First Amendment interests. In concluding that the press should have no greater visitation rights than do members of the public, the Court ignored the separate and substantial democratic dialogue function of the press not present when prisoner speech is addressed simply to members of the public. It also ignored the fact that security precautions against visitation abuses are much more feasible if only the press, and not the public generally, is permitted to designate given prisoners for interview. This is not to suggest that on balance the speech-press interest necessarily outweighs the prison administration interest. The point is, rather, that the Court cannot properly weigh these respective interests without examining separately the respective claims of speech and press. Either interest alone might not outweigh the prison administration interest, while the combined speech-press interests might. It is, then, submitted that the Court was wrong in blithely concluding in *Saxbe* that "it is unnecessary to engage in any delicate balancing [because] the sole limitation imposed on newsgathering . . . is no more than a particularized application of the general rule that nobody may enter the prison and designate an inmate whom he would like to visit, unless the prospective visitor is a lawyer, clergyman, relative, or friend of that inmate."

In the defamation cases the speech and press interests again pull in the same direction, *i.e.,* immunizing defamatory expression against the counter-interest in reputation. But here, unlike the prisoner visitation cases, the speech and press interests are not necessarily combined. If Mr. Justice White's characterization of the scope of the majority opinion in *Gertz* is correct, then the Court has articulated a First Amendment rule of immunity for defamatory expression regardless of whether such expression is channeled through the media. The majority opinion itself, however, appears to be limited to media expression. One could construct an argument, based upon an evaluation of the speech and press interests outlined above, as to why the *Gertz* doctrine should be limited to media expression.

Defamatory statements appearing in the media generally consist of expressions by persons not themselves connected with the media, quoted in the media as "news." In such circumstances the speech values of self-fulfillment and, to some extent, democratic dialogue and safety valve which pertain to the speech of the person quoted are combined with the considerable democratic dialogue press interest. Together these may be said to outweigh the counter-interest in reputation. The balance might shift in favor of reputation if the democratic dialogue press interest is removed, as would be the case in nonmedia defamatory speech. The point, once again, is not that these respective balances are necessarily correct; it is only that the Court cannot properly assess the balance in each situation without distinguishing between the separable press and speech interests.

There is, moreover, an additional concomitant of media expression which may at times justify extending First Amendment protection to it though not to the same communication expressed through nonmedia channels. This relates to the public nature of media communication. Justice Brandeis told us: "If there be time . . . to avert the evil . . . the remedy to be applied is . . . not enforced silence." Objectionable public statements via the media generally may be countered with "more speech." This is not usually the case with respect to nonmedia speech, wherein the fact of the communication itself may not be known until it is too late to counter it by corrective speech or other action. The application of this principle to the law of defamation is obvious, and it is clear that the injury to reputation may be no less devastating where there is a nonmedia defamatory communication.

Similarly, disclosure of governmental "secrets" to a foreign agent will not be known by the government, and hence corrective action by the government will not be possible. Disclosure to and publication by a newspaper will sometimes permit of such corrective action (this is in addition to the fact that the democratic dialogue interest of the public is served by newspaper disclosure and not by foreign agent disclosure). This is surely not to suggest that disclosure of governmental secrets to newspapers is necessarily protected by the First Amendment. Rather, it is to argue that in some circumstances the First Amendment line should be drawn differently depending upon whether there is a press disclosure or a nonmedia speech disclosure.

Finally, we may consider those instances in which speech and press interests are in conflict. The access cases are a paradigm example. Unlike prison visitation and defamation, here the pull of press and of (nonmedia) speech is not in the same direction. The press does not wish to communicate the same expression as that urged by members of the nonmedia public. The Supreme Court in *Tornillo* and in *Democratic National Committee* opted in favor of "press," and in effect, but not explicitly, against "speech." One wonders whether the Court would have reached this same result had the nature of the opposing forces been more squarely faced. The impact on the democratic dialogue function is essentially the same regardless of whether a given matter appearing in a newspaper originated from its editorial staff or from outsiders who gain access to the press by reason of a right of reply statute or some similar device. But that dialogue is in fact furthered if proponents of more than one side of an issue are allowed to address the same media audience. Moreover, the self-fulfillment and safety valve functions are more readily applicable to the outsiders who seek access than to those within the confines of the editorial room. Thus, in these circumstances the claims of "speech" may actually outweigh those of "press."

There are, of course, counterarguments to be made. Serious questions of governmental control of the media and of the watering down of media messages that may result from state-enforced access requirements are not without substance. But the issue cannot be resolved merely by noting, as did the Court in *Tornillo,* that a right of reply statute "constitutes the [state] exercise of editorial control and judgment." This is but one half of the equation. The Court in *Tornillo* ignored the strong conflicting claims of "speech." Perhaps on balance the press should still prevail, but those who doubt the efficacy of such a result are hardly persuaded by an approach that apparently fails to recognize that any balancing of speech and press rights is required.

In sum, the last term of the Supreme Court provided vivid illustrations of the variety of circumstances in which the First Amendment freedoms of speech and of the press may represent different interests, be they harmonious or discordant. Whatever the eventual results of any rebalancing of First Amendment rights in light of such a differentiation, freedom of the press as a right recognizably distinct from that of freedom of speech is an idea whose time is past due.

Commentary

CONSIDERING how important the role of the press is in our democratic process, it may come as a surprise to learn from one of its members that "the Supreme Court has not until very recently been called upon to delineate their constitutional role in our structure of government." The press? Why, it has been protected by the First Amendment for nearly 200 years! What Justice Stewart is suggesting is that the Supreme Court only in the last few decades has begun to confront the problem of giving distinct meaning to the words of the free press clause.

Like most good legal writing, this article sets out clearly the scope of the problem to be addressed. Most of it is simple and direct and it even offers a few tentative solutions.

However, after reading Melville Nimmer's longer essay on the same subject some doubt may have emerged. Why did Justice Stewart fail to examine, as Nimmer did, the issue of freedom of speech v. freedom of the press? What had seemed to be a tidy problem in search of an equally tidy answer in Justice Stewart's view suddenly became complicated.

Moreover, when David Lange, professor of law at Duke University, examines the writings by Justice Stewart and Professor Nimmer in the *U.C.L.A. Law Review,* the issues become much more complex. Langer writes:

> At first reading, Justice Stewart seems explicit. He thinks of the organized press, of the business, the institution. He refers in his speech to "the publishing business," but it seems clear that he would include broadcasters and perhaps other representatives of the mass media as well. Thus, for example, in his dissenting opinion in *Branzburg v. Hayes* he acknowledges "the first amendment rights of mass circulation newspapers and electronic media to disseminate ideas and information. . . ." It is not clear, however, who might be excluded from the press as he views it. Is "the lonely pamphleteer" protected by the press clause? What of the novelist and the film maker? The "underground press?" The traditional, if perhaps unthinking, answer of the Court would appear to be that they are included. And Justice Stewart's own opinions have not suggested clear disagreement with that response. Yet none of these is necessarily a part of the mass media and some, by definition, have virtually no institutional identification. Is it a misreading, after all, to suppose that Justice Stewart means to define the institutional press in terms of structure?

Would he define it in terms of role or function instead? . . . With misgivings, then, one is forced to conclude either that the Justice does not know himself what he means by "the press" or, more probably, that he has not yet had the occasion to express himself fully.

Also, Professor Lange disagrees with Nimmer:

one simply cannot accept the distinctions between speech and the press which Professor Nimmer offers. It is not at all evident that speech contributes less to the dialogue than does the press. It is no more evident that the function of the press can be considered adequately apart from the personal interests of the individuals who compose it.

What had first appeared to be a single well-defined problem in Justice Stewart's article has become a series of interrelated problems, each involving different factors to balance and each approachable from a variety of starting points about the First Amendment, one seemingly no less valid than the next. Nimmer analyzed cases from the 1973–1974 Supreme Court Term to study, by legal snapshot, Court trends on the press/speech issue. Several of these decisions are discussed in the chapters that follow. At this point, however, it is important to note that when the Court rules in a narrow substantive area, there is a fallout effect on the general meaning of the First Amendment. Thus, when the Court attacks the problem of the "public figure" in the defamation context, it introduces language to describe First Amendment "values" that will have precedent in a different corner of First Amendment law.

The problem for us is: What can we believe? Should we trust the judgment of Justice Stewart? Perhaps, but what if the other justices disagree? Can we ignore the complexities of the problem articulated by Professor Nimmer or Professor Lange without being too simplistic?

As we attempt both to frame and address the many issues raised here, we can begin our analysis with the absolutist view of the First Amendment. It was articulated by the late Justice Hugo Black of the Supreme Court:

My view is, without deviation, without exception, without any ifs, buts, or whereases, that freedom of speech means that you shall not do something to people either for the views they have or the views they express or the words they speak or write.

Only one other justice, William O. Douglas, agreed with Black, and their views ultimately were relegated to concurring and dissenting opinions. While acknowledging the nobility of the absolutist position of Black and Douglas, the rest of the Court found themselves having to balance the strong presumptions in favor of free speech and free press against competing interests of society. Sometimes those other interests—from safeguarding public safety or wartime security to preventing one individual from defaming another—won out in the balance.

The balancing process has produced a series of precedents both of facts and, more significantly, literary formulations of tolerable and intolerable First Amendment impact of actions by the state. These shadings of language import emphasis or nonemphasis on different characteristics of free speech. What emerges is an array of First Amendment "values" that exist independently of the First Amendment itself.

When a court reviews a regulation for compliance with the First Amendment, resort is made to language describing these values, say, "chilling effect" or "robust debate," to characterize the perceived impact of the law. A cynic might describe this use of past language to analyze cases as a sort of "code word" jurisprudence. Indeed, Justice Stewart has written of "the dangers that beset us when we lose sight of the First Amendment itself, and march forth in blind pursuit of its values." But when the "plain" meaning of the First Amendment is not so plain, courts may have no other choice than to measure impact by brushing the facts of a case against the language evoked in prior decisions.

The Stewart-Nimmer-Lange controversy surrounds one aspect of the First Amendment: what is meant by "press" as opposed to "speech." Let us look at nonjudicial precedents for a different approach to this controversy. In 1976 an executive producer at New York City radio station WMCA, Joe Bogart, who had worked there for twenty-eight years, was dismissed. Malachy McCourt, a broadcaster for WMCA who has an enviable wit, thought that Bogart's dismissal was outrageous. He said so on the air. Immediately, Strauss Broadcasting, licensee of WMCA, suspended him for three weeks. Unfortunately for McCourt, the *New York Daily News* published the story. McCourt then was fired.

The dismissal had a spin-off effect. In reporting McCourt's firing in the *Village Voice,* Nat Hentoff reported his own grumblings about the *Village Voice* itself. Hentoff is a columnist for the *Voice,* but he is not a staff member. He wrote:

> In a recent issue of the *Columbia Journalism Review,* I wrote—with Ellen Frankfort's book on *The Village Voice* as a basing point—an essay on the history of this newspaper. I was critical of certain journalistic practices of both the "old" and the "new" *Voice,* coming down somewhat harder on the latter, though not without hope for what might come. At the time, I was negotiating for a staff position here, having served more than a Biblical apprenticeship, certainly to be judged on competency or the lack of it. Because of that essay, however, I was informed by the editor of *The Voice* that I had not manifested the degree of loyalty and of shared values which are most fundamentally required of staff writers.

What rights accrue to "the press" under the First Amendment might be answered differently depending on whether you ask Hentoff, the *Voice,*

McCourt, or Strauss Broadcasting. As we read the specific topics in the chapters that follow, we need to bear in mind that each of them shades the overall meaning of "speech" and "press," although none does so directly. Moreover, *what* the First Amendment means in each of these contexts depends on *whose* interests are being affected. A broadcaster, a viewer, an editor, or a reporter may agree on the importance of the First Amendment and its values but utterly disagree on what they mean in a particular situation.

3

Different Media, Differing Treatment?

THE AUTHORS

In 1971 BRUCE M. OWEN was serving as an economist in the Office of Telecommunications Policy in the Nixon White House. David Bazelon was ten
blocks away, leading the United States Court of Appeals for the District of Columbia Circuit in some of its most far-reaching liberal decisions concerning
rights of the accused and the mentally ill. He was, as well, forging strong consumer rights before the federal agencies, including the Federal Communications Commission.

The book from which this excerpt was drawn was completed in 1975 while
he was on the economics faculty of Stanford University. It analyzes not only
the electronic media but trends in newspapers and films as well. Owen moved
on to teach at Duke University and then joined the Carter administration as
chief economist in the Antitrust Division of the Department of Justice, one of
the most important economic posts in government. He now heads an
economics consulting firm in Washington, D.C., with Dr. Nina Cornell, who
headed the FCC Office of Plans and Policies, 1977–1981.

DAVID L. BAZELON has been one of the most outstanding liberal jurists in
American history. Born in 1909, Bazelon received a law degree from North-
western University in 1931. After a stint in private practice and as a government attorney, Bazelon was appointed to the United States Court of Appeals in
1949 and became its Chief Judge in 1962. Chief Justice Warren Burger served
with Bazelon before being appointed to the Supreme Court.

Bazelon is best known in the law as chief architect of modern tests of in-
sanity in criminal proceedings. In addition to his formidable studies of
psychiatry, Bazelon's long tenure on the court overseeing the FCC and other
regulatory agencies gave him an important opportunity to shape our administrative jurisprudence. He currently serves as Senior Judge on the Court
of Appeals. In some ways one could not put together two gentlemen with more
opposite political profiles, at least in the early 1970s.

Radio and Television

BRUCE M. OWEN

INTRODUCTION—EARLY HISTORY OF BROADCASTING

BROADCASTING is unique among the mass media in America, for it is the
only medium subject to direct government regulation and licensing.
Licensing of the press has always been contrary to the spirit of the First
Amendment. It was initiated for broadcasting in an era when sober men
did not regard broadcasting as a part of the "press," and it continues today for rather different reasons.

Aside from its peculiar status as a regulated medium, broadcasting

---

From *Economics and Freedom of Expression: Media Structure and the First Amendment,*
Ballinger, 1975. Courtesy, Bruce M. Owen.

seems to have enormous social import. The survey firms that supply ratings of programs claim that Americans spend an almost unbelievable number of hours each day watching television. Children especially view television a great deal, and there is considerable controversy concerning the effects of this on their development. Many (perhaps most) adults depend on television for news and entertainment to a greater degree than on newspapers and other print media.

In this chapter we are concerned with the economics of television, the theory and practice of regulation, and the ways that economic analysis can give insight into policies designed to increase freedom of expression in broadcasting, both radio and TV.

The early history of broadcasting has left an unfortunate legacy for freedom of expression. From the beginning, congressional committees and courts, with no real understanding of the technology of spectrum utilization, combined with happenstance to produce a framework of legal and policy attitudes favoring what now seem to be exactly the wrong institutional structures for the broadcast media.

Four factors were influential from the beginning. The first was the obvious usefulness of radio to military units and to safety and rescue services. This invited early government control. The second was that broadcasting emerged first as an amateurish novelty, used, for example, by department stores for publicity stunts, and that these uses challenged use of the spectrum for safety purposes. The third factor was the absence of any serious attempt to establish by legislation a system of transferable property rights in the spectrum. Finally, early broadcast technology was characterized by the absence of any practical mechanism for enforcing payment by listeners for the service they received.

Speculation about historical events that take the "for want of a nail" line are seldom fruitful. Nevertheless, the consequences of the early history of broadcasting are sufficiently important that some insight may be gained from a few "what if" questions. For instance, if initial uses of the electromagnetic spectrum had not involved military and safety services, it is possible that the governments of the world would have been less ready to exercise control over the allocation of this resource. In that event, commercial users who faced the problems of interference and chaotic allocation conditions would presumably have exerted pressure on courts and Congress to establish a system of property rights in the spectrum. In any event, this trend was thwarted by the government's direct resort to fiat allocation. Similarly, broadcasting might have begun with wire transmissions rather than over-the-air transmissions, or it might have begun with sufficiently complex receivers that broadcasters could have exercised control of a rental market in receivers in order to collect from listeners for the broadcast service. In either case, the dominant role of advertising in determining industry structure might not have developed.

The climate of opinion generated by early uses of the technology resulted, however, in fiat allocation and in free (zero price) radio service.

These "accidental" beginnings were incorporated in the Radio Act of 1927 and later in the Communications Act of 1934. Fiat allocation of the spectrum in the public interest by a group of administrative agencies (chiefly the FCC and IRAC) became imbedded in the law, and it was not long before a body of judicial philosophy evolved to defend this state of affairs. Of course, no one in the early days of radio could foresee the enormous importance that television would come to have. Probably few people saw radio, in 1927, as an important source of news and opinion, or as a part of the "press" contemplated by the First Amendment.

The Federal Radio Commission and its successor, the FCC, embarked on a program of awarding radio broadcast licenses. Initial concern was centered on technical questions of interference: power levels, antenna locations, hours of operation, and the like. But at a zero price there was more demand for licenses than the amount of spectrum the government wished to make available for this particular use. Some criterion was needed for selecting among the applicants and for renewing existing licenses.

Congress's instructions on this point were far from clear: the Commission was to award licenses in a way that served the public interest. Since no reasonable application of this criterion by the Commission could avoid examination of the content of communications, that content became the subject of regulation. It is true that at first this regulation was quite general and benign. But as we shall see, the foundation was laid for increasingly detailed federal regulation of content in the electronic media.

The remaining major implication of early decisions was equally profound. The Commission allocated less spectrum to broadcasting than was demanded at the price of a license. The result was the creation of scarcity rents or excess profits associated with the license itself. This in turn established a class of firms with a vested economic interest in the status quo of regulation and technology—an interest group with both economic and political power—and this precedent was perpetuated and worsened when television frequencies were allocated.

The elementary economic and political error involved in this allocation decision might have been avoided either by providing more spectrum for broadcasting (and therefore less for other services) or by changing technical standards so as to accommodate all the demand, or by charging a license fee that cleared the market at the supply level preferred by the Commission. These things might have been done at the onset with little political cost. The moment they were not done, the vested interests created a formidable block to reform which has continued to the present day. Perhaps worse, a myth was created that there was a limited supply of spectrum for broadcasting, and this myth provided the rationale for a long series of judicial decisions confirming the Commission's policies, and undermining freedom of expression in the electronic media.

The major point can be illustrated vividly by a hypothetical example. Suppose the government decided that because of its (considerable) effect on the environment, the papermaking industry should be nationalized as a public resource: "trees belong to the people." Moreover, the "Federal

Paper Commission" would grant licenses to individuals allowing the consumption of paper produced by the government. The licenses would be awarded in a manner that served the public interest, and at a zero price. Obviously, at a zero price, demand would exceed supply at present production levels, and the government would either have to expand production or allocate licenses on some other basis. Since expansion of production would harm the environment, licenses would have to be awarded only to a limited number of individuals who used the paper in a manner that served the public interest. The Commission would have to inquire into the content of matter printed on the paper. Before long, government control of print media content would be full blown. This example seems silly only because no one is frightened by the technology of paper production. But the historical development of radio regulation has no greater justification, save only the absence of a preexisting set of rules governing property rights in the resource itself.

SPECTRUM ALLOCATION

The electromagnetic spectrum is a medium of communication as well as an input to various noncommunication production processes. Among the uses to which the spectrum can be put, besides radio and television broadcasting, are: radar, military communications, microwave relay systems, police radio systems, ham and amateur services, taxicabs and delivery vehicle dispatch, microwave ovens, and communication satellites. The signals involved in these uses can, in many cases, be sent over wires (or otherwise be "contained") as well as over the air.

The physical characteristics of the spectrum are such that a full specification of the signal requires a multidimensional enumeration of characteristics. Among these are frequency or wavelength, modulation technique, polarization, geographic space, and time. A crucial characteristic of the signal for reception purposes is the signal to noise ratio, where "noise" is the presence of unwanted interference from various sources. Thus the "quality" of a signal is a function not merely of its own characteristics but also the character of interfering signals. In the absence of a property right, this phenomenon can be regarded as an externality. The nature of the externality is such that negotiation among users is difficult. . . .

There are two solutions to the interference problem. The first is the use of private markets and private property rights. These could evolve either through common law adjudication of infringement suits, or by legislation. Some parts of the spectrum have an international character, requiring that the problem be dealt with on that level. The second approach is government or monopoly allocation. This internalizes the interference externalities. In either case, the spectrum can be allocated more or less efficiently among users and uses by equating marginal social costs and benefits, to the extent that appropriate information is available. One way to generate this information in a centralized system of allocation is to auction off leasehold or rental rights. Any of these alternatives can in principle achieve economic efficiency in the use of the spectrum; if this were all that was at stake, the choice among them would be purely pragmatic.

But more is at stake. The use of part of the spectrum (not a large part) for broadcasting means that both the monopoly solution and the government allocation solution raise certain First Amendment issues. These difficulties are not insuperable. There is no necessary conflict between centralized spectrum allocation and freedom of expression, provided that the allocation rules are neutral with respect to the content of the signals. But even this is too strong a statement; since the content of signals has something to do with the economic value of the signal, the allocation system can take this into account without losing its neutrality. For instance, the government can allocate spectrum by auction, and adjust the rights definitions until the criteria for efficiency are met as nearly as possible.

The spectrum is not a limited resource in any sense beyond the sense in which other economic resources are limited. Indeed, physically, the spectrum is infinite, although only parts of it are usable for communication under current technology. The spectrum can thus be used more or less intensively. The best analogy is that as the price of paper goes up, one would expect people to use narrower margins. The "margins" in spectrum use are also variable: if more money is spent on equipment quality, less spectrum is needed for a given signal. Similarly, spectrum has many substitutes, including wires, paper, and travel. The presence of substitutes, and the fact that spectrum can be used in variable proportions with equipment to produce signals, means that the allocation mechanism, whether centralized or private, must take account of the prices of substitutes and complementary inputs in order even to approximate efficiency.

The preceding analysis of spectrum allocation, when contrasted with the actual manner in which the allocation is presently carried out, leads directly to two serious indictments: (1) The present allocation scheme cannot be economically efficient; society would, from a purely economic point of view, be better off with some allocation other than the present one. (2) The present allocation scheme is quite unnecessarily in conflict with the First Amendment.

These two indictments are based on the fact that the allocation of spectrum is now based on what are, from an economic point of view, entirely arbitrary rules and traditions. The FCC allocates spectrum in the public interest. In practice, this means spectrum is allocated according to tradition and current political equilibria, equilibria in which the consumers' interest is not in fact well represented. Since license fees are minimal, no user has anything like the proper incentives to use inputs in the right proportion, or to substitute other media appropriately.[1]

---

1. This is aggravated by the fact that much of the spectrum is allocated for government use, where incentives for internal efficiency are slack to begin with.

Moreover, in broadcasting, the allocation is far from independent of the content of messages. Allocation is not neutral from the First Amendment viewpoint; instead, the government decides what kinds of messages, and how many, shall be broadcast, purely from the point of view of its own ill-defined standard of public welfare. This is to be distinguished from an attempt to simulate the results of a private market, which is for some reason thought to be impractical. In the latter case there must be an explicit attempt to determine the parameters of consumer demand, while in the former there is reference only to what consumers "ought" to see and hear. The process by which the government determines what messages shall be broadcast includes both direct regulation of these messages and the selection of licensees on the basis of their representations as to what programs they will broadcast in the future.

CURRENT STATUS OF BROADCASTING

Broadcast stations sell audiences to advertisers. They attract the audiences, of course, by broadcasting "free" programs. In this respect also, broadcasting is a unique medium: other media combine advertiser and subscriber support, or depend on subscribers entirely. There are more than 900 TV broadcast stations in the United States, and upwards of 7,500 radio stations. Many of these (220 of the TV stations) are educational or public broadcasting stations. . . .

Networks dominate TV broadcasting, which is a result of the economies of sharing program costs over large audiences. The overwhelming majority of viewer hours are spent watching shows produced or selected by the three networks, rather than by stations themselves. Stations can of course choose to produce or purchase their own shows, but it is nearly always less profitable to do so. Independent stations are independent because there are not enough networks to go around in cities with more than three stations. Nevertheless, stations are responsible for program selection in the legal sense, since they and not the networks are licensed. In practice, stations have little power to select programs, especially if there are more than three stations in a city; the network whose programs are not "cleared" often enough will simply threaten to switch affiliations. A station that carries network programs is paid by the network for the audiences thus produced. Of the $1,835 million in gross network revenues in 1973, $229 million was paid to affiliated stations. The stations are also allowed to sell commercial time during station breaks in the programs. Stations are interconnected with their networks by microwave communication channels supplied by the telephone company, for about $50 million per year. In the future these links may be supplied by domestic communication satellite systems.

For our purposes, the most important role played by local stations—both TV and radio—is in the production of local news stories. Local TV news is popular and profitable. It is often the only source of local news other than a local monopoly newspaper. Unfortunately (perhaps by virtue of its very form), television news on the local level leaves much to be desired. Even leaving aside the recent trend toward "happy talk" local news, dripping with banality, the medium is not a good substitute for print when it comes to detailed coverage of complex events—there simply is not time. Moreover, for reasons to be discussed, local news stories avoid controversy, and avoid catering to minority tastes.

Local stations are of course in competition with each other and with local newspapers for audiences and advertisers, but this competition is attenuated by the dominant role of network programming. The networks are a three-firm oligopoly with the usual features of oligopoly behavior. There is rivalry among the networks in those dimensions where implicit cooperative behavior is difficult or impossible, especially in program quality.

It is difficult to characterize viewer behavior in general. The evidence is consistent with the view that viewers are rather passive, on average, in their choice of programs: it takes extreme provocation to switch channels. (Network executives apparently believe that a large part of the audience for a given program is determined by the popularity of the preceding program.) On the other hand, viewers may appear to act in this way simply because the programs available are all pretty much alike. In any event, TV viewers spend an enormous amount of time at it—upwards of six hours per adult per day, on average, it is claimed. A successful prime time network TV show reaches about 15,000,000 homes, giving it an audience larger by far than that of most other media messages.

Entertainment programs are produced by program producers or series packagers in Hollywood. This industry is rather competitive. Although the major studios as a group dominate it, independent producers can and do succeed quite often in entering the market. The main market, of course, is for network sales. The syndication market is dominated by shows that have previously run successfully on the networks, and is limited to independent stations and a few hours per day on affiliates of the networks.

THEORY OF BROADCAST REGULATION

. . . .
The premises of the theory are straightforward. The electromagnetic spectrum, so the story goes, is a valuable public resource, and it is in scarce supply. In the absence of government regulation the resource would be unusable because interference among users would result in chaos. Therefore some regulation of private users is essential, and this implies that some persons who would like to use the airwaves must be excluded. To compensate for this, those who are allowed to use the airwaves must adopt a fiduciary relationship to the public, serving as proxies for those who cannot speak directly. Some say, going further, that licensees become in effect instrumentalities of the state. In any event, the behavior of the licensees must be carefully regulated to ensure proper

fiduciary behavior. In particular, they must be required to act "in the public interest." This regulation would not be required if it were not for the scarcity of licenses (or frequencies) and for the role of the licensees as public fiduciaries.

These premises, it is said, require a balancing between the First Amendment rights of the licensee and the public's "right to hear." This balancing permits certain kinds of regulation of the behavior of licensees that would not otherwise be tolerable from the First Amendment viewpoint.

From these premises a number of more specific conclusions are said to follow. Among these are:

1. The ability of a licensee to perform his public service responsibilities is not unrelated to his economic viability. Hence, the government is not free to ignore the effects of its allocation policies on the profits of existing licensees.
2. The FCC can require a licensee to behave in a certain specified way with respect to his carriage of opinions and views on controversial public issues.
3. There does not exist a right of access by the public to the facilities of licensees.
4. The Commission may extend its regulatory jurisdiction to institutions (networks) or technologies (cable television) if this is necessary in order to preserve the Commission's scheme of broadcast regulation.
5. The public interest in broadcast service precludes a general right on the part of the public to enter into contracts with broadcasters to pay for programs.

The implementation of this theory of regulation requires that the government select licensees who promise to perform in the public interest. At certain times, as at license renewal or license challenge, the Commission must evaluate performance in terms of this criterion—that is, the public interest and the promises. This requires examination of program content. While the theory of broadcast regulation clearly and explicitly requires active responsibility by the licensee for program content, and is grounded on the notion that the editorial function is performed solely by licensees, the reality is far different. In practice, broadcasters relinquish control of program content to networks, because this is more profitable than local control.

Advertising time is, for most purposes, sold on a common carrier basis to a well defined subclass of customers. That is, the station or the network publishes a rate card setting forth the prices at which it will accept advertising matter. Commercial advertisers who wish to buy time simply pay the rate; so long as they are advertising standard products or services there is no discrimination among them. This would not be true of someone who wished to advertise noncommercial ideas. The audience, far from being the object of service, is merely an intermediate product.

Audiences are not served in the sense of the legal theory; they are instead attracted and then sold to advertisers. The broadcaster's concern for his audience is akin to the farmer's concern for his cattle.

Finally, the government does not live up to its own theory of regulation—that is, notions of the public interest that might generally be considered consistent with the paternalism of the overall theory are not in fact employed in the process of license award and renewal. Activities that from the paternalistic viewpoint could be regarded as rather atrocious violations of the fiduciary role are tolerated by the Commission until overwhelming external pressure is brought to bear. Examples include the quiz show scandals, cigarette advertising, and violence on children's programming.

What I have called the paternalistic view of media regulation has perfectly respectable roots in philosophical thought, going back to the Platonic notion that art should serve some social purpose. This is in contrast to the Aristotelian view of art as an emotional purgative. Thus Plato and the Puritans would endorse prohibitions on televised violence while Aristotle would defend such programming as a vicarious substitute for real action. Neither argument is concerned with notions of freedom, but the Aristotelian view is of course more consistent with freedom of expression. (One can, I think, make the case that political expression and news are "art.") One of the problems faced by modern day conservatives is that they are apt to believe in both freedom of expression and the Platonic view of art; libertarians seldom wish to be libertines.

The premises of broadcast regulation are largely false. The conclusions which have been asserted to follow from those premises are not, in fact, logical derivations, and are in any event not unique—that is, there are other conclusions that could be drawn which are more consistent with freedom of expression. Finally, the reality of broadcaster behavior and the practice of regulation do not accord with the theory. There are a number of levels on which the theory of broadcast regulation can be criticized. One can attack the premises, or the logical consistency of the conclusions, or the departure of reality and theory.

It is important to point out at once that one of the principal reasons why reality and theory diverge is that the legal theory contains no recognition of economic incentives. There is a pretense that licensees can be expected to act in a fiduciary role without regard for their own self-interest. Moreover, because the theory recognizes no divergence between the economic interests of the licensee and his fiduciary trust, it fails to provide any mechanism for balancing or channeling these conflicting incentives—much less a mechanism for actually harnessing the economic incentives to achieve the public interest objectives. To the extent that such a mechanism exists, it lies in the threat of license revocation or nonrenewal, a brutal and awkward tool.

What lies behind this failure of law and policy? We have already examined the historical and technological "accidents" involved. There seem to be at least two factors at work. The first is simple ignorance on the part of courts, commissions, and congressional committees of the economics and technology of broadcasting. They are uninformed about the first and frightened by the second. The other factor is a certain psychological attitude toward the electronic media. Many people regard television, for instance, as being too powerful and influential to be allowed freedom from government control. This attitude is not at all limited to liberals; many people who would otherwise regard themselves as conservative have this feeling.

Of course, a good deal of the "power and influence" of television is due to government policies limiting spectrum allocations to broadcasting and otherwise tending to produce concentration of control. This is somewhat Orwellian. The power of the networks, often cited as a rationale for government control, is the *result* of government control. But the feeling is deeper than this. Perhaps it has something to do with McLuhan effects—the nature of the medium conditioning and interacting with sociological phenomena. Hard as it may be to defend, this feeling plays an enormously important role in determining media policy. There may be something to it. If so, there exists a range of tools available to policy makers for dealing with it: tools which are less intrusive on First Amendment freedoms (and certainly more effective) than present regulatory policy and practice. If television is dangerous to society, maybe we would be better off without it. That is an acceptable proposition. What is not acceptable is the notion that a dangerous medium should or can safely be "controlled" by the government, in the sense of content regulation and licensing.

It may be that all of this is no deeper than the fear with which the medieval church and state viewed the technology of printing. (The *Index Liborum Prohibitorum* was first published in 1564.) That technology certainly did have "dangerous" sociological and cultural implications for the status quo, though these are easily exaggerated. If television is only dangerous in that sense, then we have a real conflict between the principle of free expression and the interest of the state in internal order. It would be unfortunate if the argument were put in these terms, since the Court has generally favored the latter interest in balancing these goals.

The analysis of the theory of broadcast regulation can, however, proceed in a less general plane. Let us turn to the premises:

1. The electromagnetic spectrum is a valuable public resource only because the government has chosen to nationalize it; otherwise it is in no wise distinguishable from paper, ink, land, or other resources.
2. The spectrum is not in "scarce supply" to any greater extent than steel, plastic, or pencils.
3. A chaos of interference would accompany the end of government regulation only if private property rights could not be (and were not) defined. But such rights can be defined.
4. Broadcasters need not be fiduciaries of the public. The law that makes

them so is subordinate to the Constitution. There is no technological or economic necessity for this role.

5. If licenses are peculiarly scarce it is only because the FCC has chosen to make them so. Moreover, some licenses (e.g., UHF assignments) are not scarce; they go begging. In any event, the necessity for regulation of content does not follow from the premise of scarcity. A more reasonable proposition from this premise is the necessity for common carrier status. By this I mean that broadcasters be required to sell time to all comers at published rates. This may or may not be accompanied by profit regulation. The Communication Act's rejection of common carrier obligations must be subordinated to the Constitution.

6. There is no reasonable interpretation of the Constitution which endows the public with a "right to hear" (be informed by) a government conceived scheme of regulation; on the contrary, the Constitution appears to say that government is to have no direct control over the process by which people are informed.

In sum, broadcasting does not logically possess any peculiar characteristic that would enable one to distinguish it from the print media for First Amendment purposes. Moreover, even if it did—that is, if the spectrum could only be allocated by fiat or if the spectrum were peculiarly scarce—there would logically flow from this certain different propositions more consistent with freedom of expression, such as a public right of paid access to broadcast transmitters.

Pragmatically, if one wanted to achieve the most obvious sorts of paternalistic goals, there are perfectly straightforward tools available by which broadcasters can be led, as if by an invisible hand, to provide such programs—e.g., subsidies, tax incentives, and the like, perhaps tied to spectrum use fees. These economic incentives are not employed, and the theoretical coercive powers of the FCC are (luckily) not in practice much used either. That is, licenses are seldom actually revoked. This does not mean that the threat of revocation does not significantly affect behavior. Nuclear deterence does not require actual explosions. Even on pragmatic grounds, the structure of broadcast regulation is bankrupt.

Many of the people involved in producing network television news and documentaries believe that the present structure and regulation of broadcasting is essential to their survival and to the survival of their product. Whether or not one has sympathy for their essentially arrogant and elitist view that the public ought to see what they (the producers of these programs) regard as "good" programming, we can evaluate the strength of the claim itself.

The problem, of course, is that this material is now regarded by the networks as unprofitable by itself. Its costs exceed its advertising revenues. It is, however, profitable in the broader sense that it helps to retain FCC licenses and serves as a justification for government restriction on competition from new technologies. But the notion that the material is unprofitable in the direct sense is due to the dependence on advertising and the fewness of competing outlets. A program that produces an audience of "only" a million homes is unprofitable when only three networks split a potential audience of 65 million homes. It might look better if there were ten networks, and it would certainly look better if the one million were allowed to pay 10¢ each for the program.

Although the preceding considerations are of course irrelevant to the constitutional question, one suspects they underlie much judicial thinking on these issues. The ultimate point is that speakers, operating without constraints in the marketplace, must produce what people will see and hear; neither the government itself nor its licensees are appropriate or proper proxies for speakers. Moreover, it is not technically or economically necessary that there be proxies for speakers in broadcasting, as the courts and Congress seem always to have assumed—usually without further support than 40-year-old congressional committee reports.

THE *Carroll* DOCTRINE AND TAXATION BY REGULATION

The ability of regulators to require broadcasters to provide programming other than that programming which maximizes profit depends on the extent to which broadcasters are protected from competition. If broadcasters were subject to free entry of competitors, their profits would be reduced in equilibrium to normal levels. At these profit levels, any attempt by the government to alter program content would push broadcasters over the brink of bankruptcy. Accordingly, broadcasters must be allowed to earn more than normal profits in order to be able to provide public service programming.

For many years the FCC refused to accept this elementary economic fact, and tried to have things both ways. Finally, the court of appeals in the *Carroll* case educated the Commission. The specific issue in the case was the complaint of an existing licensee that the FCC's proposed grant of a competing license in his market would destroy his economic ability to perform his public service obligations. The Commission refused to accept this argument, and the court had to tell the Commission that it could not have its cake and eat it too. (However, in practice, no broadcast license application has ever been denied on *Carroll* grounds.)

Richard Posner has aptly called this behavior "taxation by regulation." Certain services which the government decides ought to be provided are made over into obligations of regulated firms. These firms can perform the obligation only if protected from entry, and thus enabled to earn monopoly profits on their nonpublic service functions. The cost of this falls on the purchasers of the unsubsidized services, and on profits. There are many examples of this outside broadcasting, one case being the ICC's insistence that railroads provide passenger service.

Taxation by regulation is usually bad policy, and this is so for several reasons. First, there may exist a number of more efficient ways to produce the revenue required to support the public services in question, ways which do not produce the dead weight loss of monopoly pricing. In this respect taxation by regulation is in the same category as the old monarchical practice of granting chartered monopolies in order to raise revenues. Second, the consequence of this practice is the creation of a vested interest with claims on the scheme of regulation. These claims serve as a rationale for protecting the interests against institutional and technological change. In broadcasting the best current example of this is cable television. Broadcasters have more or less successfully argued that cable, with its multiplicity of channels, must not be allowed to compete freely with broadcasters because this would destroy the broadcasters' ability to perform their public service obligations.

The Commission, mesmerized by its own theory of regulation and the myth that public service programming really exists, has largely accepted the argument, as have the courts. Thus the Commission's interest in an objective (public service programming), which bears no obvious relationship to consumer wants, is allowed to dominate the valid consumer interest in greater choice. Finally, of course, from the First Amendment viewpoint, the *Carroll* doctrine creates an unfortunate alliance between the government and an artificially small group of media interests, an alliance which is in necessary conflict with forces promoting greater competition and hence freedom in the marketplace of ideas. In a word, the effect is to raise the price of access to the public through the media higher than it needs to be, and to create unnecessary monopoly of control over the channels of mass communication. This monopoly is reinforced by the notion that only the licensee can control content on his facilities.

Even if one accepts the public service thesis, there are better ways of proceeding. For instance, auctioning of property rights or leasehold rights in the spectrum would produce a great deal of revenue that could be used to subsidize public service programming.

A natural corollary of the *Carroll* doctrine is that new technologies and institutions cannot be allowed to disturb the monopoly profits of broadcasters; otherwise, the base of taxation would be destroyed. Accordingly, the courts and Congress have upheld or extended the Commission's right to regulate these new technologies or institutions. The first instance of this was the extension of FCC power to networks, which do not themselves use the spectrum and accordingly are not subject to Commission licensing. The Commission now makes rules for the networks by forbidding station affiliation with a network which does not behave. Later, the FCC's authority was extended to certification and specification of equipment produced by electronics manufactuers, to communication satellites, and to cable television. In some of these cases Congress has acted; when Congress had not, the courts simply endorsed FCC extensions of power. In each case, however, the theory by which the extension is justified is the protection of the FCC's regulatory schemes. In practice, the extensions are promoted by vested interests seeking to protect monopoly profits, and sometimes by unregulated firms seeking federal protection from local regulation or relief from "excessive" competition.

Certainly the effect of the extensions has been to remove or control threatened sources of competition or institutional arrangements that respond better to the incentives of the marketplace—that is, to consumer demand. Consumers did not want to purchase UHF converters for their TV sets, so Congress and the Commission required manufacturers to install them. Consumers still did not use them, so the Commission required manufacturers to put "clicks" on the UHF tuning dials. Consumers showed that they were willing to pay for additional channels provided by cable systems. The Commission limited the number and kind of channels that could be thus supplied, and proceeded to impose a series of regulatory taxes on the cable systems.

This behavior is consistent with the hypothesis that the Commission is simply a tool of rich and powerful broadcasters. There is some truth in the hypothesis, but the reality is more subtle. In practice, the Commission responds to political pressures exercised through Congress and the executive branch, and these pressures reflect all of those interests to which the broader political process is responsive. Many of the failures of the Commission can be traced to fundamental imperfections in the democratic process itself, of which one is the well-known underrepresentation of large groups, each of the members of which has a small stake in the issue at hand. Such groups are not readily organized, and their weight is small in political decisions, particularly obscure decisions involving apparently complex technological or institutional policies.

Probably the only way in which such groups can be protected—and by "such groups" I mean principally consumers—is by broad legislation affecting a wide range of administrative behavior. Thus it is probably best to argue for laws that proclaim that "no regulatory agency may . . ." do this or that, than to take individual cases seriatum. But the development of a general theory of regulatory behavior must precede such policy making, and that theory does not yet exist.

LOCALISM

A persistent theme in FCC regulation of broadcasting is the doctrine of localism. There are two levels at which this can be discussed. The first is the political and economic motivation for the doctrine, and the second is the economic viability of localism as a goal—that is, its economic costs.

Localism is a goal with deep roots in the American political experience. It is associated very closely with representative democracy and populist suspicions of large national corporations. In the context of broadcasting, localism means three things: local ownership of broadcast facilities, a preference for smaller as opposed to larger service areas for each station, and actual program control and selection being exercised at the station level. The source of this doctrine can be traced to early decisions about spectrum allocation. There was a trade-off to be made between the creation of stations that would cover large areas, so that every viewer could have access to many channels, and the creation of less powerful stations, each covering a single city, giving viewers fewer choices but, in return, a locally owned facility. The latter course was taken.

From the point of view of freedom of expression, there are arguments on both sides of this question. The regional station approach provides greater direct competition among stations, and provides each viewer with a wider range of choice. The local station provides an opportunity for discussion of local issues, and perhaps reduces the power of monopoly local newspapers. Politically, the right choice is not obvious. In practice, the FCC allowed 30 percent of the stations to be owned by local newspapers, and in any event the local stations do not in fact serve as a significant forum for the discussion of local issues—in part for economic reasons, and in part because the fairness doctrine inhibits controversy on television.

In practice localism is futile because it is much more profitable for stations to affiliate with a network than to produce or select their own programs. This is due to the "public good" nature of programs, or the economies of scale in program supply relative to audience size. This is not inevitable, of course; it simply turns out that local tastes in TV programming are not sufficiently strong or unique to offset the economies of national programming, given the number of outlets. As a result, local programming is limited to local news and a few programs whose audiences are small, put in to satisfy the FCC's penchant for localism.

Given the economic facts both on the demand and supply sides, it is doubtful that pursuit of localism is worth its cost. The cost can be measured by the consequences of the doctrine for the number of competing voices in the marketplace of ideas. One consequence of localism in spectrum allocation is that only three national networks are viable, because not enough cities have more than three VHF-TV assignments. A reformation of the allocation scheme could provide all viewers with more choices and insert greater competition in the marketplace of ideas, without in practice giving up any of the unobtainable benefits of localism except local news shows. The reader must judge for himself whether local TV news shows are worth the cost involved in maintaining them.

ECONOMIC BIASES IN PROGRAM SELECTION

Firms in a market environment must choose not merely the price or quantity of output they will produce (the variables emphasized in traditional economic theory) but also the character of their product. The problem of firm location in product space has not received the same attention as the traditional price-quantity relationships have. But partly because broadcasters do not charge consumers a price for their programs, there is a good deal of economic literature on the problem of program choice. The ultimate question, of course, is whether broadcasters under one or another structure of incentives will produce the "right mix" of programs.

There are two different notions of what constitutes the right mix of programs. The notion explicit in the traditional legal theory of broadcasting is that programs ought to serve the public interest. This is not very helpful. In practice, it means that entertainment programs ought to be leavened with news, public affairs, educational, and other program types that appeal to the paternalistic standards of regulatory theory. The economic standard of an optimal program mix is that mix which maximizes the sum of consumers' and producers' surplus, given whatever constraints are relevant on the production side.[2]

The traditional theory of program patterns in broadcasting put enormous emphasis on the distortionary role of advertising support. Moreover, the traditional analysis did not utilize the surplus welfare measure, but instead emphasized audience sizes and the number of viewers receiving their first choice program. According to this analysis, since broadcasters sell audiences to advertisers rather than programs to viewers, consumers can exercise choice only on a one man, one vote basis, and are not free to express the intensity of their preferences for programs.

Depending on the structure of competition in broadcasting, the number of channels, and the nature of preferences, this could have varying results. If there are only a few channels, then noncollusive competition among broadcasters tends to produce duplication of programs—i.e., excessive sameness. This is a phenomenon recognized for many years in two party political systems and other contexts. Monopoly control of the few channels, on the other hand, elicits a tendency toward "common denominator" programs. These are programs that most people will prefer to turning off their sets, but which are not anyone's first choice. As taxonomic concepts, both duplication and common denominator programs have certain infirmities. The existence of either phenomenon depends critically on the nature of consumer preferences, about which little is known.

It had been thought that the underlying problem was advertiser rather than viewer payment to broadcasters. Given this constraint, a possible solution is to have competing broadcasters but lots of channels, or to have competition for audiences over time on the few channels. But for some combinations of tastes, costs, and channel capacity, monopoly control of all channels did produce the best economic result in these models, and this is a difficulty for First Amendment goals.

More recent works suggest that advertiser support per se is not the problem. Firms competing in product space always have a bias against certain kinds of products, provided there are any fixed costs of production. In particular, there is a bias against products demanded by a relatively small group of consumers with rather intense preferences—that

---

2. "Consumer surplus" is the difference between what the programs are worth to consumers and what is actually paid for them. Producer surplus is essentially profit.

is, products for which demand is relatively insensitive to price. Broadcasting would have this problem even if consumers could pay directly for programs, because fixed costs are very important. But advertising support and limited channel capacity almost certainly make the problem worse.

Given the present structure of broadcasting, this means that minority taste programs, opinions, and views are probably systematically discriminated against, strictly as a result of economic incentives facing broadcast firms. (Minority taste here means preferences for material that are held by relatively small groups, each member of which might be willing to pay quite a lot for them.) Even with direct viewer payment and lots of channels there would still be some tendency in this direction, although things probably would not be as bad.

The political implications of this are obvious, and they are worsened by the fairness doctrine's incentive to avoid controversy. (Controversy is in this context closely related to minority tastes—that is, tastes or views held by a minority of the population that are likely by virtue of their unpopularity to be controversial.) Given the existence of these effects, one has to ask what structure for the broadcasting industry would produce the best possible results in terms of consumer welfare. An "optimal" result is not obtainable unless centralized planners or discriminating monopolists know everything about individual consumer preferences. This is, of course, impossible, and even if it were not impossible it would be undesirable for First Amendment reasons.

The structure of the broadcast industry is, as we have seen, entirely the creation of government policy regarding spectrum allocation, pay TV, cable television, and the like. Hence this is the crucial policy variable. The present structure of broadcasting, with artificially limited channels and rules against pay TV, is very nearly the worst structure that can be imagined. The solutions are clear: . . . remove the artificial barriers to channel expansion, and let people express the intensity of their preferences by paying directly for programs. These policies are not going to produce a perfect result, but they will almost certainly improve matters.

Fortunately, these policies are also consistent with greater freedom of expression, with this caveat: it is conceivable that FCC regulation does result in the airing of some programs of very limited appeal that would not be produced in a competitive, multichannel pay TV system. I regard this as a doubtful proposition, but it cannot be dismissed out of hand. The real import of these bias effects is that the current system of broadcasting is very far from being the best that is available, almost no matter what set of premises are made about spectrum allocation, channel capacity, or consumer preferences. This is a serious indictment. What the present structure of regulation and policy does do is to ensure excess profits for existing broadcasters, and provide a rationale for continued direct government intervention in program content.

. . . .

The First Amendment and the "New Media"— New Directions in Regulating Telecommunications

DAVID L. BAZELON

TEN YEARS AGO, in the landmark *Red Lion* case,[1] the Supreme Court rejected a First Amendment challenge to the FCC's so-called "personal attack" rules, part of the broader "fairness doctrine." Justice White, writing for the Court, observed: "[D]ifferences in the characteristics of new media justify differences in the First Amendment standards applied to them."

The *Red Lion* decision stirred widespread controversy about the role of the First Amendment in telecommunications regulation. Yet the problem has plagued thoughtful observers of the broadcast industry since radio first transformed the way we learn about the world, more than a half century ago. I have observed the strains between the First Amendment and the orderly use of the airwaves for thirty years. My vantage point has been the court that is charged with a major responsibility for reconciling those two, often antagonistic concerns.

I would like to explore with you, practitioners, students and critics of "the new media," the assumptions underlying Justice White's observation. This is an opportune moment for such an exploration. For the first time in fifty years of regulation, we stand on the brink of major changes in the regulatory framework governing telecommunications. New technologies call into question time-worn assumptions about the need for government regulation. At the same time, these technologies open unprecedented vistas in communications, entertainment, news and cultural affairs. It is a fitting time to look back on our experience in fashioning First Amendment standards for the new media, and to hazard some suggestions about where we should go in the next fifty years.

By 1927, it was clear that the government would have to regulate the use of the electromagnetic spectrum. The chaos from unfettered access threatened to drown out all productive uses of the airwaves. "With everybody on the air, nobody could be heard."[2] For a variety of reasons, Congress did not opt for government operation and control of the airwaves, which was the choice of most countries. This decision was influenced in part by our historical preference for private enterprise. But Congress also wished to preserve something of a traditional journalistic role for broadcast licensees. We should recall that the Radio Act con-

This address was delivered to the UCLA Communications Law Symposium—1979, "The Foreseeable Future of Television Networks," Los Angeles, California, Feb. 2, 1979. Copyright © 1979, David L. Bazelon. Reprinted from *Federal Communications Law Journal* 31(1979):201–13. Courtesy, David L. Bazelon.
    1. Red Lion Broadcasting Co. v. FCC, 395 U.S. 367 (1969).
    2. NBC v. United States, 319 U.S. 190, 212 (1943).

tained explicit restrictions on government censorship, at a time when the press had yet to win a significant First Amendment victory in the courts.

The model of regulation adopted by the Radio Act, and extended to television in the Communications Act of 1934, differed sharply from the government's role in regulating the print media. When it comes to the written word, the basic rule has been "hands off." The First Amendment has been read to give the government very little authority to interfere with publishing, particularly when reporting the "news." The print press, like any business, has been subject to incidental regulation. For example, the press is subject to federal tax, antitrust and labor relations laws. But the editorial process has been almost inviolable.

In contrast, the broadcast media is extensively regulated. Every three years the FCC scrutinizes the broadcaster's performance to determine whether the broadcaster has fulfilled its obligation to serve the public interest. The FCC has imposed a myriad of specific requirements to flesh out the public interest obligation. The broadcaster must "ascertain" the most important public issues in his community. The broadcaster must devote a reasonable amount of time to public issues and present conflicting viewpoints. While the print editor's discretion is bounded only by the laws of libel and slander, the TV editor's judgment is significantly constrained by the law, the FCC's rules, and the need for periodic license renewal.

These different First Amendment standards traditionally have been justified by the scarcity of the electromagnetic spectrum. From the Radio Act of 1927 to *Red Lion,* we have been guided by the notion that there is "room for only a few" on the broadcast spectrum. Those few who receive a license must therefore serve those who are barred from entry, as well as the licensee's own interest.

To understand the tension created by this "public trustee" doctrine, it is necessary to reflect for a moment on the meaning of the First Amendment. The First Amendment provides: "Congress shall make no law . . . abridging the freedom of speech, or of the press." It is a firm barrier against government interference with the content of the spoken and written word. This barrier serves many purposes in our society. In part, the First Amendment protects the right of self-expression; the right to "speak your mind." But the First Amendment also serves a second, instrumental role. It prohibits government from suppressing unpopular or unconventional viewpoints, and therefore contributes to the diversity of the political and cultural life of our society. In this instrumental role, the First Amendment rests on the premise that, in an "uninhibited marketplace of ideas, truth will prevail," that political and social justice will emerge from robust and unrestricted debate, and that cultural life will flourish.

The first function of the First Amendment, protecting self-expression, is primarily for the benefit of the speaker himself. But the second role bans government interference with speech primarily for the benefit of the listeners, and not for the benefit of the speaker. The value served is not the speaker's interest in speaking his mind, so much as the listener's interest in hearing the widest possible variety of ideas.

Applying the First Amendment to the spoken and written word, we have held firmly to the belief that a "hands-off" approach will in fact promote the desired diversity of ideas. Government noninterference has taken on particular significance in applying the First Amendment to the press. We have come to see the press as a fourth branch of government, constantly questioning and challenging official truths. Without a substantial degree of independence from government control, the press of course could never serve this function. Indeed, Justice Stewart has argued that it is precisely for this reason that the Founders included special protection for the press in the First Amendment, beyond the protection afforded speech generally.[3]

In broadcast, however, protecting the speaker's right to say whatever he wants does *not* necessarily lead to a flourishing of diverse viewpoints. On the contrary, because the licensee can exclude others from his frequency, protecting the speaker's right may tend to *suppress* viewpoints—the viewpoints of those who do not have a broadcast license. In the broadcast media the formula "non-interference yields diversity of views" simply may not hold true. In fact, non-interference and diversity can be in sharp conflict.

In applying the First Amendment in the broadcast context, the courts have clearly felt that the instrumental function of the First Amendment was preeminent. "It is the right of the viewers and listeners, not the right of broadcasters, which is paramount."[4] The Communications Act excluded some voices from the air altogether, in the name of orderly broadcasting. It therefore seemed necessary, in the name of the First Amendment, to find other means of promoting diversity.

To compensate for those silenced voices, the Communications Act imposed an affirmative obligation on broadcasters to air a wide variety of viewpoints regardless of the wishes or the inclination of the broadcaster. The FCC was not to assume that, as in print, the market would generate diverse material to suit different tastes. Rather the FCC, through the licensee, was to ascertain the public's different interests, and each broadcaster would have to serve those interests.

The record of fifty years of regulation suggests that the mandate to promote diversity is unfulfilled. In part this is due to decisions of the FCC, often at the instigation of the networks, completely disregarding the need to promote diversity. For example, the FCC's decision to intermix VHF and UHF stations within a single market significantly impeded the growth of UHF outlets, killed a then-viable fourth network, and effectively precluded the development of any new networks. In so doing, the FCC squandered a valuable opportunity to expand program variety. Similarly,

---

3. *See* Stewart, *"Or of the Press"* [Chapter 2].
4. Red Lion Broadcasting Co. v. FCC, 395 U.S. at 390.

the FCC's long-standing hostility to rapid expansion of the cable industry is another instance of the failure of the FCC to promote diversity.

But even when the FCC has tried to promote diversity, the results have been questionable at best. The most notorious vehicle for promoting diversity has been the fairness doctrine. The rationale behind the fairness doctrine was to limit the ability of a broadcaster to use his quasi-monopoly position to promote only a single side of an important public issue. But the fairness doctrine has not fostered wide-ranging debate spanning the full spectrum of political and social ideas. Rather, it has contributed to suppressing programming on controversial issues almost entirely. Rather than risk charges that they have covered only one side of an issue, broadcasters have chosen not to cover the issue at all. Far from promoting diversity in programming, the fairness doctrine has reduced television programming to homogeneous, bland fare.

Under this regime, the networks have flourished. To a large extent the triumph of telecommunications as the preeminent medium of our times is the victory of the networks. Every index—ratings, revenues, public opinion surveys—confirms our impression that the networks are the dominant source of entertainment, news and information. Our national political life has been moved from the meeting hall to the living room by the pervasiveness of the network camera.

Yet despite their tremendous influence, the networks have never developed a leverage to free the broadcast media from government influence. On the contrary, the tremendous stakes in the highly concentrated television medium make the networks particularly sensitive to the prevailing political winds at the FCC, in Congress, and in the White House. And the government has fostered network sensitivity to government wishes by making clear that the failure to respond to the government's concept of appropriate program content would jeopardize the all-valuable license. I am reminded of one broadcaster who observed: "We live or die . . . by the FCC gun."

Thus, at the same time that FCC policies have failed to achieve or even promote the First Amendment value of diversity, they have threatened the other important First Amendment value, the right of the press to be free from government control over the content of speech. To enforce the fairness doctrine, for example, the FCC must inevitably evaluate the content of programming. When a fairness complaint is filed, the FCC must determine which viewpoints must be expressed on a particular issue, how much time to allot to each of the viewpoints and when in the broadcast schedule those opposing viewpoints must be aired to afford a "reasonable balance." The result is nothing short of placing a government editor in the programmer's booth.

Nor has the FCC shied away from using its power over license renewals to influence broadcasters' behavior. When the right to continue to operate a lucrative broadcast facility turns on periodic government approval, even a governmental "raised eyebrow" can send otherwise intrepid entrepreneurs running for the cover of conformity. The history of the Family Viewing Hour dramatically illustrates the susceptibility of even the powerful networks to government pressure on programming decisions.

In many ways, we now have the worst of all possible worlds. The FCC's policies, such as intermixture, restrictions on cable and the fairness doctrine, have hindered diversity, suppressed creativity, and fostered the domination of three large, but virtually identical networks, which exercise an unprecedented influence over the national political and cultural life. Yet these networks, far from being a bulwark of independence from the government, have been made to cringe at the slightest questioning glance of the regulator. We reluctantly accepted content regulation in order to promote diversity. Yet we have not achieved significant diversity, and all we are left with is content regulation.

This abysmal record alone would justify a reexamination of the First Amendment standards for telecommunication regulation. But recent events have not only cast doubt on the political assumptions behind regulation, they have also called into question the technological predicate of regulation—scarcity. Advances in the technology of communications satellites, fiber optics, and improved broadcasting and cable facilities, offer the potential of nearly limitless access to the living room. The technical limitations that have inhibited the development of UHF and contributed to the dominance of the three networks are being overcome. At least in the long run technology offers the promise of diversity without the painful compromise of government oversight of content.

But the elimination of "scarcity" does not in itself eliminate the justification for regulation. A second rationale has come to supplement, and now, even supplant scarcity as the justification for "different First Amendment standards" for television regulation. Some proponents of the "different" First Amendment standard argue that the pervasiveness of television undermines basic assumptions of consumer freedom of choice that apply to other forms of speech. I call this the "impact" rationale. This justification for regulation received the Supreme Court's imprimatur in the *Pacifica* case.[5] In *Pacifica,* the Court ruled that the very limited First Amendment rights afforded broadcasters were not violated when the FCC held that a station's daytime broadcast of "indecent" language could justify administrative sanctions. The Court thought its decision justified in part because "the broadcast media have established a uniquely pervasive presence in the lives of all Americans."

But the impact rationale does not explain the different First Amendment standards for the telecommunications media and the press. After all, many of our important cities have become one newspaper towns. Surely those papers have a "uniquely pervasive presence." We have never thought that the power of the printing press justified govement in-

---

5. FCC v. Pacifica Foundation, 438 U.S. 726 (1978).

trusion into the editorial process to guarantee fairness. On the contrary, in the *Miami Herald* case,[6] the Supreme Court struck down a Florida law requiring newspapers to grant a right of reply. Yet that requirement is no different than the requirement imposed routinely on broadcasters. On its face, it would appear that we need the fairness doctrine more for newspapers than for broadcast outlets. Even if the number of channels or networks is limited, they generally exceed the number of print news outlets in any community.

If the traditional justifications for regulation are so inadequate, why do courts remain so reluctant to embrace traditional First Amendment standards for telecommunications? In part, I must agree with Benno Schmidt. We, as a society, are ambivalent about a strong "hands off" attitude toward the press.[7] As Dan Schorr has observed, the press used to wear only white hats, but more and more Americans see the press, and particularly television, as the guys with black hats.

But even among those who firmly believe in a strong and unfettered press, there remains a basic uneasiness about providing nearly absolute independence for television broadcasters. This may be due in no small measure to the performance of TV thus far in its history. The vast potential of television has become lost in an orgy of programming geared only to the statistical "average family."

Certainly after thirty years we may question whether television will ever bring us the multitude of voices that would enhance our political and cultural life. Newton Minow's prophesied wasteland appears to become more arid year by year, as television becomes even more homogenized, and the few oases dry up one after another. I join those who lament television's apparent inability to promote creativity and variety. But I fear direct government intrusion into program content even more. What promise telecommunications may hold must largely depend on the market and the potentials of the new technology. But I do not think that as a nation we must be wholly dependent on market forces. There are a variety of approaches to fostering diversity which promise significant gains without imposing substantial government control over the content of program.

The key, in my view, is to move away from "behavioral" regulation toward what I call "structural" regulation of the media. Let me illustrate. The press has long been subject to the antitrust laws. Although challenged initially, it has been widely accepted that antitrust regulation of the press poses few First Amendment problems precisely because it is content neutral. The antitrust laws, by limiting concentration of the media, substantially increase the likelihood of diversity in programming. Regulations strictly limiting cross-ownership of media outlets present similar prospects for encouraging diversity. Although the benefits from

---

6. Miami Herald Publishing Co. v. Tornillo, 418 U.S. 241 (1974).
7. *See* B. SCHMIDT, FREEDOM OF THE PRESS VS. PUBLIC ACCESS (1976).

diversified ownership are hard to predict with accuracy, surely it is reasonable to assume that concentration will tend to stifle, rather than promote a multitude of tongues. Of course, diversification of ownership does not, in itself, guarantee quality programming, or indeed even diverse programming. The economics of programming with substantially increased channels is still uncertain, and even with an expanded number of channels, entry into programming is not costless. But entry into book or magazine publishing is not costless either, and yet there is still significant diversity.

There are also some measures that government can take to promote the voices of those kept off the air by economic or social barriers. One approach is to establish mandatory access requirements limiting cable operators' right to exclude some speakers from the cable system. Such regulation is content neutral, yet substantially increases the number of voices that can reach the home. Access requirements may provide a way of promoting diversity without straining the First Amendment.

Public broadcasting offers another promising avenue for stimulating diversity. But even in public broadcasting, we have fallen into the trap of content regulation. Only today are we learning the full extent of the Nixon White House efforts to stifle PBS news and public affairs programming, because it reflected, in Clay Whitehead's phrase "the northeast liberal media establishment." We now have a record of the attempt by the White House to force out Robert MacNeil and Sander Vanocur, two experienced journalists who were the focus of administration animosity.

Our experience need not cause us to abandon government support for public broadcasting altogether. With public broadcasting, as with telecommunications policy generally, our goal must be to minimize direct government interference with the content of programming. Public broadcasting must be given a substantial degree of financial and policy independence from the changing political winds of Washington. . . .

I don't mean to minimize the dangers that arise anytime government involves itself with promoting programming. No one is alarmed by the White House's practice of sending out press releases. But when the White House offers radio stations a tape of that press release, read by a voice that sounds like a conventional reporter, we become queasy. Of course, the station need not use the tape, or may label it for what it is—a government production. But for too many low budget stations, it may prove a tempting way of presenting the "news." This country has never examined closely the problem of government propaganda. We tend to think that propaganda is confined to communist or fascist dictatorships. But every time the government promotes some programming, it does so because it believes that such programming is in the national interest. I believe strongly that the government has a duty to inform. But we must be alert to the subtle influence of government sponsored perceptions of the "public interest," and we must maintain vigorous non-governmental journalistic and cultural counterweights.

This is an important time in the history of broadcast and telecommunications. . . . The technologies that have developed since the Act was written in 1934 are nothing short of mind boggling. We now have satellites that can transmit television programming over great distances, cheaply and efficiently. These satellites have the potential for direct broadcasting to the home. The digital revolution, fueled by the microprocessor, continues, with digital television on the horizon. At some not too distant future, there will be a broadband pipeline into the home, with astonishing channel capacity, based on the still emerging potential of fiber optics. In turn, these technological developments are spurring new consumer services, such as pay TV and teletext. Truly, we are on the threshold of the "television of abundance."

Our past history with regulating telecommunications cannot be undone. But it does provide us a laboratory, to see what works, what doesn't, and why. I urge you to examine that history closely before creating the regulatory framework for the next fifty years of telecommunications. We must not repeat the mistakes of the past. I believe we can draw three important lessons from our fifty-year experience with applying First Amendment standards to broadcast regulation.

First, the "print model" of the First Amendment, the "hands off policy," has proven more durable and more congenial to our national political values than the "different" First Amendment standards endorsed in *Red Lion*. We should hesitate to stray from it in the name of diversity. If past efforts are any indication, government intervention is as likely to suppress diversity as to promote it.

We must stress, wherever possible, the values of independence. One obvious way of promoting independence is through eliminating unnecessary regulation of telecommunications. The call for deregulation echoes throughout the land. At the present time, however, I do not think we can launch into full deregulation of television. The egg is too scrambled now for us to unscramble it in a single stroke. Nor am I sure that complete deregulation of TV is warranted. But I do applaud the suggestion that we deregulate radio. This should provide an opportunity to test some of the assumptions behind deregulation, and may provide useful insights for further deregulation of the broadcast industry in the future.

Second, when we do regulate, we should avoid behavioral regulation in favor of structural regulation. The nature of the markets in telecommunications may preclude total deregulation. Natural monopolies, economies of scale and high entry barriers may counsel against leaving telecommunications entirely to market forces. But structural regulation, through antitrust policies, cross-ownership limitations and content-neutral access requirements permit rectifying undesirable aspects of the market without government involvement in program content. But even when regulation is limited to structural intervention, we must take care that government policies are consistent with the goal of diversity. We must remember that the FCC policies that most impeded diversity are not the content-oriented regulation, but rather structural decisions such as intermixture and the restriction of cable.

Third, when the government does promote specific programming, in the name of diversity, we must be on guard to prevent abuse, and to insulate such efforts from political pressure. As we go about the task of creating a new charter for telecommunications, I urge you to examine the time-worn assumptions that underlie regulation. There is a tremendous danger that we will unthinkingly apply old bromides about broadcast and the First Amendment to new technologies, both broadcast and non-broadcast. Oliver Wendell Holmes once observed: "It cannot be helped, it is as it should be, that the law is behind the times." Perhaps there is wisdom in Holmes' notion that by progressing slowly, the law lends stability in a rapidly changing world. But we must not allow the law to remain too far behind the times. The technologies of the next half century will pose new and difficult challenges to the venerable principles of the First Amendment. It is vital that we make good use of technology's potential. At the same time, we must remain faithful to the First Amendment values that have served us well for almost two hundred years. The distinctive character of American society, liberty through law, depends on it.

Commentary

AFTER READING these selections, one might conclude that when it comes to free expression values, broadcast regulation is in dreadful shape, the product of an intellectually dishonest birth and a destructive adolescence. My guess is that most people who have studied the question would agree with that conclusion. Of course, the situation in the 1980s rather differs from the summer of 1926, when Congress set about trying to fashion a bill to control a situation in radio out of control since the end of World War I.

The Radio Act of 1912 had failed to set aside frequencies for the exclusive use of broadcasters, so the Secretary of Commerce, Herbert Hoover, selected two and licensed all stations to one of these two. Takers soon outpaced spaces. After two national radio conferences were convened to straighten out the mess, and failed, the government divided the radio spectrum into different bands, each allocated to a different service. Again babble ensued, and the government adopted the licensing scheme in place today, conditioning the grant of licenses on a finding that the public interest would be served thereby.

Neither Bazelon nor Owen is impressed with the results of this scheme. The concept of the broadcaster as designated community trustee embodied in such FCC policies as the fairness doctrine has reduced television programming, in Bazelon's words, "to homogeneous, bland fare." Owen excoriates the regulatory scheme for failing to recognize that economic incentives motivate all business executives, and the trustees of the airwaves are such people. The price we pay for programming that would otherwise not be carried—public interest programs and some news broadcasts (local news is generally profitable)—shows up in the higher-than-normal profits earned by broadcasters. The *Carroll* doctrine established in 1958 by the U.S. Court of Appeals that Judge Bazelon sits on permits the FCC to deny a license to a competing new station if an existing licensee offers substantial proof that the economic effect of the new station would be detrimental to the public interest.

For some this is just the beginning of how bad things are under the United States system of broadcast regulation. Consider the FCC's regulation of commercial broadcast networks. Concern with the power of networks is not new. The 1941 FCC *Report on Chain Broadcasting* concluded that the radio networks had expanded their influence over the industry beyond owning and operating stations by controlling the scheduling of their affiliates. The FCC adopted rules to limit the networks' ability to control station time.

In television, network economic power can be traced not to decisions of a cabal of New York executives trying to divide up the market but to the commission's spectrum allocation plan for television adopted in 1952. At the time, the uppermost desideratum of the FCC was to bring local VHF service to as many communities as possible. Other proposals, such as Dumont's regional broadcast system (for example, Washington, Baltimore, and Philadelphia might all be part of the same regional market) were rejected. The 1952 Table of Allocations resulted in three VHF outlets only in most markets.

This plan has made creation of a fourth full-time network difficult and has forced ad hoc networks to rely on weaker UHF stations in many markets. And it virtually assured creation of the three networks because nationwide distribution of entertainment programming would always be more efficient than creating programming at each station individually.

These findings were basic to the two studies of television networks made by the commission: the 1958 *Barrow Report,* named after its principal author, law professor Roscoe Barrow, and the *Final Report* of the FCC Network Inquiry Special Staff in 1980. In the words of the *Final Report,* if the three networks did not exist today, they would have to be created, given the pattern of allocation created by the commission in 1952. The 1980 report sharply criticized the commission's network regulations which were, in Bazelon's terminology, behavioral, for example, limitations on the negotiable rights networks can specify in contracts with affiliates or program suppliers.

The report found that the costs of regulating network contracts outweigh the benefits. Disputes between affiliates and networks do not involve program control or content but how the profits from a telecast are split. Regulating the bargaining power between networks and affiliates or networks and program suppliers is fruitless work, according to the *Final*

Report, because an advantage denied by regulation can be regained in a nonregulated aspect of contract negotiations.

Overall it looks as though the commission made a mess of doling out the television spectrum, and subsequent attempts to rectify the situation made things worse, not better. But let us take it a bit further. Who are the commission's broadcast licensees?

While 80 percent are radio broadcasters and many of these are still mom-and-pop operations, the economic clout—VHF licensees in the top markets—resides with major corporations. The 3 commercial television networks hold licenses in the top 3 markets, New York, Los Angeles, and Chicago. These 3 markets, out of the nation's 214, cover 17.4 percent of all television homes in America. For purposes of comparison, if one owned outlets in all markets numbered 30 to 60, including communities like Phoenix (No. 30), Dayton (No. 50), and Tulsa (No. 56), 18.3 percent of the homes would be reached, less than 1 percent more than the top 3 markets alone deliver.

Group ownership is commonplace in broadcasting as are cross-media interests. The FCC required television broadcasters who also owned competing newspapers in the same market to divest one or the other in certain "egregious" cases in the mid-1970s and banned future combinations, but co-located media properties are still plentiful. Bazelon views divestiture as consistent with the multiplicity-of-voices objectives of the First Amendment. No doubt, the one television–one newspaper towns pose the greatest threat of a monopoly of ideas. But beyond asserting this hazard, how should the FCC measure monopolization of ideas? Or can the FCC proceed upon the assumption that the threat of control inherent in ownership justifies divestiture? Before we answer we must consider that the FCC could not do a thing about a community where the newspaper cross-owned the cable system, and there was no other medium in the market—it is beyond its federal jurisdiction.

Multiple ownership is another area where the FCC for decades placed limits (for example, no one may be licensed for more than seven AM stations, seven FM stations, and seven television stations, of which no more than five may be VHF stations). Group ownership can produce significant economies of scale in costs of production. In terms of producing independent programming, groups such as Westinghouse's Group W or Metromedia's MPC Corporation pose a viable alternative to network supplied shows. Group ownership and groups also provide a useful organizing block for productions by others. In the world of syndicated programming, multiple ownership deals are critical to establishing a base for funding. Few shows "go to series" without a major group of television stations committed to airing them.

The foregoing discussion suggests that the question of broadcast regulation can be approached in quite different ways. Economists such as Owen view the broadcast spectrum as an asset which will be utilized best if left to marketplace forces. To imbue it with a public interest character leads to such market distortions as higher-than-normal profits to cover the costs of program services that would not be provided if left to market forces.

Lawyers have tended to look at broadcasters not in marketplace terms, but as carriers of a fiduciary responsibility to the communities to which they are licensed. What they own, and where, bears on their fitness to serve. The best broadcasters, under the rationale, are not necessarily those who will pay the government the highest price for use of the spectrum or will use it most "efficiently." They are those who will provide the highest level of "service," as it is determined by the FCC.

Broadcast regulation today reflects both philosophies. Economists were vindicated when the commission "deregulated" radio in 1980 by eliminating logging requirements, advertising guidelines, news and public affairs time guidelines, and the rigors of formal ascertainment. While stations are still licensed, they may, for example, change formats without fear of facing a day of reckoning at the commission for doing so. Or they may discontinue news broadcasts if the news and information needs of the community are adequately served by other stations in the market.

The commission decided to abandon these requirements because of the diversity of formats in most major markets. The marketplace, the commission concluded, is doing a satisfactory job of providing the radio services the public wants. Even if there are imperfections, the FCC is a poor surrogate to articulate and enforce what the unserved portion of the community wants.

Opponents of radio deregulation insist that there is no "market" in radio. Advertisers, not subscribers, pay for most radio programs. The formats that will woo the listeners that advertisers want to reach may not be the ones the aural majority wants to listen to. Turning over decisions about formats to the marketplace is, according to this viewpoint, an abandonment of regulation in the public interest.

To me, both are right. There is no true "market" as we might define that term for such goods as handbags or hamburgers. On the other hand, the FCC has no clear guidelines when it finds that the marketplace has failed to produce the programs some want.

For me the answer for radio (and, ultimately, television) lies in deregulation but charging stations a reasonable spectrum use tax for the right to distribute programs over airwaves. The fees in turn could be used to support programs that might be termed marketplace "failures"—public affairs and the like. In radio, National Public Radio provides the offbeat, experimental service that is unlikely to emerge in a risk-averse, "all the hits, all the time" marketplace. Support for alternative radio through a spectrum tax would provide a way to assure variety in radio's diet without forcing each licensee to provide a smorgasbordlike format.

Off-the-air television regulation has been a different matter, at least until recently. Many markets have but three VHF stations, plus an educational station and perhaps an independent one. This "scarcity" has led to regulating the medium with "trusteeship" features. In the final chapter we will revisit the video marketplace and the "scarcity" question. But I suspect the "impact" rationale mentioned by Bazelon, quite apart from "scarcity," has something to do with the heightened regulatory sense for television.

In the following chapters the sharp differences between the traditions accompanying the electronic press, particularly television, and all other information suppliers should be considered. Is television so different that it will never enjoy the "hands-off" approach mandated by the First Amendment for the press? Does television's role as the most powerful news *and* entertainment medium in history make it ineligible for the same treatment that less powerful media receive? What does it mean for the Constitution to be a "living" document if it cannot embrace new media in its protections?

DLB

4

Access to Information: Protecting the Gatherer

THE AUTHORS

FRED P. GRAHAM, whose Little Rock, Arkansas, youth and Vanderbilt University Law School education can be detected in the slightly southern accent that still flavors his broadcasts as legal correspondent for CBS News, is a member of the steering committee of the Reporters Committee for Freedom of the Press. In addition to an LL.B. from Vanderbilt, Graham holds degrees from Yale (B.A., 1953) and Oxford (diploma in law, 1960) universities.

After private practice in Nashville for four years, Graham moved in 1963 to the United States Senate Subcommittee on Constitutional Amendments as its chief counsel. He served as Assistant Secretary of Labor under W. Willard Wirtz, 1964–1965. Shifting to journalism, Graham next became the United States Supreme Court correspondent for the *New York Times.* In 1972 he joined CBS News, guiding his network colleagues and much of the public through the legal intricacies of Watergate. In 1975, Graham was awarded one of broadcasting's coveted honors, the George Foster Peabody award, for his legal affairs reporting.

JACK C. LANDAU, also a lawyer and journalist, has covered the United States Supreme Court beat for the Newhouse newspapers. He was graduated from Harvard University (1956) and from New York University School of Law (1961) and in 1968 was selected for a Niemann Fellowship at Harvard University. Currently, he directs the Reporters Committee for Freedom of the Press. This committee is a highly efficient, public interest research and legal defense fund established in Washington, D.C., to report on judicial and legislative actions that impinge on the First Amendment freedoms of reporters and to assist in their defense.

The Federal Shield Law We Need

FRED P. GRAHAM AND JACK C. LANDAU

[On] June 29 [1972], the U.S. Supreme Court ruled that the First Amendment does not grant newsmen a privilege to withhold from grand juries either confidential information obtained during legitimate newsgathering activities or the source of that information. In addition to this specific 5 to 4 holding in the *Caldwell-Pappas-Branzburg* cases, Justice Byron R. White implied even broader limitations against the press by repeatedly stating, in one form or another, that reporters have no more rights than "all other citizens":

> We see no reason to hold that these reporters, any more than other citizens, should be excused from furnishing information that

From *Columbia Journalism Review* 11(1973):26–35.

may help the grand jury in arriving at its initial determinations. . . . Newsmen have no constitutional right of access to the scenes of crimes or disaster when the general public is excluded, and they may be prohibited from attending or publishing information about trials if such restrictions are necessary to assure a defendant a fair trial before an impartial tribunal.

What is important about these statements is that the issue of press access to public disasters or public trials was extraneous to the *Caldwell* case; and in fact the statements appear to be erroneous as a matter of public record.

1) A great many "other citizens" have privileges not to testify before grand juries. There are more than 300,000 attorneys who may, in all federal and state courts, invoke the attorney-privilege to protect confidential information from clients which might solve a case of heinous murder or treason; about 300,000 physicians who may withhold confidential information about crimes under certain conditions in federal and state courts; and several hundred thousand clergymen who have a recognized privilege, in one form or another, in federal and state courts to protect confidential information obtained from penitents. (The priest-penitent issue, however, is somewhat murky because there has never been a Supreme Court case in that area.)

2) So far as we know, newsmen may not be prohibited from attending public trials. In fact, the only Supreme Court cases on the subject state that newsmen must be admitted and that they may not be held in contempt of court for publishing public trial events.

3) It has never been decided that a representative of the public—in the person of the news media—is not guaranteed some access to public disaster areas. It is true that public officials would have a strong argument against admitting 1 million persons to a disaster area in New York City. But the current concept is that the public "has a right to know" and that, while the number of visitors may be restricted, to guarantee a flow of information the public is entitled to be represented by a reasonable number of journalists.

The point here is that Justice White felt so strongly about the *Caldwell* case that he interpreted issues against the news media which were not even litigated and made statements of constitutional policy which, consciously or unconsciously, appear to misrepresent existing constitutional law to the detriment of the media. It is therefore imperative for journalists to realize that, while they must continue activity in the courts—meeting every censorship challenge head-on—they must seek a redress of their grievances at the legislative level—an invitation, no matter how gracelessly offered, by Justice White in *Caldwell:*

Congress has freedom to determine whether a statutory newsman's privilege is necessary and desirable and to fashion standards and rules as narrow or as broad as deemed necessary to address the evil discerned and equally important to refashion those rules as experience . . . may dictate.

Congressmen responded by introducing twenty-eight bills granting various types of newsmen's privileges in [1972] and twenty-four bills within the first fortnight of the [1973] session. Hearings were held on some of these bills [in 1972] by a Subcommittee of the House Judiciary Committee chaired by Rep. Robert W. Kastenmeier of Wisconsin. Both Rep. Kastenmeier and Sen. Sam Ervin of North Carolina, who chairs the Constitutional Rights Subcommittee of the Senate Judiciary Committee [held hearings in 1973].

The Kastenmeier hearings were perhaps more educating for the press than for Congress. The news media displayed a disturbing lack of unity (with various organizations supporting different bills); a disheartening public exhibition of intramedia rivalry between a book author representative who accused TV of producing "warmed-over" documentaries, and a broadcasters' representative who declared, "I see the authors didn't mention Clifford Irving" (both comments were edited out of the formally published committee hearings); and a failure to present convincing factual evidence of the necessity for new legislation.

In an effort to consolidate the media position, Davis Taylor, publisher of the Boston *Globe* and chairman of the American Newspaper Publishers Assn., invited major media-oriented organizations to participate in an Ad Hoc Drafting Committee to prepare a bill which could be used as a model. The committee included representatives of the ANPA, the American Society of Newspaper Editors, the Newspaper Guild, the National Assn. of Broadcasters, the Sigma Delta Chi journalistic society, the American Civil Liberties Union, the Reporters Committee for Freedom of the Press, the New York *Times, Newsweek,* ABC, CBS, and NBC. The ANPA has endorsed the whole bill; many other groups support only various portions of the bill or have not yet taken a formal position. The operative language of the bill is:

> SECTION 2: No person shall be required to disclose in any federal or state proceeding either
> 1) the source of any published or unpublished information obtained in the gathering, receiving or processing of information for any medium of communication to the public, or
> 2) any unpublished information obtained or prepared in gathering, receiving, or processing of information for any medium of communication to the public.

Because there are so many bills and they vary so widely, the following discussion will only briefly note particular bills—mainly the ANPA absolute privilege bill introduced in this session and the Joint Media Committee qualified privilege bill, and the Ervin bill (both of which were introduced [in 1972]). The Ervin bill is the most restrictive of those that appear to have some chance of widespread support.

Problem One: Which members of the "press" should qualify for a federal "shield law" privilege which at least protects the source and content of "confidential" information? (Underground newsmen? Freelance news writers? Lecturers? Researchers? Book authors?)

Pending suggestions: The narrowest commonly used definition is contained in several state shield laws which grant only protection to "newspaper, radio, or television . . . personnel." All of the pending Congressional legislation is considerably more expansive, ranging from bills which protect "persons directly engaged in the gathering of news" to the broadest possible definition of "any person who gathers information for dissemination to the public." This would appear to include even dramatists and novelists.

Comment: This threshold question—of who should receive shield law protection—poses most disturbing moral, political, and legal problems which could easily fragment the media.

Those who argue for the broadest definition—describing researchers and would-be authors as members of the press—present a strong historical and constitutional case that the First Amendment was written against a background, not of multinational communications and great news empires, but of individual letter writers, Committees of Correspondence, and citizen pamphleteers. Justice White, in the *Caldwell* opinion, emphasized the historical validity of a broad definition for members of the press by noting that the "liberty of the press is the right of the lonely pamphleteer who uses carbon paper or a mimeograph machine." The Authors League, in its testimony, stressed that many major political scandals of recent years have been unearthed by individual authors working alone, rather than by investigative reporters for major newspapers, magazines, or TV networks. In effect then, a broad definition—including authors, researchers, and freelances unconnected to any established news organizations—would, in many ways, make the newsman's privilege virtually coordinate with the freedom of speech protection of the First Amendment and would mean, in practical terms, that any person interested in public affairs could probably claim shield law protection.

Those who argue for a narrower definition favor limiting the privilege to persons connected with recognized news organizations. They argue that the author-researcher definition is so broad as to create the privilege for virtually any person interested in public events. Such a broad definition might invite many fraudulent claims of privilege, perhaps even "sham" newspapers established by members of the Mafia (as Justice White hinted); would alienate Congress and the Courts; and would give opponents of a shield law their most powerful political argument against creating any privilege at all. Furthermore, they argue that while the legendary individual author from time to time does engage in muckraking on a grand scale in the most hallowed traditions of Lincoln Steffens, the great majority of investigative reporting is conducted by employees of established news organizations. It is they who are going to jail and it is they who need the coverage more than any other identifiable group.

Suggested solution: While politics and pragmatism would dictate limiting the privilege to news organization employees, morality and history would dictate that the greatest possible number of journalists be covered without attempts to include all purveyors of information and opinion. Therefore we suggest that the bill grant the privilege to "recognized members of the press" and permit the courts to decide who should and should not qualify. The bill should specifically state that the privilege covers the underground and minority press (the true heirs of the eighteenth century pamphleteers), the student press, and at least previously published "legitimate" freelance nonfiction writers.

Case examples: The Justice Department has claimed recently that Thomas L. Miller, a writer for the Liberation News Service and other underground publications, is not a "news reporter" and should not be accorded any of the protections under the Justice Department Subpoena Guidelines for members of the press. The District Attorney for Los Angeles County has claimed that William Farr should not qualify for the newsman's privilege in California because at the time he was asked to disclose his confidential sources he was not regularly employed by any news organization. He obtained the information sought while he was a reporter for the Los Angeles *Herald-Examiner* but then left its employ.

Problem Two: Which proceedings should be covered by a shield law (grand juries, criminal trials, civil trials, legislative investigations, executive agencies)?

Pending suggestions: These range from the narrow coverage in the Ervin bill, which would grant the privilege only before federal grand juries and criminal trials, to the broadest coverage, which would protect a news reporter before any executive, legislative, or judicial body.

Comment: There is general agreement among the press as to which government proceedings should be covered—all of them. If a newsman is protected only from testifying at a criminal trial, his testimony can still be coerced by a legislative body or by an executive agency which has the contempt power, such as state crime investigating commissions. Furthermore, it seems unfair to deny to a criminal defendant confidential information which might help to acquit him but at the same time give the information to a state legislative committee which may have no better purpose than to further some ambitious Congressman's stepladder toward the governorship.

Suggested solution: News reporters should be privileged before all judicial, executive, and legislative proceedings.

Case examples: While the current subpoena problem originated with federal grand juries (Earl Caldwell), and with state grand juries (Paul Pappas and Paul Branzburg), the infection is spreading. Joseph Weiler of the Memphis *Commercial Appeal* and Joseph Pennington of radio station WREC were called before a state legislative investigating commission. Dean Jensen, Stuart Wilk, and Miss Gene Cunningham of the Milwaukee *Sentinel* and Alfred Balk of the *Columbia Journalism Review* (in a case involving an article in the *Saturday Evening Post*) were asked to disclose confidential sources during civil hearings before federal district courts. William Farr resisted a county judge's personal investigation into violations of his Manson trial publicity order. Three St. Louis area reporters appeared before a State Ethics Committee which appears to be some kind of executive committee authorized by the state legislature to investigate state judges. Brit Hume of the Jack Anderson column and Denny Walsh of *Life* resisted libel case subpoenas.

Problem Three: What types of information should be protected?

a) Confidential sources of published information (e.g. Earl Caldwell was asked to disclose the confidential source of material published in the New York *Times*. William Farr was asked the confidential source of a Manson trial confession published in the Los Angeles *Herald-Examiner*)?

b) Confidential sources of unpublished information (e.g. TV news reporter Paul Pappas was asked what occurred inside Black Panther headquarters; CBS News was asked the identity of the person in New York who supplied a Black Panther contact in Algiers in connection with a *60 Minutes* story on Eldridge Cleaver)?

c) Unpublished nonconfidential information (e.g. Peter Bridge was asked further details of his nonconfidential interview with a Newark Housing Commission member; CBS News was asked to supply outtakes of nonconfidential interviews in *The Selling of the Pentagon;* the St. Louis *Post Dispatch* was asked for unpublished photos of a public antiwar demonstration)?

d) Published nonconfidential information (e.g. Radio station WBAI in New York City was asked for tapes of published interviews with unnamed prisoners involved in the Tombs riot; WDEF-TV in Chattanooga was asked for the tapes of a published interview with an unnamed grand juror)?

Pending suggestions: The narrowest commonly accepted protection is contained in several state shield laws which protect only the "source" of "published" information, giving no protection, of course, to the confidential source of background information never published and no protection to the unpublished confidential information itself. All the pending Congressional bills protect both the *source* and the *content* of "confidential" information whether or not the information is published. Interestingly, all the congressional bills also protect the source and content of "nonconfidential information," which could even protect TV outtakes or a reporter's notes of a Presidential speech ("nonconfidential information").

While the broadcasters generally support the printed media's desire to protect "confidential" sources and information, the real TV interest in the shield law debates will center on the nonconfidential information problem, from both a practical and philosophical point of view. The classic cases cited by the TV news executives concern the difficulties of television cameramen covering riots, dissident political demonstrations, and student disorders—"nonconfidential" events whose film records could be used by the FBI or local law enforcement to identify participants for criminal prosecution. TV executives and, to a lesser extent, news cameramen recite incidents of stonings by demonstrators, breaking of cameras, and destruction of equipment because demonstrators believed that journalists were collecting evidence for the police. The TV news executives argue that their news operations are not an "investigative arm of the Government" and that their cameramen must be able to represent to hostile demonstrators and to the general public that the only film the FBI will see is the film that is actually shown on the tube. But this raises a logical dilemma: Is a film outtake of a public demonstration to be given the same protection from subpoena as a "confidential" source in the Watergate bugging scandal?

Television also has a practical financial objection to permitting its film to be subpoenaed. It is expensive and time-consuming to run through reel after reel of film, an objection similar to that of newspapers whose morgues have been subpoenaed.

Suggested solutions: It is our suggestion that the shield law privilege might be bifurcated like the attorney-client privilege: There could be an "absolute" privilege to refuse to disclose the source or content of confidential information; there could be a "qualified" privilege to refuse to disclose nonconfidential information—such as outtakes of a public demonstration. The outtakes would be available only if the Government demonstrates an "overriding and compelling need."

This two-level absolute-qualified privilege would be similar to the privileges available to attorneys. Attorneys may refuse to disclose the content of confidential communications from their clients and in some cases even the identity of their clients. However, attorneys have only a limited privilege to refuse to turn over nonconfidential "work product" evidence—such as an interview with a witness to a crime who is now unavailable. There are three advantages to offering to a news reporter or cameraman the absolute-qualified privileges held by attorneys.

FIRST: The press is not asking Congress to create a novel or unique concept by establishing a specially privileged class of citizens. In fact, the press is merely saying that confidentiality is as important for the performance of newsgathering as it is for the performance of legal representation; and to deny the press a privilege which Congress has granted to an attorney would be saying that the right of the public via the press to learn about the Bobby Baker or Watergate scandals is to be accorded less protection than the right of a member of the public, via his lawyer, to be represented in a land transaction or a patent case.

SECOND: The attorney-client relationship is so well established that a whole new body of law would not have to be developed for the multitude of unanswered questions which naturally arise with establishment of a new and untested right. (How is the privilege asserted? Who has the burden of proving it is properly invoked? etc.)

THIRD: [The] federal rules of evidence . . . grant . . . federal confidentiality privileges to the attorney for his client, to the policeman for his informer, to the priest for his penitent, and to the psychiatrist for his patient. . . . [I]t might be advisable for the press to obtain its privileges in connection with [these] rules.

Problem Four: Should there be any specific exceptions to the privilege to refuse to reveal confidential and nonconfidential information or sources? (Libel suits? Eyewitness to a murder? Information about a conspiracy to commit treason?)

Pending suggestions: The Congressional bills vary. The Joint Media Committee qualified privilege bill would permit confidential and nonconfidential information to be obtained if "there is a compelling and overriding national interest." The Ervin bill would not protect information which "tend[s] to prove or disprove the commission of a crime." The CBS bill would permit the confidential information to be disclosed "to avoid a substantial injustice." The Pearson bill would force disclosure of confidential information to prevent a "threat to human life." The ANPA absolute privilege bill permits no exceptions.

Comment: Most of the bills would not have protected Earl Caldwell because the grand jury in the *Caldwell* case was allegedly investigating a threat by Eldridge Cleaver to assassinate the President. Once the Congress suggests that newsmen may protect confidential information except for national security or libel or felonies or to prevent injustices, the media will end up with a bill which is full of procedural loopholes, moral dichotomies, and legal inconsistencies.

Furthermore, judges have proved ingenious in discovering ambiguities in statutes in order to force reporters to testify in situations that would boggle the nonlegal mind. Paul Branzburg was ordered to name his source of a drug abuse story despite a state law protecting reporters' sources! The Kentucky courts ruled that he saw the sources making hashish and thus they became "criminals" and not news sources. A California law protects reporters' sources, but a Los Angeles judge waited until William Farr temporarily became an exnewsman and then ordered him to talk; the California legislature promptly passed a new law protecting former newsmen. The moral is that shield laws should be as broad and tight as words will permit, or judges will find ways to evade the intent of the statutes.

Critics of the unqualified privilege often fall back on a stable of horribles ("what if a kidnaper had your child and a reporter knew where"?) to argue for leeway to compel testimony in extreme situations. But some states have had unqualified laws for years and no such incident has ever occurred. Either a reporter believes that it is his duty to talk or he feels so strongly against disclosing the information that no judge or turnkey could break his silence.

Of all the qualified bills, the Joint Media Committee bill is closest to the absolutist approach. Its exception for the "national interest" would place a heavy burden on the Government or a private litigant—a burden that would appear to be satisfied in those rare situations similar to the Pentagon Papers litigation.

The conceptual difficulties of attempting to cover all confidential and nonconfidential information under the same broad legal standards have persuaded us that the privilege perhaps could be tailored to the major problems of confidential and nonconfidential information rather than attempting to make a series of subjective evaluations for certain types of crimes or proceedings. Libel presents an unusual situation; in other testamentary confidentiality situations such as the attorney-client privilege, if the client refuses to waive the privilege then he is subject to an automatic default judgment as the penalty for invoking the right.

Suggested solutions: Attorneys, clergymen, and psychiatrists cannot be forced to violate the confidences of their clients, penitents, and patients, even upon a showing of an investigation into espionage or murder. In fact, how many attorneys know that their own clients or other persons are guilty of heinous crimes but are protected by the attorney-client privilege? It seems grotesque to accuse a news person of being an unpatriotic citizen because he has a privilege to refuse to disclose confidential information of a serious crime, when attorneys (50 per cent of the Congress are lawyers), physicians, and clergymen are considered upstanding citizens if they invoke their privileges to refuse to divulge the same criminal information to a grand jury or a trial. Therefore it is suggested that any exemptions for confidential information be drawn as narrowly as possible and that there be a heavy burden of proof for forced disclosure of nonconfidential information.

Problem Five: Should the shield bill apply only to newsmen involved in federal legislative, executive, and judicial proceedings? Or should the bill cover newsmen involved in attempts by state government agencies to obtain confidential sources and information?

Pending solutions: All of the Congressional bills apply to federal proceedings. The ANPA bill would cover both federal and state proceedings.

Comment: No single issue divided the ANPA Ad Hoc Drafting Committee more than the question of federal-state coverage. While lawyers all agree that Congress can cover federal proceedings, there is serious disagreement—both on constitutional and political grounds—as to whether the press should aggressively push for state protection in the federal bill.

If statistics were the only issue, then the media would all agree that Congress should cover state proceedings because the subpoena problem is much more serious now in the states and counties than in federal jurisdictions. Ever since Atty. Gen. John N. Mitchell promulgated his Justice Department Subpoena Guidelines in July, 1970, the Justice Department, which had issued a large number of subpoenas to the press in the prior eighteen months, issued only thirteen subpoenas [through spring 1973]. The celebrated cases today are mostly state cases: William Farr, Peter Bridge, Harry Thornton, David Lightman, James Mitchell, Joseph Weiler, Joseph Pennington. . . .

A federal-state law would fill the void in states [without shield laws], thus eliminating the necessity of new legislation in these states and of corrective legislation in most of the existing states whose laws offer less protection than the ANPA bill. A subcommittee of the Conference of Commissioners on Uniform State Law is now working on a model reporters' privilege law. But even if the commissioners eventually approve a model statute, it might be years before any substantial number of state legislatures adopt it.

Then there is the potential legal impact of the *Farr* decision in the California courts. They held that the state legislature has no power under the state constitution to pass a shield law which invades the inherent constitutional power of the state courts to protect their own integrity by forcing news reporters to disclose confidential information. What this means potentially is that California and perhaps other states must pass a state constitutional amendment—rather than a shield law—to give complete protection to news reporters involved in many types of contempt proceedings.

There are, however, serious constitutional and political problems with a federal-state shield law. Constitutionally, the ANPA bill attempts to give Congress two different methods to intervene in state court and legislative proceedings. First: It notes that news is in commerce and therefore the ANPA bill uses Congress's power to control "interstate commerce." Second: It notes that, under the Fourteenth Amendment, Congress has the power to pass legislation protecting rights guaranteed in the First Amendment. While Congress has used its power to protect federally guaranteed rights by passing the Civil Rights Acts of 1965 and 1968, Congress has never attempted to pass legislation implementing the Bill of Rights.

. . . .

Suggested solution: The federal government is only one of fifty-one jurisdictions. In fact, when one remembers that the *Farr-Bridge-Thornton* cases were processed in the county courts, there are the federal government; fifty states; and some 3,000 county court jurisdictions. Under the Justice Department guidelines, there is a lessening danger from the federal government. Therefore, we consider it absolutely essential that, despite the political difficulties of this position, the shield law protect every news reporter in the nation—not just those who, by happenstance, are involved in federal proceedings.

Assuming that the media can agree on which bill they want, can the press persuade Congress to pass the legislation? [In 1970] the newspaper publishers succeeded in obtaining passage of the Newspaper Preservation Act with its exemption from the antitrust laws, over the public opposition of the then antitrust chief, Richard McLaren. [In 1971] the broadcasters, within forty-eight hours, were able to muster enough support to protect CBS president Frank Stanton from being held in contempt of Congress, over the objections of Rep. Harley Staggers, who was attempting to obtain nonconfidential outtakes of *The Selling of the Pentagon.* The conclusion is quite simple: What the media owners want from Congress, the media owners get from Congress. The only question that remains is whether the First Amendment is of as much concern to the media owners as was exemption from the antitrust laws.

Commentary

A FEDERAL STATUTE defining the breadth of a reporter's testimonial privilege regarding confidential communications appears to be the soundest means of recovering the ground lost by the 1972 *Caldwell* decision (*Branzburg* v. *Hayes*). The United States Supreme Court denied the assumption that the free press clause of the First Amendment arms a reporter with a shield of immunity from testifying in investigative proceedings at which citizens generally can be compelled to reveal what they know. But the Court's decision leaves open statutory relief, an avenue that could become one way to guarantee a certain though limited privilege made applicable to both state and federal proceedings.

The statutory approach has developed on a state by state basis rather than by national law. Congress has yet to pass a federal shield law. The issues commented upon by Fred Graham and Jack Landau remain so unsettled that a compromise bill eludes passage. Some media voices, notably the *Washington Post,* would rather rely on the protective potential inherent in the First Amendment's absolute language than on a modern interpretation. Yet the concept of immunizing news reporters by statute from the obligation to testify is not new.

Maryland passed a newsperson's privilege law in 1896. Eighty-five years later, twenty-six states have such laws. These statutes typically relieve the journalist from compulsory testimony about a source of information in any legal proceeding. About half the statutes qualify that privilege with balancing standards of varying strictness. For instance, the Arkansas statute removes the shield if disclosure relates to information "published or broadcast in bad faith, with malice, and not in the interest of the public welfare."

The premise of a shield law is simple. By determining that society's interest in obtaining evidence for use by Congress, by criminal investigators, or by grand juries should be subordinated to the press's and society's interests in newsgathering free of government intrusion, state legislatures bypass balancing of competing constitutional interests by the courts. But such statutes, whether state or someday, perhaps, federal, only supplement the right found in the free press clause.

The *Caldwell* case established that the free press clause does not guarantee press immunity in all cases. Accordingly, the outcome of assaying the claims of privilege against the need for disclosure will depend on the particular circumstances in which the need arises. As Graham and Landau point out, the subpoena power has not arisen as an issue in extreme cases. For example, a reporter could have confidential knowledge of evidence that would acquit an innocent defendant accused of first degree murder. Or a reporter might know the location of a street gang's hideout, knowledge which might prevent a felony.

The three cases decided in *Caldwell* are more typical: subpoenas issued to elicit the testimony of journalists who in the course of investigative reporting have obtained what a prosecutor believes would help the grand jury in deciding whether to issue a criminal indictment. This duty of citizen participation in investigations and subsequent trials is supported by well-established common law doctrine. As early as 1612, Sir Francis Bacon in the *Countess of Shrewsbury's Trial* held that the public has a right to every person's evidence. For government effectively to combat crime, to assure a criminal defendant's Sixth Amendment right to all evidence, as well as to guarantee to civil litigants an informed, government dispute-solving mechanism, it is vital that all citizens holding relevant information be required to disclose what they know.

But when the citizen involved is a journalist, generalizations about the need for "every person's evidence" break down. First, as a matter of privacy, reporters often establish confidential relations with their sources to gain access to information. The right to keep what they have collected to themselves should be recognized. Indeed, in the *Caldwell* trio, the privacy claim sounded strongest in the case of Paul Pappas, a reporter-cameraman for a New Bedford, Massachusetts, television station, who was allowed to spend the night at a Black Panthers' headquarters by agreeing to report on police methods if there was a raid, but to write nothing if there was not. No raid occurred, and yet the grand jury sought out Pappas's testimony regarding confidential observations.

Still, you might argue that a reporter sheds any expectations about the privacy of his or her information once it is converted into a published account. But the claim of privacy should not be overcome by any state interest when a reporter has not disclosed any of the information collected. The Court, of course, was of another mind.

In addition to claiming a privacy interest, a reporter's protected right under the First Amendment to gather news is severely hampered by any government investigation forcing access to press information. Sources dry up. Confidants become suspicious, even when a reporter promises to remain silent before the grand jury at the peril of risking contempt. If you were a confident, how could you be sure what a reporter would do in the closed chambers of the grand jury? What if he were denied the aid of counsel or the right to public disclosure of the grand jury transcript? Stripped of a vital two-pronged spear of the investigative arsenal (the ability to promise broad dispersal of otherwise concealed information as well as absolute silence as to source) a reporter becomes an impotent steward of the public interest.

Consider that the most celebrated of our investigative reporters, Carl Bernstein and Bob Woodward, dedicated *All the President's Men:*

To the President's other men and women—in the White House and elsewhere—who took risks to provide us with confidential information. Without them there would have been no Watergate story told by the *Washington Post.*

The power to compel the press to testify, according to this argument, is the power to harass a reporter out of his or her job as watchdog of the Government. The reporter is then in the position of a compliant investigative arm of any prosecutor holding the cracking whip of the subpoena power. The ultimate loser becomes the public, its source of neutral information necessary for self-governance reduced today to a trickle, tomorrow to a bone-dry gully.

Unfortunately the atmosphere for striking that proper balance between the competing claims of press and government, whether on strictly First Amendment grounds or in the context of a shield statute, has been clouded in the recent past by controversies surrounding government attempts to learn what the press knows. Often a subpoena has been issued in the course of undirected inquiries into the activities of political or cultural radicals. The *Caldwell* and *Pappas* cases involved the Black Panthers; Branzburg's information dealt with the inner workings of the marijuana trade.

Furthermore the grand jury itself, historically a much-valued restraint on a prosecutor's reach, has become suspect in many communities. Some see it as the permanently chartered vessel of prosecutors, used primarily for fishing expeditions conducted not to catch but merely harass political dissidents. And demands for information have usually gone well beyond the identity of a confidential source. In some situations, such as those involved in *Caldwell* and *Pappas,* the names were already known but further confidential information was desired by the prosecutor. In others, the government demanded photographs or television films that actually showed peaceful demonstrations but were identified by the prosecutor to the grand jury as overt acts in unlawful conspiracy.

Press subpoenas have not always arisen in such an adversarial climate. During the Lyndon Johnson years the press had voluntarily cooperated with federal investigators. For instance, in an article written for the *1972 Report of the Twentieth Century Fund Task Force on Government and the Press,* Fred Graham notes situations in which the media and the government engaged in preliminary negotiations resulting in consented-to subpoenas, particularly when investigations involved violence against civil rights advocates in the South, and organized crime. Of course, the information turned over was not usually the product of a confidential relationship between reporter and source.

But even without the suspect political considerations that infected some investigations in the late 1960s and early 1970s, the proper balance remains elusive, at least short of an unqualified press privilege, and this the current Court is not likely to establish.

One complication involves the hazardous task of trying to define the scope of "confidentiality." When radio station KPFK-FM, Los Angeles, received a communique from the New World Liberation Front claiming credit for a bombing in October 1974, did a confidential relation suddenly spring into existence? Although the station did not solicit the information, did its past willingness to serve as a conduit establish a confidential privilege? The attorney-client relationship, after all, does not come into being so haphazardly. Moreover, that privilege is held for the advantage of the client, not the attorney. The privilege exists primarily to provide an atmosphere of complete confidentiality for the client's benefit.

Perhaps the clergyman-penitent privilege, which accords a testimonial privilege to both priest and confessor, is an apter model than the attorney-client privilege. Indeed, the free exercise clause found in the First Amendment, like the adjacent free press clause for subpoenaed reporters, provides the constitutional basis to secure a priest's right to seal his lips as to what is conveyed during confession. Moreover, the informalities that often accompany creation of the privilege (the priest may not even know the identity of the confessor) resemble the "Deep Throat" atmosphere surrounding a newly struck confidential relationship between source and reporter. However, this comparison may be less than convincing, particularly when one considers the longstanding sanctity accorded penitential prayer.

While many journalists believe in the sanctity of the reporter's interview, society has traditionally considered only the special dialogue of the penitential confession to be a direct communication with the Divine. Still, there is no time like the present to embark on new traditions, and Graham's and Landau's reference to this confidential privilege may find greater acceptance than a claim rooted entirely in the free press clause.

It is one thing to probe a reporter's mind, another to obtain documents or other materials in the reporter's possession. The problem of how the police or others can collect these materials was taken before the Supreme Court in 1978 in *Zurcher* v. *Stanford Daily.* Armed with a search warrant, police entered the office of the *Stanford Daily,* Stanford University's student newspaper, searching for photos to identify suspects connected with a hospital sit-in. The issue was whether the police ought to have proceeded with a warrant or should have obtained the documents with a subpoena *duces tecum.* With the subpoena approach, a hearing is required before surrender of the documents. There, the target of the subpoena can argue why the documents should not be released.

The Court ruled that the state's interest in enforcing the criminal law and recovering evidence of crime outweighs the interests of a third party in a hearing preceding surrender of evidence. A third party is, of course, not suspected of committing a crime. Preventing harm to the investigation (mainly by lost or destroyed evidence) was deemed more significant than the interest of nonsuspects in avoiding a surprise visit from the police. The Court did not believe that reporters deserve special treatment, either. The police are entitled to "every person's evidence," and that includes the press.

The issue differed from the *Caldwell* situation; in particular the photos were not entrusted to a reporter. But similar considerations apply, since a reporter's notes or documents could become fair game in an open season of search warrants. Should reporters do the evidence-gathering work of the police? Should they be entitled to some special protection above the average citizen, because they gather evidence as a part of their business? Where does that leave private investigators? Does the ability of the police to enter a newsroom armed with a less-than-precise warrant (if it were a subpoena it could be resisted in a hearing before having to comply) cripple the press's ability to cultivate sources or to make investigations?

The *Stanford Daily* case triggered efforts in Congress to prohibit the use of search warrants in gathering evidence from third parties. The result was a mixed bag: the Privacy Protection Act of 1980. Searches directed at the press were restricted, but not third party searches generally. Instead the Attorney General was ordered to promulgate regulations to define the limits of a nonpress third party search.

Under the act, the type of material determines the scope of permissible searches. "Work product materials" (notes, for instance) are more tightly protected against searches, while such "documentary material" as the photos in the *Stanford Daily* case receive less protection. A search is permissible if imminent destruction of such documents is likely, but not for the destruction of a reporter's notes. Whether the exceptions will swallow the rule that generally prohibits third party searches of the press remains to be seen.

For me the special protection owed the press in honoring its confidences remains a matter of continual testing, one case at a time, balancing articulated needs of police and prosecutors and the heavy presumption against asking the press to betray trusts to do the prosecution's work. Each time a court finds that a state's interest is compelling enough to overcome the presumption, our independent press tradition, rooted in the First Amendment, is compromised. A federal shield law might remove some of the uncertainty of ad hoc press-police relations. The exceptions in the Privacy Protection Act suggest the limits of that statutory solution, however.

DLB

5

Access to Information: What Should Be Available?

THE AUTHORS

HARRY KALVEN, JR., professor of law at the University of Chicago from 1945 until his death in 1974 at age sixty, was a scholar of the first order in the two areas of law that privacy law touches—torts and the First Amendment.

Kalven wrote scores of technical and popular articles and six books on the law, including *Cases and Materials on Torts,* written in 1959 with Charles Gregory, which soon became a standard text for first-year students in many law schools. Beloved by his students at a school better known for its austere competitiveness than for Kalven's brand of gentle but persuasive pedagogy, he wrote with a wit and precision seldom found in legal literature.

As Edward H. Levi, former Attorney General of the United States and a colleague and teacher of Kalven's at the University of Chicago said of him at a memorial tribute in the school's law review: "His contribution to the understanding of the law and legal institutions is among the most significant of our time. Nothing he touched was left without added insight."

Although his studies of the United States Constitution rank among his best writing, Kalven gained greatest attention as the leader in the 1950s, along with Professor Hans Zeisel, of the University of Chicago "Jury Project," a study of how juries work. It stands today as the most complete analysis of the deliberative aspect of our trial system.

THOMAS I. EMERSON received the A.B. (1928) and a law degree (1931), both from Yale University. During the Roosevelt administration he served as an attorney for the National Recovery Administration and the Social Security Board; as special assistant to the Attorney General, 1940–1941; and as general counsel of the Office of War Mobilization and Reconversion, 1945–1946. He returned to Yale to join the law school faculty in 1946 and has remained there since. He is best known for two landmark books on free speech, *Toward a General Theory of the First Amendment* (1966) and *The System of Freedom of Expression* (1970).

Privacy in Tort Law— Were Warren and Brandeis Wrong?

HARRY KALVEN, JR.

". . .NO OTHER TORT HAS RECEIVED SUCH AN OUTPOURING OF COMMENT IN ADVOCACY OF ITS EXISTENCE." —*Prosser, Torts 1051 (1st ed. 1941).*

PRIVACY is one of the truly profound values for a civilized society, and it is heartening to find it today the subject of active interest and concern on many fronts. Several popular books have sounded alarm about the threats of surveillance that modern technology may carry, and an impressive

Reprinted by permission of Duke University School of Law © *Law and Contemporary Problems* 31(2)(1966):326–41.

committee of the Association of the Bar of the City of New York has for some years now been at work exploring the matter. At the constitutional level, there have been the new emphases of some of the opinions in the birth control cases, finding in privacy a touchstone for constitutional policy, a sort of culminating right derived from the specific provisions of the Bill of Rights read together. In jurisprudence, there has been the sustained debate between Lord Devlin and Professor H. L. A. Hart on the limits of legal enforcement of morality, a debate which can well be said to turn on the protection to be afforded consensual adult conduct when private.[1] The psychologist tells us the importance to the child of a room of his own, and the sociologist describes for us the terrible attrition of places of privacy in modern life. And, if necessary, our still vivid experiences with totalitarianism remind us that a major tactic for the dictator is to subjugate by eliminating privacy.[2] I start, therefore, from the premise that privacy is surely deeply linked to individual dignity and the needs of human existence.

It is perhaps still too early in the day to tell whether privacy, however great a value, can function as a constitutional concept. Can, that is, the protection of privacy provide a base from which to reason, a clue for policy? There are at least two difficulties. First, privacy seems a less precise way of approaching more specific values, as, for example, in the case of freedom of speech, association, and religion; second, there is always the possibility that it cannot be used to delimit the public sphere but will turn out invariably to be residual, simply what is left after the state or society has made its demand.

My immediate concerns, however, are not with these larger issues but with the fate of the law's most direct effort to respond to privacy—the development of a tort remedy for invasions of the right of privacy. And I find myself enmeshed with a paradox. Although privacy is for me a great and important value, tort law's effort to protect the right of privacy seems to me a mistake.

It takes a special form of foolhardiness to raise one's voice against the right of privacy at this particular moment in its history. As we all know, it did not exist as such at common law, and the first case clearly recognizing it dates from the twentieth century.[3] Its development is a bit of legal culture we are all likely to be proud of: it shows that the "eternal youth" of the common law is still green; it is a reflection of civilized sensitivity to subtle harms; and, above all, it traces its lineage back to that most influential law review article of all, Warren & Brandeis, *The Right to Privacy.*[4]

---

1. The several exchanges can be readily traced in H. L. A. HART, LAW, LIBERTY AND MORALITY (1963), and PATRICK A. D. DEVLIN, THE ENFORCEMENT OF MORALS (1965).
2. Compare GEORGE ORWELL, 1984 (1949).
3. Pavesich v. New England Life Ins. Co., 122 Ga. 190, 50 S.E. 68 (1905).
4. 4 HARV. L. REV. 193 (1890). It is to be noted, in view of the popular impression, that the authors speak of the right *to* privacy rather than the right *of* privacy and that Warren, not Brandeis, is the first author.
    In view of the probable importance of Spahn v. Julian Messner, Inc., 23 App. Div. 2d 216, 260 N.Y.S.2d 451, *motion to dismiss appeal denied,* 16 N.Y.2d 1082, 266 N.Y.S.2d 405, 213 N.E.2d 696 (1965), as a precedent in the privacy field, for one brief, delirious moment I flirted with the idea of calling this essay "Brandeis and Warren Spahn."

Further, all indications are that the tort has come of age, after hesitant beginnings until the 1930s. Our most authoritative commentator advises that there are now some 300 reported cases on privacy in American law reports, and the roll call of states recognizing the right has grown in the interval between the first and third editions of *Prosser on Torts* from eight to thirty-one with only a handful of states expressly rejecting it. Moreover, the tort has not only grown; it has, so to speak, multiplied and prospered. Dean Prosser a few years ago, after carefully reviewing the cases, argued persuasively that the right of privacy is not one right but is in reality four different ones.[5] And to make things as awkward as possible for my stance, Dean Wade, following up a Prosser suggestion, then argued that privacy now overlaps defamation to a significant degree, and predicted that we may well see the right of privacy gradually replace the torts of libel and slander, a development of the law he would applaud.[6] Finally, Professor Bloustein, joining in the remarkable renaissance of serious writing about the tort of privacy in the past five years, has flung the gauntlet at Dean Prosser and has ably attempted to rehabilitate privacy as a single tort, protecting a single fundamental interest.[7]

To reduce my thesis at the outset to capsule form, it is this: I suspect that fascination with the great Brandeis trade mark, excitement over the law at a point of growth, and appreciation of privacy as a key value have combined to dull the normal critical sense of judges and commentators and have caused them not to see the pettiness of the tort they have sponsored.

I

There is special sense in going in this instance back to the source, not only because the famous article has influenced courts and legislatures but equally because its touch of grandeur and its emphasis on the spiritual side of man seem indelibly to have set the tone for subsequent discussion of the tort. There is a point here for the legal historian to ponder. The impact of the article resides not so much in the power of its argument as in the social status it gave to the tort. In the vernacular of the sports pages, it lent it "class."

The rhetoric is lofty indeed. Thus, at the start: "Political, social, and economic changes entail the recognition of new rights, and the common law, in its eternal youth, grows to meet the demands of society." And again: "Later, there came a recognition of man's spiritual nature, of his feelings and his intellect." Or again:

> This development of the law was inevitable. The intense intellectual and emotional life and the heightening of sensations which came with the advance of civilization, made it clear to men that only a part of the

---

5. Prosser, *Privacy,* 48 CALIF. L. REV. 383 (1960).
6. Wade, *Defamation and the Right of Privacy,* 15 VAND. L. REV. 1093 (1962).
7. Bloustein, *Privacy as an Aspect of Human Dignity: An Answer to Dean Prosser,* 39 N.Y.U.L.REV. 962 (1964).

pain, pleasure, and profit of life lay in physical things. Thoughts, emotions, and sensations demanded legal recognition, and the beautiful capacity for growth which characterizes the common law enabled the judges to afford the requisite protection, without the interposition of the legislature.

And later on, in dismissing the analogy to libel and slander, the authors tell us: "In short, the wrongs and correlative rights recognized by the law of slander and libel are in their nature material rather than spiritual."

Yet while the view is long and the right is placed on high ground, there is a curious nineteenth century quaintness about the grievance, an air of injured gentility. "The press is overstepping in every direction the obvious bounds of propriety and of decency. Gossip is no longer the resource of the idle and of the vicious, but has become a trade, which is pursued with industry as well as effrontery." And again:

> When personal gossip attains the dignity of print, and crowds the space available for matters of real interest to the community, what wonder that the ignorant and thoughtless mistake its relative importance. Easy of comprehension, appealing to that weak side of human nature which is never wholly cast down by the misfortunes and frailties of our neighbors, no one can be surprised that it usurps the place of interest in brains capable of other things. Triviality destroys at once robustness of thought and delicacy of feeling. No enthusiasm can flourish, no generous impulse can survive under its blighting influence.

One may perhaps wonder if the tort is not an anachronism, a nineteenth century response to the mass press which is hardly in keeping with the more robust tastes or mores of today.[8]

More surprising is the fact that the article reads so much like a brief and rests on an incomplete argument. The key analogy is to common law copyright, and the case is rested almost in full in *Prince Albert v. Strange*.[9] There is a neat point contrasting statutory copyright, which depends on publication and is thus designed to protect property, with the common law rights which exist prior to publication and "are, it is believed, but instances and applications of a general right to privacy, which properly understood affords a remedy for the evils under consideration."

There can be no objection to the tactic of locating a broader principle behind the protection of intellectual, artistic, and literary property at common law. The difficulty goes rather to the selectivity with which this is done. Even in 1890 it must have been abundantly clear that the common

---

8. It is now well known that the impetus for the article came from Warren's irritation over the way the press covered the wedding of his daughter in 1890. Warren and Brandeis had been classmates together at Harvard Law School and had practiced law together. . . . There is, from my special point of view, poetic justice in the circumstance that so petty a tort should have been spawned by so petty a grievance.
9. De G. & Sm. 652, 64 Eng. Rep. 293 (V.C. 1848).

law had a highly cautious and ambivalent set of reactions toward giving protection against dignitary and emotional harms, that the law was atomized into pockets of doctrine that pointed in different directions. *Alcorn v. Mitchell,* for an easy example, was on the books in Illinois when Warren and Brandeis wrote. It was a supreme instance of an offensive battery,[10] the defendant having spat upon the plaintiff in the courtroom. Judgment for a thousand dollars was affirmed. It is transparent that it was the offensiveness, the indignity, and not the physical battery that infuriated the plaintiff, the jury, and the judge. Yet one might have argued, using the Warren and Brandeis logic, that the principle underlying the case supports recognition of insults and indignities as torts, regardless of whether they are accompanied by a technical battery. But surely such an argument would have been simplistic. It is hard to see that the Warren and Brandeis argument for the inevitable growth of an underlying principle is much better.

There are three final points to note about the article. First—and this is particularly relevant in terms of the current Prosser analysis of the multiple aspects of the right of privacy today—Warren and Brandeis were concerned *only* with public disclosure in the press of truthful but private details about the individual which caused emotional upset to him. Second, there is the question of whether the argument does not prove that if any adjustment in law is to be made, a much broader right ought to be recognized than the one Warren and Brandeis sponsored. If infliction of emotional harm in this special way is now actionable on the grounds of underlying principle, why should not all intentional infliction of emotional harm be recognized? There has long been criticism of the entire dignitary area of tort law for its lack of coherence, consistency, and adherence to general principle. Yet the Warren and Brandeis effort serves really to add another little *ad hoc* category.

Finally, while the article is admirable in the care with which it specifies certain limitations on the new right, it makes it apparent at the birth of the right that there are certain major ambiguities. These are all points which haunt the tort today and to which we will return, but we would note here that there is no effort to specify what will constitute a prima facie case; no concern with how damages are to be measured; no concern, other than to dismiss actual malice, with what the basis of liability will be; and finally there is the projection of a generous set of privileges but no effort to assess whether they do not engulf the cause of action. And, of course, there is no hint that any but gentlemen will ever be moved to use the new remedy.

II

Dean Wade has said that the publication of Dean Prosser's article, *Privacy,* in 1960[11] is an event rivalling in importance for the law in this

---

10. "An exasperated suitor has indulged the gratification of his malignant feelings in this despicable mode." 63 Ill. 553, 554 (1872).
11. Prosser, *supra* note 5.

area the publication of the original Warren and Brandeis work. There is, therefore, a certain logic in now moving our discussion from the source to, as it were, the second source.

The earliest cases, *Roberson v. Rochester Folding Box Co.*[12] and *Pavesich v. New England Life Ins. Co.,*[13] and the enactment in 1903 of the New York statute have long made it apparent that the right of privacy was mixing at least two ideas. One was that kind of invasion by the press of private life that Warren and Brandeis has as their grievance; the other was akin to appropriation, the use commercially of another's name or likeness without his consent. The rationale for the latter protection, although the matter may be more complex than first appears,[14] is the straightforward one of preventing unjust enrichment by the theft of good will. No social purpose is served by having the defendant get for free some aspect of the plaintiff that would have market value and for which he would normally pay. In the last decade this point has become fully apparent, and we have had talk of the right to publicity.

What Dean Prosser did was to isolate two additional themes in the privacy cases. One involves intrusions where there is no trespass, as for example the Peeping Tom case or the wire tap on a telephone. It is an interesting challenge to fit in these cases conceptually, but the problem appears *de minimis*. There is not even a handful of such cases where there is no trespass. It seems dubious doctrine, therefore, to dignify this cluster as a major subcategory.

The fourth and final Prosser category encompasses what he terms the "false light" cases. A prime example is *Hinish v. Meier & Frank Co.,*[15] where the plaintiff's name without his consent was signed to a telegram to the governor urging defeat of certain legislation. The use of plaintiff's name or picture in advertising without his consent may also often present this form of grievance as well as appropriation. The analogy here is, of course, to defamation, and the overlap might have been thought substantial enough to make an approach via privacy superfluous. It appears, however, that courts are finding it more congenial to assimilate defamation cases to privacy. It is in this group of cases that Dean Wade sees as carrying the promise that some day privacy will replace defamation, a thesis we will examine later.

It is an important part of Dean Prosser's argument that these aspects of privacy are not only analytically different—as one might say the action of trespass to land protects a variety of interests—but that they are func-

---

12. 171 N.Y. 538, 64 N.E. 442 (1902).
13. 122 Ga. 190, 50 S.E. 68 (1905).
14. The point is best put by Bloustein. . . . He argues that relatively few of these cases have involved the use of names or likenesses that had a true commercial value; this seems to have been true in *Roberson* and *Pavesich* and in such recent cases as Eick v. Perk Dog Food, 347 Ill. App. 293, 106 N.E.2d 742 (1952), which established the right in Illinois. He argues further that the grievance goes to being "used" by another. I think he is correct that it is possible to have an "appropriation" case that involves not a commercial tort but exactly the same affront to peace of mind that is involved in the disclosure cases. But I am saying simply that the commercial grievance makes sense as a distinct rationale for a tort.
15. 166 Ore. 482, 113 P.2d 438 (1941).

tionally different so that the measure of damages and the appropriate limitations and defenses differ.

It is not easy to know just what to make of this new schema, except that given the legal mind's weakness for neat labels and categories and given the deserved Prosser prestige, it is a safe prediction that the four-fold view will come to dominate whatever thinking is done about the right of privacy in the future. It is difficult to say whether this reformulation represents a radical revision in analysis, new insight based on the many cases since 1941, or simply new rhetoric. In any event, Warren and Brandeis did not have any such network of privacy protection in mind, and the new analysis dramatically relocates the place of their specific tort of the invasion of private life by the press. On a very small scale, it effects a Copernican revolution.

There may be two consequences from this in addition to useful clarification of messy law, and they may move in opposite directions. On the one hand there is the lament eloquently voiced by Professor Bloustein that the whole spirit, dignity, and deep rationale for the tort has now been lost. In place of the grand underlying principle of inviolate personality and individual dignity, we have now four *ad hoc* categories. Or, to put this another way, the deadening common sense of the Prosser approach cuts the tort loose from the philosophic moorings Warren and Brandeis gave it, from, that is, the excitement of association with the grand norm of privacy. Bloustein's gallant article is in effect an attempt to return analysis of the tort to the moral tone of Warren and Brandeis.

The other consequence of the Prosser schema is paradoxically to inflate the importance of the Warren and Brandeis subcategory of privacy, to lend it a kind of vitality by association. Courts confronted with privacy cases in the future are likely to "hear" only the message that privacy is thriving as a legal concept, with its over 300 cases and thirty-one jurisdictions, that it is complicated and technical, and that it still bears the Warren and Brandeis name.

III

We come at last to our point, the critique of the Warren and Brandeis category of privacy. We do not aspire here to take on the other three categories. The appropriation tort, as indicated, makes sense; the intrusion tort hardly exists; and the case for the "false light" category, given the law of defamation, will be examined briefly in the next section. Our concern then is with the mass communication tort of privacy.

To begin with, the tort has no legal profile. We do not know what constitutes a prima facie case, we do not know on what basis damages are to be measured, we do not know whether the basis of liability is limited to intentional invasions or includes also negligent invasions and even strict liability.

The conduct, I take it, will involve some reference to the plaintiff in the mass media without his consent, which reference must involve the use of his name, his likeness, or some recognizable personal detail of his personality or biography. And, since we are putting the "false light" cases to one side, the reference will be an accurate one. The problem of definition then is to state *what less than every such unconsented-to reference* is prima facie tortious. This is the problem unless we are to emulate some primitive tribe that believes that any use of one's name somehow magically reduces one's potency. We cannot here follow the strategy the law has been able to use on battery. There can be no analogue to the formula that every unconsented-to touching is prima facie a tort.

What then is the threshold for actionable disclosure in the press of details of privacy? At one time we were told that the invasion must be "conduct which outrages the common decencies. . . ."[16] This formula, it should be noted, would have limited the tort to a few exceptional cases and presumably to cases where punitive damages would be appropriate. This might have provided a viable stopping point; the only difficulty is that few if any of the privacy precedents would satisfy it. Today it is said the formula is that the disclosure must be "one which would be offensive and objectionable to a reasonable man. . . ."[17] Whatever the success of the reasonable-man standard in negligence cases, in this context it can only mean that the jury will know better than the court what the sensitivities of the day are. The upshot is that every unconsented-to reference in the press creates prima facie a cause of action that could take the plaintiff to the jury.

The theory of damages is equally vague and mysterious in so far as damages are supposed to be compensatory. It is said that special damages need not be shown and that the difficulty of measuring damages here is no more reason for denying recovery than it would be in defamation. But it remains odd to give recovery for emotional disturbance without any showing that plaintiff suffered or was upset. And defamation at least has the rationalization that it is trying to infer what degree of injury there has been to reputation and what degree of emotional upset a false and defamatory statement has caused. Surely it is even more conjectural to price the emotional impact of a truthful nondefamatory statement.

Nor has there been much interest displayed in what the underlying basis of liability is, although this has been *the* standard topic of analysis for all other tort categories. Does it matter whether the defendant knew the disclosure would be so offensive, or whether he meant to refer to plaintiff at all, or whether he thought he was privileged by the public interest in the item? We are concerned, it must be emphasized, with a mass media tort where malicious intention is not likely to appear. In *Cason v. Baskin,*[18] would the distinguished author-defendant have had reason to anticipate the outrage with which the plaintiff greeted her portrayal in a novel? In *Mau v. Rio Grande Oil, Inc.,*[19] was the defendant on notice that the re-enactment of the crime story in which plaintiff had been a victim would so intensively upset the plaintiff? In *Kerby v. Hal Roach Studios, Inc.,*[20] where the defendant employed an advertising gimmick of letters

---

16. WILLIAM L. PROSSER, TORTS 1062 (1st ed. 1941).
17. WILLIAM L. PROSSER, TORTS 837 (3d ed. 1964).
18. 155 Fla. 198, 20 So. 2d 243 (1945).
19. 28 F. Supp. 845 (N.D. Cal. 1939).
20. 53 Cal. App. 2d 207, 127 P.2d 577 (Dist. Ct. App. 1942).

from "your ectoplasmic playmate, Marion Kerby" and was unaware
there was an actual Marion Kerby living in Los Angeles, was liability imposed for a negligent failure to check the telephone directory, or did the
defendant risk invasion of privacy at its peril? It is once again characteristic of the indifference to the legal profile of the tort that there is virtually
no discussion in the books of whether or not privacy is an intentional tort.
And this is especially striking since the underlying basis of liability for
defamation has been so famous a point of tort doctrine.

This is perhaps the place to pause to reflect on the rule that truth is a
defense in defamation. Although the rule has considerable venerability,
there has been some controversy over its policy in recent years. There
have been articles urging that truth as a defense be qualified, and about
ten jurisdictions have by statute made moves in this direction. What is ar-
resting here is that none of the critics argue for more than a change that
would make truth a defense only if uttered with good motives. If we come
at the matter from the angle of defamation, liability for disclosing a truth
about the plaintiff would at most be actionable only if the defendant
published with bad motives. If this is as far as we have been willing to go
in defamation, where the disclosure is negative enough to injure reputation, why do we expand the liability rule when we come at the grievance
as an invasion of privacy? If privacy were to have been made consistent
with the old tort of defamation, it would have been a stringent form of intentional tort requiring something akin to ill will. Perhaps as Dean Wade
suggests it is the old that should conform to the new; defamation should
now be made consistent with privacy. But in any event the strained relationship of truth in privacy to truth in defamation is one more indication
that the law has been oddly indifferent to working out any serious definition of the newer tort.[21]

The fact that we have no intelligible version of a prima facie case is
only half the difficulty; the other half is that since Warren and Brandeis
wrote, it has been agreed that there is a generous privilege to serve the
public interest in news. And today, since *New York Times Co. v.
Sullivan*,[22] the privilege may arguably have some constitutional status.

---

21. It may lend perspective to the right of privacy too if we approach it for a moment as
an instance of the emerging generic tort of intentional infliction of emotional harm, as Wade
. . . has urged. For example, the formula proposed by Prosser, *Insult and Outrage*, 44 CALIF.
L. REV. 40, 43 (1956), was this: "One who, by extreme and outrageous conduct, intentional-
ly or recklessly causes severe emotional distress to another is subject to liability for such
emotional distress and for bodily harm resulting from it" (all italicized in original) (quoting
RESTATEMENT (SECOND), TORTS § 46(1) (Tent. Draft No. 1, 1957)). Has there been a single
privacy case that satisfies this standard?

22. 376 U.S. 254 (1964). See generally Kalven, *The New York Times Case: A Note on the
Central Meaning of the First Amendment*, 1964 SUP. CT. REV. 191. There is a possibility that
the newsworthiness privilege in privacy will acquire constitutional status and thus become
independent of state policy. This would alter some of Dean Wade's expectations of flexibly
incorporating any free speech privilege in privacy cases into a negligence-like calculus.

The constitutional issue is now on appeal before the U.S. Supreme Court in Hayes v.
Hill, 15 N.Y.2d 986, 207 N.E.2d 604, *prob. juris. noted sub nom.* Time, Inc. v. Hill, 382 U.S.
936 (1965), *reargument ordered*, 384 U.S. 995 (1966). See generally Franklin, *A Constitutional Problem in Privacy Protection: Legal Inhibition on Reporting of Fact*, 16 STAN. L. REV.
107 (1963). See also, Franklin, *The Origins and Constitutionality of Limitations on Truth as a
Defense in Tort Law*, 16 STAN. L. REV. 789 (1964).

What is at issue, it seems to me, is whether the claim of privilege is not so overpowering as virtually to swallow the tort. What can be left of the vaunted new right after the claims of privilege have been confronted?

To begin with the Warren and Brandeis dictum, privacy inherits all the privileges of libel and slander together with an additional privilege to publish, in their words, "matter which is of public or general interest." In other words in privacy, unlike defamation, there is a privilege to report news. I need not for my purposes push the point to its logical extreme, but surely there is force to the simple contention that whatever is in the news media is by definition newsworthy, that the press must in the nature of things be the final arbiter of newsworthiness. The cases admittedly do not go quite this far, but they go far enough to decimate the tort.

In *Jenkins v. Dell Publishing Co.*,[23] Judge Hastie found a sufficient public interest to exonerate defendants for republishing in a magazine called *Front Page Detective,* a year after the event, the story of how Jenkins had been kicked to death by a teen-age gang. The story was told in a one-page account with 150 words and several photographs. Judge Hastie declined to distinguish furnishing news for entertainment and for information.

In *Metter v. Los Angeles Examiner,*[24] the plaintiff's wife committed suicide by jumping from a high building, and the news accounts featured photographs of the event despite the request of the anguished husband. The court, in finding the newspaper coverage privileged, argued that, by the method she chose, Mrs. Metter had made herself a public figure forfeiting all right to privacy. "For a brief period and in the pitiful and tragic circumstances attending her demise she became an object of public interest."

And again in *Kelley v. Post Publishing Co.*[25] the defendants published a photo of the body of plaintiff's daughter immediately after her death in an auto accident. The court stoically confronting the needs of the public interest observed: "But if the right asserted here were sustained, it would be difficult to fix its boundaries. . . . A newspaper could not safely publish the picture of a train wreck or of an airplane crash if any of the bodies of the victims were recognizable."

The lack of legal profile and the enormity of the counterprivilege converge to raise for me the question of whether privacy is really a viable tort remedy. The mountain, I suggest, has brought forth a pretty small mouse. Let me sum up my complaint by citing three cases which in my view frame the weaknesses of the tort: *Cohen v. Marx,*[26] *Cason v. Baskin,*[27] and of course *Sidis v. F-R Publishing Corp.*[28] In the *Cohen* case the plaintiff, a former boxer, sued the comedian, Groucho Marx, for having said on a radio show: "I once managed a fighter named Canvasback Cohen. I

23. 251 F.2d 447 (3d Cir. 1958).
24. 35 Cal. App. 2d 304, 95 P.2d 491 (Dist. Ct. App. 1939).
25. 327 Mass. 275, 98 N.E. 2d 286 (1951).
26. 94 Cal. App. 2d 704, 211 P.2d 320 (Dist. Ct. App. 1949).
27. 155 Fla. 198, 20 So. 2d 243 (1945).
28. 113 F.2d 806 (2d Cir. 1940).

brought him out here, he got knocked out, and I made him walk back to Cleveland." It is true that the court in this instance declined to protect Mr. Cohen's privacy. I offer the case simply as an example of the unbeatable triviality of some privacy litigation.

Cason involved the effort of Marjorie Kinnan Rawlings to use plaintiff as a character in her book, *Cross Creek*. The following is a fair example of the characterization of which plaintiff complained:

> Zelma is an ageless spinster resembling an angry and efficient canary. She manages her orange grove and as much of the village and county as needs management or will submit to it. I cannot decide whether she should have been a man or a mother. She combines the more violent characteristics of both and those who ask for or accept her manifold ministrations think nothing of being cursed loudly at the very instant of being tenderly fed, clothed, nursed or guided through their troubles.

The case went up to the Florida Supreme Court twice. On the first occasion the court reversed, holding plaintiff stated a prima facie case, and thereby entered Florida among the states recognizing a right of privacy. The case came back on appeal after a trial resulting in a verdict for the defendant. The court again reversed, this time because evidence about defendant's status as an author had erroneously been admitted; it went on, however, to note that plaintiff had failed to offer any evidence on the matter of compensatory damages and to remand with directions that the judgment for the defendant be reversed and that plaintiff recover only nominal damages. 'Twas, as the poet said, a famous victory.

Sidis involved the *New Yorker* profile of a one-time child prodigy who in adulthood, after a brilliant youth, had dwindled to a career as an "insignificant" clerk desirous of anonymity and given to odd enthusiasms such as elaborately collecting streetcar transfers. The facts in *Sidis* present a very appealing case, if there is to be a legal right of privacy. Here we have a detailed disclosure of personal life at the expense of one who manifestly wished "to be let alone." Yet even here, as the logic of Judge Clark makes inexorable, there is no liability. Sidis, argues Judge Clark, was inescapably public. Originally at the height of his brilliance he was a public figure. "Since then Sidis has cloaked himself in obscurity, but his subsequent history, containing as it did the answer to the question of whether or not he had fulfilled his early promise, was still a matter of public concern."

The final point to make against the tort rests to a considerable extent on a surmise. It goes to claims consciousness. It goes to who will be recruited as plaintiffs under this tort, and we need some empirical data about the handling of privacy claims. We know a little something about claims consciousness in the personal injury field,[29] and we know there is a

---

29. See ROGER B. HUNTING & G. S. NEUWIRTH, WHO SUES IN NEW YORK CITY? (1962); HANS ZEISEL, HARRY KALVEN, JR. & BERNARD BUCHHOLZ, DELAY IN THE COURT 223 (1959).

pronounced and interesting difference between English culture and our own in terms of readiness to sue for libel. We can at this point only guess about privacy.

I have two guesses. The first is that the victims on whose behalf the privacy tort remedy was designed will not in the real world elect to use it and that those who will come forward with privacy claims will very often have shabby, unseemly grievances and an interest in exploitation. I would think, for example, that a parent ruthlessly photographed at the terrible moment of picking up the body of his child seriously hurt or perhaps killed in an accident would have an appealing case against the intrusion into his moment of grief; this is "news" we might well ask the public to forgo.[30] But I would also think that the parent I have in mind would not deign to sue for money damages.[31] I am emboldened, therefore, to assert that privacy will recruit claimants inversely to the magnitude of the offense to privacy involved.

It is an old story that law must tolerate some fraud and exploitation of its processes, but the challenge here is narrower. In the law at large there is a rough favorable balance between claims we would wish the law to honor and exploitative claims. Hence, most remedies seem worth their price in shabby assertions of right. But it is possible for the balance to get thrown off, for primarily unattractive claimants to seek to use the remedy. Perhaps the one major experience the law has had with the balance of claims going askew is with redress for breach of promise. The balance finally became so bad that in many jurisdictions the remedy was abolished. As one commentator put it: "The plaintiffs who do recover are not the ones who should, and the persons who are wronged in this way practically never bring suit." Of course, breach-of-promise suits had come to involve fraud and blackmail, and there is no parallel strain on privacy actions. What is similar, however, is that in both instances the cause of action on paper looked attractive and meritorious and that the victim that society had in mind when it created the means of redress was not the one who used the remedy. Thus, my question is this: Would we have created the tort remedy for invasion of privacy had we foreseen what the cases brought under it to date have amounted to?

My second guess about the handling of privacy claims is that they take their toll in the settlement process. The lack of legal profile for the tort makes any sort of unconsented-to reference to the plaintiff look colorable, and there is the threat of indeterminate damages. I suspect, therefore, that the achievement of the new tort remedy has been primarily to breed nuisance claims.

I have put my suspicions in the form of guesses. It would have been more appropriate perhaps simply to state them as questions. I am writing

---

30. *But see* Kelly v. Post Publishing Co., 327 Mass. 275, 98 N.E.2d 286 (1951), holding there is a privilege.

31. Yet the father did sue in *Kelley, supra* note 30; the husband did sue in Metter v. Los Angeles Examiner, 35 Cal. App. 2d 304, 95 P.2d 491 (Dist. Ct. App. 1939); and the parents of the deformed baby did sue in Bazemore v. Savannah Hospital, 171 Ga. 257, 155 S.E. 194 (1930).

from a most inadequate sample of legal anecdotes and bare impressions gained from case reports. The dynamics of claims consciousness is a tricky business, and I could easily be wrong. Dean Wade, after all, has told us that experience in the three Southern states which have insult statutes has been quite satisfactory; a priori the insult statute would seem as open to claimant abuse as the right of privacy.

The right of privacy is preeminently an instance where the law in action may change the significance of the law in the books. What we need to know for further discussions of this tort is this: Who sues in privacy?

IV

The mysterious way in which the common law grows and changes has never found better illustration than in the current tendency of privacy actions to move into the traditional field of defamation. Warren and Brandeis, despite their tributes to the "eternal youth of the common law," would have been astonished to learn that the precedent they launched would grow so that today, in Dean Wade's wording, "the great majority of defamation actions can now be brought for the invasion of the right of privacy . . ."; they would have been further amazed to be told as of the 1960s that "the action for invasion of the right of privacy may come to supplant the action for defamation." They had scrupulously set their new tort beside the traditional rules for libel and slander and had accepted the argument that a limitation that applied to redress of a statement that was defamatory and false should apply a fortiori to redress of one that was nondefamatory and true. It would have been expected that the relationship of privacy to defamation would be that privacy would now make some *true* statements actionable and thus qualify the defense of truth in defamation. What the "false light" cases suggest, however, is a role for privacy actions where the statement is *false*.

I find both conceptual and practical difficulties in this new development. Conceptually I am not sure I see what the invasion of privacy consists of. Is it an invasion of privacy to say falsely of a man that he is a thief? What is his grievance? Is it that, on analogy to *Melvin v. Reid*,[32] it would have been an invasion *if true* and no one had known it? Or is it that it is false? Or is it that his name has been used in a public utterance without his consent? The first idea seems to me preposterously oblique and complex; the second is surely covered by the law of defamation; the third is trivial.

Is the case for the use of privacy better if we assume that the statement, although false, would not be actionable in defamation? The literal and total overlap with defamation is then avoided, but is our judgment of the grievance any more intelligible? If the statement is not offensive enough to the reasonable man to be defamatory, how does it become offensive enough to the reasonable man to be an invasion of privacy? Or is the point again that plaintiff's name has been used without his consent?

---

32. 112 Cal. App. 285, 297 Pac. 91 (Dist. Ct. App. 1931).

And if the desire is to relax somewhat the criteria of what is defamatory, would it not be more rational to do that openly and directly?

The result seems to be the emergence of privacy cases that define a hybrid tort, cases where the use of a name without consent is held to be offensive because the attribution is false and where the answer to its being nondefamatory is that it is a use of the name without consent!

All this does not do justice to the elegance of Dean Wade's review of the cases or his argument from them. He argues first that the plaintiff surely cannot be worse off because the statement is false, that, therefore, he should be able to sue without regard to whether it is true or false, and finally that, if this step is taken, a majority of all defamation actions can be restated as privacy actions. I would agree, of course, that the plaintiff should not have to prove the truth of the assertion in order to state a cause of action for privacy. He should not, however, be allowed to bolster a claim for privacy on the ground that the statement is false. It seems to me an extraordinary torturing of categories now to view defamation as resting ultimately not on the falsity but on the use of plaintiff's name without his consent.

Dean Wade further argues that use of privacy permits defamation at last to recover from what Pollock called "its going wrong at the outset," that is, treating the matter as injury to reputation rather than to feelings; that it permits the use of a "negligence calculus" structure rather than the rigid prima facie case-privilege structure of defamation; that it permits escape from the arbitrariness of the libel-slander distinction; and that it will permit a more flexible and candid appraisal of the free-speech issues involved in defamation cases. These are all beautiful points about the possibility of the new reforming the old by the slow evolution of common law processes, and Dean Wade may well be right in his prediction.

But if the colonization of defamation by privacy does take place, it will only be because by the use of a fiction the courts have turned at last to the reform of the law of defamation. It will not be because they have perceived that logically defamation is subsumed in privacy. They will simply be calling false statements by a new name.

Finally, one may wonder if this trend represents even good judicial statesmanship.[33] The technical complexity of the law of defamation, which has shown remarkable stamina in the teeth of centuries of acid criticism, may reflect one useful strategy for a legal system forced against its ultimate better judgment to deal with dignitary harms. Perhaps the famous Pollock dictum had the matter exactly wrong!

In any event, it would be a notable thing if the right of privacy, having, as it were, failed in three-quarters of a century to amount to anything at home, went forth to take over the traditional torts of libel and slander.[34]

---

33. Prosser has expressed some dismay at the ease with which defamation bastions seem to be falling to privacy. "Are they of so little consequence that they may be circumvented in so casual and cavalier a fashion?" Prosser, *supra* note 5, at 401.

34. "All this is a most marvelous tree to grow from the wedding of the daughter of Mr. Samuel D. Warren." *Id.* at 423.

The Right of Privacy and Freedom of the Press

THOMAS I. EMERSON

AS AN INDEPENDENT CONCEPT the right of privacy is a relative latecomer to the system of individual rights. It made its first appearance in American law as a tort, a civil suit for damages or an injunction to protect against an unwarranted invasion by others of the vague "right to be let alone."[1] Originated by Samuel D. Warren and Louis D. Brandeis in their famous article in the *Harvard Law Review* in 1890, the privacy tort was given structure by Dean William L. Prosser in 1960 and broader dimensions by Professor Edward J. Bloustein and Professor Alan F. Westin[2] shortly thereafter. In the form of a constitutional right against governmental interference with the inner zones of space necessary to individual dignity and autonomy, a right of privacy was first established in *Griswold v. Connecticut*[3] in 1965. A right of privacy, in the form of protection against government disclosure of the personal affairs of an individual under right-to-know principles, came to the fore with the passage of the Federal Freedom of Information Act[4] in 1966. And a right of privacy in the form of limitations upon the power of government or private enterprises to obtain, store in computers, or disseminate large quantities of information about a particular person, is just now struggling to be born.

It is unsurprising, therefore, that the theoretical foundations of the right of privacy are relatively unformed and, indeed, are the subject of much current controversy. Efforts to formulate a comprehensive or unified concept, embracing all aspects of the right of privacy, have thus far not met with overwhelming success. And the application of such principles as do exist to particular concrete situations has not yet marked out fully discernable patterns.

On the other hand, freedom of the press has a long and well-established history in American law. Its origins stem from the abandonment of the English censorship laws at the end of the seventeenth century. It received public attention and legal support in America as early as the trial of Peter Zenger in 1735. And it has been placed upon firm constitutional footing in recent times by such Supreme Court decisions as *New York Times Co. v. Sullivan*[5] in 1964, substantially limiting the ancient law of libel in the interest of freedom of the press; *New York Times Co. v. United States*[6] in 1971, the Pentagon Papers case, which upheld freedom of the

This article is based on a paper prepared for delivery at the Privacy Conference, Pacific Lutheran University, Tacoma, Washington, April 19–22, 1978. Reprinted from *Harvard Civil Rights–Civil Liberties Law Review* 14(2)(1979):329–60.
   1. This phrase was introduced by Judge Cooley in his T. COOLEY, TORTS 29 (2d ed. 1888).
   2. A. WESTIN, PRIVACY AND FREEDOM (1967).
   3. 381 U.S. 479 (1965).
   4. 5 U.S.C. § 552 (1976).
   5. 376 U.S. 254 (1964).
   6. 403 U.S. 713 (1971).

press even against insistent claims of national security; *Miami Herald Publishing Co. v. Tornillo*[7] in 1974, protecting the press against legislative efforts to mandate a right of access for persons attacked in the press; and *Nebraska Press Association v. Stuart*[8] in 1976, forbidding judicial interference through the use of gag orders on the press. The wall of immunity thus constructed for the press has some gaping holes, including the unwillingness of the Supreme Court to close off all exceptions in the cases just mentioned; the Court's refusal to accept reporter's privilege;[9] the necessary government intervention in the electronic media because of the scarcity of physical facilities;[10] the extension of government search and seizure powers into the operations of the press;[11] and similar weaknesses. Nevertheless, as a general proposition, the constitutional foundations for a free press are solidly established in American law and show no signs of serious deterioration.

Against this background the urgent need for a right of privacy in the system of individual rights is manifest. The constantly increasing scope of governmental intercession in most areas of national life, the development of modern technology for ferreting out and monitoring everyone's affairs from womb to tomb, the closing in of physical and psychic space for the average person, all make the need for creation of an adequate law of privacy imperative for the future health of our society. It is essential, therefore, to reconcile this new area of individual rights with the established principles of freedom of the press. There are, of course, manifest dangers in this undertaking, because governmental interference with freedom of expression in any form inevitably poses a threat to the system of individual rights. Nonetheless we must make room for the new right of privacy. The press would be well-advised to accept the fundamental necessity of a privacy right and to assist in the search for an appropriate accommodation.

Actually, the areas of conflict between the right of privacy and freedom of the press are quite limited, and the task of reconciliation is by no means insurmountable. At most points the law of privacy and the law sustaining a free press do not contradict each other. On the contrary, they are mutually supportive, in that both are vital features of the basic system of individual rights. At other points there is only a minor likelihood of conflict. This is true, for instance of the protections afforded privacy through the law of trespass, theft, copyright and the like, where the press has long adjusted to limitations on the gathering of news, and the issues are hardly matters of controversy. There are, however, two major areas where an accommodation must be developed. One concerns the privacy tort, where the privacy right comes into sharp contrast with the right to publish. The other involves the right of the press to obtain information from the

---

7. 418 U.S. 241 (1974).
8. 427 U.S. 539 (1976).
9. Branzburg v. Hayes, 408 U.S. 665 (1972).
10. Red Lion Broadcasting Co. v. FCC, 395 U.S. 367 (1969).
11. Zurcher v. Stanford Daily, 436 U.S. 547 (1978).

government, where invocation of right-to-know principles to force disclosure may run squarely into an individual's claim that data about one's personal affairs should not be disseminated to others. The two problems involve somewhat different considerations and will therefore will be discussed separately.

I. THE RIGHT TO PUBLISH AND THE PRIVACY TORT

A. THE PROBLEM. Protection of the right of privacy through a civil suit for damages—the privacy tort—has developed slowly and uncertainly, but firmly, partly through legislation and partly through expansion of the common law. Analysis of privacy tort cases by Dean Prosser revealed that they fell into four categories. It has been a matter of dispute whether all four categories can be embraced within a single, comprehensive theory of privacy or whether each category represents a separate and distinct aspect of the privacy tort. Passing over that controversy for the moment, one can say that Prosser's clarification does fairly describe the actual results reached in the privacy decisions.

The four categories into which Dean Prosser divided the cases are: (1) intrusion upon a person's solitude or seclusion; (2) appropriation, for commercial purposes, of a person's name, likeness, or personality; (3) public disclosure of embarrassing private facts about a person; and (4) publicity that places a person in a false light in the public eye. Of these, the first two have not raised serious problems in terms of a conflict with freedom of the press. Intrusion upon solitude or seclusion can ordinarily be dealt with through concepts of trespass law. Limitations upon newsgathering imposed by the law of trespass have never been thought to infringe upon any right of the press. Appropriation of a name, likeness, or personality for purposes of advertising or similar commercial gain raises issues that are normally treated under principles of property law. Although the line between advertising for commercial gain and publication of news or information may be difficult to draw at times, the courts have generally been able to mark out satisfactory boundaries. Commercial speech is entitled to some protection under the first amendment but no one has suggested that freedom of speech or press authorizes impairment of copyright or similar property rights solely to promote the sale of commodities or services for a profit.

The two other Prosser categories do raise serious first amendment problems. Publication of true facts about a person, even though they are critical or embarrassing, is a core feature of the freedom of the press. The false light cases also raise issues that threaten freedom of the press. These fall into two subcategories: those where the facts are represented as true but are in fact false or misleading, yet are not defamatory; and those where the facts are presented as wholly or partly fiction. Limitations upon either subcategory can seriously curtail an "uninhibited, robust and wide-open" press. Established legal doctrines other than the concept of privacy do not afford any grounds for restrictions upon the press as to either of these categories.

It is necessary at this point to compare the law of privacy and the law of defamation. Three major differences should be noted, In defamation law only statements that are false are actionable; truth is, almost universally, a defense. In privacy law, other than in the false light cases, the facts published are true; indeed it is the very truth of the facts that creates the claimed invasion of privacy. Secondly, in defamation cases the interest sought to be protected is the objective one of reputation, either economic, political, or personal, in the outside world. In privacy cases the interest affected is the subjective one of injury to the inner person. Thirdly, in defamation cases, where the issue is truth or falsity, the marketplace of ideas furnishes a forum in which the battle can be fought. In privacy cases, resort to the marketplace simply accentuates the injury.

Conversely, there are marked similarities between the two bodies of law. The major common ground involves the dynamics of government intervention. Particularly in false light cases, but also in other privacy cases, as in defamation cases, the chilling effect of government controls inevitably tends to produce self-censorship. Any rules of law developed to deal with the situation must allow the press sufficient "breathing space" to perform its traditional function.

B. THE CURRENT STATE OF THE LAW. State and lower federal courts have on a number of occasions found invasion of a statutory or common law right of privacy in embarrassing disclosure cases and in false light cases despite freedom of the press claims. In the former category they have essentially endeavored to balance the degree of intrusion on an individual's privacy against the "newsworthiness" of the publication. If the communication is considered sufficiently newsworthy there is no liability; if it is not, and if its publication is felt to be offensive to a person of ordinary sensibilities, the privacy claim is allowed. In false light cases the courts tend to follow the rules employed in defamation matters, allowing greater leeway where the publication involves a "public figure" than where the subject is a more private person. These decisions thus establish that the right of privacy can override first amendment defenses under certain circumstances. But the rules of law are exceedingly vague, the theory not clearly formulated, and the results by no means consistent.

The Supreme Court has thus far not clarified the situation to any substantial degree. It has dealt with privacy tort questions in three cases, but has avoided addressing most of the core issues.

The first Supreme Court ruling was in *Time Inc. v. Hill,*[12] decided in 1967. In that case *Life* magazine had published a story about the opening of a new play, *The Desperate Hours,* which was based on a widely publicized episode three years before in which the Hill family had been held

---

12. 385 U.S. 374 (1967).

hostage in their home by three escaped convicts. The Hills had attempted to avoid further publicity and had moved to another state. The *Life* account of the events was not entirely accurate in that it depicted the father and son as having been beaten and the daughter as having been subjected to verbal sexual abuse. The portrayal, however, was not defamatory. Hill sued for damages, under a New York statute, alleging that *Life* had revived a painful episode, causing serious emotional and nervous illness to his wife. In the New York courts he recovered $30,000 compensatory damages.

The Supreme Court reversed and sent the case back for a new trial. Six Justices were of the opinion that *Life* could be held liable for "false reports of matters of public interest," but only if there was proof of "actual malice." The standard of "actual malice" had been previously established in *New York Times Co. v. Sullivan* as a constitutional requirement for finding liability in defamation cases. It required proof that *Life* had published the statements knowing they were false or in reckless disregard of whether they were false or not. Justices Black and Douglas concurred in the reversal on the broader ground that the first amendment prohibited any restriction on communications relating to matters in the public domain.

The Supreme Court in *Time, Inc. v. Hill* was careful to limit its opinion to the false light situation before it. In a footnote the Court disclaimed any intention of considering other aspects of the privacy tort: "This limitation to newsworthy persons and events does not of course foreclose an interpretation of the statute to allow damages where 'Revelations may be so intimate and so unwarranted in view of the victim's position as to outrage the community's notions of decency.' "

The second case in which the Supreme Court touched on privacy issues, *Cantrell v. Forest City Publishing Co.,*[13] decided in 1974, was also a false light case. A newspaper story about a poverty stricken family, whose husband and father had been killed in the collapse of a bridge, contained false but not defamatory statements about the attitude of the mother and the living conditions of the family. The Court, applying the actual malice rule, upheld a judgment for the family. Justice Black was no longer on the Court and Justice Douglas alone dissented, contending that the first amendment protected any report on "matters of public import."

After *Time, Inc. v. Hill* but before *Cantrell* the Supreme Court had held in *Gertz v. Robert Welch, Inc.*[14] that the actual malice rule applied in libel cases only where the false statement involved a public official or a "public figure," and that in cases of a private person the State could adopt any standard except one of absolute liability. In *Cantrell* the Court found it unnecessary to decide whether the same modification of the actual malice rule would apply in false light privacy cases. Since actual malice had been proved in *Cantrell*, "this case present[ed] no occasion to

---

13. 419 U.S. 245 (1974).
14. 418 U.S. 323 (1974).

consider whether a State may constitutionally apply a more relaxed standard of liability for a publisher or broadcaaster of false statements injurious to a private individual under a false-light theory of invasion of privacy, or whether the constitutional standard announced in *Time, Inc. v. Hill* applies to all false light cases."

The third Supreme Court decision, *Cox Broadcasting Corp. v. Cohn,*[15] decided in 1975, did reach the issue of whether liability could be imposed, under a privacy theory, for a truthful statement. The case involved a suit under a Florida statute which prohibited publication of the name or identity of a rape victim. The name had been obtained from court records, which were open to public inspection, and broadcast in the course of a news report about the court proceedings in the case. The Supreme Court, with one Justice dissenting on other grounds, held that the broadcast was constitutionally protected.

The majority opinion in *Cox Broadcasting* noted the growing trend toward recognition of a privacy right and the broader implications of the case: "[P]owerful arguments can be made, and have been made, that however it may be ultimately defined, there *is* a zone of privacy surrounding every individual, a zone within which the State may protect him from intrusion by the press, with all its attendant publicity." The Court continued, after citing the Warren-Brandeis article: "More compellingly, the century has experienced a strong tide running in favor of the so-called right of privacy." And it observed that the broadcasting station had urged "upon us the broad holding that the press may not be made criminally or civilly liable for publishing information that is neither false nor misleading but absolutely accurate, however damaging it may be to reputation or individual sensibilities." The Court nevertheless refused to plunge into deeper waters and confined its decision to the narrow position that the state could not "impose sanctions on the accurate publication of the name of a rape victim obtained from public records—more specifically, from judicial records which are maintained in connection with a public prosecution and which themselves are open to public inspection."

Thus the Supreme Court has held that interests of privacy, like interests in reputation, can be protected against false statements, at least where actual malice has been demonstrated. And it has made clear that truthful statements derived from public records may be published even though they may impinge on areas of privacy. Beyond this point the Court has not gone. The constitutional basis for the privacy tort thus remains largely an open question. Exploration of that issue requires examination of the value structures underlying the right of privacy and the right to freedom of expression.

C. THEORIES OF THE RIGHT TO PRIVACY. The right of privacy is clearly a vital element in any system of individual rights. Essentially it is designed to support the individual, to protect the core of individuality, in the rela-

---

15. 420 U.S. 469 (1975).

tions of the individual to the collective society. As such it is designed to mark out a sphere or zone in which the collective may not intrude upon the individual will. It thus differs from time to time, and from society to society, depending on where the line is drawn between individual autonomy and collective obligation.

So far there is general agreement. Beyond this point, however, great difficulty has arisen in defining the right of privacy in such a way as to give it specific content and to distinguish it from other elements in the system of individual rights. Warren and Brandeis, going back to Thomas Cooley, originally defined privacy as a broad "right to be let alone." Subsequent attempts were made to refine and narrow the concept. Dean Prosser, as we have seen, broke it down into four disparate rights. Professor Alan Westin takes as his definition "the claim of individuals, groups, or institutions to determine for themselves when, how, and to what extent information about them is communicated to others." Professor Richard Parker considers privacy to be "control over when and by whom the various parts of us can be sensed by others."[16]

On the other hand, some recent efforts to delineate the privacy areas have reverted to more sweeping language. Professor Edward Bloustein considers privacy as involving the "interest in preserving human dignity and individuality." Professor Milton Konvitz refers to it as the "claim that there is a sphere of space that has not been dedicated to public use or control."[17] Professor Paul Bender defines privacy as "the freedom to be one's self" and stresses that it is confined to activities that "do not affect the legitimate interests" of others.[18] And Professor Tom Gerety, in what is perhaps the most successful effort to date, postulates three elements as comprising privacy: "autonomy, identity, and intimacy."[19]

These brief formulations do not, of course, do justice to the efforts of the authors just quoted to give meaning to the concept of privacy. Yet they do demonstrate how elusive the concept can be. A further dimension is added to our conception of privacy, however, if we look at the problem in terms of the more specific functions that privacy performs in our society. These have been summarized by Professor Westin as including (1) protection of personal autonomy—being free from manipulation or domination by others; (2) permitting emotional release—relief from the pressure of playing social roles; (3) opportunity for self-evaluation—a chance to integrate one's experience into a meaningful pattern and exert one's individuality on events; and (4) allowance of limited and protected communication—permitting one to share confidences and to set the boundaries of mental distance.

Similarly, Professor Bloustein has described the role of privacy in maintaining autonomy:

16. Parker, *A Definition of Privacy*, 27 RUTGERS L. REV. 275, 281 (1974) [emphasis deleted].

17. Konvitz, *Privacy and the Law*, 31 L. & CONTEMP. PROB. 272, 279–80 (1966).

18. Bender, *Privacies of Life*, HARPER'S MAGAZINE, Apr. 1974, at 36, 41–44.

19. Gerety, *Redefining Privacy*, 12 HARV. C.R.-C.L.L. REV. 233 (1977).

The man who is compelled to live every minute of his life among others and whose every need, thought, fancy or gratification is subject to public scrutiny, has been deprived of his individuality and human dignity. Such an individual merges with the mass. His opinions, being public, tend never to be different; his aspirations, being known, tend always to be conventionally accepted ones; his feelings, being openly exhibited, tend to lose their quality of unique personal warmth and to become the feelings of every man. Such a being, although sentient, is fungible; he is not an individual.

Professor Charles Fried has stressed a somewhat different aspect of the significance of privacy in our lives:

It is my thesis that privacy is not just one possible means among others to insure some other value, but that it is necessarily related to ends and relations of the most fundamental sort: respect, love, friendship and trust. Privacy is not merely a good technique for furthering these fundamental relations; rather without privacy they are simply inconceivable. They require a context of privacy or the possibility of privacy for their existence.[20]

An understanding of the functions of privacy illuminates the problem. But it does not supply a unified theory which can serve as a foundation for development of a comprehensive law of privacy. At least so far as the privacy tort is concerned, perhaps the best we can do at this time is to accept Professor Gerety's formulation. According to his analysis the right of privacy consists of protection for the three elements which are at the core of individuality. The first is autonomy, which is necessary in order to retain control over one's destiny as an individual. The second is identity, which is necessary to develop one's potential as an individual. The third is intimacy, which is the element that distinguishes privacy from the more general concept of liberty. All three elements take on form and substance in the light of the functions served by privacy in a modern technological society.

Even if we agree on these outlines of a value structure, however, it must be admitted that we are still some distance from having a definite, workable theory of privacy. A unified concept, which will embrace the privacy protected by the tort action, the privacy safeguarded by the constitutional right against government control, the privacy necessary to limit the collection or dissemination of information about us, and perhaps other aspects of privacy as well, has thus far escaped our grasp. In my judgment, however, this state of affairs is not necessarily a cause for alarm. Privacy is a developing right. It must emerge gradually from the traditions, experiences, and needs of our society. One cannot expect it to take final, concrete shape at this point in our history.

If the evolution of a privacy right is to be successful, however, we

---

20. Fried, *Privacy,* 77 YALE L.J. 475, 477 (1968).

must keep in mind that it is a theory of privacy that we are searching for. We will not make much progress if we frame the problem in terms of a broader quest for "liberty." The recent tendency of the Supreme Court to look upon privacy as merely an undifferentiated aspect of an amorphous right to "liberty" is a regressive step. We must start from the premise that there exists a concrete area of privacy, not merely a generalized right to "liberty," and that the boundaries of that area can over a period of time be ascertained.

D. FORMULATION OF LEGAL DOCTRINE. Our next problem is to translate the basic right of privacy theory into legal doctrine in the privacy tort area. So far as possible the individual must know to what extent privacy will be protected, the press must be able to assess its potential liability for infringement, and the judicial system must have appropriate guidelines for accommodating these often conflicting interests.

The first issue in this process concerns the fundamental tension between the right of privacy and freedom of expression. In broad outline the resolution of the conflict between the two seems reasonably clear. The purpose of establishing a right of privacy is to protect certain areas of individual autonomy, identity, and intimacy from any intrusion by society at large. This exclusion of collective action would extend to the rules developed by the society for safeguarding freedom of expression. Insofar as the guaranty of freedom of expression serves social interests—in discovering the truth, assuring participation in decisionmaking, and facilitating social change—the individual right of privacy would plainly take precedence over the collective interest. Insofar as freedom of expression serves individual interests—primarily in encouraging self-fulfillment—the two individual rights would seem to be in conflict. In such a situation, however, the guiding principle would be that the exercise of an individual right which injures another person would not be favored. Hence, here too the right of privacy would prevail over freedom of expression.

If we accept this analysis, then the preferable legal doctrine would be expressed in definitional terms. That is to say, the task would be to define the right of privacy and accord that right full protection against claims based on freedom of the press. In view of our inability to articulate a precise theory of privacy, however, the definitional approach faces serious problems. Moreover, the courts have not been willing to follow this course, and show little disposition to do so in the immediate future.

The alternative is the formulation of legal doctrine in terms of a balancing process, whereby the interest in privacy is balanced against the interest in freedom of the press. While this approach lessens the need for a clear-cut definition of privacy, it contains all the disadvantages that inhere in balancing tests used in the area of individual rights. It is difficult to find comparable units to balance against each other, the social interests are likely to prevail over the individual interest, and the whole process is so loose and vague that it affords few guidelines for those applying the test or those affected by it. Nevertheless, it may be possible to refine the balancing process by isolating specific types of interests, rejecting some claimed interests, giving special weight to others, utilizing presumptions, and otherwise laying the basis for a common law development of the issues.

One starting point is to give special weight to publications that are "newsworthy" or relate to "matters of public interest." This solution, however, is hardly satisfactory. The terms used are completely open ended. Anything that is published is by definition "newsworthy" and a "matter of public interest." Otherwise it would not be published. Such a standard, therefore, either evades the issue or gives exclusive weight to first amendment rights. Indeed, this standard was used by Justice Black and Justice Douglas to achieve exactly the latter result.

A more attractive formula is that suggested by Professor Bloustein: to focus on the public's "need to know." Communication about matters of which the public has a substantial "need to know" would not be subject to liability; otherwise the right of privacy would prevail. This standard would give weight to the major social interests protected by the system of freedom of expression: the search for truth, participation in decisionmaking, and facilitation of social change. And in some respects it is more manageable than other formulations. But there are serious problems with this approach. The formula is still vague. It gives almost exclusive weight to social interests rather than to the individual interest. And it requires the government to make a determination as to what speech is of value and what speech is not, a dangerous threat to any system of free expression. In short, while the need-to-know doctrine has possibilities it is not necessarily the best answer.

Another approach, and one that seems to me more fruitful, would place more emphasis on developing the privacy side of the balance. It would recognize the first amendment interests but it would give primary attention to a number of factors which derive ultimately from the functions performed by privacy and the expectations of privacy that prevail in contemporary society. Such an approach would involve the following:

(1) Emphasis would be put on the element of intimacy in determining the zone of privacy. Thus, so far as the privacy tort is concerned, protection would be extended only to matters related to the intimate details of a person's life: those activities, ideas or emotions which one does not share with others or shares only with those who are closest. This would include sexual relations, the performance of bodily functions, family relations, and the like.

(2) Disclosures incidental to the formal proceedings for enforcement of the law by judicial or administrative tribunals would not be protected on privacy grounds. Administration of the legitimate rules of the collective society would be considered a proper function of government, which must be conducted in the open, and hence even unwilling participation in such events should not be grounds for invoking protection of the right to privacy.

(3) The extent to which a person has waived claims to privacy would be considered in the equation. Thus, a person who had voluntarily injected himself or herself into public affairs would not be protected by the privacy right as to matters relevant to his or her public status.

Other considerations could be added to this list. Their substance and weight would depend on developing experience. Over a period of time they would give specific content and greater predictability to the balancing process.

There is one final factor which is of prime importance in formulating legal doctrine in privacy tort law. It concerns the dynamics of imposing governmental controls upon the press. Any satisfactory standard of liability must allow the press "breathing space." It must not force the press into self-censorship, or in any way force it to refrain from legitimate expression, by reason of uncertainty as to where the boundaries lie, fear of costly litigation, or a desire to avoid possible trouble. Pressures on the press of this nature were given decisive weight in formulating the actual malice rule in defamation cases. The same considerations are applicable in privacy tort cases. They operate, of course, in the direction of imposing strict limitations upon the liability of the press.

Finally, it should be emphasized that the foregoing attempt to frame legal doctrine is addressed only to the problems of privacy tort cases. The proposals made here do not necessarily apply in all areas of privacy law. Such a comprehensive formulation must await development of a unified theory of the privacy right.

E. APPLICATION OF LEGAL DOCTRINES. In order to give some content to the above proposals for creation of legal doctrine it is necessary to apply the various formulae to typical fact situations that arise in the area of privacy tort. Only a brief summary, by way of illustration, is possible here.

With respect to the false light cases, those that involve mere fictionalization do not seem to pose a problem under any theory. If the author, while writing about an identifiable person, makes clear that some of the events recounted are fictitious, the reader is on notice of that fact and no invasion of privacy occurs. The most that can be claimed in such a situation is the appropriation of an identity, in violation of a property right; but surely such a property claim should not be recognized. Were this not the case historical novels, such as Doctorow's *The Book of Daniel,* a fictional account of the two sons of Julius and Ethel Rosenberg, would not be publishable without their consent.

In false light cases where false but nondefamatory statements purporting to be true are made, different issues arise. If the Black-Douglas doctrine of no liability for publication on "matters of public interest" were followed there would, of course, normally be no cause of action. The Bloustein "need-to-know" theory would probably result in liability in most cases where any misrepresentation of a person's identity occurs. The courts have consistently taken the position that false statements have no social value and they would almost certainly conclude that false information was not something the public needed to know. The argument of John Stuart Mill that even expression that is false has social importance, in that it evokes response, stimulates rethinking and otherwise stirs debate,[21] does not seem to have enough appeal to counteract this trend. The only limitation here would lie in recognition of the dynamics of controls. This might result in application of the "actual malice" rule.

A balancing theory with emphasis on delineating the right of privacy would probably arrive at different results. The invasion of privacy in false light cases normally consists only in the distortion of identity. There would be no intrusion on privacy, however, unless the element of intimacy were also present. In *Time, Inc. v. Hill,* for instance, the intimacy factor was weak or nonexistent. As Justice Douglas concluded, that case was really not a privacy case at all. The same may be said of the *Cantrell* fact situation; if any recovery were to be allowed in such a case it would be under a libel theory for injury to reputation. In other words these so-called false light cases would be treated the same as the embarrassing disclosure cases. Truth or falsity would in effect be irrelevant. Again, the opposite result would mean that a biography, such as Leonard Mosley's account of the Dulles family, could only be published on condition that it was completely accurate in all respects. Even an actual malice rule would not eliminate the risks, and costs, of litigation.

The embarrassing disclosure cases are undoubtedly the most difficult to resolve. The Black-Douglas doctrine of "matters of public interest" would constitute the most narrow rule, allowing recovery in only the most extreme cases if at all. The Bloustein "need-to-know" doctrine would result in liberal recovery. And a balancing theory with the focus on privacy factors would occupy an intermediate position.

The proper result in some embarrassing disclosure cases is relatively clear, except under the Black-Douglas theory. Thus the situation in *York v. Story,*[22] where police officers took and circulated nude pictures of a woman who had complained to them of an assault, presents a plain case. So also would *Barber v. Time, Inc.,*[23] in which a story with photographs was published about a woman confined to a hospital with a disease that resulted in gross obesity. The alleged facts in *Doe v. Roe*[24] that a psychiatrist had published a case study of a patient without sufficiently concealing the patient's identity—is another example. Likewise publication of private telephone conversations illegally obtained by wiretapping, or of the recording of a private party at which Martin Luther King was present, further illustrates the type of case where liability should result.

Another line of privacy tort cases involves the publication of embar-

---

21. J. S. MILL, ON LIBERTY (London 1859).
22. 324 F.2d 450 (9th Cir. 1963), *cert. denied,* 376 U.S. 939 (1964).
23. 348 Mo. 1199, 159 S.W.2d 291 (1942).
24. 42 A.D.2d 559, 345 N.Y.S.2d 560, *aff'd,* 33 N.Y.2d 902, 307 N.E.2d 823. 352 N.Y.S.2d 626 (1973), *opinion amended,* 34 N.Y.2d 562, 310 N.E.2d 539, 354 N.Y.S.2d 941 (1974), *cert. dismissed,* 420 U.S. 307 (1975).

rassing facts about a person's past after that person has reformed or changed lifestyles. In *Sidis v. F-R Publishing Corp.*,[25] one of the most famous of these, the Second Circuit denied recovery in a case involving a story in the *New Yorker* about a child genius, well-publicized at one time, who later sought to live a life of quiet and solitude. In contrast, the California Supreme Court in *Briscoe v. Reader's Digest Association*[26] upheld the privacy claim of a former hijacker based on an article, published eleven years after he had reformed, which referred to his previous conviction. Under the Bloustein doctrine liability would exist in these cases unless the name of the person involved was withheld; the public's need to know would extend to the information, but not to the identity of the individual. Under a theory based on a more careful delineation of privacy, however, the opposite result would be reached in most of these cases. Usually the element of intimacy is not present in such cases. Moreover, as in *Briscoe,* the facts often relate to a law enforcement situation. By and large these cases concern facts that were clearly publishable at the time they occurred and the lapse of time would not ordinarily change the result.

Legislation prohibiting disclosure of the names of rape victims, or of other victims such as in spousal abuse cases, would fare differently under different theories. The Bloustein approach would lead the courts to uphold such laws. Unless there is some unusual circumstance which makes the name of the victim particularly significant, it would be argued, the public has no need to know the identity of the person. Such a conclusion would, of course, run counter to the Supreme Court's decision in *Cox Broadcasting,* at least in some aspects. The theory proposed here, on the other hand, would not sustain such legislation. Where public proceedings are commenced to enforce a valid law, the personal affairs of those involved cannot be preserved. This rule would not require, however, that government officials release the name of the victim prior to the institution of a prosecution. Such an issue concerns, not the right to publish but the right to obtain information in the government's possession. This result is therefore consistent with the *Cox Broadcasting* case, in which the Court reserved decision on the right of the government to withhold information in its files.

Other problems involve matters which face the press frequently but are not ordinarily litigated in privacy tort cases. For example, to what extent is it proper for the press to publish stories about the sexual actitivies of public officials, public figures, or others? The Bloustein theory and the theory proposed here would be likely to reach very much the same result in such situations. The need-to-know standard would sanction publication only where the information related to the performance of official duty or otherwise touched upon public matters. A similar outcome would flow from application of waiver rules, that persons who operate in the limelight cannot expect the same degree of privacy about their personal lives.

25. 113 F.2d 806 (2d Cir.), *cert. denied,* 311 U.S. 711 (1940).
26. 4 Cal. 3d 529, 483 P.2d 34, 93 Cal. Rptr. 866 (1971).

This last example suggests a further factor which plays an important role in the practical application of privacy tort law. The mere institution of litigation greatly accentuates the original loss of privacy; in fact, it normally multiplies the very effect from which relief is sought. Nor are the results in money damages collected or deterrence achieved likely to be significant, unless the law is pressed to the point of serious self-censorship. In other words, a lawsuit is rarely a satisfactory way of assuring the privacy of the individual. By and large, protection against invasions of privacy must be sought in other areas and by other means.[27]

F. REMEDIES. A final, and difficult, problem in privacy tort law concerns the question of remedies. Since a choice of one remedy over another would not impair the constitutional right of privacy, the issues do not involve a direct confrontation between freedom of the press and the right of privacy. They do bring into play, however, other constitutional doctrines as well as policy judgments.

A claim to money damages is the normal remedy in such tort cases and, while the measure of damages poses some intriguing questions, that matter will not be considered here. The main problem concerns the remedy of injunction. Where an injunction is sought against physical intrusion upon privacy, or other illegal methods of gathering news, no infringement on freedom of the press would appear to be involved. But where an injunction is sought against publication, an issue of prior restraint is presented.

The case for allowing prior restraint in privacy tort cases is appealing. In many situations it would provide the only remedy that would not expand the injury originally caused by the invasion of privacy. In that sense there is more warrant for prior restraint here than in other types of cases, including national security cases, where whatever damage is done by publication is done once and for all. Moreover, the courts have taken the position that, while prior restraint is disfavored, it is not totally excluded.

Nevertheless, a balance of considerations impels the conclusion that prior restraint should not be permitted in privacy tort cases. The controlling factor lies in the dynamics of that remedy. A prior restraint is so easy to apply and so destructive in its impact upon freedom of the press that its use cannot be justified. The only safe course is to confine restrictions upon the right to publish to an award of damages.

II. THE RIGHT OF PRIVACY AND THE RIGHT TO OBTAIN INFORMATION

The right of the press to obtain information, either from government or from private sources, frequently comes into conflict with the right to privacy. Both rights have taken on added importance in our modern technological society. Never has it been more true that information is

---

27. *See* Kalven, *Privacy in Tort Law—Were Warren and Brandeis Wrong?*, 31 L. & CONTEMP. PROB. 326 (1966) [this chapter].

power. And never has there been more information collected in the files of government and in private centers of power. The vitality of the democratic process itself rests upon citizens having access to this information. And the citizenry must depend in large measure upon the capacity of the press to discover it and to disseminate it to the public. At the same time the autonomy, identity and intimacies of the individual have never been put under greater strain by the collection and storage of data. The dangers to privacy have been exacerbated not only by the vast increase in information assembled but by the availability of that information through computer networks.

Reconciliation of the individual and social interests at stake involves somewhat different considerations from those relevant to the conflict between freedom of the press and the privacy tort. For a number of reasons the tensions are not as stressful, and the solutions are more manageable. Before attempting to delineate the basis for an accommodation, however, it is necessary to set forth briefly the legal foundations of each of the rights with which we are concerned.

A. THE LEGAL BASIS OF THE RIGHT OF THE PRESS TO OBTAIN INFORMATION. The press has a constitutional right to obtain information from private sources on a voluntary basis, but it does not have any constitutional power to compel the production of such information. Moreover, there are a number of limitations upon the methods that may be employed. Thus the press is controlled in its quest for information by traditional laws against trespass, theft, fraud, wiretapping, and so on. These recognized restrictions, which are similar to those protecting the right of privacy against any physical intrusion, have not occasioned any serious conflict and need not be considered further.

The right of the press to obtain information from government sources stands on a different footing. In this situation the press can call upon the constitutional right to know. The Supreme Court has for a number of years recognized that the first amendment embodies a right to receive information—to see, read or hear communications protected by that constitutional guaranty—and this includes by implication a right to obtain information for the purpose of disseminating it to others. The Court has invoked the right to know in cases where the government has sought to interfere with the receipt of communications.[28] And it has hinted that the right to know could be used to compel the government to produce information. In *Pell v. Procunier*[29] and *Saxbe v. Washington Post Co.*,[30] the Court upheld regulations which prohibited journalists from interviewing inmates of prisons. But it indicated that the decision might have been otherwise if the regulations operated "to conceal from the public the conditions prevailing in federal prisons." Unfortunately the Court has not

---

28. Stanley v. Georgia, 394 U.S. 557 (1969); Lamont v. Postmaster General, 381 U.S. 301 (1965).
29. 417 U.S. 817 (1974).
30. 417 U.S. 843 (1974).

gone beyond this point. Thus the constitutional right to know remains as a potential weapon of first importance against unjustified government secrecy, but thus far it has not been utilized for that purpose.

As a consequence the primary legal basis for the press to obtain information which the government does not wish to divulge rests upon legislation. The Federal Freedom of Information Act, adopted in 1966 and amended in 1974, provides that every government agency, upon request for identifiable records, "shall make the records promptly available to any person." Nine exceptions to this blanket obligation are set forth in the statute. One such exemption provides that the disclosure requirement does not extend to "personnel and medical files and similar files the disclosure of which would constitute a clearly unwarranted invasion of personal privacy." The term "similar files" has been broadly interpreted to mean that information in any government records, not merely files of the same category as "personnel" or "medical," would fall within the privacy exception. In addition the Government in Sunshine Act[31] of 1976 requires that meetings of federal agencies must be open to the public. Again, various exceptions are made, including one which allows closed meetings that deal with "information of a personal nature where disclosure would constitute a clearly unwarranted invasion of personal privacy."

Similar legislation exists in many states. As a result the press now has access to vast amounts of government information, but its right to obtain such material is limited by broad exceptions for matters that would invade personal privacy.

B. THE LEGAL BASIS OF THE RIGHT OF PRIVACY. It would appear self-evident that the constitutional right of privacy should operate to prevent the government from revealing to the public, including the press, certain types of information about the private affairs of a person. Disclosure of information is a classic example of an invasion of privacy. If the government is prohibited by the Constitution from infringing privacy by prohibiting an individual from using contraceptive devices or obtaining an abortion, it should likewise be prohibited from invading privacy by publishing information about an individual's private life. Moreover if the constitutional right of privacy allows the government to provide a civil remedy under privacy tort law, the same constitutional right should protect the individual against publication by the government of the same kind of material. Yet there is no clear-cut decision of the Supreme Court vindicating such a constitutional right.

The Supreme Court came close to considering these issues in *Doe v. McMillan*,[32] decided in 1973. That case involved a report issued by a congressional committee with reference to the District of Columbia school system. The report mentioned particular students by name and revealed

---

31. 5 U.S.C. § 552b (1976).
32. 412 U.S. 306 (1973).

their absence sheets, their test papers, and their disciplinary records. Parents brought suit against members of the committee, staff members, the public printer and the superintendent of documents, alleging an invasion of privacy. The Court held that members of the committee and staff members were entitled to immunity under the speech and debate clause of the Constitution, but that the suit could be maintained against the other defendants. As to these defendants, the court remanded the case to the district court for consideration of whether their actions in publishing and disseminating the report served a legitimate legislative function. Thus it was not necessary to pass on the privacy issue. Justice Douglas, joined by Justice Brennan and Justice Marshall, concurred on the ground that Congress had " 'no general authority to expose the private affairs of individuals without justification in terms of the function of the Congress.' "

Likewise in *Whelan v. Roe,*[33] upholding a New York statute which required that the state be provided with a copy of every prescription for certain drugs, the Supreme Court noted that the constitutionally protected right of privacy embraced "the individual interest in avoiding disclosure of personal matters," and recognized that "in some circumstances" the duty of the government "to avoid unwarranted disclosures . . . arguably has its roots in the Constitution." Justice Brennan, concurring, stressed these dicta in the majority opinion, saying that "[b]road dissemination by state officials" of medical information "would clearly implicate constitutionally protected privacy rights." On the other hand, Justice Stewart, also concurrintg, rejected "the proposition advanced by Justice Brennan" that prior cases had recognized "a general interest in freedom from disclosure of private information."

Some state and lower federal courts have come nearer to recognizing a constitutional right to prevent disclosure of personal matters. These decisions, however, are scattered and inconclusive.

When the courts come to deal with this aspect of the right to privacy, as they undoubtedly will in the near future, they will face the problem of determining the scope of the privacy right in this context. Obviously constitutional protection should be extended at least as far as the privacy rights which would be recognized in privacy tort law. There are strong arguments to support the proposition, however, that the right of privacy should have a broader scope in the government disclosure area than in the private tort situation. The first amendment claims of the press to publish information are far wider, and deserve far more protection, that its claim to obtain material from government files. Moreover, the dynamics of the two situations are entirely different; the chilling effect upon the press which inevitably accompanies penalties on its right to publish does not come into play when the issue concerns its right to gather news. Furthermore, the remedy available in the latter situation is more readily invoked and applied than in the former. In the disclosure situation all that is necessary is for the government to withhold the information; no protracted litigation is required.

33. 429 U.S. 589 (1977).

When these factors are entered into a balancing test, they clearly produce more favorable results, from the standpoint of the right of privacy, than would otherwise be the case. If the outcome of such a weighing of interests is ever to provide much certainty of result, however, the privacy rights protected in government disclosure cases will have to be more precisely defined. Such an effort is similar to that involved in marking out the boundaries of the privacy right in the area of informational privacy, that is, the extent to which the constitutional right of privacy limits the collection and storage of personal data. In the present state of our knowledge and experience that task is a formidable one and will not be pursued further here. Fortunately, it is less urgent because legislative protections against disclosure of government information in many instances now supercede the need to rely on the constitutional right.

One form of legislative protection against government disclosure consists of the privacy exceptions to the freedom of information acts and the sunshine laws. These provisions, however, are not fully adequate. They authorize the government to withhold information, but they do not mandate that it do so. Discretion as to whether to disclose or not still rests with the government agency. Additional protection is necessary and is frequently provided by privacy acts or personal data acts.

The Federal Privacy Act of 1974[34] provides that no agency "shall disclose any record which is contained in a system of records . . . to any person, or to another agency, except pursuant to a written request by, or with the prior written consent of, the individual to whom the record pertains." The term "record" is defined to mean "any item, collection, or grouping of information about an individual," and the term "system of records" means "a group of any records under the control of any agency from which information is retrieved by the name of the individual or by some identifying number" or symbol. Hence the act covers most of the information in the possession of the government that is specifically connected to a particular individual.

There are, of course, a series of exceptions to the blanket prohibition against disclosure without the consent of the individual. Most of these are concerned with the official use of the records, but one extends to records that are "required" to be disclosed under the Freedom of Information Act. Thus the Privacy Act prohibits the disclosure of any information "which would constitute a clearly unwarranted invasion of personal privacy." Similar protections are to be found in state legislation, although in some instances the prohibition against disclosure is limited to enumerated categories of "personal data."

Several conclusions can be drawn. In the first place, the restrictions on disclosure embodied in the Federal Privacy Act were intended to embrace a wider area than the protections afforded by the constitutional right of privacy. This appears from the fact that "personal privacy," the term used in the act, is protected only against a "clearly unwarranted" invasion. If "personal privacy" were intended to be coextensive with con-

---

34. 5 U.S.C. § 552a (1976).

stitutional privacy it would have to be fully protected; since less than full protection is afforded, Congress must have had in mind a broader meaning for the words "personal privacy."

It is also evident, from the language as well as the legislative history, that determination of what constitutes a "clearly unwarranted" invasion involves a balancing process. The right of the individual to "personal privacy" is to be weighed against the right of the public to government information.

A third consideration must be taken into account: the constitutional right of the press and the public, under right-to-know doctrine, to obtain information from the government. For reasons already stated where the refusal to disclose information is based on the constitutional right of privacy, that guaranty prevails over rights grounded in the first amendment. Where privacy protection is extended beyond the point required by the Constitution, a different issue is presented; the right to know becomes a relevant factor in the equation. In view of the weak support the Supreme Court has given to the right to know, however, it is unlikely there would be many situations in which the courts would find that the right to know overcame a legislative judgment to protect "personal privacy."

The foregoing principles, whether considered as constitutional requirements or as statutory policy, supply few guidelines for deciding concrete cases. The result reached in any particular matter is more likely to be grounded on general judgment and intuition than on any more certain basis. A brief examination of some typical problems which arise in this area, however, may help to throw light on the issues. And it may also allow us to judge whether the ultimate accommodation hammered out is likely to interfere with the functions performed by a free press.

C. APPLICATION OF THE PRIVACY PROTECTION. Health and medical records represent an obvious example of information that should be protected from disclosure. Such material concerns the intimate details of one's life and would be considered private under any definition of the word. Ordinarily such information has no relation to matters of public concern. Even in those rare cases where the public interest is in question, such as those where the health of a high government official is involved, the issue of disclosure should be decided by some official body and not left to the choice of a single member of the general public.

There are also various kinds of information in the area of education which should not be open to public inspection. Such files include those which reveal a student's work product, test scores, evaluations, disciplinary record, and similar matters. Here allowance for youthful experimentation, growth, and rebirth becomes important, and outweighs the value of making such data public knowledge. It is to be noted that the Supreme Court in *Department of Air Force v. Rose,*[35] its only decision construing the

---

35. [425 U.S. 352 (1976).]

privacy exemption of the Freedom of Information Act, assumed that the disciplinary record of identifiable cadets at the Air Force Academy would be protected against public disclosure by that provision.

Employment records are a third category of materials that require some privacy protection. These records include much information of a highly personal nature, such as test scores and evaluations by superiors which have not been subject to rebuttal or investigation. They also are likely to contain data about personal habits, family relationships, and finances. An exception should be made, however, allowing disclosure of the salaries of government employees. In this case public money is being spent and there is a significant and immediate public interest in disclosure. Moreover, the general expectation is that the salaries of public servants should be public knowledge.

Other materials in government files, such as tax returns, social security wage records, and the like, relate to individual finances. In our free enterprise society these matters are considered personal. Most citizens would probably agree that they should be protected against public disclosure. There are some situations, of course, where the public interest in disclosure would outweigh the individual right to privacy. For example, tax delinquencies ought to be made public, and there may be other similar exceptions to the right to privacy in one's financial affairs.

Much personal information is also to be found in the records of welfare agencies. These files contain material that reveals a great deal about family relations, living conditions, income and expenditures, mode of life, and similar matters. The same is true of information held by other types of agencies, such as those which administer public housing. This material deserves protection.

More difficult problems arise in the area of criminal history. Most people would probably agree that records of criminal convictions normally ought not to be protected. Arrest records present a closer case. Certainly current arrest records, such as the police blotter, ought to be open to public view. But a strong argument can be made that arrest records where no conviction was obtained should, after a period of time, not be disclosed. Perhaps the best solution to this problem is not to deal with it under constitutional or general statutory protection of privacy, but to deal with it by separate legislation providing for the expunging of arrest records, and to some extent records of convictions, under specified conditions. There are times when the public interest in these records is substantial, but the privacy interest in allowing a person to alter a lifestyle or embark upon a new mode of self-fulfillment is at least equally important. Records of juvenile delinquency, which relate to young persons who have not yet achieved maturity, present a special case; existing rules for their protection against disclosure seem fully justified.

In addition to the foregoing, there are many situations which are not easily classified and which cannot be foreseen. An example would be the records of private conversations obtained by illegal wiretapping or bugging. The existence of such material makes it imperative that the privacy exception to freedom of information legislation be stated in general terms. Any effort to spell out in advance every type of material that deserves protection is doomed to failure.

Finally, several qualifications of the right to privacy protection need to be emphasized. First, the Federal Freedom of Information Act provides that where exempt and nonexempt information is included in the same record "[a]ny reasonably segregable portion of a record shall be provided to any person requesting such record after deletion of the portions which are exempt." This provision, which is also included in most state legislation, requires the government agency to pare down any material withheld to the bare essentials required by the privacy exemption. Second, the privacy exemption allows the disclosure of much material, for statistical or other purposes, from which data that would link it to a particular person have been removed. The application of this technique does no injury to privacy and satisfies most significant public needs. Finally, disclosure of material required in judicial or other formal proceedings is governed by quite different rules. In such cases specific public needs more readily outweigh private interests.

Taken as a whole, reconciliation of the right of privacy and the right of the press to obtain information from the government along the lines indicated seems entirely feasible and fair. Privacy interests are protected, and incursions upon the liberties of the press are minimal.

CONCLUSION

Freedom of the press in America has an ancient lineage. The right of privacy has developed recently out of the needs of a technological civilization. Both are now vital features of our system of individual rights and some accommodation between them must be made. Structuring that accommodation entails some difficulties and dangers. Yet upon analysis the problems do not appear insuperable. In most areas there is no serious conflict; in fact, the two rights reinforce each other. Only in the case of the privacy tort and the privacy exception to the right to know does one find any clash of interests.

In strict theory the reconciliation should be accomplished through development of a careful definition of privacy, and material falling within that carefully defined sphere would then be afforded full protection. This approach would seem to follow from the very nature of the right to privacy—protection for the individual against all forms of collective pressure. Unfortunately there has been no agreement on such a definition. Hence no unified theory of the right of privacy, which would serve as the foundation for constitutional protection of the various kinds of interests, which we intuitively group under the notion of privacy, has been forthcoming. This Article has not solved that problem.

Nevertheless, it is possible to make some progress in formulating an accommodation between the right of privacy and freedom of the press.

Accepting a balancing theory, the effort should be directed toward developing, refining, and giving specific weight to the various considerations which go into the balancing process. This Article suggests that greater advances will be made by concentrating more on the privacy side of the equation than has been done in the past. The balancing operation will be somewhat different in the case of the privacy tort than in the case of the privacy exception to the right to know. Yet many factors are common to both areas, and the process is much the same.

In applying the suggested legal principles to the problem before us, the practical prospects for a fair accommodation seem favorable. As to the privacy tort, it is most unlikely that developments in this area will pose a serious threat to the press. The basis for recovery against the press can and should be held to narrow grounds. Moreover, the remedy itself is in many ways counterproductive; it widens rather than relieves the claimed invasion of privacy. One finds it hard to believe that the courts will ever move very far in the direction of penalizing the press for the publication of truthful material. The press is strong, healthy, and well-organized; the individuals whose privacy is at stake are scattered and weak. The press will continue to be free.

With respect to the right to obtain information from the government, the claims of the press are much less direct and immediate. It has never been asserted that the press ought to have open and unlimited access to all information in the government's possession. Some regulation of the process is inevitable. Moreover, that regulation does not present the problems of self-censorship that penalty for publication does. Further, as one examines each of the separate issues raised for decision the solution does not appear unreachable. No one should underestimate the inclination or the capacity of the government to withhold information from the public. But these dangers are more likely to come from other directions, such as claims to national security. The possibility that the government can successfully evoke the right of privacy to undermine the people's right to know seems somewhat remote. The press will continue to perform its function.

Commentary

IT MAY HAVE COME as a surprise to learn that the right to privacy is a relatively recent development, emerging primarily as a result of a law review article by Louis D. Brandeis, who later served as Associate Justice of the United States Supreme Court, and his law partner, Samuel D. Warren. Harry Kalven returned to the source of this far-flung legal interest to ask whether the evils that Justices Warren and Brandeis identified are still, or were ever, within the reach of the law's power to cure.

On first reading it is difficult to pinpoint exactly what the commotion is about. Does Kalven object to creating a legal right to protect personal sensibilities, which are sometimes petty, incapable of definition, and even lacking a requirement of bad intention in order to collect? Or is it that, while the privacy interest is not always a petty one, the suits brought in its name allege injuries that should not be recoverable? Is it that the cure for true privacy invasion—a public proceeding—only aggravates the injury? Or is it that the tort of invasion of the right to privacy, with its proclivity to swallow all of defamation law with no clearly defined bounds, is too ambiguous for courts to rule on intelligently?

The privacy interest—"the right to be let alone"—poses a mountain of tasks for courts, journalists, and the public. Kalven's emphasis on the problem of defining the right in terms of traditional legal categories is deserved. Although "privacy" arises in many legal contexts (for example, it is relevant, if not entirely dispositive, to determining the permissible scope of a police search under the Fourth Amendment), in tort law it refers to a cause of action for which money damages may be recovered.

A tort is a civil, private wrong. Trespassing on another's property, negligently damaging another's car in an auto accident, or bopping someone on the nose in a fist fight, these are familiar, centuries-old instances of torts. They arise in the law when implied duties imposed by society on individual conduct are breached: running a tractor over a neighbor's field, daydreaming while driving on the highway, or losing one's temper only to find it after the other person has been socked. Torts are part of Anglo-American law, necessary appendages to the criminal law to control socially undesirable conduct and compensate injured parties.

When a new tort is recognized (such as invasion of the right to privacy) it must find its place among existing torts without upsetting an already hard-to-define ordering of personal interests. Privacy is an especially difficult right to define because, in one sense, its violation goes on unceasingly. Each time a person walks on the sidewalk, his or her right to be left alone may be violated. The violations may range from offensive stares to eavesdropping; from hand-bill solicitors to obnoxiously loud talkers.

But to recognize every intrusion into one's personal sanctuary would be to encourage endless lawsuits and paralyze social intercourse. Where to draw the line in this context becomes problematical. In light of this difficulty, and of the history of privacy litigation, it is worth wondering, as Kalven does, whether society would have been better off without Warren's and Brandeis's scholarly perturbation of 1890.

Another difficulty with right to privacy law involves the widening scope of potential encroachments as a result of expanding technologies. In 1890 the concern of those proposing the new tort centered on printed accounts of the personal lives of Boston Brahmins. Today we live in a world of live remote broadcasting from any street corner of major cities, a wide use of sound and picture recording devices in a variety of situations, and an accompanying desire to collect and air news in the making. The severity of the objected-to media activity upon the privacy interest has shifted from an invasion to a blitzkreig. The scope of the tort must be adjusted to meet the need for personal autonomy and the collective desire for the free flow of news and information.

These are contrary goals and the desirability of both values has expanded considerably in the last decade. When viewed in connection with other nonmedia assaults on privacy—computer data banks, television cameras used to prevent shoplifting, direct mail solicitations, to name a few—the legal right to one's privacy becomes all the more important. But from a legal technician's viewpoint, it becomes harder and harder to define what the scope of the right should be.

Thomas Emerson agrees with Kalven's assessment that cabining "privacy" in a tight definition is an exercise in frustration. But it remains an important task because the interest, whatever its limits, is so important. There is something intuitively right about struggling with this kind of issue. When the media reveal something of "human interest," it lets us in on activities that can be most heartfelt. Sometimes we seek this information out of lurid curiosity. Other times the revelation of intimacies about others can teach us about ourselves. In mass society, made massive by mass communications itself, focusing on the human angle is socially desirable, even if it sometimes winds up in the *National Inquirer.*

While I find value in allowing the media to make public the nearly private without being liable for money damages, I am concerned about the mass of otherwise private data that floats around in government and business. Kalven's misgivings about privacy do not reach this issue. Perhaps this omission reflects the year, 1966, in which his article appeared. Since then, government and industry have computerized our identities at a soaring rate. From traffic violations to credit card charges, computers collect, store, and retrieve many of our forays into society.

Much of this information does not, to use Gerety's formulation, bear on intimacy, identity, or autonomy. The world may know, for all I care, what my credit card company will accept from me as a minimum payment on my outstanding balance. But should persons be able to gain access to the names of restaurants I have been frequenting? Or whether I have a reservation on a flight to Acapulco? Or the destination of my long distance calls last month?

Worse, what can I do to prevent storing erroneous information about myself? One insufficient funds check, written in error, can be spun out and out as data banks are exchanged. With no control over who gets access, I can be denied credit or a job—all over town or the country.

These are not always media-related problems. But they can be, as reporters seek information as part of an investigative report. The Freedom of Information Act (FOIA) is one lawful way access can be had to information collected by government. For instance, FOIA has been used by the trade press to find out how much officers of trade associations earn. Watergate's "Deep Throat" personifies a less official way in which details of government become public.

Invasions of privacy through publication of embarrassing telephotos or intimate details overheard from the next hotel room may be impossible to prevent. But data that we know are being collected, such as credit information, juvenile arrest records, or medical histories, can be protected through encryption. The most primitive form of encryption might be considered the lock and key. No one gets into my safety-deposit box without my key. Personal identification numbers used in 24-hour bank teller machines represent a more sophisticated method of running interference in front of data base snatchers.

But concealment costs. As we develop more efficient ways of storing data for legitimate purposes, we will want to consider how sophisticated we want privacy safeguards to become. How much, for instance, would we pay a travel agent to make sure that nobody, including the air line we were flying, could find out our travel plans? To find out whether we passed a state bar examination? To learn our average money market fund balance? Finding a way to code this information so that only you have access to it can be done—but at a cost.

Even when journalists are not faced with a question of releasing information of an unquestionably private character, problems remain. Take the 1975 *Cox Broadcasting* case discussed by Emerson. There the Supreme Court was faced with the complaint of the father of Cynthia Cohn, a seventeen-year-old Georgian who died after a rape attack. At the time of the rape, Cynthia's name was not released, but eight months later a television reporter broadcast it after seeing it on indictment papers filed by prosecutors against her alleged assailants. Cynthia's father sued the broadcaster for invasion of privacy.

The Court ruled that where information is released to the public in official court records, the media cannot be liable for invasion of privacy. In such circumstances, the Court observed that "reliance must rest upon the judgment of those who decide what to publish or broadcast."

I find it difficult to conclude that the public interest value of identifying the victim in this case outweighed the harm to the family. The Court did not; only that it is sounder policy, where publicly available information is involved, to leave the decision to the discretion of journalists.

But what kind of discretion is involved? What judgment will be exercised by a reporter about to go on the air in weighing the feelings of a victim's family? Grieving families make great picture stories, and with a live mini-cam there may be no time for journalists or the public to rely "upon the judgment of those who decide what to publish or broadcast."

Still, the abuses of unseemly forays into private lives may be preferable to the impacts on journalists that liability for such activities would create. A willingness to punish reporters would chill the atmosphere in which they work; reporters would abandon significant, if intimate, news leads fearful of subsequent liability. And had *Cox Broadcasting* gone the other way, we would have the anomaly of press liability for reporting a fact that anyone who visited the courthouse could have learned.

The trick is to know when and when not to allow the private to become the irretrievably public. Responsible exercise avoids the hazards at both ends: too little reported and we conceal truth; too much reported and we debase the reasons for searching for truth in the first place. As a song sung by Bette Midler put it: "Have I seen all that I could? Have I seen more than I should?"

DLB

6

Distributing Information: When the Executive Tries to Stop Release

THE AUTHOR

DON R. PEMBER serves as director and professor, School of Communications, University of Washington. He received the M.A. degree from Michigan State University, 1966, and the Ph.D. degree from the University of Wisconsin, 1969. His books include *Mass Media in America, Mass Media Law,* and *Privacy and the Press: The Law, the Mass Media and the First Amendment.* The last work traces the slow growth of the tort of invasion of privacy in the United States.

Pember, while not a lawyer, frequently writes about the law, and belongs •to a school of communications researchers who approach First Amendment problems from an operational viewpoint. The following article, which originally appeared in *Journalism Quarterly* a few months after the "Pentagon Papers" case was decided, emphasizes the political aspects of the Supreme Court's decision.

The "Pentagon Papers" Decision: More Questions Than Answers

DON R. PEMBER

IN ITS LEAD EDITORIAL on July 1, 1971, the day after the Supreme Court of the United States had "freed" the Pentagon Papers, the New York *Times* exulted:

> The historic decision of the Supreme Court in the case of the United States Government vs. The New York Times and The Washington Post is a ringing victory for freedom under law. . . the nation's highest tribunal strongly reaffirmed the guarantee of the people's right to know, implicit in the First Amendment to the Constitution of the United States.

Most libertarian scholars viewed the same decision with far less excitement. In fact, Justice Oliver Wendell Holmes' comment in his dissent in the Northern Securities case of 1904 seemed more appropriate— "Great cases like hard cases make bad law." For while the case certainly generated widespread public interest, it provided few guidelines for future reference, and clearly posed more questions than it answered.

The short per curiam decision and the nine accompanying concurrences and dissents offered few insights to those seeking resolution of the

From *Journalism Quarterly* 48 (1971):403–11.

problems inherent in balancing freedom of the press and the national security. At the same time little comfort was given those hoping for a strong assertion of the liberty of the American press. The Supreme Court decision in *Organization for a Better Austin* v. *Keefe*[1] provided a far clearer condemnation of prior restraint. And those seeking a lucid and at times eloquent argument on the value of a free press in a democratic society might better look toward the Court's . . . decision in *Rosenbloom* v. *Metromedia, Inc.*

A majority of the court—six members—did reaffirm an opposition to prior censorship of the press. But most students of the First Amendment believed that this was a fairly well-settled principle of law. If anything this case only succeeded in raising new doubts about the viability of this old legal precept.

THE DEVELOPMENT OF THE CASE

Sometime in March (this is an educated guess based on the court testimony) the New York *Times* came in possession of a 47-volume study entitled "History of the U.S. Decision-Making Process on Vietnam Policy" and assorted other documents. All were classified Top Secret under provisions of the 1953 Executive Order 10501. On Sunday, June 13, the *Times* began publishing a series of nine articles based on the documents, with the first editions of the newspaper hitting the streets of New York on Saturday night.

About 48 hours later the government reacted—first with a telegram from Attorney General John Mitchell to the *Times* asking the newspaper to stop the series on the grounds that it would "cause irreparable injury to the defense interests of the United States." The *Times* refused. James Reston wrote: "For the first time in the history of the Republic, the Attorney General of the United States has tried to suppress documents he hasn't read about a war that hasn't been declared."

In the face of this refusal by the *Times* the government asked Federal District Court Judge Murray I. Gurfein to enjoin the publication of the material. Gurfein, who was beginning his first day on the federal bench, temporarily stopped the series on June 15 and the legal battle was joined. During the next 15 days the *Times* case, and a similar suit brought against the Washington *Post,* wound their way through the United States court system to the Supreme Court. Briefly, this was the record the High Court encountered.

Gurfein temporarily enjoined the *Times* from continued publication of the series, but refused a government request to order the newspaper to return the purloined documents. On June 19, Gurfein denied the government's request for a permanent restraining order, but let the temporary

---

1. 402 U.S. 415 (1971). The case involved an attempt by a Chicago real estate broker to protect his privacy by using a court injunction to restrain a community organization from distributing leaflets describing the broker's alleged "panic peddling" or "blockbusting" activities.

injunction stand until the United States could be heard by the Second Circuit Court of Appeals. The district court judge said the government had
failed to show good cause why the newspaper should be stopped from
publishing the papers. "Without revealing the content of the testimony,"
Gurfein wrote, "suffice it to say that no cogent reasons were advanced as
to why these documents, except in the general framework of embarrass-
ment previously mentioned, would vitally affect the security of the nation."

On June 23, the U.S. Court of Appeals, in a five-to-three vote, reversed Gurfein's decision. The court ruled that after June 25 the
newspaper could resume publication of its series, but could not use
material that the government contended would damage national security.
The court also instructed Judge Gurfein to hold secret hearings to determine which portions of the study posed security problems. The *Times* appealed to the Supreme Court, which was close to its summer recess.

As the case with the New York *Times* progressed, a similar suit began in Washington, D.C., when the Washington *Post* offered readers a
series based on the Pentagon documents. On June 18, District Judge
Gerhard A. Gesell ruled, without taking testimony, that the *Post* could
continue its series. Gesell wrote:

> What is presented is a raw question of preserving the freedom of the
> press as it confronts the efforts of the Government to impose a prior
> restraint on publication of essentially historical data.

The U.S. Court of Appeals for the District of Columbia overruled Gesell and restrained the *Post* from continued publication of the series. The
judge was ordered to take evidence in the case. After one day of
testimony Gesell again permitted the series to be printed on the ground
that the government failed to show that continued publication of the *Post*
series would present "an immediate and grave threat to the national
security." This was essentially the same conclusion reached by Judge
Gurfein. The government appealed but the Circuit Court affirmed the ruling in a seven-to-two vote. Again the U.S. appealed and the *Post* case
reached the Supreme Court as well.

On June 25 the Supreme Court agreed to hear arguments in the case
on the following day in a rare Saturday session. Justices Hugo Black,
William Douglas, William Brennan and Thurgood Marshall dissented
from the court order, saying they favored freeing both newspapers to
print the series without hearing arguments. But a majority of the court
wanted to see briefs and hear testimony. Meanwhile, the restraining
orders stayed in effect.

THE LEGAL ARGUMENT

The government's argument in the case varied substantially over the
short span of the two-week period. Initially, the Justice Department relied

on a section of the United States Code on espionage and censorship for its case. The section makes it a crime for an unauthorized person to willfully "communicate" any information relating to the national defense which he has reason to believe could endanger the national security. Defense department spokesmen admitted they had reservations about "certain ambiguities" in the law which made its application in this case questionable. There were two problems. The key word in the section was "communicate" rather than "publish," a word used in other sections of the same law. Did "communicate" include the *Times'* publication of the material? Also, the legislative history of the measure suggested that it was not intended to be used to censor newspapers, but was designed to stop espionage. Judge Gurfein ruled that the statute did not apply, and the government changed its tactics in the next stages of the case. Instead of using the statutory authority as a basis for the injunction, government attorneys argued that the President had "inherent power" under his constitutional mandate to conduct foreign affairs to take the necessary steps to protect the national security. This included the right to classify documents. Freedom of the press was not an impediment to this power, according to U.S. Attorney Whitney North Seymour Jr., who argued:

> National defense documents, properly classified by the Executive, are an exception to an absolute freedom of the press, and should be protected by the courts against unauthorized disclosure.

Acceptance of this argument, of course, would mean that the government could stop the publication of any document—merely by stamping it classified—without proving danger to the nation. Arthur Schlesinger Jr. responded to this assertion, "If the stamp decided the issue, then any fool or knave in government service could acquire immunity by classifying papers that display his stupidity or venality."

By the time the case got to the Supreme Court the government had modified its argument again, placing less emphasis on the top secret classification of the documents, and stressing instead the harm which might result from publishing them. In argument before the Supreme Court, Justice Potter Stewart asked Solicitor General Erwin Griswold whether the government's case depended more upon top secret classification of the material or upon the basic nature of the material. Griswold conceded that while some "responsible officers" of the government felt that the classification question was the key, he believed that the character of the documents—the publication of which would cause an immediate and grave threat to the security of the nation—was the key issue. The government also contended before the Supreme Court that it had not been given enough time in the lower courts to document the dangerous nature of the papers.

The *Times* and the *Post,* on the other hand, consistently used two basic arguments—that the First Amendment precluded prior restraint of the press, and that the entire government classification system was a sham. With regard to the latter, both newspapers presented affidavits from many of their reporters who said that the government routinely declassified material whenever it believed it could sway public opinion on important issues, or to win a reporter's favor, or to influence a reporter's story.

But the primary structure of the *Times* and *Post* argument rested on the First Amendment. Prof. Alexander Bickel, representing the *Times* in the case, sounded the theme early when he told District Judge Gurfein, "A newspaper exists to publish, not to submit its publishing schedule to the United States government." Before the Supreme Court, Bickel framed the issue in this manner:

> The question that I do argue is whether there is inherent Presidential power to make substantive law, . . . which can form the basis for a judicially issued injunction, imposing a prior restraint on speech.

Bickel asserted that prior restraint was clearly the exception under the First Amendment. "If the criminal statute 'chills' speech, prior restraint 'freezes' it," he argued.

But the newspapers, unfortunately, did not take the position that all prior restraint was unconstitutional. Bickel even suggested a standard which might be applied in restraining the press: whether the publication of a document would have a direct link to a grave event which was immediate and visible. The admission that in some circumstances prior restraint was acceptable, prompted Justice Douglas to remark, "This is a strange argument for the *Times* to be making."

Indeed it was. Apparently, the attorneys for both newspapers decided, together or separately, not to attempt to defend the case on an absolute reading of the First Amendment—that is, that in no circumstance would prior restraint be acceptable. But by making this concession, the press pushed the argument away from the abstract but important question—can a government precensor the press in the name of national security?—to a fact question—did circumstances exist in this case which would permit prior restraint? And this shaped the entire case.

THE CONCEPT OF PRIOR RESTRAINT

Generally when prior restraint is considered, licensing is the first subject which comes to mind. The British had an effective system beginning in 1530 under Henry VIII. The system remained in effect, one way or another, until 1695 when the licensing law expired, and Commons refused to pass a new one. While philosophical arguments were raised against licensing, the system was finally killed for practical reasons. Both Torys and Whigs feared that the other party might use such a system to stifle the opposition press, a medium through which both parties at various times had gained considerable support. Hence, members of Parliament were reluctant to support licensing.

Licensing lasted in the colonies a bit longer, until about 1721 or 1722. Of course other measures were available to control the press both here and in England. Sedition laws, taxes and legislative contempt citations provided for punishment after printing. But with the exception of the abortive Stamp Tax of 1765 and similar colonial measures in this country, there was little pre-publication government interference. In the 18th century's great compilation of the common law, Blackstone laid down a definition of freedom of the press which in all likelihood summarized the thinking of the jurists of the era. "The liberty of the press is indeed essential to the nature of a free state;" he wrote, "but this consists in laying no previous restraints upon publication, and not in freedom from censure for criminal matter when published."

Most historians and legal scholars agree that the guarantees of the First Amendment, approved in 1791, precluded prior restraint of the press by the government. Some persons, such as Hugo Black and the late Zachariah Chafee, have argued that it precludes a good deal more.[2] Even revisionist historian Leonard Levy agrees that the phrase freedom of the press in the First Amendment was "an assurance that Congress was powerless to authorize restraints in advance of publication."[3]

During the next 140 years the courts had little opportunity to explore the problem of prior restraint, as the period was notably free from instances of direct pre-publication censorship. Prosecution of the Alien and Sedition Acts of 1798 involved post-publication action. The Abolitionists were harassed, but beyond the occasional refusal of the Post Office to deliver their pamphlets, there was no prior restraint. Lincoln closed down two New York newspapers during the Civil War. General Ambrose Burnside closed the Chicago *Tribune* during the same period. But these were short-lived exceptions to the norm. Even during the First World War, which saw recorded some of the most vicious press persecution, there is little evidence of pre-publication censorship.

It wasn't until the 1930s that the federal courts began to encounter instances of direct prior restraint. The most important case of the decade— one of the most important of the century—was *Near v. Minnesota.*[4] The Supreme Court struck down a Minnesota "gag law" which was used to enjoin H. M. Near from publishing the *Saturday Press* unless he could convince the state authorities that his paper would no longer be a "public nuisance." This dramatic example of prior restraint was condemned by Chief Justice Charles Evans Hughes who declared that the chief purpose of the liberty of the press was to prevent previous restraints upon publication.

But unfortunately Hughes didn't stop there. He added:

The objection has also been made that the principle as to immunity

2. See Zachariah Chafee, Jr., *Free Speech in the United States* (1941).
3. See Leonard W. Levy, "Liberty and the First Amendment: 1790–1800" in *Origins of American Political Thought* 257 (John P. Roche, ed. 1967).
4. 283 U.S. 697 (1931).

from previous restraint is stated too broadly, if every such restraint is deemed to be prohibited. That is undoubtedly true; the protection even as to previous restraint is not absolutely unlimited.

Hughes said in exceptional cases during wartime, such as obstruction of the recruiting service or publishing sailing dates of transports, or with regard to obscenity or incitements to violence, pre-censorship would not be unconstitutional. This unnecessary dicta by Hughes has probably been quoted more often than the rule in the case—that prior censorship is fundamentally unconstitutional. Consequently, the 1931 *Near* case, a great hallmark of press freedom, has time and again been hauled out to support prior restraint—especially in obscenity rulings. In the case involving the Pentagon Papers, both sides used *Near* to bolster their arguments.

The Supreme Court considered prior restraint at other times during the past 40 years and the result followed the rule in *Near*—prior censorship violated the First Amendment.

The New York Times Co. v. U.S. and U.S. v. The Washington Post Co.

The decision of the court was announced in a short, per curiam opinion. "Any system of prior restraints of expression comes to this Court bearing a heavy presumption against its constitutional validity," the opinion read. "The government 'thus carries a heavy burden of showing justification for the imposition of such a restraint.' " The District Court in the New York *Times* case and the Court of Appeals in the Washington *Post* case held that the government had not met that burden, the opinion continued. "We agree," the six justices announced.

The Supreme Court rested its decision on a principle which holds that the normal presumption of constitutionality afforded most legislation and govenmental action is not applicable when the action appears on its face to be within a specific prohibition of the Constitution, such as the First Amendment guarantee that Congress shall make no law abridging press freedom. This doctrine was first announced in a footnote in Harlan Fiske Stone's opinion in the 1938 decision of *United States* v. *Carolene Co.*[5] It has been developed since then in numerous cases. The presumption concerns the technical, but very important question of which party in a lawsuit must bring forward evidence. Usually, the party challenging the law or action is required to show why the measure is unconstitutional—it is presumed to be constitutional.

However, in cases involving rights guaranteed by the First Amendment or other civil liberties, the burden usually rests with the government to defend and justify its action. In the *Times* case the Supreme Court ruled that the govenment had failed to meet this standard.

In addition to the short majority opinion, nine other opinions were prepared as well.

---

5. 304 U.S. 144, 152–53 n.4 (1938).

Justices Black and Douglas argued from their traditional absolute positions—that is, the prohibition in the First Amendment that "Congress shall make no law" means *no* law. "In the First Amendment," Black wrote,

> the Founding Fathers gave the free press the protection it must have to fulfill its essential role in our democracy. The press was to serve the governed, not the governors. The government's power to censor the press was abolished so that the press would remain forever free to censure the government.

Black argued that no one could read the history of the adoption of the First Amendment "without being convinced . . . that it was injunctions like those sought here that Madison and his collaborators intended to outlaw in this nation for all time."

Justice Douglas asserted that secrecy in government was fundamentally antidemocratic, perpetuating bureaucratic errors. "Open debate and discussion of public issues are vital to our national health," he said. On public questions there should be "open and robust debate," he noted, quoting *New York Times* v. *Sullivan.*

Justice Brennan argued that the government had not proved that the injunction was needed to protect national security. ". . . only governmental allegation and proof that publication must inevitably, directly and immediately, cause the occurrence of an event kindred to imperiling the safety of a transport already at sea can support even the issuance of an interim restraining order," he said. And the government had failed to do this, he asserted.

Justice Stewart, concurring in the court's ruling, also asserted that the government had failed to meet the heavy burden of proof needed to sustain an injunction. But in addition he attacked the notion of excessive secrecy in government. "For when everything is classified," he wrote, "then nothing is classified, and the system becomes one to be disregarded by the cynical or the careless, and to be manipulated by those intent on self-protection or self-promotion." This is antithetical to a democracy, Stewart said, where often the only effective restraint upon executive policy lies in an "enlightened citizenry—an informed and critical public opinion. . . ."

Justice Byron R. White, while concurring in the majority opinion, appeared less certain that what the two newspapers had done would somehow strengthen the democracy. White said he believed that publication of the documents would probably cause "substantial damage to the public interest." But the government had failed to meet the heavy burden of proof required to justify prior restraint. Nevertheless, White wrote, "That the government mistakenly chose to proceed by injunction does not mean it could not successfully proceed in another way"—namely a criminal prosecution for violation of the espionage statutes. In fact, White said, he could easily sustain a conviction of the newspapers under these laws on facts which would not justify the imposition of a prior restraint.

Justice Marshall said the key question in the case was whether Congress or the Court had the power to make law in the United States. Noting the legislative history of the various espionage acts cited by the government, Marshall said that Congress had consistently rejected giving the President the kind of power the government now asserts the Executive branch inherently has. "It would . . . be utterly inconsistent with the concept of separation of power for this Court to use its power of contempt to prevent behavior that Congress has specifically declined to prohibit," he wrote.

Chief Justice Warren Burger was one of three members of the court to dissent. But Burger said he did not dissent on the merits of the case, that other circumstances forced his decision. "This case is not simple," he wrote. Two important rights—the liberty of the press and the constitutional power of the executive—must be balanced, the Chief Justice said. But also it is not a simple matter because "we do not know the facts of the case," he added. Haste, he asserted, precluded a proper judicial treatment of the substantive issues in the matter. And, the Chief Justice added, "It seems reasonably clear now that the haste . . . was not warranted." Then the Chief Justice assailed the two newspapers:

> The newspapers make a derivative claim under the First Amendment; they denominate this right as the public right-to-know; by implication, the *Times* asserts a sole trusteeship of that right by virtue of its journalistic "scoop."

Burger suggested that the *Times* and the government should have considered the matter before coming to the courts, narrowed the issues and then presented the judiciary the problem of developing a standard to apply to the few documents which remained in dispute.

Justices Harry Blackmun and John Marshall Harlan criticized the dearth of facts in the case, but nevertheless dissented on the merits.

Harlan presented perhaps the most conservative argument of the court, asserting that with few exceptions, the President was solely responsible for the wide ranging conduct of foreign affairs—including the classification of documents. With reference to this latter power, the aging jurist wrote:

> I agree in performance of its duty to protect the values of the First Amendment against political pressures, the judiciary must review the initial Executive determination to the point of satisfying itself that the subject matter of the dispute does lie within the proper compass of the President's foreign relations power.

Moreover, Harlan wrote, the courts may insist that the determination that disclosure of the material would irreparably harm the national security be made by the head of the executive department concerned. "But in my judgment the judiciary may not properly go beyond these two inquiries and redetermine for itself the probable inpact of disclosure on the national security," the justice wrote. Hence, Harlan concluded the court should accept the government's assertion in this case—in the absence of contrary evidence—that harm would result from disclosure.

The junior member of the court, Justice Blackmun, echoed the sentiment of Burger and Harlan, that excessive speed had interrupted the normal orderly judicial process in this case.

Blackmun said he would like to have the cases remanded to the trial courts for a slower, more deliberate and fuller examination, an examination in which evidence could be carefully and thoughtfully considered. "The First Amendment, after all, is only one part of an entire Constitution," Blackmun wrote. "What is needed here," he added, "is a weighing, upon properly developed standards, of the broad right of the press to print and of the very narrow right of the Government to prevent."

CONCLUSIONS

The legal and political impact of *The New York Times Company* v. *United States* and *United States* v. *The Washington Post Company* remain to be determined by the future. But certain conclusions are suggested now.

This was not a great case. It left little legal residue which future courts may use for guidance. It will be remembered far longer for its political implications than for its legal stature. The controversy surrounding the case will remain far more significant than the one decided in the courtroom.

At least two factors dictated the minimal legal importance of the case. Haste precluded the careful thought and planning that goes into arguing and deciding a great case. Lawyers for all litigants were forced to work around the clock on occasion just to meet deadlines. Hence, the arguments were shallow, lacked the deep insights one might expect in a case of this magnitude.

Second, and perhaps more importantly, the great issue in the case— whether the First Amendment prohibits prior restraint even when the national security is placed in jeopardy—was never joined. Attorneys for both newspapers wanted to win this case, not make constitutional law. Consequently, they made the tactically sound decision to concede that in certain instances prior restraint was permissible even under the First Amendment.

The case then degenerated into an argument over whether this was such an instance. Great law cases are not built of "such stuff."

In the end, the Supreme Court answered this question negatively, but left no standard on the record for use in future cases. *Near* v. *Minnesota,* and all that is good and bad about it, is still the law.

. . . .

The great importance in the case, then, might be an old lesson—one which each generation must learn anew. It is simply that freedom of the press is never secure, never certain, even in a constitutional democracy such as ours. The guarantees of the past can become meaningless in an instant if the people drop their guard. For 15 days the government of the United States successfully stopped the presses of two of the nation's most influential newspapers. For 15 days the freedom of the press was held in abeyance. For 15 days the people were denied the right to read a report prepared by their government about a war in which they have fought and died. The rights of a citizen are only as strong as his will to defend them. This, perhaps, is the lesson of the case.

Commentary

FOR A DISCLOSURE that former Defense Secretary Clark Clifford would later describe as "an event of outstanding significance," the release on Sunday morning in June 1971 of the first of the *New York Times*'s distillation of a "History of U.S. Decision-Making Process on Vietnam Policy, 1945–1967" was greeted by other members of the press with general disinterest. In chronicling this extraordinary episode of media-government relations, *Washington Post* writer Sanford J. Unger noted in *The Papers & The Papers* that most of the newspaper clients of the *Times*'s news service, who were given an early exclusive start, made little use of the story. The *Portland Oregonian* waited more than seven days before running articles on the Pentagon Papers; the *Chicago Tribune* did not print them at all.

United Press International, which had obtained the story by early Saturday night, waited until Sunday afternoon to put its first item about the Papers on its press wire and did not include it in its "budget" of the most important news of that day. The Associated Press carried nothing at all until Monday afternoon. While NBC featured the *Times*'s disclosure as a lead item on its dinner hour news, CBS and ABC remained silent, although CBS diplomatic correspondent Marvin Kalb had called the CBS New York headquarters after seeng the *Times*'s article in Washington, urging that some mention be made.

Even the Sunday news interview programs ignored the *Times*'s disclosure, although the guests that day included Hubert Humphrey on ABC's "Issues and Answers" and Secretary of Defense Melvin Laird on CBS's "Face the Nation." Indeed, Laird had conferred with Attorney General John Mitchell on the phone in advance, anticipating that he would be questioned about the documents stolen from the defense department.

Despite the sluggish initial reaction, the disclosure of the Papers and the efforts to suppress their publication became the most significant news story of that summer. As to the legal consequences, Don Pember's general conclusion that the "Pentagon Papers" case was lean on precedent, thereby leaving the qualified rule announced in *Near* v. *Minnesota* intact, seems sound. So, too, does his concluding suggestion that this case illustrates the verity that the price of freedom is eternal, and at times litigious, vigilance. But the case also reflects three aspects of the relationship between media and government that transcend the particular historical context of the on-off-on–again saga of the "Pentagon Papers."

First, *New York Times Co.* v. *United States* provides a constitutional law textbook case of how wayward our system of interpreting the First Amendment is. The United States Supreme Court, after all, cannot pick the fact patterns of the cases it will rule upon. Indeed, under the "case or controversy" provision of Article III of the United States Constitution, the Court is forbidden from giving advisory opinions in matters not properly before it as part of a live dispute. In a case like the "Pentagon Papers" involving an urgent need for immediate publication, neither the parties nor the Court majority could spend more than the minimally necessary hours needed to decide whether an injunction was proper under *Near.*

The litigative process itself involved delay and delay was what the case was all about. An extra minute used by counsel for the *Times* or *Post* to fashion elegant and elaborate constitutional arguments; an extra hour spent by the Justices to circulate drafts of a proposed opinion that could be embraced by the largest number of Justices; each delay constituted a form of prepublication punishment, no matter how the Court ruled.

Above everything else this case had to be decision oriented. If a majority could agree only on the short three paragraphs that ultimately became the entirety of the opinion of the Court, so be it. Finespun constitutional theories, such as the absolutist positions advocated by Justices Hugo Black and William O. Douglas, could be offered in concurring opinions, potentially significant as influencing future thinking of the Court but of no precedential value. Although counsel for the defendants had considered making the absolute, every-prior-restraint-is-invalid argument, as a lawyer who represented the *Washington Post* explained:

> We were of the view that if Justices Black and Douglas were unable, over a period of several decades, to convince their brethren that the First Amendment was absolute, we certainly would not be able to devise a series of arguments that would do so between 3:30 P.M. Friday and 5:00 A.M. Saturday morning.

Because a moment expended in arguing the bounds of the First Amendment is a moment scored by those who would circumscribe the scope of the constitutional standard, the defendants in this, or any prior restraint case, must rush their work. Especially in these cases, the law must be made to fit the cases, and hurriedly; the reverse, unfortunately for those who like their law developed in a more orderly manner, simply never is true.

A second significant revelation about media-government relations that can be drawn from the "Pentagon Papers" case involves the judicially underdeveloped distinction between prior restraint and postpublication punishment. As Justice Byron White noted in a concurring opinion in which Justice Potter Stewart joined, his objection to the government's case was not rooted in a belief that newspapers were immune from punishment for the type of publication involved here; rather, they could not be punished by the extraordinary equitable remedy of injunction. It is arguable that in terms of the public's short-range interest, the crucial issue in the "Pentagon Papers" case was immediate and widespread disclosure, not what inconveniences or monetary fines were ultimately suffered by the newspapers. So long as the presses were not blocked by an injunction, the argument goes, the aims of the First Amendment were served.

Yet, such an appraisal of the holding in this case takes inadequate account of which newspapers were involved and under what circumstances publication resumed. The *New York Times* and the *Washington Post* represent two most powerful voices in newspaper publishing. With an ability to afford in-house and outside counsel in such matters, these newspapers can wage a fight against postpublication prosecutions, pay fines, and even suffer the temporary loss of a few journalists if one should be jailed. Indeed, the prestige and influence of these newspapers, quite apart from their actual culpability under the federal criminal statutes involved, made the risk of severe sanctions, let alone actual prosecution of the newspapers, distant. As it turned out the Department of Justice did not exercise its prosecutorial discretion against the newspapers.

Nor in light of the awful truth revealed by these and the other newspapers that subsequently obtained portions of the Papers (for instance, that the Eisenhower administration played a "direct role" in undermining the Geneva Settlement of 1954; that the Johnson administration waged a covert war and planned an overt one long before revealing it to Congress or the public; and that consistent with the forecasts of government intelligence, the United States bombing of North Vietnam was completely ineffective in neutralizing pressure on American and South Vietnamese troops would such a prosecution have been politically viable. The government had been caught in a lie, albeit not entirely of the current administration's making. To attempt to punish only the messengers would have made an already embarrassed administration look vengeful.

What about secrets not about the past, but the present? In 1979, the *Progressive,* an iconoclastic monthly founded in 1909 by Robert La Follette, decided to publish the "secret" of how to make a hydrogen bomb. If the article contained data restricted by the Atomic Energy Act, the publisher could receive a $10,000 fine and ten years in jail. The article was submitted to the Atomic Energy Commission for clearance. Upon reading it the government decided to seek an injunction to bar publication.

The "secret" turned out not to be so secret, but discoverable with some basic college physics. Yet the District Court judge issued an injunction based on his view that the article could spread the use of nuclear weapons. While the case was on appeal, a letter containing some of the "secret" was published in the *Press Connection,* a small Madison, Wisconsin, newspaper, although the same letter was enjoined by a California court from running in the Berkeley, California, *Daily Californian.*

Publication of the letter, along with (or resulting in) the government's decision to drop its injunction action, mooted the case, and the court dismissed the appeals. For the *Progressive,* the dollar costs of resisting the injunction were dear. Yet, after the costly legal battle, the magazine, which had sought to publish the article to show how accessible information about nuclear weapons is, got to exercise what it thought the First Amendment granted it in the first place—the right to publish.

Revelations of official secrets do not always emerge on the front page of the *New York Times,* nor do they concern matters that are likely to generate public interest, like an ongoing war or atomic formulas. Disclosing a county administrator's defalcation of public funds based on stolen financial records; uncovering serious highway design defects by publication of suppressed safety reports unlawfully obtained; these are matters that may be the subject of scoops by any daily newspaper in the United States.

For many newspapers, however, the knowledge that prior restraint cannot be exercised against them is small comfort if the prospect of postpublication indictment is assured by the prosecutor. The impact of subsequent punishment on the precarious financial footing of some newspapers is enough to shake loose an editor's courage to publish material of vital public interest based on data gathered from stolen documents. As a result, postpublication punishment is far more coercive a force for a shoestring publishing operation (which, incidentally, characterizes much of what remains of the underground and alternative press) than the inability to publish one particular story.

Such newspapers must read Justice White's concurrence, distinguishing between enjoining speech and punishing it after the fact, as standing for the proposition that they can win the immediate battle but lose the war by judicial liens placed on their typewriters and printing facilities and by casualties in the form of imprisoned journalists. As a result, for many newspapers an after-the-fact prosecution presents no less a threat to the right of the press to transmit and, accordingly, the right of the public to receive; for some, it comprehends an even greater hazard to the long-term well-being of the newspaper.

A third lesson to be drawn from the "Pentagon Papers" case has been offered by law professor Louis Henken in his *University of Pennsylvania Law Review* article, "The Right to Know and the Duty to Withhold: The Case of the Pentagon Papers" (1971). Henkin suggests that the case illustrates a typical example of how the public must depend on the "unhappy game of trial by cleverness between Executive and Press" to obtain disclosure of the brand of critical intelligence illustrated by the Pentagon Papers. Henkin writes:

> For, as regards governmental documents and information, the Constitution is apparently interpreted as ordaining that a branch of government can properly conceal, even from other branches, surely from the public; but the Press is free to try to uncover, and if it succeeds it is free to publish.

What happens as a result, Henkin argues, is a haphazard, sporadic release of otherwise "confidential" information that depends for its disclosure on the political consciousness of a Daniel Ellsberg, who delivered the documents, and the tenacity and editorial skill of a Neil Sheehan, who headed the *Times*'s distillation of the 7,000 pages of the Pentagon Papers for nearly three months while secreted on the eleventh floor of the New York Hilton Hotel. Ellsberg (and Anthony Russo, who helped Ellsberg remove and reproduce the documents) were subsequently prosecuted for stealing and knowingly converting the Papers, although the charges were dismissed eventually because of improper government conduct in the prosecution of the case. Nevertheless, for some years after his trial, Ellsberg was viewed by many Americans as having acted more like a traitor than a patriot in releasing the Papers; surely, Ellsberg paid an emotional price for his bold conduct.

What is necessary, Henkin argues, is for government to release any information to the press that does not legitimately deserve the label TOP SECRET, instead of the public's having to rely on the occasional snatch of what should have been made freely available. Yet, even if executive declassification of papers undeserving of their confidential status (a reform set in motion by the "Pentagon Papers" case) and the Freedom of Information Act do reduce reliance on this cloak-and-dagger method of informing the public on matters of keen public importance, they cannot eliminate illegitimate concealment of information that the public has a need to know.

The tenacity with which Richard Nixon clung to his tapes, not to mention the incriminating eighteen-minute gap "discovered" in them, suggests that the solution cannot lie wholly in better systems of declassification or increasing liberality of Freedom of Information Act provisions. The remedy for the incompetent government official, whether local, state, or federal, will unfortunately continue to depend in part on Henkin's "unhappy game of trial by cleverness." Ultimately, however, the solution resides in public insistence on greater honesty and accountability by those elected to govern.

DLB

7

Distributing Information: When Courts Try to Stop Release

THE AUTHORS

WILLIAM H. ERICKSON serves as an Associate Justice of the Colorado Supreme Court and has had a rich, varied career in the law. His credits include appointment as a Judicial Member at Large on the Board of Governors of the American Bar Association, 1975–1979; Chairman of the ABA's Special Committee on Standards of Criminal Justice, 1973–1975; and Chairman of the ABA Criminal Justice Section, 1971–1972. This experience well equips him to discuss the problems of bench and bar relating to free press rights at trial. This article is part of a symposium on the *Nebraska Press Association* v. *Stuart* decision sponsored by the *Stanford Law Review*.

BRUCE W. SANFORD is a former reporter for the *Wall Street Journal* and now is a communications lawyer in Washington, D.C., with the Cleveland based firm of Baker and Hostetler. Among the clients handled by the firm is the Scripps-Howard newspaper group. It is worth noting that the First Amendment Congress Sanford talks about, held in 1980, was the first attempt by the print and broadcast media to join forces to articulate what the First Amendment ought to mean to modern society. Scores of resolutions were passed by the Congress, but the effort, while earnest, produced few national results.

Fair Trial and Free Press: The Practical Dilemma

WILLIAM H. ERICKSON

JUSTICE BRENNAN aptly described the problem raised by *Nebraska Press Association v. Stuart*[1] as one of exploring the "interface" of the first and sixth amendments. However, in examining the relationship of the two amendments in the context of a judicial gag order imposed directly on the press, the unanimous Court did not seem perplexed by the practical difficulties inherent in simultaneously maintaining loyalty to both constitutional principles.[2] In suggesting that a more realistic appraisal of the con-

---

From *Stanford Law Review* 29 (1977): 485–92.
1. 427 U.S. 539.
2. The question of the proper accommodation of the values of free press and fair trial is not unique to the age of modern journalism and media technology. In 1846, it was observed that "[o]urs is the greatest newspaper reading population in the world; not a man among us fit to serve as a juror, who does not read the newspapers. Every great and startling crime is paraded in their columns, with all the minuteness of detail that an eager competitor for public favor can supply. Hence the usual question, which has now become almost a necessary form in empaneling a jury, 'have you formed or expressed an opinion?' is virtually equivalent to the inquiry, 'do you read the newspapers?' . . . In the case of a particularly audacious crime that had been widely discussed it is utterly impossible that any man of common intelligence, and not wholly secluded from society, should be found, who had not formed an opinion." *Trial by Jury in New York*, 9 L. REP. 193, 198 (1846), *quoted in* ABA STANDARDS RELATING TO FAIR TRIAL AND FREE PRESS 21 (1968).

stitutional difficulties was in order, this Comment will analyze *Nebraska Press Association* and assess the options currently available to a trial judge faced with protection of the defendant's rights at trial.

I. THE PRACTICAL DIMENSIONS OF THE INTERFACE BETWEEN THE FIRST AND SIXTH AMENDMENTS

The sixth amendment by its terms guarantees that "the accused shall enjoy the right to . . . an impartial jury."[3] Without belaboring the perhaps irresolvable problem of absolute priorities in the Bill of Rights, it is clear that this right always has been considered both a fundamental right, and one at least on a par with those embodied in the first amendment.

The first amendment, on the other hand, provides that "Congress shall make no law . . . abridging the freedom of speech, or of the press."[4] The profound importance of that principle is a theme that has been repeated throughout our national experience. Certainly a fundamental aspect of first amendment jurisprudence has been the Court's resistance to prior restraints upon either the content or the timing of publication. In *Near v. Minnesota*[5] the Court stated that "The main purpose of [the first amendment] is 'to prevent all such previous restraints upon publications as had been practiced by other governments.'" In practical terms, however, the right to trial by an impartial jury often implies the necessity of an abridgement of the freedom of the press. If the ideals embodied in the constitutional phrases are examined with some scrutiny, there emerges a dilemma of significant practical dimensions: a press operating without "abridgement" would be immune from restrictions on the timing and the content of published material; an impartial jury would be insulated from factors which could prejudice its determination in a court of law.

A. THE THEORY OF THE IMPARTIAL JURY. The modern concept of the jury in the criminal trial process is remarkably refined. The Supreme Court's efforts to insure "impartiality" in the parameters of racial, sexual, and religious composition of the panel, and to insulate the jury from extrinsic and inadmissible evidence, are significant guides to the affirmative steps required to safeguard this "most fundamental of all freedoms." The character of the juror mandated by this pervasive dictate of "impartiality" is based upon the theory that the guilt or innocence of the defendant must be decided on the basis of *evidence* that the court properly determines to be admissible. The juror, above all, is no longer a witness as he once was at common law. He is, theoretically at least, a *tabula rasa* as to

---

3. U.S. CONST. amend. VI. The sixth amendment right to trial by an impartial jury was made applicable to the states through the fourteenth amendment in Duncan v. Louisiana, 391 U.S. 145, 149 (1968).

4. U.S. CONST. amend. I. The restrictions imposed upon Congress by the first amendment are applicable to the states via the fourteenth amendment. *See, e.g.*, Hughes v. Superior Court, 339 U.S. 460, 465–66 (1950).

5. 283 U.S. 697 (1931).

the particular facts of the case before the court. Thus, insofar as the juror is incapable of fairly receiving and evaluating this evidence, or is merely considering the evidence along with extrajudicial facts relating to the particular events, he is "partial" and constitutionally defective.

B. THE IMPACT OF THE MEDIA ON JURORS. The often profound impact of the communications media upon the public audience, hence potential jurors, is too basic to question. Courts have not hesitated to recognize that impact and its implications for diluting the constitutional requirement of impartiality. No judge can fail to perceive that the communications media operate with the potential for near instantaneous dissemination, that they can convey information in psychologically sophisticated terms with attractive auditory and visual dimensions, and, while variable, they often enjoy a credibility that is the envy of other social institutions. Moreover, the role of the press must be frankly assessed in light of the fact that intense inter- and intra-media competition may exist, with pressures that may promote both comprehensive coverage and, at times, a sensational style.

It is at the point where press commentary threatens to preclude the existence of a reasonable number of impartial veniremen that the constitutional interface confronted in *Nebraska Press Association* is encountered. The dilemma in the case was that, arguably, the values of an unabridged press and of ultimately empanelling an impartial jury were mutually exclusive. Whether or not one chooses to adhere to Justice Black's proposition that the Constitution cannot tolerate implied priorities within its structure,[6] the effect of the media upon virtually every potential juror creates profound practical problems in seeking to maintain both values intact.

II. THE *Nebraska Press Association* DECISION

In light of the nature of the problem, it is not surprising that *Nebraska Press Association* turned primarily upon facts rather than constitutional distinctions. In evaluating the failure of the Nebraska district court to establish a "record that supports the entry of a prior restraint on publication, one of the most extraordinary remedies known to our jurisprudence," the Court apparently adopted the classic balancing analysis of Judge Learned Hand as the test for the burden of proof: Whether "the gravity of the 'evil,' discounted by its improbability, justifies such invasion of free speech as is necessary to avoid the danger."[7] This "balancing" was guided by three key areas of consideration that must be reflected in the record before a gag order directly affecting the press may

---

6. With regard to the first and sixth amendments, Justice Black stated that "[f]ree speech and fair trial are two of the most cherished policies of our civilization, and it would be a trying task to choose between them." Bridges v. California, 314 U.S. 252, 260 (1941).
7. *Quoting* Dennis v. United States, 183 F.2d 201, 212 (1950), *aff'd*, 341 U.S. 494 (1958).

be upheld as constitutional: "(a) the nature and extent of pretrial news coverage; (b) whether other measures would be likely to mitigate the effects of unrestrained pretrial publicity; (c) how effectively a restraining order would cooperate to prevent the threatened danger."

To evaluate compliance with the balancing test based on these three factors, the Court turned to the record. Newspaper clippings and, interestingly, the testimony of the county court judge whose initial restraining order was under review were deemed a sufficient evidentiary basis for the trial judge's conclusion that "there would be intense and pervasive pretrial publicity concerning this case." The Court found that the trial judge "could . . . reasonably conclude, *based on common human experience,* that [such] publicity might impair the defendant's right to a fair trial."[8] However, the Court considered the record essentially devoid of evidence relevant to "determining whether measures short of an order restraining all publications would have insured the defendant a fair trial." In addition, the Court noted that the record lacked both an evidentiary foundation and a judicial determination as to the probable efficacy of the gag order itself. Thus, the district court failed to establish the requisite "showing" in two of the three crucial areas. Apparently insisting upon a full evidentiary basis and judicial analysis in each area as a condition precedent to the exercise of the "balancing" required in assessing the propriety of issuing a gag order, the Court concluded that the requirements were "not demonstrated with the degree of certainty our cases on prior restraint require."

The Court thus resolved the dilemma by invoking or, more correctly, defining the burden of proof faced by the trial judge who issues a gag order directly affecting the press, and by suggesting some types of evidence sufficient to meet that burden. The beauty of such analysis is that it allows resolution of the case without defining the outer limits of the constitutional values involved. The defect is that, given the Court's tacit encouragement of some form of gag order,[9] and the enduring responsibility of the trial judge to insure jury impartiality, the emergence of factual backgrounds and gag orders in seeming conformity with the strict requirements in *Nebraska Press Association* may be inevitable. The resulting demand for clarification of the balancing test ultimately may force the Court to delineate the constitutional boundaries so neatly avoided in *Nebraska Press Association.*

The burden of proof developed in the case may also create significant analytical problems of its own. It is, of course, pedestrian to criticize a "balancing test" as imprecise: That is its very purpose and virtue. On the other hand, the unstructured balancing proposed in *Nebraska Press Association* reaches unprecedented levels of obscurity. First, there is the

---

8. Emphasis added.
9. The Court did not condemn all prior restraints in this context as unconstitutional. It merely concluded, on the facts of this case, that "[g]iven these practical problems, it is far from clear that prior restraint on publication would have protected [the defendant's] rights." The Court also noted "that the guarantees of freedom of expression are not an absolute prohibition under all circumstances, but the barriers to prior restraint remain high and the presumption against its use continues intact."

bedrock unpredictability inevitably involved in purporting to measure the gravity of the evil, discounted by its probabilities, and weighing this against the justification of avoiding the danger. Second, consider the imponderables involved in each of the three areas of consideration. While a trial judge may rely on "common human experience" in "reasonably concluding" that a certain predicted level of publicity will result in the impairment of a fair trial, he is admittedly making a "necessarily speculative" decision that involves "factors unknown and unknowable." By contrast, he apparently cannot rely on a similar intuitive analysis in making the "more difficult . . . predictive assessment" of the efficacy of a prior restraint or of alternative devices. This tension between what is a matter of *prediction* and of *proof* strikes a discordant note when compared with the more definitive proposition that "when this Court has reversed a state conviction because of prejudicial publicity, it has carefully noted that some course of action short of prior restraint *would have* made a critical difference." Yet, if ascertaining the impact of pretrial publicity upon a juror is an exercise in speculation and intuition based on common human experience and ultimately on the "unknown and unknowable," is "demonstrating" the remedial effect, for example, of an admonition of impartiality to each juror a more concrete type of inquiry?

The ultimate problem with the "balancing" test in *Nebraska Press Association* is not merely that it compounds a loose verbal formula with a mandate to somehow "demonstrate" some imponderables and to intuit others. The more disturbing defect is that the test purports to establish a heavy burden of proof, yet offers only marginal guidance, even though the opinion tacitly invites further attempted refinement of the gag order.

III. POST-*Nebraska Press Association* GUIDELINES FOR THE TRIAL JUDGE

It is the trial judge, of course, who initially must face the practical pressures generated by the conflict between the values of an unabridged press and impartial jurors. When confronted with a factual situation in which the values of the constitutional tenets appear to be mutually exclusive—where the sensational facts of the case and the limited universe of veniremen together with the nature of the press coverage make full press disclosure incompatible with a reasonable likelihood of ultimate juror impartiality—what should he do?

It is unfortunate that the theoretical balancing analysis applied in *Nebraska Press Association* may prove to be more of a procedural obstacle than a guide. However, it is at least clear that the case did not establish a per se rule as to the invalidity of prior restraints. In the wake of *Nebraska Press Association*, the trial judge contemplating the utility and constitutionality of a gag order may benefit from the following considerations:

(1) Timing may be the most crucial element in the court's determination. Failure or inability to act in a timely manner precludes any arguable efficacy in imposing a gag order.

(2) The determination that a gag order is necessary should be based

on a careful analysis in each of five key areas. That analysis, together with explicit findings of fact based on plenary evidence, should be fully reflected in the record, as indicated in the following guidelines:

(a) An appreciation of the *Nebraska Press Association* balancing formula should be demonstrated.

(b) A factual determination should be made that prejudicial pretrial publicity which will preclude a fair trial is a reasonable certainty unless a restraint on the press is imposed.

(c) At a minimum, the following alternative devices should be individually considered and their aggregate efficacy should be determined to be inadequate to prevent or erase the effects of pretrial publicity:

    (i) Voluntary compliance with any applicable bar-press compacts,[10]

    (ii) Closure of pretrial hearings,

    (iii) Continuance,[11]

    (iv) Change of venue,[12]

    (v) Voir dire of prospective jurors,[13]

    (vi) Preliminary admonitions of impartiality to each juror,[14]

    (vii) Final instructions to the jury,

    (viii) Sequestration of the jury.[15]

(d) A determination should be made that the ultimate remedy of

---

10. Largely as a result of the ABA STANDARDS RELATING TO FAIR TRIAL AND FREE PRESS (1968), numerous jurisdictions have developed voluntary bar-press compacts designed to guide the conduct of members of both professions in relation to trials.

11. *See* Sheppard v. Maxwell, 384 U.S. 333, 363 (1966). The theory behind this device is that the passage of time may dilute the effect of prejudicial publicity. . . .

The efficacy and costs of this device have been criticized: "While a lengthy continuance might sufficiently protect the accused in some cases, it does not do so here. Delays may be an efficacious antidote to publicity in medium and large cities, but in small communities, where a major crime becomes embedded in the public consciousness, their effectiveness is greatly diminished." Maine v. Superior Court, 68 Cal. 2d 375, 387, 438 P.2d 372, 380, 66 Cal. Rptr. 724, 732 (1968) (footnotes omitted).

Moreover, a continuance, if it is to be long enough to dissipate the effects of the potentially prejudicial publicity, may require the defendant to sacrifice his right to a speedy trial and its purpose will be defeated if the publicity is renewed when the case finally comes up.

12. The utility of this device may be constrained by statutory limitations upon movement of the trial.

13. The judicial faith in this device has waned since its utility was first expounded in United States v. Burr, 25 F. Cas. 49 (C.C.D. Va. 1807) . . . Thus, the Supreme Court has held that a juror's assurance on voir dire may be unreliable if "deep and bitter prejudice is found." Irvin v. Dowd, 366 U.S. 717, 727 (1961). . . .

In addition, as Judge Learned Hand once noted, "any examination on the voir dire is a clumsy and imperfect way of detecting suppressed emotional commitments to which all of us are to some extent subject, unconsciously or subconsciously." United States v. Dennis, 183 F.2d 201, 227 (2d Cir. 1950).

14. To the extent that voir dire is insufficient to detect impartiality due to the subconscious character of some preconceptions of guilt, it is unlikely that admonitions or instructions will have a remedial effect in erasing prejudice, even in the usual case of the well-intentioned juror.

15. Sequestration, of course, is an effective means of insulation only after empanelling of the jury. As to *pretrial* publicity, therefore, it is almost completely inefficacious as a technique for assuring impartiality. Only minimal curative effects may be found in the *Nebraska Press Ass'n* Court's suggestion that sequestration "enhances the likelihood of dissipating the impact of pretrial publicity and emphasizes the elements of the jurors' oaths."

appellate reversal after conviction by a prejudiced jury would be an inadequate alternative because it is speculative, it deprives the defendant of at least interim due process, and it is inconsistent with the duty of the trial judge to take affirmative steps to insure a fair trial.

(e) The probable efficacy of the gag order should be carefully considered and documented in light of each of the following variables:

    (i) The number and types of persons affected by the order,[16]

    (ii) The specificity demanded by the first amendment requirement that the order create only the minimum abridgement of press freedom necessary to achieve its objective.

    (iii) The effect of lack of jurisdiction over press organs or persons,[17]

    (iv) The possibility of overreaching by members of the press.

(3) The fullest degree of precedural due process consistent with the exigencies of the case should be accorded all interests potentially affected by the gag order.[18]

To the degree that the defects in the restraint order in *Nebraska Press Association* were, as the Court intimated, problems of the requisite "showing" or of inadequate documentation, a determination in accord with the above considerations should largely erase the constitutional frailties that led to the invalidation of the gag order in that case.

IV. THE "EVIL WITHOUT REMEDY" SYNDROME

Underlying the ambiguity of the burden of proof analysis developed in *Nebraska Press Association* are some indications of a movement toward protection of the press from prior restraint at any cost. The possibility that the Court may, in a case where the "demonstration" required in *Nebraska Press Association* has been met, ultimately consider the conclusion that press-induced jury partiality is "an evil for which there is no

---

16. This would include members of the press, publishers, officers of the court, and affected parties.

17. The issuing court's lack of jurisdiction over nonlocal press and media organizations may limit significantly the prospective efficacy of any gag order. As the Court itself pointed out, modern long-arm jurisdiction statutes may remove any constitutional problems in reaching the press and media "at large"; *see* New York Times Co. v. Sullivan, 376 U.S. 254 (1964) (jurisdiction over the New York Times Co. by Alabama based upon the distribution of 394 copies of an allegedly libelous copy of the *Times* in Alabama). However, as the Court went on to note in *Nebraska Press Ass'n*, the practical problems of enforcing nationwide gag orders in a multijurisdictional legal system may be immense.

18. Thus, the court carefully should consider the feasibility of affording adequate notice and a prior hearing to members of the press and publishers who will be subject to the order. Some members of the *Nebraska Press Ass'n* Court were sensitive to the dangers of abuse inherent in a procedure of ex parte prior restraints. . . . The better rule with respect to gag orders, therefore, requires that all orders which potentially affect the press by restricting access to information or imposing outright publication restraints be treated as analogous to other temporary injunctive relief, allowing all affected parties to be heard.

remedy" is disturbing. The harbingers of such apparent resignation should not be ossified into an implicit priority between values of constitutional magnitude.

This comment suggests that the appropriate construction of *Nebraska Press Association* is a narrow one, and that the decision should not discourage trial courts from exploring the utility and constitutionality of carefully refined prior restraint or gag orders when it is manifest that the right to trial by an impartial jury is at stake. While the public interest in the "news" of all crimes is undoubtedly a matter of legitimate concern, the deprivation of the right to a fair trial should be of equal concern and may well be as "irreparable" as restraints upon the press. The effect of a prior restraint is only "irreversible" in the same sense that the denial of a fair trial is: The satisfaction of each right is postponed, with the accompanying permanent loss of the benefits of immediacy.[19] The difference, however, is that, because of the competitive nature of journalism, the "public's right to know" has reasonable guarantees of ultimate satisfaction. Given the costs, delays and vagaries of appellate relief, the public's right to the guarantee of fair trials is not similarly protected when a trial judge is precluded from insuring juror impartiality in the first instance.

---

19. . . . Professor Bickel noted that "[p]rior restraints fall on speech, with a brutality and a finality all their own. Even if they are ultimately lifted they cause irremediable loss—a loss in the immediacy, the impact of speech." A. BICKEL, THE MORALITY OF CONSENT 61 (1975). However, the "immediacy" of speech, like its content, should not stand as a naked, absolute value in the context of the first amendment. The loss in "impact" is, of course, exactly the result that may be required in order to preserve the defendant's right to a fair trial. The conflicting values involved are incommensurable and not subject to a simple weighing. The dilemma appears when the "impact" of the speech also will create an irreparable prejudice in the minds of veniremen. The resolution must lie between absolute protection of one right or of the other.

Richmond Newspapers: End of a Zigzag Trail?

BRUCE W. SANFORD

IT WAS ONE of those bright moments when a youth punctures hours of adult contrivance with a simple question. Neither Jean Otto, president of the Society of Professional Journalists, Sigma Delta Chi, nor the other tireless organizers of the First Amendment Congress, meeting last March in Williamsburg, Virginia, could have planned it better.

The congress had been convened initially in January at Philadelphia's historic First Bank building where, with the help of Dan Rather, Anthony Lewis, and other speakers, delegates celebrated the First Amendment and worried about the erosion of its protections at the hands of the U.S. Supreme Court. Two months later, delegates to a second meeting in co-

From *Columbia Journalism Review* 19(1980):46–47.

lonial Williamsburg were charting a program for educating the public about First Amendment freedoms. After all, George Gallup, Jr., had told the Philadelphia assembly that 76 percent of polled Americans didn't even know what the First Amendment was.

A candlelight tour of Williamsburg's reconstructed capitol, with its colonial courtroom, concluded a long day of speeches and enough discussion to weary a founding father. Much of the talk denounced the Supreme Court's baffling 5–4 decision in *Gannett Co., Inc.* v. *DePasquale* on July 2, 1979, which permitted the closing of pretrial proceedings to the press and public on the grounds of an accused's Sixth Amendment right to a fair— but not necessarily open—trial.

Seventy or so delegates crammed into the small courtroom to listen to a lavishly gowned guide describe how trials were conducted in eighteenth-century Virginia. Finished with her spiel, the guide sought the audience's questions. Silence. Then an abrupt hand from Allan Hoffman, a junior high school student from Upper Dublin, Pennsylvania. "Were the trials always open to the public?" Allan asked.

Amid the laughter, which perplexed her, the guide allowed as how, yes, she thought they always were.

The guide was right. History, as it turned out, is the foundation for the Supreme Court's self-proclaimed "watershed" decision in *Richmond Newspapers, Inc.* v. *Virginia,* which the Court handed down a year to the day after *DePasquale.* It is at once an unsurprising decision, given what the Williamsburg guide sensed—the presumption of openness inherent in Anglo-American justice—and the most surprising First Amendment decision of the past decade.

Most observers had been betting that if the Court decided to reverse the Virginia courts' closure of the fourth murder trial of John Paul Stevenson, it would do so only on the narrowest of grounds. Faced with the *DePasquale* majority of five justices who had ignored the entire question of the public's First Amendment right to attend pretrial proceedings, and worried about the Court's increasingly undisguised irritation with the fourth estate, media lawyers were understandably apprehensive.

But when the Court handed down its decision, it confounded everyone by the historic scope of its pronouncement. In crisp and emphatic language, a 7–1 majority held that: "Absent an overriding interest articulated in findings, the trial of a criminal case must be open to the public." At the same time, Chief Justice Burger startled his critics by articulating, for the first time, the broad contours of a First Amendment right of access to governmental information and proceedings.

"People in an open society do not demand infallibility from their institutions, but it is difficult for them to accept what they are prohibited from observing," the Chief Justice wrote. Along with a clear majority of the Court, he was recognizing, as never before, a right that the press had sought more assiduously than any other throughout the 1970s—constitutional protection for newsgathering.

The decision has for this reason been universally heralded as a "victory for the American people and only secondarily for the American press," in the words of J. Stewart Bryan III, publisher of Richmond Newspapers, Inc. "It's one of the two or three most important decisions in the whole history of the First Amendment," says *Miami Herald* lawyer Dan Paul.

Robert C. Bernius, the Rochester lawyer who argued *DePasquale* for Gannett, and lost, feels "vindicated" by *Richmond Newspapers.* He sees it as a "one-hundred-and-eighty-degree policy shift for the Court." Other news media lawyers think that's overstating matters a bit since the Chief Justice and Justices Stewart and Stevens justify their seeming change of position by breezily explaining that *DePasquale* dealt only with pretrial proceedings—not trials—and was decided on Sixth Amendment—not First Amendment—grounds. Nonetheless, there has been a shift, or at least a new willingness to address the First Amendment arguments about the public's right to view court proceedings—arguments which Bernius made in his *DePasquale* brief two years ago.

Whatever the reason for the Court's shift, the effect of *Richmond Newspapers* will almost certainly be to reduce the nationwide epidemic of courtroom closings. Footnotes in the various opinions place vague limitations on the sweep of the decision. Thus, Burger notes that "whether the public has a right to attend trials of civil cases is a question not raised by this case, but we note that historically both civil and criminal trials have been presumptively open."

But the "general perception of the case is more important than the footnotes," says CBS News correspondent Fred Graham, "and it will be perceived by lower courts as broadly discouraging the closing of courtrooms." Attorney General Benjamin Civiletti has drafted new Justice Department guidelines that may limit strictly the occasions when the government will seek closure in trials and pretrial proceedings.

Underestimating the bureaucratic reverence for secrecy may be naive, however; just one week after *Richmond. Newspapers* was handed down, United Press International and several Utah news organizations had to challenge the U.S. Comptroller of the Currency and two of Utah's largest banks, which were attempting to exclude the public and press from large segments of a major antitrust trial in Salt Lake City. When pressed, the comptroller and the banks failed to show any compelling or overriding reason for excluding reporters, and the judge indicated that all aspects of the trial would be open except certain so-called sensitive and confidential records of bank examinations, which he may open up after inspection.

The most troublesome problems for the press will probably continue to erupt in pretrial proceedings, due to whatever life is left in *DePasquale*. Even though *DePasquale* is not overruled, "you can make an awfully strong argument that the same rigorous standards articulated for trials in *Richmond Newspapers* should also apply to pretrial proceedings," argues

First Amendment lawyer Floyd Abrams. "We are probably back to where we were two years ago with open trials, and now and then a closed pretrial suppression hearing, when a criminal defendant can make a strong showing."

Essentially, news media lawyers will argue that the paramountcy of First Amendment considerations compels a judge to use all available alternative measures to closing a courtroom in pretrial proceedings as well as in trials. A mounting number of state court decisions, including those handed down by the highest courts in Pennsylvania, New York, West Virginia, Arkansas, and Oregon, have already accomplished this collaterally by making closure, as a practical matter, the very last resort. "The arguments are now First Amendment arguments and *DePasquale* is no longer the law," concludes *New York Times* lawyer James C. Goodale.

Besides keeping courtroom doors open, *Richmond Newspapers* will be a powerful tool in the hands of news media lawyers who wish to assert the right of access to other kinds of governmental proceedings, such as closed city council or school board meetings—and even to such governmental data as police blotter entries. "One will start with *Richmond Newspapers* in all future access cases," says Floyd Abrams.

The logic for applying the decision to nonjudicial matters comes from what Justice Brennan calls the "public access component" of the First Amendment. In his concurring opinion, Brennan sketches two principles to help determine when the right of access should be granted. "The case for a right of access has special force when drawn from an enduring and vital tradition of public entree to particular proceedings or information," he writes, and "what is crucial in individual cases is whether access to a particular government process is important in terms of that very process." Thus, Brennan finds a First Amendment right to attend trials because, first, it is a historical practice, and, second, public scrutiny is of value to the trial process itself.

The right of access may be extended even beyond those proceedings that meet Brennan's "structural" test. Justice Stevens counts noses in his concurring opinion and implies that there is now a majority of five—Brennan, Powell, Marshall, Blackmun, and himself—that would overrule the 1978 plurality decision in *Houchins* v. *KQED, Inc.,* which denied the news media a constitutional right of access to a California prison.

James Goodale also expects the language of *Richmond Newspapers* to strengthen the position of reporters subpoenaed to testify in court proceedings; they will now be able to argue that the Supreme Court has upheld their right to preserve the confidentiality of sources since this is part of their constitutionally protected right to gather the news.

Nevertheless, the euphoria generated by the Court's decision has been tempered by lawyerly caution. Most lawyers are understandably timid about predicting a brave new world of constitutional access. A Court that can swing from *DePasquale* to *Richmond Newspapers* within a year does not, after all, inspire a great feeling of confidence about what it may do in the future. *"Richmond Newspapers* validates the press's claim as the surrogate of the public in covering courtrooms," says Alice Neff Lucan, an attorney for the Gannett Co., Inc., "but it will not be terribly useful in opening up other proceedings." "There have been seeds that have been sown before which have dried up and shriveled away," says Jack Landau of the Reporters Committee for Freedom of the Press, adding that the decision could be enormously useful but that it will take another opinion to clarify it.

In addition to their doubts about the distance *Richmond Newspapers* can be stretched beyond its specific holding, Abrams and others fear the possibility of an insidious side effect. There is some risk that as courts become accustomed to performing balancing acts in right of access cases, the balancing mood will extend to a totally different and inappropriate area—prior restraints. The danger here is that courts may confuse these two wholly separate areas of First Amendment law, and relax the long-standing rule that any attempt at prior restraint of publication bears the heaviest constitutional burden against its validity. Thus, in a future *Pentagon Papers* or *Progressive* case a court might start balancing the government's rights against other rights instead of requiring the government, if it wants to block publication, to show a clear and present danger to national security.

Commentary

LET US BEGIN with the background of *Nebraska Press Association* v. *Stuart.* In 1976 a Nebraska judge put a gag order on the press, prohibiting reports of testimony given in open court during a preliminary hearing for a defendant accused of killing six members of a neighboring family. On appeal, the United States Supreme Court, after reviewing prior restraint cases (primarily *Near* v. *Minnesota* and *New York Times* v. *United States*), stressed, "The thread running through all these cases is that prior restraints on speech and publication are the most serious and the least tolerable infringement on First Amendment rights." In the *Nebraska Press Association* case, as in previous cases, the Court declined to put an outright ban on prior restraints, leaving the door open for the future: "We reaffirm that the guarantees of freedom of expression are not an absolute prohibition under all circumstances, but the barriers to prior restraint remain high and the presumption against its use continues intact."

The First Amendment prescribes a free press. The Sixth Amendment prescribes a fair trial. If the press uses the full extent of its freedom to report and comment on an accused person, can his trial actually be fair?

This dilemma is an old, difficult one. It began to be debated seriously by attorneys and journalists in the 1930s when Bruno Richard Hauptmann, a carpenter, was tried for the kidnaping and murder of the infant son of Charles A. Lindbergh. Lindbergh had recently become an international hero for his solo flight across the Atlantic in 1927, and the Hauptmann trial was front-page news for months. In a highly emotional atmosphere, Hauptmann was convicted and executed. Did news coverage prejudice the trial? Walter Lippmann sketched the issues:

> We are concerned with a situation spectacularly illustrated in this case, but typical of most celebrated criminal cases in the United States which may be described by saying that there are two processes of justice, the one official, the other popular. They are carried on side by side, the one in courts of law, the other in the press, over the radio, on the screen, at public meetings—and at every turn this irregular popular process interferes with, distorts and undermines the effectiveness of the law and the people's confidence in it.
>
> Because there are two pursuits of the criminal, two trials and two verdicts—the one supposed to be based on the law and a thousand years of accumulated experience, the other totally irresponsible—the self-appointed detectives get in the way of the regular detectives, the self-appointed judges and jurymen and advocates for the prosecution and defense get in the way of the officers of the law, and the official verdict becomes confused with popular verdict, often in the court itself, almost always in the public mind.

Lippmann made it clear that the media were far from alone in trying defendants and encouraging popular verdicts. He emphasized that, "without the connivance of the regular officers of the law, the abuses of publicity would have been reduced to manageable proportions." The opposing attorneys "by their public statements violated No. 20 of the Canons of Ethics of the American Bar Association." (Canon 20: "Newspaper publications by a lawyer as to pending or anticipated litigation may interfere with a fair trial in the Courts and otherwise prejudice the due administration of justice. Generally they are to be condemned. . . .") Nonetheless, the media were blamed. Two years after the trial the American Bar Association passed Canon 35, which sought to ban from courtrooms photographers and electronic media (meaning chiefly radio at that time). In 1952 television was added to the ban.

It should not be forgotten that the mass media represent the right of the public to know whether its courts are dispensing justice and how. There are two approaches to this responsibility. One consists in reexamining and reevaluating all the evidence and, in effect, conducting a second trial to check the verdict of the court. Such investigations, carried on after the legal trial, have turned up many miscarriages of justice. A reporter for the *Miami Herald* won a Pulitzer Prize in 1966 for such a discovery.

The second approach to this responsibility requires checking the performances of the police, the judges, the other officials, and the lawyers to determine whether they are dispensing justice. This approach is more difficult, for it surely includes calling officials to account for making comments and leaking facts that should come out in the course of the trial, not in a press conference or interview—and comments and facts are, of course, the lifeblood of mass communication. Journalists, then, not only must refuse to accept some of the proffered news but must also criticize the officials who offer it.

As a result of sensational and apparently prejudicial reporting, the debate on free press and fair trial has moved beyond the simple question of whether cameras and other modern reporting devices should be allowed in the courtroom. Skirmishes between the bar and the mass media over that issue were elevated to the plane of warfare as a consequence of events beginning in Cleveland in 1954. The pivotal event was the trial of Dr. Sam Sheppard. The case had all the elements of high drama: Dr. Sheppard was a handsome young osteopath accused of the brutal murder of his lovely young wife. The family was prominent. There was another woman. A mysterious man was alleged to have been in the house on the murder night.

Many of the patterns of the Hauptmann case were repeated. Hordes of reporters and photographers descended on Cleveland. Information was leaked. Notes were passed to reporters by the accused. Lawyers talked. Self-styled crime experts analyzed the evidence, even added to the evidence, in public print. Biographies of the accused were published and broadcast. The photographic coverage was extensive. The sex element was played up in a big way and the crime itself was described in gruesome detail.

Dr. Sheppard was convicted and sentenced to life in prison. Then, in 1966, after he had served ten years, the Supreme Court ruled that the "carnival atmosphere" of the 1954 trial had deprived Dr. Sheppard of his constitutional rights.

It is clear that the Court held the trial judge chiefly responsible, but this finding should not be allowed to obscure the role of the news media. The Court cited the *Cleveland Press* for a vicious series of headlines and news accounts, and among the many prejudicial reports was a broadcast carried by station WHK in Cleveland in which Bob Considine likened Sheppard to a perjurer and compared the episode to Alger Hiss's confrontation with Whittaker Chambers. The Court decided that Dr. Sheppard should be retried promptly or granted freedom. A retrial was held in November 1966 under closely controlled conditions and Dr. Sheppard was found not guilty.

In 1981 the Court ended the debate about whether, in itself, the presence of television cameras in the courtroom deprived a defendant of a fair trial. In *Chandler* v. *Florida* the Court held that it did not. While a judge need not grant television crews the right to set up shop in the courtroom, the mere televising of court proceedings is permissible under the Sixth Amendment. Trials are now routinely televised in many states. Reductions in size and noise of cameras, lights, and microphones doubtless aided television's entry into courts.

The *Chandler* case as well as the *Nebraska Press Association* and *Richmond Newspapers* cases tend to point to greater press power on the First Amendment–Sixth Amendment teeter-totter. But are there dividends to a defendant that can come from greater press attention? Surely defendants and plaintiffs desire publicity for their causes in what are styled as political cases, for example, the Chicago Seven trial in the late 1960s and the MCI Corporation antitrust suits against AT & T in the early 1980s.

And think about it in another way. For particularly complicated and wide-ranging defenses the defense counsel must rely on the media to attract public attention in the hope that individuals will contact the lawyers with evidentiary leads, legal theories, or other information that might prove useful. Often, those who try to be helpful provide useless tips or crank information. But sometimes information indirectly solicited by means of media exposure can prove useful.

During the bank-robbery trial of Patricia Hearst, her defense counsel, F. Lee Bailey, received ten to forty unsolicited letters each day with a variety of tips, some of which were followed up. One such tip from a New York attorney, who was following the case in the newspapers, became the foundation for an important defensive evidentiary motion. Hence, a defendant's access to the press, even if it may tend to unsettle the calm of the trial, may be an invaluable defense tool.

The tension between assuring both the constitutional guarantees of a fair trial and a free press will continue, although the *Nebraska* case has doubtlessly resulted in a more restrained use of press gags as a means to alleviate it. However, the ultimate problem facing journalists and jurists alike lies not with a sensationalistic press or an overwrought judge, but with the unpredictable jury. Eventually, the controversy is reduced to inquiring about the jury's ability (or lack thereof) to remove from its deliberations *any* prejudice, whether spawned by the media or by purely personal experiences. Press coverage is one, but only one, source of juror prejudice. In examining prospective jurors a trial judge asks not whether they have heard about the case but whether what they have heard will impair their ability to decide the case impartially. No one is without preconceptions about the aspects of a defendant's appearance or courtroom personality. The defendant may be low in intelligence or physically unattractive or from a racial minority. These factors cannot help but be noticed by jurors.

Our system of law does not pretend that the prejudices resulting from these factors do not exist. But as the Supreme Court in the 1961 case of *Irvin* v. *Dowd* noted: "It is sufficient if the juror can lay aside his impression or opinion and render a verdict based on the evidence presented in court."

Court-ordered gags may be able to reduce the impact news stories can have on juror prejudice, but they can never remove all sources of prejudice. In the end, trial by jury will remain a vital and valuable right only if individual jurors can themselves lay aside preconceptions, press-induced or otherwise, and decide guilt or innocence based on what they hear and see in the courtroom.

WLR

8

"Unprotected" Expression: Obscenity

THE AUTHORS

WALTER GELLHORN, who was graduated from Amherst College in 1927, earned a law degree from Columbia University four years later. He worked first as a law clerk to Supreme Court Justice Harlan F. Stone, then as attorney in the office of the Solicitor General of the United States, and then became a member of the law faculty at Columbia.

Like his sister Martha, who has written many nonfiction books, Walter Gellhorn has a delightful way with words. His books center on legal problems, but are written in a style that makes reading them uncommonly pleasurable—for legal tracts.

HARRIET F. PILPEL was graduated from Vassar College, then earned the M.A. in international relations as well as a law degree from Columbia University. Since her admission to the bar of New York State in 1936 she has emphasized the rights of those who write. She is published regularly in the trade magazine *Publisher's Weekly* in a signed column called, "You Can Do It." She has also written four books: *Your Marriage and the Law, Rights and Writers, A Copyright Guide,* and *Know Your Rights.*

Dirty Books, Disgusting Pictures, and Dreadful Laws

WALTER GELLHORN

SOME YEARS AGO an irreverent Columbia law student asserted that if a certain professor were to lecture on sex for two solid hours, he would not manage to say a single interesting thing. Fearful that students might make the same comment about me at the end of the two hour lecture I am about to give, I proposed to Dean Beaird that I be allowed to enliven my talk by interspersing it with old stereopticon slides showing the graffiti in the ruins of Pompeii. He rejected the proposal, saying that it ran counter to the policy of the Department of Physical Education, which seeks to deemphasize spectator sports and, instead, to encourage direct participation in intramural contact athletics. Then I suggested reading from the works of Joyce, Lawrence, Hemingway, Hawthorne, Shaw, Whitman, Shelley, and other who had had losing battles with the antiobscenity forces. But he told me that all of the pertinent passages were required to be committed to memory during this university's Freshman English

[This article is] the second John A. Sibley Lecture in Law for the academic year 1973–74 delivered at the University of Georgia School of Law on February 8, 1974. It was published originally in the *Georgia Law Review* 8(2)(1974):291–312. Reprinted by permission.

course, so nothing would be gained by reciting them anew. I am therefore thrown back on my own meager resources.

I propose, as the title of my talk will have suggested, to discuss the law of obscenity. In an ideal world this topic might be exhausted speedily, since even if, like me, a person dwelt always in an ivory tower and therefore had no contact whatsoever with obscenity, one should in any event be able to grasp the law of the subject readily enough. But this, alas, is not the case here.

Consider, for example, the national law, which in one of its parts prohibits "importing into the United States from any foreign country . . . any obscene book . . . or other article which is obscene or immoral."[1] Several years ago a traveler returning from Mexico sought to bring back with him certain photographs and films, which were uncontestedly meant for his personal use and enjoyment. They were seized as being obscene. In an earlier case, the Supreme Court had held that possessing and reading and looking at obscenity in the privacy of one's own home could not be penalized.[2] In 1973, however, the Court ruled that the traveler was properly forestalled in his effort to carry the assertedly offensive materials to his hearthside; the home does not extend as far as a port of entry into the United States.[3] That sounds straightforward enough. But the law becomes a bit fuzzy when applied. What, exactly, is an obscene or immoral article, whose importation is forbidden? Not long ago the customs official who decided whether or not motion pictures were excludible because of their prurient nature was asked how he reached his conclusions. He answered: "As to how I go about making that judgement [sic] this is just—it seems to me it would be based on the reaction I had to seeing the film. . . . I think my answer would have to depend on my own judgment, my own experience: I couldn't define it."

Well, that clears that up, and we can now pass to the next question. Before doing so, however, I should tell you that some officials are more precise. A postal inspector charged with responsibility akin to that of the customs official just quoted, said that he preferred to rely on explicit tests of impermissibility, of which the following is a sample: "Breasts, yes, but nipples, no! Buttocks, yes, but cracks, no!"

Still, despite a few lingering uncertainties (including four dissenting Justices), the Supreme Court has settled for the time being that legislatures may constitutionally prohibit obscenity, whether printed or pictorial, notwithstanding the constitutional denial of legislative power to abridge freedom of expression. In *Miller v. California*[4] the Court upheld a

---

1. 19 U.S.C. § 1305(a).
2. Stanley v. Georgia, 394 U.S. 557 (1969).
3. United States v. 12,200-Ft. Reels of Super 8MM. Film, 413 U.S. 123 (1973). *See also* United States v. Orito, 413 U.S. 139 (1973), upholding 18 U.S.C. § 1462 (1970), which penalizes using a common carrier to transport "any obscene, lewd, lascivious, or filthy book . . . or other matters of indecent character." Orito had argued that the right to possess obscene material in the home included the right to get it there.
4. 413 U.S. 15 (1973).

statute aimed at distribution of "any obscene matter." The defendant had conducted a mass mailing campaign to advertise several books bearing such titles as "Intercourse," "Sex Orgies Illustrated," and "An Illustrated History of Pornography." The advertising brochures consisted largely, as the Court noted, of very explicit depictions of "men and women in groups of two or more engaging in a variety of sexual activities, with genitals often prominently displayed." The situation could therefore fairly be characterized as one "in which sexually explicit materials have been thrust by aggressive sales action upon unwilling recipients who had in no way indicated any desire to receive such materials." The Court's decision did not rest upon that fact, but, rather, undertook to chart the entire field of permissible state regulation.

First, the Court repeated a declaration it had made in 1957, when it had rejected arguments that the First Amendment's protection of free expression should be extended to expression regarded as obscene. "All ideas having the slightest redeeming social importance," the Court had then said, ". . . have the protection of the [First Amendment] guaranties . . . But implicit in the history of the First Amendment is the rejection of obscenity as utterly without redeeming social importance"—and therefore fair game for suppressive laws.

Defining what is obscene and, for that reason, subject to suppression remained a problem. To this the Court next turned, since a careless proscription might constrict expression to an unconstitutional degree. During the sixteen years since the 1957 decision had declared open season on obscenity, the Supreme Court of the United States had passed upon more than thirty cases involving allegedly unprotected expression. Most of these thirty-odd cases had been decided without an opinion because no view of what is obscene could command the support of as many as five Justices. At last, in 1973, Chief Justice Burger was able to muster four votes besides his own for what was no doubt believed to be a clear test. Regulation of expression because it is thought to be obscene, the Chief Justice declared, must be confined to "works which depict or describe sexual conduct. . . . specifically defined by the applicable state law . . ."; these works must be only those ". . . which, taken as a whole, appeal to the prurient interest in sex , which portray sexual conduct in a patently offensive way, and which, taken as a whole, do not have serious literary, artistic, political, or scientific value."[5]

Then, to help legislatures which might wish to adopt restrictive laws without fear of transgressing the Constitution, the Court added "a few plain examples" of what can be forbidden, as follows:

(a) Patently offensive representations or descriptions of ultimate sexual acts, normal or perverted, actual or simulated.
(b) Patently offensive representation or descriptions of masturbation, excretory functions, and lewd exhibition of the genitals.

5. Miller v. California, 413 U.S. 15, 23, 24 (1973).

Of course even these, the Court said, might have "serious literary, artistic, political, or scientific value," as in the case of medical books with graphic illustrations of human anatomy. Juries would have to be relied upon to differentiate between the valuable and the valueless.

What standards should a jury apply in deciding whether material appeals to "prurient interest" or is "patently offensive"? The juryman must determine what would be the view of "the average person applying contemporary community standards." What, then, is the "community" whose standards are to be applied? It is not the nation as a whole, the Chief Justice answered; he declared it to be "[N]either realistic nor constitutionally sound to read the First Amendment as requiring that the people of Maine or Mississippi accept public depiction of conduct found tolerable in Las Vegas, or New York City."[6]

Four Justices remained unpersuaded. Justice Douglas adhered to his often expressed "absolutist" view that expression which, as he puts it, is unbrigaded with action may not constitutionally be subjected to governmental regulation.[7] Justices Stewart and Marshall joined Justice Brennan in concluding that the Court's decision could not succeed in stabilizing the law without jeopardizing fundamental First Amendment values. The progeny of the 1957 opinion written by Justice Brennan himself had shown, the dissenters thought, the impracticability of formulating manageable standards for judging what could and what could not be suppressed by law. Surely not all sexually oriented matter is beyond constitutional protection, since, as the Court has said, sex is a "great and mysterious motive force in human life, which has indisputably been a subject of absorbing interest to mankind through the ages. . . ." For more than fifteen years the Court had struggled manfully (should I say personfully) but unsuccessfully to differentiate between the allowably sexual and the unprotected area of obscenity. Its present effort to map the boundaries of state power led the majority to "resort to such indefinite concepts as 'prurient interest,' 'patent offensiveness,' 'serious literary value,' and the like," whose meaning must perforce vary "with the experience, outlook, and even idiosyncracies of the person defining them." Justice Stewart on an earlier occasion had said that though he might not be able to define hardcore pornography intelligibly, still he knew it when

---

6. *Id.* at 32. The concepts just summarized were used also to sustain state power to control films shown in a so-called "adult" theater, Paris Adult Theatre I v. Slaton, 413 U.S. 49 (1973); federal power to prohibit imports of obscene matter, United States v. 12,200-Ft. Reels, 413 U.S. 123 (1973); federal power to prohibit interstate common carrier transportation of obscene material, United States v. Orito, 413 U.S. 139 (1973); and state power to punish the proprietor of an "adult" bookstore which sold an unillustrated obscene book, Kaplan v. California, 413 U.S. 115 (1973).

7. In an address delivered at Staten Island (N.Y.) Community College on October 23, 1973, Justice Douglas noted that he and Justice Black had been criticized for being "absolutists." But, he added, that epithet "never bothered us. It was the First Congress and the people who were the absolutists when they made the First Amendment say that Congress shall make 'no law' abridging freedom of speech or of press."

he saw it.[8] But now he joined his dissenting colleagues in declaring that the Justices were "manifestly unable to describe it in advance except by reference to concepts so elusive that they fail to distinguish clearly between protected and unprotected speech." The consequent vagueness constitutes a danger for persons who cannot know with certainty what the law forbids; when the boundaries of the allowable remain uncharted, exercising the constitutionally protected right of expresson becomes too hazardous for the unadventurous. Moreover, as the dissenters remarked, the vagueness of the line which separates the protected from the unprotected speech places a heavy burden on the courts, forced as they are to function "in a system in which almost every obscenity case presents a constitutional question of exceptional difficulty."

My sentiments concerning the constitutionality of anti-obscenity laws, I am frank to say, approach those of the minority rather than the majority of the Supreme Court. Objections to the Court's judgment are multiple.

First, the Court has persistently assumed that when the Constitution was adopted, obscenity (whatever it is) was already widely outlawed and was therefore not deemed to be among the kinds of expression meant to be safeguarded from governmental interference. This is untrue. A drunken Englishman who had cavorted in the nude on the balcony of a London tavern, whence he had thrown on the heads of passersby a number of bottles which he had filled with what the judge euphemistically called an "offensive liquor," had been convicted of obscenity in the seventeenth century. That was the common law beginning, and it plainly has little to do with words or graphics. Among the American colonies in pre-Revolutionary times only Massachusetts had adopted a law relating to obscenity, and it had to do with mockery of preaching or divine worship, rather than with sexual nervousness.[9] What was indeed a commonplace in preconstitutional days was legislation which penalized blasphemy.

---

8. Jacobellis v. Ohio, 378 U.S. 184, 197 (1964) (concurring). E. van den Haag, in CENSORSHIP: FOR AND AGAINST 143, 158 (H. H. Hart ed. 1971), maintains that separating pornography from literature is "fairly easy." He asserts that
> material is pornographic if, in the opinion of the deciding body (best, a jury), two of the following three criteria are met: 1) if the pornographic intention is proved by admission, testimony, or circumstances; 2) if the marketing, in the main, is directed at prurient interest; 3) if the prevalent effect is sexual arousal. (Since effects differ, a jury would consult witnesses and its own reactions.)

He adds that he has yet to meet anybody who is unable to separate most pornography from most literature, though he acknowledges that lawyers "have invented interpretations which obscure and nullify the statutes." Id. at 158, n. 13.

9. Ch. 6, § 19, [1711–12] Mass. Province Laws. Justice Douglas remarks in dissent in the Paris Adult Theatre case, 413 U.S. at 70, that he had found no colonial law which excluded obscenity "from the regime of freedom of expression and press that then existed." And he added that the late distinguished legal historian Julius Goebel, whom Justice Douglas described as "our leading colonial expert," could find none, either. According to the REPORT OF THE COMMISSION ON OBSCENITY AND PORNOGRAPHY 300, 301 (1970), the first American statute about obscenity was enacted in Vermont in 1821; the early statutes were aimed at sexual works which had anti-religious implications, and obscenity as such did not become the focus until much later, when literacy had been increased by free education and when church influences on community life had decreased. See generally, P. BOYER, PURITY IN PRINT: THE VICE-SOCIETY MOVEMENT AND BOOK CENSORSHIP IN AMERICA (1968).

Statutory reinforcement of the Biblical command not to take the name of the Lord in vain was, of course, meant to preserve the spiritual well-being of persons who might otherwise hear blasphemous or sacrilegious expressions. Nobody, so far as I know, argues today that the community can constitutionally be immunized against moral debilitation by suppressing words which our forefathers thought would endanger society.

Second, I deplore the Court's insistence that depiction or description of sexual conduct can be suppressed unless it appears in a work which, taken as a whole, has serious literary, artistic, political, or scientific value. Many persons—the late President Kennedy was among them, and I am, too—like to relax with silly novels about spies and manhunts. In them the hero usually conceals in his trousers personal equipment resembling a twenty-shot repeating rifle, to be used against any female target; every girl whom the hero encounters is beautiful, pneumatic, horizontally gymnastic, and ready at a moment's notice to enjoy a roll in the hay. What harm is done by trash of this kind? The suspense novel deserves its name because readers temporarily suspend contact with reality. Sooner or later, however, most readers return to real life no worse for their bookish exposure to lust, larceny, and lifelessness. Who can pretend that a published study of Agent 007's bedroom athletics has enduring literary worth? Still, it may entertain—and that, too, is socially worthwhile.

You will no doubt remind me that the Supreme Court did not condemn sex or nudity as such, but only works which appeal to prurient interest and which are patently offensive. The words have a confident ring, but, plainly, they mean different things to different people in different circumstances. Our great grandfathers, if one can believe serious novels of the nineteenth century, were thrown into paroxysms of concupiscence when they glimpsed a prettily turned ankle. When I was a boy the sight of a girl's knee occasioned lewd thoughts, and *La Vie Parisienne,* a long dead precursor of *Penthouse* and similar magazines, drove young males mad with pictures a good deal less explicit than today's department store advertisements of brassieres and bikinis.[10] Not until the 1960's did the motion picture industry dare to show a woman's navel. Today, as I understand, pubic hair is a generally respected tabu, and a showing of genitalia (the possession of which is thought to be fairly widespread and therefore unlikely to come as a complete surprise to a patron of the movies) is presumably a rather blatant "appeal to prurient interest." Some years ago college women were asked what had aroused their libidinous thoughts, if any. An overwhelming majority answered, simply, MEN—whose appeal to prurient interest one hopes will be allowed to continue.

---

10. A few legislators do not leave these matters to chance, TEX. PENAL CODE, art. 534(b), § 3(b) (1969) (repealed 1973), for example, said that prurient interest is very likely to be triggered if a woman's breast is depicted "below the top of the nipple." And ORE. REV. STAT. § 167.060 (1971) forbids, among other things, furnishing to a minor any representation of nudity, which is defined as "uncovered, or less than opaquely covered, post-pubertal human genitals, pubic areas, the post-pubertal human female breast below a point immediately above the top of the areola. . . ." A wag has expressed the hope that no Oregon child will wander unescorted by his parent into the art galleries of the Vatican or into the Metropolitan Museum.

Moreover, the process of judging whether or not particular matter is offensive to the community does not inspire confidence. What exactly is the community whose attitudes supposedly determine the labeling of material as inoffensively sex-oriented or, on the contrary, as objectionably pornographic? The Chief Justice has said that the community is not the nation as a whole; the country's makeup is too diverse to permit a nationwide norm.[11] Maine, the Chief Justice observed, might have different standards from Las Vegas. Is the community, then, to be the state or the city—or even in the case of the larger metropolitan areas, a segment of the city?[12] "Can a man be prosecuted for reading a dirty book in a plane occupying air-space over eastern Kansas? What recourse will the publisher of Baudelaire have against the city council of Ogallala, Nebraska?"[13] Must a California publisher or film producer gear himself to San Clemente or San Francisco? A prominent federal judge believes that "community" will come to be related to small geographical units, since nobody can determine the standards of an entire state which like California has a population of more than 18,000,000, "notoriously diverse in culture and life style." In short, he foresees not fifty standards, but thousands and thousands—and even then uncertainties will remain. "Is a college bookstore," he asks, "governed by the standards of the college community or of the town or county in which the college is located?"[14]

No matter how the "community" may be defined, who knows it well enough to compute the average of the degrees of its sensitivity? The omniscient juror, of course. Approximately eighty-five percent of adult males and seventy percent of adult females in the United States, according to recent surveys, "have been exposed at some time during their lives to depictions of explicit sexual material in either visual or textual form"; most of the exposure occurred during adolescence,[15] and yet the young

---

11. Miller v. California, 413 U.S. 15, 31, 32 (1973). The Chief Justice did not explain how anything other than a nationwide standard could be used in applying federal laws such as those forbidding obscene importations, 19 U.S.C. § 1305(a) (1970); obscene transportations, 18 U.S.C. § 1462 (1970); obscene mailings, 18 U.S.C. § 1461 (1970); and obscene language on radio broadcasts, 18 U.S.C. § 1464 (1970).

12. A motion picture adjudged not to be obscene in Manhattan has been found to be obscene in the Bronx, another part of New York City. N.Y. Times, Aug. 5, 1973, at 51, col. 1. After the city of Denver adopted a "strict" anti-pornography ordinance in accord with the Court's most recent utterances, the mayor expressed belief that book stores and theaters would now simply move to the suburbs, and then to rural areas if suburbs adopted similar laws. N.Y. Times, July 28, 1973, at 8, col. 6.

13. Adams, Dirty Stuff: The Redeeming Cultural Importance of the Obscene, 2 COLUM. FORUM (no. 3) 2, 7 (1973).

14. Leventhal, The 1973 Round of Obscenity-Pornography Decisions, 59 A.B.A.J. 1261, 1263 (1973).

15. The REPORT OF THE COMMISSION ON OBSCENITY AND PORNOGRAPHY 19, 20, (1970) [hereinafter COMMISSION REPORT]. The Commission was appointed by President Johnson in 1968 to study the relationship of obscenity to misbehavior and to consider how "to deal effectively" with the "traffic in obscenity and pornography." The Commission's chairman was William J. Lockhart, a well known professor of Constitutional Law who was then the Dean of the University of Minnesota Law School. The Commission majority concluded that adults should be allowed to read, obtain, and look at sexual materials if they wished to do so. President Nixon, to whom the report was delivered but who may just possibly not have read its 700 pages and its nine additional volumes of research reports, promptly repudiated the study, saying: "So long as I am in the White House, there will be no relaxa-

people survived. Since this exposure had been chiefly voluntary and has been both extensive and intensive, one might reasonably assume that the material had not offended most jurors. But that would not prevent their finding that it offended the community, since almost everybody supposes that he is different from, and very probably superior to, the rest of the human herd.[16] In actuality, however, the determiners of offensiveness are unlikely to be jurors, anyway. Much more probably they will be judges, sitting in declaratory judgment or equity proceedings or engaging in de novo review of others' findings, for the Supreme Court, as the late Justice Harlan once complained, has tied itself to the "absurd business of perusing and viewing the miserable stuff that pours into the Court," an unedifying task the Court has recently declared its intention of continuing to perform.

All of these uncertainties and imperfections would be more readily acceptable if only the cause for being socially concerned were more solidly established. The reason for social concern about pornography is—what? Is it that pornography stimulates sexual fantasizing, impure thoughts, "genital commotion" (as a well known cleric phrased it)? Some who favor regulation do indeed seem to be concerned with what goes on in the mind and, consequently, in one's physiology. But a moment's reflection reassures us that lustful thoughts, which can be aroused in myriad ways, are beyond governmental control. Verbal or pictorial expression which simply stimulates *thoughts* about sexual activity cannot be suppressed, whether the expression be an advertisement for a provocatively named perfume or a book showing provocatively undraped humans, mailed in a plain brown wrapper. Thanks to the Constitution, Americans are free to have sex on their minds often, indeed constantly. They are allowed to think what they wish, and not merely what legislators regard as pure thoughts. As a corollary, expresson which goes no farther than causing

---

tion of the national effort to control and eliminate smut from our national life . . . American morality is not to be trifled with. . . ."

16. This explains why policemen, prosecutors and judges, who see more "hardcore pornography" than almost anybody else, are sure that the horrid stuff will have an alarmingly bad impact on others, though none at all on themselves. Sordid experience, the dirty linen of mankind, is presumed to have a corrupting effect on those who read about it or see pictures of it—but never on thee and me.

Speaking of a suggestion by the late Senator Dirksen that jurors be the final arbiters of community standards, a satirist wrote that were jurors "to apply local community standards—as reflected in what most people in the community seem to want—we might well expect to find an increase, rather than a decrease, in the amount of allowable obscenity." Fortunately, the satirist added, "the genius of the local jury is that it does *not* apply the local community standard as reflected in the actual behavior of the people. Rather, the local jury applies the *expected* or *anticipated moral standard*. This anticipated moral standard is that which each member of the jury thinks other members of the jury expect him to possess" (emphasis in original). When "a piece of smut" is submitted for jury consideration, no juror is likely to "be brazen enough to suggest that his moral standards are so lax that he would permit himself or his children to read or look at smut, the actual fact notwithstanding." THE OBSCENITY REPORT 110–11 (1970) [This satire is not to be confused with COMMISSION REPORT, *supra* note 15.] *See also* H. Alpert, in CENSORSHIP: FOR AND AGAINST 10, 14 (H. H. Hart ed. 1971), in which Mr. Alpert reports having found, during his study of cinematic sex, that "the very pillars of our society—veterans' groups, patriotic organizations, policemen and firemen—were the principal supporters of that hoary American institution, the 'stag party' "—often with films supplied by the police chief after he had confiscated them.

mental operations could not be penalized.[17] The power to halt expression must rest on a finding that the mental operations which expression has stirred will lead in a straight line to conduct of a kind society may reasonably seek to forestall.[18]

At this time the evidence of a nexus between pornography and antisocial acts is slim indeed. Numerous empirical studies have yielded no clear proof that reading or seeing has caused crimes, sexual aberrations, or other behavioral dislocations. To some extent, on the contrary, reading dirty books or looking at disgusting pictures seems to have had a sublimating effect, so that misconduct which might otherwise have occurred has been turned into subjective fantasies, without anyone's being hurt. The literature on the subject is vast. The available evidence is not persuasive of the harmfulness of pornography; equally, however, it fails to prove its harmlessness. If a legislature chooses to act on the intuitive judgment that pornography does jeopardize the public welfare by increasing the likelihood of undesirable behavior which would not have occurred but for the pornographic matter, courts should perhaps respect the legislative judgment. Man lives by his images of reality, not by reality alone. Belief that danger exists powerfully shapes judgment; and when a legislature cannot be shown to have acted arbitrarily in indulging that belief rather than another, courts must perhaps stand aside. Especially when the belief has been acted upon in essentially the same manner by a host of presum-

---

17. Judge Jerome Frank, in a separate concurring opinion in United States v. Roth, 237 F.2d 796 (2d Cir. 1956), wrote in part as follows:

> If the government possesses the power to censor publications which arouse sexual thoughts, regardless of whether those thoughts tend probably to transform themselves into anti-social behavior, why may not the government censor political and religious publications regardless of any causal relation to probable dangerous deeds?

Id. at 805.

This rhetorical question seems to me to capture the pertinent constitutional doctrine. Censorship's justification must be sought in its relationship to behavior, not in its relationship to thinking divorced from the real likelihood of acting in a way harmful to society.

18. Some externally able, literate, thoughtful persons who are far from being bigots have taken a different view. They believe that anti-obscenity laws can properly be aimed at protecting the social climate, as it were. *See, e.g.,* Berns, *Beyond the (Garbage) Pale,* in CENSORSHIP AND FREEDOM OF EXPRESSION 49 (H. Clor ed. 1971) ("To live together requires rules and a governing of the passions, and those who are without shame will be unruly and unrulable. . . ."); Clor, *Obscenity and Freedom of Expression,* in CENSORSHIP AND FREEDOM OF EXPRESSION, 97, 109, 110 (H. Clor ed. 1971) ("Liberal democracy and the constitutional system of government depend, for their vitality if not for their sheer survival, upon the character of citizens. . . . Beyond these political concerns, civil society has an interest in the maintenance of, at least, that level of moral sensibility that is implied in the term 'decency.' . . .Laws against obscenity constitute some of the community's rules of civility"); Anastaplo, *Obscenity and Common Sense,* in THE TOOTHING STONES 182, 190, 191 (R. E. Meagher ed. 1972) ("One does not have to read much of ordinary obscene writing to realize that the people who develop and distribute this stuff are, for the most part, corrupt or, at least, very low if not sick people. And they, in effect, attempt to make others like themselves. . . . Do we not have the right and perhaps even the duty to establish and preserve what we consider beautiful? . . . Why not when we deal with the moral beauty . . . of our people as well?"); E. van den Haag, *supra* note 8, at 150 ("Laws can protect the cultivation of feelings and penalize what might destroy them. Pornography, in exalting the instrumental use we can make of each other, depreciates and destroys the emotions that go with devotion to or consideration for others, as ends. Yet love and affection are precious—and precarious—heritages of our civilization and their socialized modes, compassion and empathy, are indispensable to it").

ably reasonable legislators, judges may well hesitate to insist upon a contrary finding whose evidential underpinnings are only debatably firm.[19] Be well aware, nevertheless, that widespread, persistent belief is not necessarily consonant with truth. The great Seventeenth Century common law judge Sir Matthew Hale, when sentencing two women to be hanged as witches, asserted to some doubters that "the reality of witchcraft" was indisputable, a conclusion he had reached at least partly because "the wisdom of all nations had provided laws against such persons, which is an argument of their confidence of such a crime."

My discussion thus far, with its focus upon the constitutionality of regulatory measures, falls into the mistake which characterizes much of the American political debate. Far too often we Americans leap to the conclusion that if a measure is constitutional, it must perforce be good. Of course this is palpably untrue. The Constitution sets boundaries beyond which a statute may not go, but it certainly does not imply that everything within the outer boundaries is socially desirable. In its most recent cases upholding measures aimed at pornography the Court itself has been at pains to remind that the States remain free to eliminate all controls if they choose to do so. In my opinion the legislature would be wise not to enact new laws (or to reaffirm old laws) which go as far as the Court now says would be constitutional, but, at the same time, the states should not abandon controls altogether.

First, the factual uncertainties about the impact of erotica on very young persons may justify efforts to reinforce parental restrictions on children's reading matter or movie-watching. A New York statute, widely copied in other states, prohibits commercially distributing to juveniles materials which stress nudity, sexual acts, or sadomasochistic abuse that is found to be harmful to minors. Harmfulness turns on a threefold test: the material must predominantly appeal to the prurient interest of minors *and* it must patently offend prevailing standards in the adult community

---

19. This approach to constitutional litigation was the main reliance of Louis Brandeis when seeking to defend the validity of social welfare legislation. The "Brandeis brief" won the day in Muller v. Oregon, 208 U.S. 412 (1908), which upheld a state regulation of working hours for women. The Court was strongly influenced by the adoption of similar statutes in many other states as well as foreign countries. The Brandeis brief also referred to many Commissions and other reports concerning the need for this type of statute:

> The legislation and opinions referred to [the Court's opinion said] may not be, technically speaking, authorities . . . , yet they are significant of a widespread belief. . . . Constitutional questions, it is true, are not settled by even a consensus of present public opinion. . . . At the same time, when a question of fact is debated and debatable, and the extent to which a special constitutional limitation goes is affected by the truth in respect to that fact, a widespread and long continued belief concerning it is worthy of consideration. We take judicial cognizance of all matters of general knowledge.

Id. at 420–21.

Similarly, before changing his mind about the validity of anti-obscenity laws, Justice Brennan had said in Roth v. United States, 354 U.S. 476 (1957), that obscenity's utter worthlessness "is mirrored in the universal judgment that obscenity should be restrained, reflected in the international agreement of over fifty nations, in the obscenity laws of all of the 48 States, and in the 20 obscenity laws enacted by Congress from 1942 to 1956." (citations omitted) *Id.* at 485.

concerning what is suitable material for minors *and* it must have no social importance for minors. The validity of this approach has been settled by the Supreme Court, and it has been widely copied by many of the other states, almost all of which have adopted statutes aimed particularly at distribution of erotica to the young.[20]

This kind of insulation against sex may not be worth the effort involved in trying to maintain it. Before 1970 roughly three-quarters of America's adult male population acknowledged having been rather fully exposed to explicit sexual materials before reaching age 21, and more than half of adolescent males had had "some exposure . . . by age 15. Exposure on the part of girls," the official report adds, "lags behind that of boys by a year or two." If these figures are even approximately correct, little Willie and little Nellie are more than likely to be more familiar with smut than their parents suspect, regardless of the laws on the books. But, even so, compassionate legislators might very plausibly decide that public welfare will be furthered by preserving parental illusions about the ethereal innocence of children. That is probably the sum total of what will be accomplished. Many boys, according to well documented researches, have noted "genital commotion" after such innocent activities as riding a merry-go-round or sitting in the sand at the beach, while girls, many of whom seem to be less sexually aroused than are many boys by portrayals of nudity or genitalia or, even, observing sex acts, seem often to be stirred by romantic stories or motion pictures which nobody would dream of censoring. One doubts, moreover, that young people's interest in sex had lain wholly dormant during the long centuries which antedated the corrupting influences of motion pictures or paperback books. So one may question whether the prohibition of pictorial or verbal erotica will produce a nation composed exclusively of Little Lord Fauntleroys and Rebeccas of Sunnybrook Farm. Still, legislation calculated to enhance parental peace of mind has something to be said for it, especially since inquisitive youths are not likely to remain permanently unenlightened about the facts of life.

The second area of control is one about which I feel much more positively. I see no reason at all not to forbid imposition of sexual expression upon an unwilling audience. As to this branch of the matter, I would happily extend the doctrine of *Rowan v. Post Office Department*[21] upholding a federal law which permits mail recipients to require removal of their names from the mailing lists of those who have dispatched material the recipient "believes to be erotically arousing or sexually provocative." This has the effect, obviously, of limiting the mailer's freedom of expression, but the limitation is permissible because the "right of every person 'to be let alone' must be placed in the scales with the right of others to

---

20. COMMISSION REPORT, *supra* note 15, at 330. The Commission notes, however, that more than ninety percent of state and local prosecutions have involved distribution of erotica to adults rather than enforcement of the juvenile statutes. *Id.* at 38.
21. 397 U.S. 728 (1970).

communicate." The Constitution, the Court said, creates no "right to press even 'good' ideas upon an unwilling recipient."

For example, one may be told not to attack a religious faith in a manner which forestalls escape from the attacks and is likely to arouse violent counterattacks. One may be forbidden to destroy residential peace and quiet by blaring political opinion through a sound truck's loudspeakers. Offensive advertising of pseudoerotica, as distinct from "neutral dissemination to consenting persons," may be a matter of social concern if it amounts to "an assault upon individual privacy by publication in a manner so obtrusive as to make it impossible for an unwilling individual to avoid exposure to it."[22]

Of course the same is true of conduct which, permissible in itself, becomes impermissible when it needlessly shocks the sensibilities of others. Laws against nudity on the highway seem to me to be explicable not on moral, but purely on aesthetic grounds. Humans rarely possess forms of unalloyed delight; to say that God created man in His own image sometimes borders on the defamatory. So the law seeks to safeguard the wayfarer against visual outrages, rather than against sexual arousal. The inadequate man who exposes his genitals in a public place engenders revulsion, not lust. The prohibition of exhibitionism of this kind is meant not to protect morality, but to protect unwilling viewers. Defecating in public is discouraged for similar reasons. So is public copulation. A live performance of a couple "locked in a sexual embrace at high noon in Times Square," Chief Justice Burger recently remarked, would not be constitutionally protected even if "they simultaneously engage in a valid political dialogue." By a parity of reasoning, display advertising which thrusts genitalia or genital contacts before the eyes of shocked passersby can be forbidden. As Justice Holmes once remarked, "[m]y right to swing my arm ends at the point at which your nose begins."

My own preference is for a community which does not shock easily. Yet I would accept, as one of the prices of being a community at all, paying generous attention to variant tastes. When so many opportunities exist for copulating, defecating, or posing in the nude without actively upsetting one's neighbors, I believe that prohibitory laws can properly reinforce what are social conventions.

I cannot close without anticipating the question—why should people of probity be disturbed by efforts to suppress the vulgarities which enrich pornographers? Writers have been able to produce successful books without possessing a vocabulary consisting chiefly of four letter words, and many a worthwhile motion picture has been produced without showing a penis in glorious technicolor. Why should we as concerned citizens

---

22. *But cf.* Cohen v. California, 403 U.S. 15 (1971), which upset the conviction of a war opponent who appeared in a county courthouse wearing a jacket on whose back were printed the words "Fuck the Draft." Justice Harlan writing for the Court, thought that the state cannot "excise, as 'offensive conduct,' one particular scurrilous epithet from the public discourse" on the theory that "its use is inherently likely to cause violent reaction. . . ."

have the slightest interest in protecting meretricious material which debases those who make it as well as those who consume it?

First, the threat or the actuality of law enforcement has a chilling effect upon expression which is in fact not meretricious at all, though some official might seek to stigmatize it. This is not an imagined danger. "The Changing Room," chosen as the best play of the 1972–1973 season by the New York Drama Critics Circle, has had difficulty in arranging a national tour because theater owners in Los Angeles, San Francisco, Detroit, Philadelphia, and Boston have been afraid to book it. They fear being shut down because the performance involves occasional frontal nudity. Motion pictures which have been exhibited without major incident before general audiences in many cities find themselves the center of lawsuits in others, as has happened with the "Last Tango in Paris" and "Carnal Knowledge" among others.[23] Because local standards multiply the threat of being found unacceptable, those who publish or produce or sell the work of writers and performers will, I think, halt well short of the line beyond which they may not step with impunity. Some of them will prudently hunt for the lowest common denominator. We lawyers are well aware that nobody likes to buy a law suit. Too much altogether legitimate expression will be stifled lest somebody's hypersensitivity be activated. This has happened already in the case of magazines, which have been driven from stores by zealous policemen or prosecutors whose threats have sufficed to discourage sales of such periodicals as *Playboy*.

Second, the First Amendment has too often been discussed as though it was meant only to protect speakers and writers. It was meant also, if indeed not mainly, to protect hearers' and viewers' freedom of choice. Our Constitution is designed to make for an unconstricted flow of spoken and written words or of pictures that take the place of words—and the flow is for the benefit of the consumer, not merely the producer of expression. We have made a constitutional commitment to a do-it-yourself system, in which each person is his own censor. So long as one remains free to read or not to read, to look or not to look, I think society would gain from leaving selection with the consumer. Like Justice Douglas, a person can go through life without being trapped into reading or seeing what offends him.

Third, selective law enforcement has hit especially hard at suppressing political communication which has appeared in publications with incidental sexual material. Underground newspapers and similarly irreverent publications have been harassed by prosecutors who found "por-

---

23. As to "Carnal Knowledge," the Georgia Supreme Court upheld a jury conviction based on the community standards of Albany, Georgia. Jenkins v. State, 230 Ga. 726, 199 S.E.2d 183 (1973). Three of the seven justices believed that the film was plainly protected. Justice Gunter thought it "inconceivable" that the picture be regarded as worthless. "My experience with this one case," he remarked, "teaches me that the 'alarm of repression' was validly sounded." [The decision was reversed by the Supreme Court of the United States in 1974, 418 U.S. 153, on the ground that the standards set in *Miller* could not support the jury's verdict. (Eds.)]

nography" a convenient peg upon which to hang proceedings brought for other purposes entirely. How frequently courts will be able to examine closely into the merits of suspect cases is problematical.

Fourth, the burdens of enforcing laws pertaining to the quality of sexual words as distinct from acts weigh heavily but unrewardingly on police, prosecutors, and judges. Successful enforcement is not commonly achieved. So far as the laws do in fact operate as deterrents of undesired forms of expression, they do so not chiefly because the risk of punishment after legal proceedings is great, but because the risk of being involved in costly litigation is great. The possibilities of arbitrarily selective law enforcement, with attendant shakedowns and subversions of official rectitude, are apparent. And in any event, "Are police forces, prosecution resources, and court time being wastefully diverted from the central insecurities of our metropolitan life—robbery, burglary, rape, assault, and governmental corruption?"

Fifth and most important, the forces in our society which constantly seek to intensify concern about pornography seem fixated upon conceptions of sexual morality, as though moral values related to sex alone. What about the other human virtues? "No book has ever been suppressed on the ground that it promoted selfishness or dishonesty or cowardice." The daily press and the television newscasts provide numerous accounts of real life skullduggery, often leading to public eminence. If words and pictures will mislead the impressionable into deplorable behavior, Americans would do well to consider the quality of life as a whole, and not merely sex life. Objected to authoritarianism reflected in obscenity legislation which he links with this country's religious heritage, a professor of religion bitingly exclaims: "In so far as the God in whom we, as a nation, officially trust is thought to be more concerned about illicit sexual pleasure than about social justice or the use of napalm, it is inevitable that attention will be diverted from these issues and concentrated on the control of pornography.[24] Like him, I favor a redirection of reformist energies toward an attack upon social evils more debilitating than erotica have been shown to be.

You may recall the fictional politician who declared that he was strongly against inflation and he was strongly against deflation; he was, however, in favor of flation. My position is less enigmatic. I take my stand with Hollis Alpert, the just retired president of the leading film critics' organization, who, after denouncing the abysmal level of taste which pornography reflects, declared: "I do not admire those who so proudly flaunt the banner of their sexual liberalism, for they mock what has meaning for me. . . . Therefore, I am not for pornography; I am merely against censoring it."[25]

---

24. Hettlinger, *Sex, Religion and Censorship*, in Censorship and Freedom of Expression 73, 81 (H. Clor ed. 1971).
25. H. Alpert, in Censorship: For and Against 10–12, (H. Hart ed. 1971).

Obscenity and the Constitution

HARRIET F. PILPEL

THE FIRST AMENDMENT to the United States Constitution prohibits the local, state and national government from passing any laws abridging freedom of speech and the press—so, as my two-year-old grandson is fond of saying, "How come?" How come we are having problems on the obscenity front? The answer is deceptively simple: for many decades the United States Supreme Court has held that what is obscene is not entitled to the protection of the First Amendment and the majority decisions of the Court of June 21 [1973] reiterate this view.

What has been the result of those decisions, and what can or should we do about them? [1973]

The portents are mixed: on Sunday, November 11, the *New York Times* carried the enlightening news that three dozen copies of Kurt Vonnegut's now famous and well-regarded book "Slaughterhouse-Five" were burned in Drake, North Dakota, on orders of the local school board. The rest of the story makes clear that the whole thing was set into motion by the complaint of a girl sophomore student that the book was "profane." The story evokes the indignant shade of Franklin D. Roosevelt, who signed the first proclamation reducing postage rates on books in the 1930s, saying with a flourish, "Here is the difference between Nazism and democracy. They are burning books, while we here are going to make them as available as possible."

Earlier this fall, on September 4th, the *New York Times* carried a story, "Crime In, Sex Out in New Film Season." Apropos of this: a great many years ago a sociologist wrote a book pointing out that we increasingly glorify violence, killing and destruction and condemn sex in all its manifestations. He forecast that the result would be a violent society; so far, he has turned out to be right and no doubt the recent United States Supreme Court obscenity rulings will make possible a further substantial lurch in that direction.

According to another recent *Times* story, headed "Film Pornograpy Flourishes Despite Court Ruling," "It is still possible to see blue movies and purchase graphically explicit books in virtually all major cities." The paper then goes on to give details. It reminds me of the famous cartoon which showed a smiling and bowing Hitler who had just swallowed the Russian sickle. The caption read, "Wait until he tries to straighten up." Maybe this is the situation with the June 21 United States Supreme Court decisions on obscenity: we haven't really stood up since we swallowed

From the December 10, 1973, issue of *Publishers Weekly*, 1180 Avenue of the Americas, published by R. R. Bowker Company, a Xerox company, Copyright © 1973 by Xerox Corporation.

them—haven't really felt their impact because the state legislatures have not been in session, Congress has had more pressing matters to attend to, and state authorities are constrained by the June 21 decisions to wait until the present generalized obscenity laws which those decisions may have rendered unconstitutional are replaced by the type of new specific statutes which the Court indicated were constitutionally permissible.

The whole situation relating to obscenity today in this country brings to mind the airplane pilot who announced over the loudspeaker to the plane's passengers that he had "good news and bad news. First the good news: we have a very strong tail wind and have an almost unprecedented ground speed of 700 miles an hour. Now for the bad news: our instrument panel isn't working so we don't know where we're going—but we're sure getting there fast."

That seems a pretty accurate description of today's obscenity volatility, and I thought I would sketch in briefly the good and the bad news on the obscenity front as of now. Before I do so, however, I would like briefly to summarize where we had got to before the United States Supreme Court redefined obscenity in its June 21 decisions, and what is the essence of the decisions.

Obscenity was not regarded as an offense in this country until the mid 19th century, when Massachusetts became the first state to adopt a law against obscenity. In the words of Justice Douglas ". . . There was no recognized exception in the free press at the time the Bill of Rights was adopted which treated 'obscene' publications differently from other types of papers, magazines and books." We might deduce from our criminal laws that we as a nation were afraid of sedition, treason, blasphemy and sacrilege. Now we're afraid of sex.

The anti-obscenity forces flowered in the Victorian era and were epitomized in the federal Comstock Act whose 100th birthday we celebrate— or more accurately should deplore—this year. It prohibited the importation, or carriage by mail or in interstate commerce of "every obscene, lewd, lascivious, indecent, filthy or vile article, matter, thing, device or substance." Many states adopted identical or similar "little Comstock Acts" of their own and a number of cities and towns followed suit. But despite the anti-obscenity laws, the courts handed down rational decisions. The test of obscenity ceased to be the probable effect of material attacked as obscene on the most susceptible person in the community, and became its probable effect on the average person. No longer could isolated passages be made the basis of an obscenity conviction—the test became the effect of the work as a whole, and defendants were held entitled to introduce expert testimony as to the merits and effect of a book. All this progress culminated in 1957 in the famous *Roth* case decisions, somewhat expanded subsequently by later decisions in the *Fanny Hill* and other cases.

In the *Roth* case, the United States Supreme Court pronounced itself unequivocally in favor of sex: "Sex and obscenity are not synonymous.

The portrayal of sex, e.g., in art, literature and scientific works, is not itself sufficient reason to deny the material and constitutional protection of freedom of speech and the press."

The Court then proceeded to formulate a three-pronged test, and material had to fail all three parts of the test before it could be held obscene. To justify a finding of obscenity, the material had to:

a) appeal to prurient interest,

b) be patently offensive under current community standards, and

c) be utterly without any redeeming social value.

It looked like "The End of Obscenity," the title of my friend Charles Rembar's book on the subject. This possibility was given further impetus in 1967 by the *Redrup* case, which seemed to be saying that the test is no longer the character of the material itself but the manner in which it is promoted, and to whom. Thus, Ralph Ginsburg went to jail among other things for what the Court called "pandering."

The Court also indicated its disapproval of the "thrusting" of obscenity on unwilling adults in public places, stating that such thrusting violated an aspect of the "right of privacy" in public of those who did not wish to see or hear it. And the Court also made clear that a different test would apply if the so-called obscene material were beamed directly to children.

It was not, of course, all good news after the *Roth* case and until the obscenity decisions this year. There was also some bad news. Two additional federal obscenity statutes were passed. These enable any person to prohibit a particular mailer from sending him *any* mail because he thinks he previously received obscene mail from that sender. Moreover, any mailer of "sexually oriented material" must on the outside of the envelope in which it is enclosed identify it as such, and no one who has asked that such mail not be sent to him can be sent such mail if he so indicates by putting his name on a public list.

At the same time, there continued to be good developments. The Report of the Commission of Obscenity and Pornography concluded after extensive study that there was no causal connection between "obscenity" or "pornography" on the one hand and criminal behavior on the other—indeed, that obscenity might well be a safety valve for those who might otherwise explode into unlawful conduct. President Nixon, of course, who is all in favor of sexual purity, rejected the Report.

Then came the case of *Stanley v. Georgia,* holding that a man had a constitutional right to enjoy any obscenity—in this case a motion picture—in the privacy of his own home. Said the Court: "If the First Amendment means anything, it means that the State has no business telling a man, sitting alone in his own house, what books he may read or what films he may watch. Our whole constitutional heritage rebels at the thought of giving government the power to control men's minds."

The United States Supreme Court also held that a draft and war opponent had the constitutional right to wear in public a sweat shirt on the back of which was printed "Fuck the Draft" (which should be contrasted with a recent decision of the New Hampshire Supreme Court which held criminally liable the proprietor of a shop where a teenage girl bought a button saying "Copulation—Not Masturbation").

The Justice writing the opinion was John M. Harlan, not generally known as a liberal or free-speechnik: ". . . The constitutional right of free expression is powerful medicine in a society as diverse and populous as ours. It is designed and intended to remove governmental restraints from the arena of public discussion, putting the decision as to what views shall be voiced largely into the hands of each of us, in the hope that use of such freedom will ultimately produce a more capable citizenry and more perfect polity."

It should be noted, however, that during this interim period between the *Roth* case and the June 21 decisions, obscenity proceedings were brought against underground newspapers, which were probably really under attack because of their dissident points of view. By and large these did not succeed.

It should never be forgotten that in addition to the evil inherent in so-called obscenity censorship itself, the agenda of those who propound it almost always includes using obscenity charges as a means of suppressing views which are dissident, satirical, irreverent or merely unpopular; in other words, that charges of obscenity are not infrequently the pretext for suppressing works because of the non-sex-related ideas which they contain.

Generally speaking, I have now summarized where we had arrived with respect to the laws on obscenity before the blows fell on June 21, 1973. But before I get to that, I'd like to say a few words on the *general* legal principles to be borne in mind when we come to our current good and bad news in the obscenity field. We should distinguish between local, state and federal law; we should remember that the United States Supreme Court's reading of the Constitution takes precedence over all else. In the obscenity field we should above all distinguish between civil and criminal law—between what lawyers call an *in personam* proceeding and a proceeding *in rem:* An "in rem" attack on the grounds of obscenity may result in a *work* but not a person being condemned. Many of us insist that no criminal prosecution on obscenity grounds should be permitted until a work has been declared obscene in a civil case. We should also bear in mind that the obscenity law is to be found not only in statutes but also in court rulings, and the rulings of such administrative agencies as the Post Office.

So now we come to the current bad news, i.e., the decisions of June 21. These decisions—all of them 5-to-4—made two changes in the basic test of obscenity formulated in the *Roth* case: Henceforth, the Court said, while the "appeal to prurient interest" and "patently offensive" tests are still in effect, they are to be applied in the light of the *local* community where the questions are presented and not a national community, as had been previously thought. The Court did not make at all clear what community it meant—the state? the city? the town? the block? It referred to the differing standards between "Maine and Mississippi"—*states* on the one hand, and "New York City and Las Vegas"—*cities* on the other. And the third of the *Roth* tests changed significantly. It is no longer true that a work can be suppressed only if it is "utterly without redeeming social value"; now a patently offensive work which appeals to prurient interest must have "serious literary, artistic, political or scientific value" if it is to be saved from being banned as obscene.

The net result of the majority's holdings is an almost complete negation of the right established in the *Stanley* case to enjoy obscenity in private. As was pointed out, all the *Stanley* case now apparently means is that you have the right to compose an obscenity in your attic, print or produce it in your basement and look at it in your study or living room—but as soon as you try to take anything obscene into or out of your house, you can be in serious trouble with the obscenity laws.

Unfortunately, it is all too clear that all this applies to books as well as other forms of expression. The Court essentially applied the same test to books as to anything else, but only after saying piously that "a book seems to have a different and preferred place in our hierarchy of values, and so it must be."

However there are also some good news aspects to these cases. Presumably we keep the gains we won before the *Roth* case, i.e., the test is the average adult—the work must be judged as a whole, and the defense in an obscenity case can introduce expert testimony on the worth of a work. Moreover, all the cases were decided 5-to-4. Thus we're only one judge away from the four who would not hold anything obscene for consenting adults and who would at the most permit to be banned as obscene only the thrusting of obscenity in public on unwilling adults and the distribution of obscene material to children. What the minority was really doing was to apply to obscenity the rule which is increasingly being applied to sex acts—i.e., the apparently emerging rule that no sex acts should be made criminal if engaged in by consenting adults in private. The majority in the June 21 obscenity cases rejected these limits—although it did seem curiously concerned at the thought of a nude couple copulating in public in Times Square.

Also, it seems still to be true that a book must fail all three tests to be held obscene, i.e., it must appeal to prurient interest, it must be patently offensive under current community standards, and it must lack any serious literary, artistic, political or scientific importance.

Moreover, the Court said that any prohibition of obscenity "must be carefully limited to areas of sexual conduct" and must be in very specific terms. In the words of the Court: "No one can be subject to prosecution for the sale or exposure of obscene material unless these materials depict or describe patently offensive 'hard core' sexual conduct, specifically defined by the regulating state laws as written or construed." The Court also, to make its decision clearer, pointed to examples of the type of patent offensiveness which could constitutionally be held obscene: "descriptions of (a) ultimate sexual acts, normal or perverted, actual or simulated, or (b) masturbation, excretory functions and lewd exhibitions of the genitals."

Perhaps the lack of clarity as to what is the community whose standards are applicable can be turned to advantage. Maybe it can be argued that when, e.g., a book or a movie is selling well in an area, it is clearly not "patently offensive" under the standards of that community. If "Tropic of Cancer" or "Fanny Hill" or their present-day counterparts are on the best seller list of a place, surely that is proof positive that they are not patently offensive under the standards of that community. Moreover, the requirement that obscenity laws specifically describe what they proscribe casts doubt on the constitutionality of all the present state obscenity laws except the very specific statute now in effect in the state of Oregon.

This is the type of specificity set forth by that statute: " 'Nudity' means uncovered, or less than covered, post-pubertal human genitals, pubic areas, the post-pubertal human female breast below a point immediately above the top of the areola, or the covered human male genitals in a discernibly turgid state."

It seems to me that because of the requirement of sexual specificity, the basic federal obscenity law may also be unconstitutional.

What to do now, to cut down on the bad news and bring about the good?

1. *On the legislative front.* Our first battle is to persuade the legislators not to pass any new general or "specific" prohibitions of obscenity but to leave the subject alone, since the Supreme Court decisions themselves show that the subject is really impossible to regulate. If an obscenity law must be passed, then try to get legislation in the mold recommended by the dissenting judges, i.e., let it prohibit only the thrusting of obscenity in public and to children. Remember and stress at all times that the United States Supreme Court obscenity decisions leave it up to the legislatures. The Court doesn't say anyone *shall* or *must* pass *any* legislation—only that if they do, the legislation must conform with and cannot go further than its decisions allow.

2. Insist that whatever the substantive law against obscenity is, there must always be a civil suit—an *in rem* proceeding against the work—i.e., a finding of obscenity in a civil suit before any criminal prosecution or conviction can be based on the work. In no other way can the "chilling effect" of mammoth self-censorship be avoided.

3. Make the applicable standard a statewide standard, if you can't persuade a state to adopt a national standard (which it can if it wants). But bear in mind that there may be some special situations where some areas in a state may do better if the standard is not statewide, e.g., New York City, as opposed to the rest of New York State; San Francisco, as opposed to Orange County, Calif.

4. *On the court side.* Continue stressing, as have Justices Black and Douglas for so many years, that the basic constitutional freedoms of speech and the press mean what they say; that they protect the recipients—the listeners and viewers—as well as the publishers and transmit-

ters; and that all obscenity laws are a form of thought control, the most virulent restraint there can be: a government effort to regulate not what we do, not even what we say, but what may come into our minds.

5. Stress also our newly won constitutional right of privacy—first declared in the Connecticut birth control cases and more recently reaffirmed and extended in the abortion cases. We can hope that the next development will be a guaranty of the privacy of the mind against obscenity prohibitions because no matter how specifically defined the prohibited obscenity is, obscenity, as the dissenting judges pointed out, is really impossible to define.

6. Develop briefs, legal papers and defense pleadings banks as part of a coordinated national effort, and make their availability known. The federal government has given a grant of federal moneys to a religious institution (not Catholic) to do this kind of thing for obscenity prosecutors. I submit it can do no less for defendants in obscenity cases. It is, after all, the defendants who are trying to preserve rather than whittle down the constitutional rights of free speech and press. Why not a comparable grant to the Media Coalition, for example?

7. Attack as unconstitutional those parts of the obscenity laws which make distributors of obscene material who are mere conduits of material criminally liable if the material they merely distribute is held to be obscene. Insist, in other words, that the laws provide that conduits like libraries and bookstores can in no circumstances be held criminally liable until after it has been held in a civil proceeding that the material on the basis of which they are attacked is legally obscene. This should apply to librarians, booksellers, printers, etc., who can be and sometimes are made the totally innocent victims of obscenity proceedings. (In practice, the book publishers and the producers of movies and television programs almost always do step up and defend the innocent distributors, but they can't in the final analysis remove from their shoulders the burden of a conviction.)

Here we really still have a chance to persuade not only the legislatures but also the courts, including the United States Supreme Court. While it appears that a majority of the United States Supreme Court has sustained a rebuttable presumption in connection with juveniles that a bookseller knows the contents of the book he sells, this has not yet been held generally applicable or necessarily applicable to librarians. As Justice Douglas noted in his June 21 dissent: "What we do today is rather ominous as respects librarians. The net now designed by the Court is so finely meshed that taken literally it could result in raids on libraries."

8. If obscenity laws there must be, either urge the position of the dissenting judges, as in point 1—or, preferably, urge that no law be passed which would limit the press or speech on any obscenity grounds unless the prosecutor proves beyond a reasonable doubt that the material challenged would give rise to a clear and present danger of illegal conduct on the part of those exposed to it.

The "clear and present danger" test appears to be still the only sound constitutional basis (and to have been held as such by the Supreme Court) for making criminal any speech and press *except* obscenity. It is Justice Douglas's position (and was Justice Black's) with regard to obscenity as well. Why shouldn't this same test apply to obscenity? There should be as free a marketplace for sexual ideas and descriptions as we have nów with reference to other kinds of ideas and descriptions.

9. And we must keep litigating. When the Supreme Court majority sees that its June 21 decision created more problems than they solved, perhaps the Court will again drift toward the position of the dissenting Justices. Moreover, experience suggests that *in fact* the United States Supreme Court majority view does not really reflect the viewpoint of the country because, by and large, juries have been and continue to be unwilling to convict in recent obscenity cases.

It seems odd to me that the United States Supreme Court majority turned out to be so uptight on obscenity that they handed down what seem to me a series of unlawyerlike decisions, inconsistent with the Court's own recent thinking on the subject of freedom of choice and freedom of the press. My guess is that this is so because the majority of the Court consists of middle-aged or elderly gentlemen of the upper middle class, basically afraid of two things:

(a) Themselves. In a sense they exemplify Walt Kelly's "We have met the enemy and it is us." Even at the risk of sounding Freudian I would venture to surmise that many of the Justices are not completely comfortable about sex and therefore objectify their subjective concerns by saying in effect "this obscene material which we must look at in the course of our judging process can't and doesn't hurt us, but we're afraid it might hurt the rest of you."

(b) In addition, I suspect that so-called obscene material is offensive to the majority Justices because it is in "bad taste." As Justice Douglas put it, the United States Supreme Court is worried about good taste. "The Court is at large because we deal with tastes and standards of literature. What shocks me may be sustenance for my neighbors. What causes this person to boil up in rage over one pamphlet or movie may reflect only his neurosis, not shared by others. We deal here with problems of censorship which, if adopted, should be done by constitutional amendment after full debate."

The majority of the Court mask this conventional middle-class distaste for bad taste and vulgarity with words like "protecting the public community," "the state's right to maintain a decent society," and "protecting the public environment." I'm all in favor of good taste, but I don't think it should be enshrined as a matter of constitutional law, and that I think is what the June 21 decisions have done.

In summary, all is not lost and needn't be. There are many specific things we can do, some of which I have mentioned, to blunt the edges of the June 21 obscenity decisions and bring them more rationally into the framework of our Constitution.

We should develop slogans like "Keep the minds of America free— Defend the Constitution—Get rid of anti-American obscenity laws."

Remember, as Dean Roscoe Pound of the Harvard Law School

pointed out, "The law of each age is ultimately what the age thinks should be the law." It would be nice if we were able to celebrate our 200th birthday as a nation in 1976 with the same obscenity laws we had when this nation was founded; namely, no obscenity laws directed against sex at all—with freedom, in other words, from the fear of sex which is really what underlies the obscenity laws and which subverts our First Freedom: that freedom of speech and the press which, as Justice Cardozo pointed out, is "the matrix," the "indispensable condition" of all our other freedoms.

Commentary

THERE IS a further interesting comment in the *Georgia Law Review* of Winter 1974, in which Walter Gellhorn's article was published. In a footnote published on the first page of that article, the student editors noted:

> It has become the policy of the *Georgia Law Review* to publish these quarterly lectures in the issue next following their presentation. Obscenity of course is currently a hotly debated issue in Georgia, with cases from the state making much of the "new law." The editors of the *Review* and the author of this article are aware that this law is still in the process of being formed in the courts, and that perhaps a more complete statement of the law could be presented after the Supreme Court renders decisions in obscenity cases it currently has under submission. Pursuant to our policy of immediate publication, the editors decided not to wait.

Had the editors actually postponed publication, eager for "a more complete statement of the law," they would still be waiting.

Perhaps nothing is more elusive than defining what is meant by "obscenity." As a consequence the United States Supreme Court has not mastered it. After reviewing the decisions since *Roth* v. *United States* of 1957, Justice William Brennan concluded: "the concept of 'obscenity' cannot be defined with sufficient specificity and clarity to provide fair notice to persons who create and distribute sexually oriented materials to prevent substantial erosion of protected speech" and to avoid "very costly institutional harms to the Nation's judicial machinery," which is charged with the task of safeguarding First Amendment freedoms.

Justice Brennan's point has been illustrated to the Court on numerous occasions. For example, filing a brief in *Alberts* v. *California*, the companion case to *Roth*, attorneys for petitioner David S. Alberts pointed out that John Keats's *Endymion*, Percy Shelley's *Queen Mab*, Walt Whitman's *Leaves of Grass*, Daniel Defoe's *Moll Flanders*, Theodore Dreiser's *An*

American Tragedy, and many editions of the Bible have been declared obscene at various times in various places.

If this disturbing record of the whimsy of past public censors is any guide to future censorship, we can take little comfort from a five-four Supreme Court decision in 1973 that apparently makes it impossible for anyone to know in advance what is obscene. More precisely, today no one can be certain *where* a given work will be judged obscene.

The starting point for modern obscenity law was the 1957 *Roth* case where the Court decided what would be the consequences of finding a work to be obscene even though the justices were unable to define the all-important term precisely. They concluded that the obscene, whatever it may be, is not protected expression under the U.S. Constitution's guaranties of freedoms of speech and press.

After *Roth,* divergence of opinion on the Court over the meaning of "obscenity" intensified. In 1966 a lean plurality of three justices in *Memoirs* v. *Massachusetts* at least agreed that the First Amendment required that three elements must coalesce for a work to be judged obscene: (a) the dominant theme of the materials taken as a whole appeals to a prurient interest in sex; (b) the material is patently offensive because it affronts contemporary community standards relating to the description or representation of sexual matters; and (c) the material is utterly without redeeming social value.

These elements offered only a general guide, and even this general statement was never adopted by a majority of the Court. The Court was so patently unable to establish that obscenity was harmful that many attorneys came to refer to the body of obscenity law as a prohibition in search of a rationale. In 1967, unable to resolve the diverging views among its members, the Court began a practice of reversing convictions for the dissemination of matter that at least five justices, applying their separate tests, agreed not to be obscene. At least thirty-one cases were disposed of in this no-stated-test manner between 1967 and 1973. In short, the "dim and uncertain line" that had long marked the difference between obscenity and constitutionally protected expression continued indistinct.

But the vagueness of the period before the Court decision of June 1973 seemed like bedrock certainty compared to that following it. For although the Court retained the first two elements of the *Memoirs* test— that the dominant theme be prurient and that the material be patently offensive—the decision changed the third. Rather than being "utterly without redeeming social value," an obscene work is one that "taken as a whole, lacks serious literary, artistic, political or scientific value." Most importantly, the decision held that whether a work dominantly appeals to the prurient interest should be decided using local standards. Chief Justice Warren Burger wrote, "People in different states vary in their tastes and attitudes, and this diversity is not to be strangled by the absolutism of imposed uniformity."

Justice William O. Douglas dissented sharply, warning that the new test of obscenity "would make it possible to ban any paper or any journal or magazine in some benighted place." He added, "To send men to jail for violating standards they cannot understand, construe and apply is a monstrous thing to do."

Justice Douglas's opinion was echoed by a great many media spokespersons, especially book publishers, magazine journalists, and filmmakers whose work circulates widely and who had become accustomed to the old standards, which had encouraged a more permissive atmosphere. Many expressed the widely held opinion that the Court should have established a standard restricting what is available to minors, leaving it to adults to make their own decision about what they buy or see. In the absence of such a ruling and with the possibility that every community will be able to establish its own standard, the laws of obscenity can only be surmised.

So it is that even a law professor such as Walter Gellhorn finds that in speaking of "obscenity," he is walking on treacherous ground. So, too, was Harriet Pilpel. No sooner had her lecture, "Obscenity and the Constitution" been published than lawyer Charles Rembar responded with an article titled, "Obscenity and the Constitution: A Different Opinion."

Although Rembar said he was not using *Publishers Weekly* as a place for "amiable argument"—in fact, he paid tribute to her as a "superb lawyer"—his viewpoints were devastating. "It is wrong to say," Rembar said, "that we had 'no obscenity laws . . . when this nation was founded' and that 'obscenity was not regarded as an offense in this country until the mid-19th century. . . .' " From there, he went on to score most of her views.

Let us put ourselves in the position of Harriet Pilpel. There is no certainty about obscenity. What do you do as an editor or legal adviser when an author brings you a manuscript that deals with sex but is not "clearly" obscene? Or what do you tell a filmmaker who comes to you with a screenplay with one sexually explicit scene? Is it your suggestion to play it safe and delete the scene, lest the whole film become banned as obscene in Boston, Bismarck, or Bogalusa? Or, delete the scene even if it detracts considerably from the author's overall message? If you would not delete it now, would your mind change if 300 first-run theater owners told you they would not accept the film without the deletion, but 150 owners told you they would not accept the film if it were deleted?

WLR

9

"Unprotected" Expression: Offensive Speech

THE AUTHORS

DANIEL L. BRENNER is coauthor of this book. In addition, he has had first-hand experience with the limits of free speech on television: in 1970 he appeared on "The Dating Game" (Bachelor No. 3) (and won!).

ABBOTT WASHBURN has been a Commissioner of the Federal Communications Commission since 1974. Former deputy director of the United States Information Agency, Washburn grew up in Minnesota, was graduated from Harvard in 1937, and spent thirteen years with General Mills. Among his services to the government was work on the "kitchen debate" between Vice-President Richard Nixon and Nikita Khrushchev at the 1959 American National Exhibit in Moscow.
    This pair of articles appeared in consecutive issues of the ABA Young Lawyers Division magazine, *Barrister.* Washburn's article was adapted from a speech made in the wake of the United States Supreme Court's *Pacifica* decision. Brenner wrote his article especially for the magazine while an attorney with the Washington law firm of Wilmer, Cutler & Pickering.

Censoring the Airwaves: The Supreme Court's Pacifica *Decision*

DANIEL L. BRENNER

ABOUT THE TIME that network censors were debating whether Barbara Eden's "I Dream of Jeannie" costume should or should not reveal her navel, NBC programmer Paul Klein coined the phrase "least objectionable programming." Klein meant that network programmers provide broadcast fare that offends the least number of people and thereby maximizes audience size.

The genie costume never descended below midriff. But if "I Dream of Jeannie" has been sent to the syndication scrap heap, the least objectionable programming concept has ascended in significance, recently receiving the *imprimatur* of the highest court of the land. For, according to a majority of the U.S. Supreme Court, young children as well as easily offended adults must be spared exposure to "indecent" expression on radio and television. This result seems anomalous in our contemporary society, in which the very same expression, concededly not obscene, is freely available to listeners and viewers of all ages in other media.

From *Barrister Magazine,* published by the Young Lawyers Division of the American Bar Association. Copyright © Fall 1978, American Bar Association.

The [1978] ruling, *Federal Communications Commission v. Pacifica Foundation,* is notable for two reasons: it seems to reduce the free [expression] interests of broadcasters to a new and disturbing low; and it provides scant guidance to mass communicators on radio and television—commercial and noncommercial radio and television broadcasters, pay cable television entrepreneurs and cable television operators—concerning the extent of their protection under the First Amendment.

On review was a broadcast by a listener-sponsored New York City FM radio station, WBAI. The station aired a monologue called "Filthy Words" from comedian George Carlin's record album, *Occupation: Foole.*

The monologue is an offbeat, earthy comedy that pokes fun at sexual and excretory slang words by isolating them from their colloquial context. (E.g., "Ah, ass is okay providing you're riding into town on a feast day.") WBAI, operated by the Pacifica Foundation, broadcast the album cut during its early afternoon program, "Lunchpail," on a late October Tuesday in 1973. Although an announcer's advisory warning had preceded the broadcast, a man who tuned in while driving with his 15-year-old son was offended by the monologue. Twenty-nine days later he filed a complaint to the FCC.

After forwarding the complaint to the station for comment, the commission ruled that the broadcast was not obscene, but "indecent" under Section 1464 of the Federal Criminal Code which forbids use of "any obscene, indecent or profane language by means of radio communications." The commission defined "indecent" as that which "describes, in terms patently offensive as measured by contemporary community standards for media broadcast, sexual or excretory activity and organs, at a time of the day when there is a reasonable risk that children may be in the audience." Had the station carried the program late at night the situation might have been different. Since it had not, the FCC warned WBAI that it would place the complaint in its renewal file, monitor whether the station misbehaved again during the rest of the license term, and take action at renewal time if it did.

The Supreme Court affirmed the commission, overturning a two-to-one District of Columbia appeals court split. Justice Stevens delivered the 5-to-4 opinion of the Court for a widely split majority. Stevens ruled that satirical comment on an issue of social significance that is available to adults or children in other media is forbidden to both when broadcast over an FM radio station on a weekday afternoon. It is this conclusion that must raise the eyebrows of those concerned with constitutional freedoms in the broadcast media.

How Stevens arrived at this outcome is almost as peculiar as the outcome itself. First, he singled out—and seemingly drained much of the relevance from—Section 326 of the Communications Act of 1934. This provides that "nothing in this Act shall . . . give the Commission the power of censorship over the radio and no regulation or condition . . . shall interfere with the right of free speech by means of radio communication."

Concluding that the history of this section "makes it perfectly clear" that it was not meant to limit the commission's power to regulate "obscene, indecent, or profane language," Stevens turned the statute into little more than a prohibition on prior restraints by the commission. But this protection is clearly implicit in the First Amendment and requires no statutory iteration.

Admittedly, the legislative history of Section 326 provides scant instruction about what Congress intended (nor does the history of the virtually identical predecessor provision in the Radio Act of 1927 help much). Section 326 might reasonably have been handled as a statutory barrier to the commission's action, thereby avoiding a difficult constitutional decision. But Stevens brushed aside Section 326 as a legislative gelding, limiting it to an injunction against prior restraints.

Stevens launched into Pacifica's First Amendment claims by first rejecting the argument that the commission's definition of "indecent" was unduly vague and that it gave too wide discretion when free speech values are involved.

To illustrate Pacifica's argument, what does a radio programmer do with a musical lyric that explicitly relates to sexual or excretory organs, no matter how pertinent the language is to the lyricist's message? Under the commission's test of indecency, the only choice would be to avoid the lyric. However, Stevens was not particularly troubled by deterring the broadcasting of "patently offensive references to excretory and sexual organs and activities." Concluding that such references "surely lie at the periphery of the First Amendment concerns," he declined to administer the "strong medicine" of invalidating the rule on the basis of hypothetical applications.

But then, citing nothing, Stevens went on to conclude "of all forms of communication, it is broadcasting that has received the most limited First Amendment protection." Stevens placed broadcasters at the bottom of the First Amendment totem for two reasons.

First, "the broadcast media have established a uniquely pervasive presence in the lives of all Americans," particularly when heard "in the privacy of the home." This may seem to be a persuasive distinction until it is remembered that newspapers, drive-in movies, direct mail advertisements and imprinted T-shirts are media that have also "established a uniquely pervasive presence" in our lives, in and out of home.

Ah, but there is a second reason: "broadcasting is uniquely accessible to children, even those too young to read." However, even if the presence of children in the broadcast audience fairly imposes a special responsibility upon broadcasters, virtually all forms of expression, save explicit sexual depictions, are "accessible to children." Indeed, Carlin's recording can be freely purchased by children. However, because broadcasting somehow is "uniquely accessible," electronic communication of a recorded monologue transmogrifies it into a substance suitable for govenment regulation.

The fourth and fifth majority votes were provided by Justices Powell and Blackmun who turned most of the three-vote opinion by Justice Stevens into The Opinion of the Court by generally adopting the foregoing arguments. Powell concluded that whatever the standard, the Carlin broadcast amounted to "a sort of verbal shock treatment" that would not be brought into the protected preserve of the First Amendment. But whereas Stevens generally would distinguish the social utility of, say, political debate, from speech which contributes somewhat less to the commonweal (in his view, the Carlin broadcast), Powell concluded that the "value," more or less, of speech should not be judged by a court.

Yet this out-of-our-hand approach remits content decisions to the commission by default, and provides for no judicial oversight. Powell seems to justify this result because of "the unique characteristics of the broadcast media" (which he never specifically identifies), "combined with society's right to protect its children from speech generally agreed to be inappropriate for their years." [What's this? A value judgment?] He also mentions the interest of "unwilling adults in not being assaulted by such offensive speech in their homes." But who judges what constitutes "such offensive speech"?

With acrimony directed from Brother Justice to Brother Justice unrivaled by any other opinion during the term, Justice Brennan's dissent stated: "I find [in the opinions of Justices Powell and Stevens] . . . a depressing inability to appreciate that in our land of cultural pluralism, there are many who think, act, and talk differently from the Members of this Court, and who do not share their fragile sensibilities. It is only an acute ethnocentric myopia that enables the Court to approve the censorship of communications solely because of the words they contain."

Concluding that the majority's attempt to divorce the content and impact of an idea from words used to express that idea was "transparently fallacious," Justice Brennan said the intrusiveness of radio and the presence of children in the audience was not enough to validate the commission's order. In addition to the majority's failure to explain how those qualities of broadcast speech translate into the commission's definition and regulation of indecency, Brennan found the justifications demonstrably lack "principled limits on their use as a basis for FCC censorship." Broadcasting the works of Shakespeare, Joyce, Hemingway, Fielding, and Chaucer—indeed, portions of the Bible—would be deemed "indecent" speech under the commission's approach.

One critical fact ignored by Stevens—and even the thoughtful Brennan dissent missed it—is that the medium of the Carlin message was a daytime weekday FM radio broadcast. Reading the majority opinions, one gets the impression that unwilling adults and unknowing children were being bombarded in their homes by filthy words spewing forth from a living room home entertainment center, like so many microwaves gone berserk.

It is perhaps arguable that this image might apply to television. The concern is somewhat intensified by the demonstrable, if astonishing, A. C. Nielsen statistic that the average household plays its television for about seven hours a day, an increase of one hour from 10 years ago.

But FM radio—*FM radio!*—hardly occupies the centerpiece in the American living room, especially a channel such as WBAI. One must almost be blessed with a safecracker's touch to tune it in on the FM dial. Television has replaced radio as the home-based medium of general consumption, while radio, especially FM, is a medium of specialty tastes and interests.

As a station presenting programs of interest to relatively highly educated audiences, WBAI exemplifies this development: it is unlikely that one would happen upon its programming in the same manner that one might catch a glimpse of something offensive on Channel 5 when switching from Channel 4 to Channel 7. The Court mixes televisions and radios when it invokes the pervasiveness of one medium in the home to justify suppression of speech of another.

In addition, contrary to the conclusion of the Court and the commission, two o'clock Tuesday afternoon is not the Children's Hour on FM radio. Market research indicates that except between midnight and 6 A.M., when listening by all age groups is minimal, child audiences nationwide are smallest during the early afternoon weekday period (when the Carlin monologue was broadcast). Besides, children young enough to be offended by the Carlin monologue ought to be in school at that hour. One can hardly be accused of being hardboiled to assume that if a kid is habitually absent from school at that hour, overhearing a few infelicitous words on radio probably will not rank as his or her greatest problem.

Perhaps the most frustrating part of *Pacifica,* though, is its meager direction to the electronic media about the scope of their First Amendment rights. Offhand comments about broadcasting enjoying "the most limited" First Amendment protection—What of comic books? Playing cards? Chinese cookie fortunes?—are not simply harmless baffle; they constitute Delphic pronouncements made at a watershed period in the development of electronic media.

For instance, the Supreme Court must be aware that cable radio and television functionally have replaced broadcast radio and television in many households. But until now, and especially in light of "the most limited" protected status of broadcasters, we are left with no Supreme Court guidance as to the First Amendment posture of cable expression. Moreover, radio continues to become more specialized, a development which the FCC recognized when it proposed to deregulate urban radio. Does *Pacifica* require radio stations to consider their operation as simply television without pictures and shape their broadcasts accordingly? Meanwhile, broadcast television is left with very little guidance other than the obvious requirement to purge excessive "filthy words" from most daytime broadcasts.

What seems basically wrong about the Stevens opinion is its attempt to infuse First Amendment law with an air of unreal civility by which we no longer conduct our private lives. This point is hardly new, but it went unheeded by the majority.

Justice Harlan in 1971 in *Cohen v. California* expressed the difficulty created by judicial arbitration of morality and taste. "[W]hile the particular four-letter word being litigated here is perhaps more distasteful than most others of its genre, it is nevertheless often true that one man's vulgarity is another's lyric. Indeed, we think it is largely because governmental officials cannot make principled distinctions in this area that the Constitution leaves matters of taste and style so largely to the individual," he wrote.

There is, to be sure, an interest in avoiding expression thought to be offensive by sensitive adults and parents of young children. But because "offensiveness" is often a very personal notion, it can seldom be the primary concern in a balancing of interests by editors, and less frequently still by a court or administrative agency. Surely, the Court goes too far when it rules that the interest in avoiding the offensive must extend to an afternoon broadcast of a recording by a specialty FM radio station that has warned its audience of the recording's content.

Perhaps the future of uninhibited broadcast expression is not so bleak as a strict reading of *Pacifica* suggests.

Shortly after the *Pacifica* decision was announced, the commission dismissed a complaint against WGBH-TV, Boston's public television station. The complaint asked the FCC to deny WGBH's license renewal for "consistently broadcasting vulgar and otherwise material harmful to children without adequate supervision or parental warnings," including "Monty Python's Flying Circus," an installment of "Masterpiece Theater," and other programs. In throwing out the challenge, the commission pointedly found that the *Pacifica* decision "affords this commission no general prerogative to intervene in any case where words similar or identical to those in *Pacifica* are broadcast over a licensed radio or television station."

The WGBH case suggests the commission may be inclined to store the regulatory powers won in *Pacifica* in a locked cabinet marked, to employ Powell's characterization, "Shock Treatment, Verbal (Sort of)," and bury the key. As FCC Chairman Charles Ferris said to the New England Broadcasting Association shortly after WGBH was announced, "The particular set of circumstances in the *Pacifica* case is about as likely to occur again as Halley's Comet. Our WGBH decision should make clear that *Pacifica* really is limited." Indeed, if *Pacifica* does receive this narrow reading, then the impact of this case on the freedom of broadcast expression may be minimal since even the "filthy words" used by Carlin will not be banned *per se;* only their jackhammer utterance can expect to feel the weight of the commission's administrative kibosh.

But even if the current commission is content to view *Pacifica* this way, there is no guarantee that other reviewing bodies will feel themselves so bound, or for that matter that a commission majority appointed by a different administration will not remember where the cabinet key is buried. Because of the uncertain way in which the opinion may be used, it does create a lingering cloud over the airwaves of broadcast expression.

Radio has become more than an advertiser-supported music box, and television has emerged from the days when wrestling matches and game shows were its trademark. But if this process is to continue, the words and ideas by which they will make their ascent must not be arbitrarily constricted. The Supreme Court's majority in *Pacifica* has done just that. By unsuccessfully trying to skim off what it perceives as the scum, the Court has stirred the confused (and confusing) waters of free expression in broadcasting, leaving them only murkier.

Regulating the Airwaves
Is Not the Same as Censoring Them

ABBOTT WASHBURN

AS OFTEN HAPPENS in our work at the Commission, we were faced in *Pacifica* with the necessity of balancing two conflicting rights, in order to make a judgment in the public interest. In this instance we came down unanimously for parental discretion and privacy over the broadcaster's prerogative to transmit indecent material into the home at any time of day.

The offensive speech in the *Pacifica* case came to be called the "Seven Dirty Words." These words had been repeated deliberately 106 times during a 12-minute radio broadcast in the middle of the afternoon with children in the audience.

After reviewing complaints about the broadcast, we did not ban the use of such speech outright, but required that it be channeled to hours when children are less apt to be a significant part of the audience. (It is interesting that Pacifica Foundation itself, in response to a listener's complaint about provocative broadcasting a decade earlier, advised the Commission that it had taken "into account the nature of the broadcast medium when it scheduled such programming for the late evening hours, after 10 p.m. when the number of children in the audience is at a minimum." Its licenses were renewed.

The U.S. Court of Appeals of the District of Columbia overturned the Commission in its *Pacifica* decision, calling the ruling "over-broad and

From *Barrister Magazine,* published by the Young Lawyers Division of the American Bar Association. Copyright © Summer 1979, American Bar Association.

vague." The Supreme Court, in July of last year, reversed the Court of Appeals, and later refused request for rehearing.

After the Supreme Court's decision last summer, there were those who expected a burst of public criticism about erosion of the First Amendment. This did not occur. No great outcry arose from the Fourth Estate, nor from the broadcast journalists. A *Washington Post* editorial welcomed the decision. The *New York Times* said it made them "uneasy" but trusted it would have the narrow application described. On *Agronsky and Company,* all four commentators expressed themselves as favorable to the action. Significantly, perhaps, most publications did not print the seven words.

What are we to make of this lack of public furor? I believe it underscores that the Commission and the Court enunciated a credible position, that most people want a line drawn somewhere on what comes into the home over-the-air. The outcome was perceived by objective observers as a reasonable balance between the rights of viewers and listeners and the rights of broadcasters.

Should this result distress broadcasters? Does it in reality erode their First Amendment rights? The answer to these questions is *no,* in my view.

Before this case there was uncertainty about the meaning of "indecent" in Section 1464 of Title 18 of the U.S. Code. Now broadcasters and the Commission have a clear understanding of the limited framework in which the Court construes it. Justice Stevens, speaking for the majority, wrote: "It is appropriate to emphasize the narrowness of our holding. This case does not involve a two-way radio conversation between a cab driver and a dispatcher, or a telecast of an Elizabethan comedy. We have not decided an occasional expletive . . . would justify any sanction . . . context is all-important."

"OBSCENITY" V. "INDECENCY"

When the "Seven Dirty Words" case reached us, the members of the Commission, in addition to myself, were Chairman Dick Wiley, Bob Lee, Charlotte Reid, Ben Hooks, Jim Quello, and Glen Robinson. Our dilemma was how to handle this and other complaints being received by the Broadcast Bureau about indecent language over the air. Congress mandated the FCC and the Department of Justice to enforce Section 1464 of Title 18, which prohibits the broadcast utterance of obscene or indecent language. But, unlike "obscenity," in the area of "indecency" we had no legal guidelines or definitions. We were searching for a way to meet the statute.

I recall Bob Lee saying at the time: "We need direction from the Court; we're not seeking authority to censor." We agreed upon this definition of indecency: "Language that describes in terms patently offensive as measured by contemporary community standards for the broadcast medium, sexual or excretory activities or organs."

This definition was ultimately embodied in the Declaratory Order which we adopted unanimously on Feb. 12, 1975. The concept of "indecent," we held, is intimately connected with the exposure of children to such language.

Our purpose was to clarify Commission authority. It was not our intention to penalize Pacifica Station WBAI, because the legal meaning of "indecent" was then so vague.

Very conscious of the sensitive First Amendment implications, we drafted the Order narrowly. We emphasized it did not "modify our previous decisions recognizing broadcasters' broad discretion in the programming area . . . it [was] not intended to stifle robust free debate on any of the controversial issues confronting our society." The hours such broadcasts are aired was the primary focus of the Order.

Our individual backgrounds inevitably affect how we approach such judgments. (This, by the way, is a persuasive argument for keeping the Commission at seven members, rather than going to a smaller one with less diversity of viewpoints.)

A longtime interest in children's programming undoubtedly influenced me in this case, as did an early experience at General Mills, Inc. In the late 1930s I was working in the Department of Public Services at General Mills. The company sponsored—indeed owned—radio shows like "The Lone Ranger," "Jack Armstrong the All-American Boy," "Betty Crocker," and numerous soap operas. One day the founder and board chairman of General Mills, James F. Bell, called us into his office. He emphasized that we should continually bear in mind what an extraordinary privilege it was to be invited into millions of homes every day, that we had an obligation to see that our programs carried nothing offensive. "Imagine," he said, "that you and I and the members of the Board of Directors are personally carrying the program through the front door and sitting down with members of the family to listen to it. Ask youself: Is there anything here that would embarrass us as guests in that home?"

TELEVISION'S AWESOME POWER

This was my first appreciation of the special responsibility borne by those who manage broadcast communications in our society. And then we only had radio. Today, with the awesome power of television and the tremendous role it plays in the lives of most Americans, that responsibility has increased enormously. It is one that has no parallel in the print media or motion pictures or the stage. TV-radio today is a socializing force comparable to the school, the church, even the home. It comes into the living room, the very core of the household where the family gathers. Whatever is allowed to enter there tends to be accepted by children as the social norm. If it's *there,* it must be okay.

Most broadcasters, I believe, recognize the uniqueness of their medium and the challenge its technology imposes. The existence of the National Association of Broadcasters' Television Code attests to this.

I have always believed and argued that self-regulation is the best course, the one most in keeping with our free enterprise system. But not everybody in the industry subscribes to self-regulation. Government regulation exists in this area because there are always a few who see themselves as totally unfettered, despite the fact that Congress and the courts have recognized from the beginning that broadcasting is different from other media with respect to First Amendment protection. *Pacifica* is but the most recent in a line of such rulings.

LIMITS ON PROFANITY SINCE DOTS AND DASHES

Rules governing offensive language go back to the beginning of commercial radio—to the dots and dashes era. The Secretary of Commerce issued the earliest regulations, pursuant to the Radio Law of 1912. These prohibited the transmission of "profane or obscene words or language." (A 1916 Bulletin reports that the Department of Commerce suspended the license of an amateur operator in Stoneham, Massachusetts, for the use of "profane and abusive language in transmitting messages."

The Radio Act of 1927 included similar language in Section 29, prohibiting utterance of "any obscene, indecent or profane language by means of radio communication." Section 29 of the Radio Act of 1927 became Section 326 of the Communications Act of 1934. Both sections contained language prohibiting censorship by the Commission and "prohibiting the utterance on the air of obscene, indecent or profane language." When the U.S. Criminal Code was revised in 1948, the obscenity and indecency part of Section 326 was removed from the Communications Act and became Section 1464 of Title 18. Section 326 of the Communications Act now deals only with censorship but, interestingly, is still headed, "Censorship: Indecent Language."

Consistent with this legislative background, I predict that similar language will be included in any "renovated" Communications Act which may be approved by Congress in the 1980s.

Nevertheless, the Commission has no intention of going on a regulatory spree as a consequence of judicial clarification of its authority in the *Pacifica* case. This was apparent from a decision rendered shortly after the Supreme Court's opinion, in which we unanimously dismissed complaints brought by Morality in Media against Boston's public television station, WGBH. Moreover, I have no doubt whatever that the result would have been the same had there been no changes in Commission membership between 1975 and 1978.

In *Pacifica*, the Supreme Court stressed the broadcast medium's "unique accessibility to children," its "uniquely pervasive presence in the lives of all Americans," and that "of all forms of communications, broadcasting has received the most limited First Amendment protection." In so doing, it put the case in perspective, but enunciated nothing new. In fact, as early as 1970, in *Eastern Educational Radio*—an indecency complaint against WUHY-FM Philadelphia—the medium's pervasiveness and its intrusion into the home "frequently without advance warning," were factors cited by the FCC.

In his concurring statement in *Pacifica,* Commissioner Glen Robinson wrote: "While I would not have the government in the business of enforcing morals and good taste . . . it seems to me legitimate that there be a limited regulation of offensive speech which is purveyed widely, publicly, and indiscriminately in such a manner that it cannot be avoided without significantly inconveniencing people or infringing on their right to choose what they see and hear. In short . . . I think *we can regulate offensive speech to the extent it constitutes a public nuisance.*"[Emphasis added.]

OVER-THE-AIR ASSAULT

There are nuisance laws to protect, for example, against a streaker coming by on the sidewalk during a family picnic in your front yard. An unwanted assault over the air, with children in the audience, is a comparable nuisance, in my opinion. In both cases the parents, absent some form of legal protection, are powerless to control what impacts on their children in their own home.

During the argument before the Supreme Court, Justice Lewis F. Powell asked counsel for the Department of Justice: ". . . what would the Department's position be with respect to this program if these 11 minutes were put on the air at, say, eight to nine o'clock on Saturday morning, which is prime time for small children?" Counsel replied that if it could be shown that the program in which it was included was aimed specifically at children, then "tentatively" that program could be reached by Section 1464. In this event the broadcaster would be liable to criminal prosecution.

Earlier, during the Appeals Court argument, when the same question was asked of counsel for *Pacifica,* the answer was that it was constitutionally protected speech, even at that hour on Saturday morning.

Justice Stevens, writing for the majority of the Court, commented that *Pacifica*'s position would mean "anything that could be sold at a newsstand for private examination could be publicly displayed on television."

As to the future, I agree with Chairman Ferris, in his speech to the New England Broadcasting Association, that it would be too bad if the *Pacifica* decision led to timidity on the part of broadcasters in their coverage of controversial subjects and in undertaking innovative entertainment programming. This would be over-reaction. But I don't think it will happen. *Pacifica* does not address the subject of controversial issues (in fact the Commission has indicated that its ruling does not apply to live newscasts or other live events), nor does it affect innovative programming unless one begins with the assumption that such programming cannot be done without the requirement of a stream of offensive speech in hours when children are apt to be in the audience.

ORPHANS OF THE FIRST AMENDMENT?

Industry spokesmen deploring their orphan status with respect to the First Amendment have never sounded very convincing. The nature of the technology itself is at the root of their complaint. It's like an orange wanting to be a banana. This medium enters the home on a massive scale. The airwave spectrum space it rides on is a limited public resource, a public trust. But there are considerable advantages to being an orange: the broad scope of coverage, the exclusive right-to-use of the signal, and the profitability.

Judge Bazelon, formerly chief judge of the D.C. appeals court, discussed the First Amendment at a UCLA seminar recently. He charged that the Fairness Doctrine "has contributed to suppressing programming on controversial issues almost entirely." With all due respect, I suggest that the judge has not been watching much television. There have been programs on abortion, nuclear power plants, prostitution, gun control, marijuana laws, airport safety, pollution, Laetrile, Proposition 13 and tax reform, the Panama Canal *ad nauseum,* Salt II, Taiwan, and now the question of a Constitutional Convention, Iranian oil and the pros and cons of gas rationing. Indeed it would be hard to find any issue that has *not* been covered by the electronic media, whether of national importance or of purely local interest.

Based on many conversations I have had with broadcasters over the past four years, the men and women on the front line of broadcast journalism do not regard the Fairness Doctrine as much of a problem. It does not inhibit them from tackling touchy subjects, nor does it turn them off controversial issues. I am convinced that the supposed "chilling effect" of the Doctrine is something that exists largely in the minds of those who make speeches and write articles about it—can you imagine a Cronkite, a Walters, or a Brinkley actually being so "chilled?"

Similarly, the vast majority of day-to-day programmers are not concerned about Section 1464. One of them said to me at a recent convention of the Association of Independent Television Stations: "We wouldn't use those words in such a context anyway, and we're not pining to put 'Oh Calcutta' on our station."

In his article, "The Case for Liberal Censorship," Irving Kristol called these words "debasing," and said they "deprive human beings of their specifically human dimension . . . reducing men and women to some of their mere bodily functions." Most broadcasters would agree.

The Commission's Order and the decision of the Supreme Court are reasoned, moderate and sensible approaches to a very difficult problem. They reduce uncertainty and add helpful clarification to existing policy. They do not constitute a new departure, nor do they signal the opening of the door to further restrictions in the name of indecency. They are narrow in application and provide valuable guidelines to broadcasters in carrying out their special responsibilities due to the "uniquely pervasive presence" of radio and television in the home.

Our Declaratory Order in *Pacifica* stated: "In this as in other sensitive areas of broadcast regulation the real solution is the exercise of licensee judgment, responsibility, and sensitivity to the community's needs, interests and tastes."

That is where we prefer to see the responsibility rest.

Commentary

IF YOU LIVE in Monroe, Louisiana, part of the Bible Belt, you can watch adult oriented television programs in your home by paying $2.95 per month to a cable system known as Premium Channels Television. In 1981 you could have tuned in R-rated features, like "Maid in Sweden," "Too Hot to Handle," or "Emanuelle, Queen of Sados." Also you could have seen "Midnight Blue," a New York cable sex show, that, well, offers the imagination a rest.

Why is Monroe, a conservative community, so lax in its standards? Ask Jerry Womack, operator of Premium Channels Television, who says about 10 percent of his subscribers have signed up for the weekend adult channel, Private Screenings. He expects that percentage to double because Home Theatre Network, a channel featuring family entertainment is so unpopular he has to drop it. "People say they want the goody-goody stuff," concludes Womack, "they just aren't going to pay for it."

After reading the Federal Communication Commission's handling of the George Carlin broadcast you may wonder why the commission doesn't swoop down on Womack's enterprise. Legally the FCC's jurisdiction over cable is limited and does not extend to program regulations. Municipalities generally license cable operators or franchises, but not all franchise agreements limit the type of programs a system may carry. And, most importantly, some viewers, given the choice to pay for the otherwise scrambled signal, choose the R-rated entertainment.

Placing limits on the timing of sexually explicit programming may be all that *Pacifica* stands for. Washburn believes that the commission has a mission to perform in this area, while Brenner tries to trace the logic of the *Pacifica* rationale and finds it garbled. Censorship decisions that fail to draw clear and predictable boundaries around themselves are dangerous precedents.

Despite the expected "chilling effect" of *Pacifica,* there has been an intermittent thaw, not only on pay cable services, but on off-the-air network television as well. Consider the following entries to understand the quiet revolution in language and depiction that is evolving in the mass media:

On October 14, 1980, an editor named David Teitelbaum broke the four-letter word obstacle at NBC. When he reviewed the transcripts of the ABSCAM tapes, Teitelbaum knew that the tape was dramatic news and that its language was troublesome. Pennsylvania Congressman Michael Myers and undercover FBI agents posing as agents for rich Arab businessmen conversed in words riddled with profanities and vulgarities (not to mention felonies). Because Teitelbaum was responsible for editing the tape to transmit to NBC affiliates, he had to decide which words to bleep, which to leave in.

"Son of a bitch"? Could Teitelbaum transmit those words to the many NBC affiliates? Yes, he decided. How about "bastard"? All right, he thought. He also decided that "bullshit" should be transmitted. He thought about one word—the vulgar word for copulation—and finally decided against transmitting it.

WNET, a public television station in New York City, consulted its lawyers, and then broadcast the entire series of tapes—including the word Teitelbaum had deleted. WNET Producer Paul Smirnoff said, "They had all the words in them."

WBRE-TV broadcast the ABSCAM tapes with most of the expletives left in. There were no complaints. WBRE is in Wilkes-Barre, Pennsylvania. Tom Bigler, vice-president for news, explained, "We're in a redneck area. This is George Wallace country, an area of fundamental Protestantism and some very conservative people." Also, WBRE publishes its own monthly magazine that once featured an article on a mental home. During a broadcast about that article, offensive language was used. Bigler stressed, "People seem to accept strong language on news programs as long as it's essential to the story, as long as it's honest."

Also, in April 1980, "60 Minutes"—the most watched news program in the United States—broadcast the phrase "horse's ass" for the first time in its history. At CBS News, Director of Affiliate Services Peter Herford emphasized that he or his assistant watches in advance each edition of "60 Minutes." If one of them sees something questionable, he sends a warning to all the 208 affiliate stations. When Herford saw the "60 Minutes" program that carried "horse's ass," he sent a warning. The reaction at WTVF-TV in Nashville, Tennessee, was typical: News Director Bill Goodman said, " '60 Minutes' has great stature and we let the word go."

When ABC used obscenities in a documentary, "Youth Terror: The View from behind the Gun," the entirety of the executive suite—Leonard Goldenson, Fred Pierce, Elton Rule, and Roone Arledge—watched it before it was broadcast. ABC Producer Dick Richter said, "The brass was reluctant. They realized that there would be repercussions. They said they feared alienating large portions of the country—people who were not ready to hear such language in their living rooms. But the expletives were near the end of the documentary, where one guy was spilling his guts on how youth gang members felt and acted. We felt toning down the language, bleeping any words, would have lost the authenticity of that moment."

ABC decided to broadcast that program without bleeping, but the executives decided to warn viewers that they would see a documentary that carried harsh language. Richter said between nineteen and twenty-two of its affiliates decided not to broadcast "Youth Terror." After the program was aired, the controversy over the language was overtaken by claims by some persons involved in the show that some scenes had been staged for the camera.

The Philadelphia ABC affiliate, WPVI-TV, rejected showing "Youth Terror" because of the offensive words. The station's general manager, Lawrence Pollock, said, "We saw them first and decided the language could have been edited out. But since we can't censor or edit network documentaries, we decided not to take them." But Pollock emphasized that he does not recall rejecting any entertainment program because of taste or obscenity. "We looked closely at *Soap* but judged it was a satire and therefore it would be acceptable."

An expletive undeleted does not a revolution make. But use of language on broadcast frequencies that we hear on the streets moves the medium from passive "Who, me?" viewer involvement to an active "'Yes, you!'" voice. It reflects the changing relation between listeners and their media: from inactive receivers to interactive consumers, sometimes paying directly for product instead of letting advertisers foot the bill.

Changing language mores are confronting print journalists and editors, too. Washburn and Brenner may simply be descendents of the debaters in the early 1800s who quarreled over whether the *New York Herald* should have published "leg" for "limb." Consider these developments in the press that track the broadcast situation:

Executive Editor Benjamin Bradlee of the *Washington Post* said: "Certainly our standards have changed. What we've done is reflect social changes. If the president of the United States says 'fuck,' then you say 'fuck.'"

The *New York Times* published the transcripts of the Watergate tapes when President Nixon was in power. Executive Editor A. M. Rosenthal explained in a published interview, "We'll take 'shit' from the president of the United States."

A recent issue of *New York* magazine carried an article in which the words ranged from "schmuck" to "fuck," and most of these words were in quotations by the late John Lennon and Ronald Reagan, Jr., the son of the president of the United States. The editor of *New York,* Edward Kosner, said, "We try to allow colloquialisms like 'ass' and 'crap,' but we almost always use dashes for more vigorous words than that. The idea is not to add ugliness to the world, but that impulse must live in tension with our desire not to muzzle people who talk in a flamboyant way."

The trend thus seems to be away from clamping down on four letter words, *Pacifica* notwithstanding. But the right of audiences to be shielded from offensive ideas or words is one that is still fought for. Individuals who might describe themselves as liberals condemn television violence and sensational newspapers like the *New York Post*. So do conservatives. The Parent-Teacher Association has vowed to make an issue about television violence on the networks. And the defenders of Saturday morning cartoon shows are seldom over the age of seven.

The crusade against immorality reached a new level in 1981 when the Moral Majority, a fundamentalist Christian group, and others decided to monitor network television for the worst offenders of their moral values under the rubric Coalition for Better Television. The punishment? A national boycott of advertisers found sponsoring the shows. Whether or not you agree with the pithy bumper sticker that reads, "The Moral Majority is Neither," it is true that even a group with its political clout decided to fight its battle to clean up the airwaves *not* by asking the government to step in, but to keep the issue in the private sector.

That does not mean that the government will always stay out. Consider the judgment of Harry Cole, a communications lawyer who represents the *Pacifica* stations, "I have already advised Pacifica stations that they should start being somewhat concerned. The trouble with the Carlin decision is that it gave the FCC lots of power. No one has been concerned about it lately because the FCC hasn't felt like using that power, but with a conservative administration. . . ."

Finally, range Cole's judgment against that of Reinhold Aman, the editor of a scholarly publication named *Maledicta: The International Journal of Verbal Abuse:*

> Over the last 15 years, beginning with the Vietnam War, many traditions and conventions have broken down. With the decline of patriotism and family values has come a decline in traditional standards of language. All levels of society are now using more four-letter words. Many people now use them to show how hip they are. In the past you might have heard someone curse his wife in private; now you'll hear it in public.

WLR

10

"Unprotected" Expression: One-sided, Deceptive, Unfair Speech

THE AUTHORS

ALBERT H. KRAMER's short article is based on a speech he delivered in 1977 to the Advertising Law Conference. As an attorney in Washington, D.C., Kramer has had a wide-ranging practice. He headed the influential public interest group Citizens Communications Center in the late 1960s and early 1970s. He returned to private practice with the noted law firm of Arnold and Porter in the early 1970s and then joined the Carter administration as director, Bureau of Consumer Protection, Federal Trade Commission. While in that position he gave the controversial address reprinted here. He returned to private practice in Washington, D.C., in 1981.

WESLEY J. LIEBELER was asked to respond to Kramer's views. He is professor of law, University of California, Los Angeles, School of Law, where the journal containing Kramer's and his remarks is edited. Liebeler was on the FTC staff during the Ford administration, serving as Director of the Office of Policy and Evaluation.

DAVID L. SINAK wrote the article appearing here during his second and third years of law school at Boston College. A 1979 graduate of the Boston College Law School, he is in practice with the Dallas law firm of Hughes and Hill.

Marconian Problems, Gutenbergian Remedies: Evaluating the Multiple-Sensory Experience Ad on the Double-Spaced, Typewritten Page

ALBERT H. KRAMER

> The unconscious depth-messages of ads are never attacked by the literate, because of their incapacity to notice or discuss nonverbal forms of arrangement and meaning. They have not the art to argue with pictures.[1]

THE INITIAL OBSERVATION that must be made about contemporary advertising is that it is enormously effective. Whatever one thinks of America's ability to solve its social problems or repair its automobiles, it is indisputable that America is very good at selling itself goods and services. The advertising community is marvelously skilled at transporting the consumer of an advertisement to a wooded mountain stream and creating the apparently contradictory impression that smoking a cigarette will cool him off.

From *Federal Communications Law Journal* 30(1)(1978):35–40.
1. M. MCLUHAN, UNDERSTANDING MEDIA 205 (Signet ed. 1964).

It is in fact this ability to successfully suggest a sensory experience to the recipient of an ad that makes advertising effective. This phenomenon has only recently come to be understood. Traditionally, both the advertisers and the regulators of advertising have viewed the effectiveness of a message in terms of the linear written word. Now, however, the media have changed. The media have left the written word behind in a cloud of dust and have created a new environment of multiple-sensory experience of which the written word is a minor part.

Communications theory experts tell us that health warning messages on cigarette advertisements are seldom noticed. The reason they are seldom noticed is that advertisers spend a great deal of money learning to make them go unnoticed. They spend their resources creating a sensory experience (the wooded mountain stream, for example) to which the health warning is extraneous. The advertiser tests different ads to determine the most effective presentation of the central message of the ad, and implicitly, the least effective presentation of the "extraneous" health warning.

We have made great progress in communication theory over the last decade or two. No other industry has exploited social science data as advertising has exploited communication theory. This exploitation is not necessarily evil. Communication theory can be abused, of course, but such techniques, as long as they are not illegal, are perfectly proper components of the American marketplace. It is imperative, however, that regulators of commercial advertising be equally well-versed in communication theory. A very serious problem arises when regulators evaluate the possible falsity, deception, or unfairness of an ad without considering it in the same "sensory experience" context that the ad sought to instill. Despite all the lessons of communication theory—lessons the advertising technicians have learned very well—the regulators and the judges who review their work persist in using a relatively ancient method for evaluation: they first reduce the total sensory experience of the ad—voices, music, graphics, movement, colors—to the written word, via the double-spaced, typewritten memo or brief.

"Those who have spent their lives protesting about 'false and misleading ad copy,' " wrote Marshall McLuhan, "are godsends to advertisers, as teetotalers are to brewers. . . . Since the advent of pictures," he continued, "the job of the ad *copy* is as incidental and latent as the 'meaning' of a poem is to a poem, or the words of a song are to a song. . . . [T]ypography is itself mainly subliminal in effect. . . ."[2]

A recent case illustrates the difficulty of the current approach to advertising regulation.[3] In 1969 and 1970, Beneficial Finance Company ran ads centered around the concept of the "Instant Tax Refund." In reality, this "Instant Tax Refund" was merely an invitation to the consumer to apply for a loan from Beneficial at the normal rates and using the normal qualification procedures—information which was not communicated by

---

2. *Id.* at 205 (emphasis added).
3. Beneficial Corp. v. FTC, 542 F.2d 611 (3d Cir. 1976).

the total impression conveyed by the radio and television commercials. An administrative law judge of the Federal Trade Commission found that the total sensory experience of those commercials was deceptive and misleading. More important, he found that there was no possible way to modify the phrase "Instant Tax Refund" so that the ad would not be deceptive and misleading. Therefore, he concluded, Beneficial could no longer use the phrase.

The U.S. Court of Appeals for the Third Circuit reversed, 2–1, on that portion of the order and held that the administrative law judge could not require excision of the phrase because of its quasitrademark value and the First Amendment's general disfavoring of prohibitions on protected speech. A "less restrictive alternative" to deletion would have to be found.

This author does not quarrel with the court's application of First Amendment theory, nor dispute what consumer perceptions of the ad might have been. He does, however, quarrel with the fact that the judges did not evaluate the potential deceptiveness of the ad via the sensory experience it created. Rather, they evaluated the deceptiveness only via the ad's script, reduced to the double-spaced, typewritten page.

A necessary corollory of this view is that as the ad is dulled by reduction to print, the gravity of any perceived falsity, deception, or unfairness is lessened. Implicit in this discussion of the *Beneficial* case is the belief that the deception of the "Instant Tax Refund" ad is far more stark when the entire commercial is viewed or heard—when one is exposed to the entire sensory experience of the ad.

Marshall McLuhan has noted that advertisers strive to find and exploit the sensory experiences to which audiences are most responsive. "The need is to make the ad include the audience experience," he wrote. "The product and the public response become a single complex pattern. . . . The steady trend in advertising is to manifest the product as an integral part of large social purposes and processes."

In his widely praised book *The Responsive Chord,* radio-TV ad creator Tony Schwartz put it even more bluntly. Both the FTC and advertising agencies focus on the "truth" of an ad, which may be a very small part of the total sensory experience. The Commission focuses on "truth" because of its statutory responsibilities and the agencies, because, as Schwartz puts it, "they want to *appear* truthful." However, he concludes that both are dealing with "an irrelevant issue. Neither understands the structure of electronic communication. They are dealing with TV and radio as extensions of print media, with the principles of literacy setting the ground rules for truth, honesty, and clarity."[4]

---

4. An analogous situation can be found in the fact that the Federal Communications Commission has recognized that visual techniques, as well as words, may be subject to regulation in its handling of "subliminal perception" advertising. Subliminal perception techniques generally involve a superimposed statement, such as "Buy It," flashed on the screen for such a short duration that the viewer may not consciously see the message. In a Public Notice on January 24, 1974, the Commission noted that "[w]hether effective nor not, such broadcasts clearly are intended to be deceptive" and are against the public interest. 44 F.C.C.2d 1016, 1017, 29 R.R.2d 395 (1974).

The only important question for the regulators to ask, according to Schwartz, is

> What are the *effects* of electronic media advertising? For an advertiser, the issue of concern should center on how the stimuli in a commercial interact with a viewer's real-life experiences and thus affect his behavior in a purchasing situation. . . .
>
> From the FTC point of view . . . government agencies responsible for safeguarding public well-being should concern themselves with understanding the effects of a commercial, and preventing those effects that are not in the public interest.

Judge Bazelon has also noted the importance of evaluating the *effect* of advertising as follows:

> In an age of omnipresent radio, there scarcely breathes a citizen who does not know some part of a leading cigarette jingle by heart. Similarly, an ordinary habitual television watcher can *avoid* these commercials only by frequently leaving the room, changing the channel, or doing some other such affirmative act. *It is difficult to calculate the subliminal impact of this pervasive propaganda,* which may be heard even if not listened to, but it may reasonably be thought greater than the impact of the written word.[5]

In contexts other than advertising, regulators seem to recognize their obligation to tailor their method of review to the sensory experience of the medium.[6] Films generally have been considered as distinct from other forms of expression for First Amendment purposes because of the inherent characteristics of the medium. Moreover, in obscenity cases, the U.S. Supreme Court has recognized that it is the dominant theme of the material taken as a "whole" that must be considered and has recognized a duty to review allegedly obscene material in its chambers before making a determination on obscenity. In the famous "sound truck" case, Mr. Justice Frankfurter made very explicit the notion that different forms of media deserve different analysis:

> The various forms of modern so-called "mass communications" raise issues that were not implied in the means of communication known or contemplated by Franklin and Jefferson and Madison. Movies have created problems not presented by the circulation of books, pamphlets, or newspapers. . . . Broadcasting in turn has produced its brood of complicated problems hardly to be solved by an easy formula about the preferred position of free speech.[7]

---

5. Banzhaf v. FCC, 405 F.2d 1082, 1100–01 (D.C. Cir. 1968), *cert. denied,* 396 U.S. 842 (1969) (emphasis added).

6. Despite this Article's emphasis on sensory advertising in electronic media, it may be possible that its analysis would be equally valid if applied to the print media. None of these remarks is intended to eliminate that possibility.

7. Kovacs v. Cooper, 336 U.S. 77, 96 (1949) (Frankfurter, J., concurring) (citations omitted) (prohibition against the use of any sound truck located upon public streets or places emitting "loud and raucous" noises).

Thus, in other contexts, the Supreme Court has often acknowledged a principle that seems to impeach the fairly widespread practice among regulators of accepting a sensory experience via the double-spaced, typewritten pages of a brief. The Court's approach is instructive for regulators who must evaluate allegedly false, misleading, or deceptive ads and shape an appropriate remedy.

The problem this Article has addressed is part of a broader one. The media have become so powerful that they have shaped many societal institutions, including the First Amendment itself. The media have molded "expression" into an image which promotes their power—because the media need the First Amendment. The time has come to recognize that the First Amendment protects expression itself, not just the *representation* of expression.[8] To the extent there is any mandate to regulate false, deceptive, or unfair advertising expression, regulators must be sure to consider the expression itself and not just a representation of the expression.

If advertising regulation is to be effective against advertising that makes its point through use of advanced communications techniques, it is imperative that both regulators and the courts take account of the media revolution, of the advanced market research that enables advertisers to know just what effect a certain message will create, and of the handicap under which they, as regulators, labor if they continue to prescribe ancient, pedestrian remedies for sophisticated but false, deceptive, or misleading sensory experiences that advertisers have created.

Only then will the regulators be dealing in the same currency as the advertisers they regulate.

---

8. Cohen v. California, 403 U.S. 15, 26 (1971) (the "Fuck the Draft" case) (A state may not, consistently with the First and Fourteenth Amendments, make the public display of a four-letter word on one's jacket a criminal offense. The Court noted that much linguistic expression "conveys not only ideas capable of relatively precise, detached explication, but otherwise inexpressible emotions as well.").

No Matter What the Sheepskin Looks Like, It's Still the Same Old Wolf: A Reply to Mr. Kramer

WESLEY J. LIEBELER

HAVING BEEN A MISFIT even at the "Old" Federal Trade Commission because of my insistence on viewing problems in a market context, it comes as no surprise that I have difficulty understanding what the leaders of the "New" Commission are all about. While I think I understand the words, I

From *Federal Communications Law Journal* 30(1)(1978):41–46.

must admit that somehow the total sensory experience of Mr. Kramer's message tends to pass me by. After some reflection though, a familiar strain comes through: it's the government that knows what's *really* good for you.

At first, Mr. Kramer's argument seems simply to be that the true meaning of some advertisements that include voices and pictures cannot be determined solely by reference to a transcript of what the voices said. That, of course, is a perfectly obvious proposition. A pictorial sequence could show the same person being carried into the baths at Lourdes as a cripple and coming out like a track star. The voices could say nothing or, more appropriately perhaps, they could provide information on train schedules in southwestern France. In a more modern context we might substitute Geritol for Lourdes, but the result would be the same. In neither case would the obvious claim of restorative power be reflected in a written transcript of the advertisement.

Few of us would attempt to evaluate advertisements like these by "protesting about 'false and misleading ad copy.' " The pictures, sounds and so on are just as much a part of the advertisement as the meaning of the words involved. Indeed, in the examples I have given, the non-verbal part of the ads carries the real message.

The usual approach would be to take the words and music (or pictures) together, to place ourselves in the "environment of multiple-sensory experience," if you must, and specify the claim which the two (or more) different forms of communication state. Sometimes, as in the Lourdes and Geritol examples, the pictures and other "multiple-sensory" part of the advertisement will expand the claim that is made by the words alone. At other times the non-verbal portion of the ad will constrict the apparent claim being made by the words alone. An example of this may be found in the recent Commission proceeding against "Dry Ban," where the pictures were used to limit and restrict the meaning of a verbal claim that the deodorant in question was "dry."[1]

In either case, however, whether the non-verbal portion of the ad constricts the claim of its verbal segment or expands that claim, the total ad is examined *so as to state the specific product claim which the ad is making.* That product claim can, of course, be expressed in words, whether it was actually made in words or in some other way. I would, indeed, have thought that it was necessary to express that claim in words if its truth or falsity were to be made a legal issue. That necessity, of course, arises out of even a modest regard for advising respondents of the nature of the claims being made against them.

Be that as it may, it would be hard to quarrel with Mr. Kramer if his only point was that we should look at all parts of an advertisement in our attempt to state the precise claim which the ad makes, the truth or falsity of which claim is to be assayed in our proceeding. As I have said, that is a

---

1. Matter of Bristol-Meyers Company, 85 F.T.C. 688, 743, 750 (1975).

perfectly obvious proposition; the Commission already does it.[2] But Mr. Kramer is saying much more than that. He is not concerned that we look to the entire ad to guide our statement of its claim. He positively rejects the idea that we should attempt to draw from the entire ad any statement whatever of its perceived claim. He objects that the old-fashioned regulators "persist in using a relatively ancient method for evaluation: they first reduce the total sensory experience of the ad— voices, music, graphics, movement, colors—to the written word, via the double-spaced, typewritten memo or brief."

Of course, if we are not to "reduce the total sensory experience of the ad . . . to the written word," of an ad claim, we need not concern ourselves with the truth of such a claim or even with the question of whether an intelligible claim has been made at all. Apparently, the only thing that counts is the effect of the advertisement:

> The only important question for the regulators to ask, according to Schwartz, is "[w]hat are the *effects* of electronic media advertising? For an advertiser, the issue of concern should center on how much the stimuli in a commercial interact with a viewer's real-life experiences and thus affect his behavior in a purchasing situation. . . .
> From the FTC point of view . . . government agencies responsible for safeguarding public well-being should concern themselves with understanding the effects of a commercial, *and preventing those effects that are not in the public interest.*"[3]

What are these effects? Which ones are "not in the public interest"? One possibility is that Mr. Kramer wants to measure effect in terms of the "sophisticated but false, deceptive, or misleading sensory experiences that advertisers have created." This, of course, would make the Federal Trade Commission the guardian of our fantasies, or at least of those fantasies that are somehow prompted by commercial speech.

A more likely possibility is that Mr. Kramer would view an ad's effect in terms of its ability to affect consumer "behavior in a purchasing situation." I suppose that we may put aside all ads that do not have the ability to induce a positive response from consumers; they will presumably not be around very long in any event. How do we determine which of the re-

---

2. In the Dry Ban case the administrative law judge not only had the filmed commercials themselves, he also had marketing surveys which had been conducted by the respondent which showed how viewers perceived the ad, i.e., what message they received from it. But there was more. Commissioner Hanford reported:

> Judge Hanscom's finding that these representations were false is based primarily on an experiment which was performed by complaint counsel in his presence and replicated on videotape. In this experiment, Dry Ban was sprayed on glass and on a human forearm and was fond to be "wet, runny, liquid and watery" and to leave an "obvious residue." Respondents, however, object to a finding of wetness based on this demonstrative evidence because of the fact that in the experiment the product was sprayed downward, contrary to ordinary usage.

Id. at 742–43.

3. Emphasis added.

maining ads, those that do have an ability positively to affect consumer behavior in a purchasing situation, produce effects that "are not in the public interest"?

I cannot avoid the conclusion that the ads that are not in the "public interest" must be those ads that effectively induce us to buy products that it is not in the "public interest" for us to buy. What is in the "public interest" for us to buy is, I venture to suppose, a matter for Mr. Kramer and his colleagues at the "New" Federal Trade Commission to decide.

The basic problem with Mr. Kramer's approach is that it turns the purpose of advertising regulation at the Commission on its head. The Commission is supposed to police advertising so that consumers can more efficiently learn about real options open to them in the market. Armed with this information they (we) then make choices that seem best to them (us). The fact that some, or even many of us will choose to eat "junk" food, smoke cigarettes, buy "gas guzzlers" or do something else that fails to meet with the approval of those who run the Federal Trade Commission is absolutely irrelevant. When the Commission acts to reduce the flow of true (non-deceptive) messages that would lead us to purchase such "unworthy" goods it substitutes its judgment for ours. It is in that way and to that extent that Mr. Kramer's approach reverses the real purposes of the Commission's program to police false advertising.

The difference between Mr. Kramer's proposal and the Commission's more orthodox approach is not merely a difference of degree or a shifting of emphasis. These two approaches are in fundamental and irreconcilable conflict with each other. Kramer would concern himself with the effects or end-state of the market process, of which advertising is only a part. If those effects or results do not measure up to some exogenous standard, one that is not derivable from the choices that consumers actually make, the process itself (or at least the advertising portion of it) stands condemned.

A market approach to the policing of advertising—the approach on which the Commission's original charter in this area is presumably based—is legitimately concerned only with the *process* by which consumers receive the information on which they base their purchasing decisions. This approach does not concern itself with the nature of the choices which consumers make. The public interest in the production and sale of particular goods and services is something that is determined by the purchasing decisions of consumers themselves.

While I could develop the differences between these two different approaches to the policing of advertising in an extended theoretical discussion, let me close by contrasting these different approaches in the context of some recent remarks by the Commission's chairman. The Commission must confront, Mr. Pertschuk is reported as having said:

> . . . the realities of a marketing system run amok, a system in which neither incentives nor rewards bear any rational relationship to society's needs, a system which most rewards the sellers of the least

healthful foods, a system which in its cumulative impact has produced a bounty of malnutrition. . . .

We are similarly witness to a bizarre market system which rewards the delivery of health care services—whether or not they are needed—but provides little or no rewards for the preventer of disease—for example, the physician who would devote his life to teaching consumers about the relationship between nutrition and health.

By removing competitive restraints on the providers of health care, we free them to communicate with consumers on the importance of diet and sound nutrition as well as on the costs of medical services. We are in effect promoting a competitive system in which medical practitioners teach consumers about the relationship between nutrition and health; consumers demand better quality food; and an increased supply of nutritious food products results.[4]

Mr. Pertschuk objects to the food marketing system because of the *result* which he claims it produces—"a bounty of malnutrition." Aside from the fact that his characterization of that system resembles more the carping of a chronic malcontent than a realistic description of the food marketing sytem, it is additionally deficient in that it does not explain what aspects of the food marketing process produce this unfortunate alleged result. The system is wrong because it produces results that Mr. Pertschuk does not like—we consumers are simply not eating enough health foods. A market approach to this "problem," if such it is, might ask what it is that prevents existing firms in the food industry, or new entrants into it, from advertising the virtues of eating nutritious foods, presumably in connection with their efforts to sell the same. What prevents these purveyors of wholesomeness from hiring doctors and other professionals to spread the word that will both meet "society's needs" for an increased demand and supply of "better quality food" and at the same time increase their own profits? Nothing as far as I know.

The Commission's approach to the health care industry, the other matter addressed by Mr. Pertschuk, was quite different. Here, and in the related fields of prescription drugs and eyeglasses, the Commission identified specific factors that directly impeded the efficient operation of the market *process* itself. With prescription drugs and eyeglasses, a skein of state laws and regulations prevented price advertising at the retail level. The Commission moved directly against those restrictions on the operation of the market for price information. With medical services, there are restrictions, both legal and "professional," on advertising of prices and other factors important to consumers in their selection of medical suppliers along with a virtually endless system of other guild-like restrictions on the effective operation of the market for medical services. The Commission is also moving against these restrictions.

The justification for the medical services, prescription drug and eyeglass programs is vastly different from what Mr. Pertschuk seems to

---

4. *See* FTC: WATCH, January 27, 1978, at 9.

have in mind as regards nutritious foods. The former programs are based on the proposition that various legal and institutional factors in those markets are interfering with the ability of consumers to get information that would enable them to make better choices in the market *in terms of their own standards.* Reduced to its fundamentals, Mr. Pertschuk's problem in the nutrition field seems to be that people are eating too many Twinkies and drinking too much Coke, when they *should be* on a diet of bean sprouts and papaya nectar. As every *sensible* person *ought* to know, that is bad for our health.

Could be. But I doubt that the harm is equal to that which would be produced by the remedy that Messrs. Pertschuk and Kramer seem to have in mind.

Application of the Fairness Doctrine to Ordinary Product Advertisements: National Citizens Committee for Broadcasting *v.* FCC

DAVID L. SINAK

THE FAIRNESS DOCTRINE in broadcasting imposes a twofold obligation on television and radio broadcast licensees: licensees must broadcast material concerning controversial issues of public importance, and they must broadcast differing views on those controversial issues.[1] The doctrine attempts to ensure that a licensee's total programming presents balanced coverage of important public issues.[2]

The fairness doctrine was developed by the Federal Communications Commission, and was later incorporated into the Communications Act[3] and validated by the Supreme Court.[4] While the FCC considered applying

---

Reprinted by permission from *Boston College Law Review* 20(1979): Case Notes, 225–38, © Boston College Law School.

1. *Report on Editorializing by Broadcast Licensees,* 13 F.C.C. 1246, 1248–49 (1949).

2. Potential sanctions for violating the doctrine run from a mild notice of violation kept on file, *see* Central Maine Broadcasting Sys., 23 F.C.C.2d 45 (1970), to non-renewal of the offending broadcaster's license, *see* Brandywine-Main Line Radio, Inc., 24 F.C.C.2d 18 (1970).

To comply with its fairness doctrine obligation, a licensee need not air opposing views on the same program, but it must make a reasonable effort to ensure balanced coverage. For example, after broadcasting a controversial issue, the licensee must make a diligent, good faith effort to solicit a spokesman to present the opposing view. *The Handling of Public Issues Under the Fairness Doctrine and the Public Interest Standards of the Communications Act,* 48 F.C.C.2d 1, 13–14 ¶37 (1974) [hereinafter cited as *Fairness Report*]. The licensee must also provide the spokesman airtime at its own expense if sponsorship is unavailable. Cullman Broadcasting Co., 40 F.C.C. 576, 577 (1963).

3. 47 U.S.C. §315(a) (1976).

4. Red Lion Broadcasting Co. v. FCC, 395 U.S. 367, 385 (1969).

the fairness doctrine to commercial advertising for over thirty years, it did not do so until 1967. In *WCBS/TV (Banzhaf)*[5] the first case in which the FCC applied the fairness doctrine to commercial advertising, the Commission held that cigarette advertising was subject to the fairness doctrine because it raised the controversial and publicly important issue whether smoking is desirable. Although the commission referred to cigarette advertising as "unique" and sought to limit the application of the fairness doctrine to cigarette advertisements, the courts soon extended the doctrine to other product advertisements.[6]

During the next several years, the debate over the proper interplay between the fairness doctrine and advertising focused on delineating the contours of the *Banzhaf* approach. Out of this debate grew the realization that it was difficult, and perhaps impossible, to decide on a case-by-case basis which advertisements should be subject to fairness obligations. Neither the courts nor the Commission clearly articulated a standard for applying *Banzhaf* to product advertisements. Faced with this confusion, the FCC investigated methods for more adequately implementing the fairness doctrine in the commercial advertising context and released its conclusions in its 1974 *Fairness Report*. The *Fairness Report* divides advertisements into three cateogries: editorial advertisements, advertisements making product efficacy claims about which there is a dispute, and standard product commercials.

Editorial advertisements consist of "direct and substantial commentary on important public issues." A typical example is an "overt" editorial, prepared and paid for by an organization or an individual, which takes a position on one side of an important public issue. The advertisement need not explicitly take a position; any advertisement that "presents a meaningful statement which obviously addresses, and advocates a point of view on, a controversial issue of public importance" constitutes an editorial advertisement. The *Fairness Report* indicates that the FCC will continue to apply the fairness doctrine to editorial advertisements.

The second category of advertisements in the *Fairness Report* encompasses advertisements making product efficacy claims about which there is a dispute. These include deceptive, false, and misleading adver-

---

5. WCBS-TV, 8 F.C.C.2d 381, *upon reconsideration*, 9 F.C.C.2d 921 (1967), *aff'd sub nom*. Banzhaf v. FCC, 405 F.2d 1082 (D.C. Cir. 1968), *cert denied*, 396 U.S. 842 (1969).

6. The first indication that the FCC's attempt to limit *Banzhaf* to cigarette advertisements would fail came in Retail Store Employees Local 880 v. FCC, 436 F.2d 248 (D.C. Cir. 1970). In that case, the Court of Appeals for the District of Columbia Circuit held that a department store's regular product advertising during a union boycott of the store inherently raised one side of a controversial and important issue—the boycott—and that the FCC had to consider a fairness complaint that a station's discontinuance of the union's boycott support advertising while continuing to broadcast the store's regular product advertising violated the station's fairness obligations. *Id*. at 258–59.

Shortly thereafter, the same court held that television advertisements for large cars and leaded gasolines raised the controversial and publicly important issue of the desirability of motorist preferences which could increase automobile-related air pollution and its attendant health hazards. Friends of the Earth v. FCC, 449 F.2d 1164, 1169 (D.C. Cir. 1971). Other parties argued that *Banzhaf* applied to everything from military recruitment commercials, Green v. FCC, 447 F.2d 323 (D.C. Cir 1971), to oil company commercials concerning the development of oil in Alaska, National Broadcasting Co., 30 F.C.C.2d 643 (1971).

tisements. Because the FCC believes that the Federal Trade Commission can better sanction false advertising, it decided not to apply the fairness doctrine to advertisements making product efficacy claims.

The third category of advertisements, standard product commercials, includes advertisements that simply promote the sale of a product. Although under the *Banzhaf* approach these advertisements were potentially subject to the fairness doctrine, the FCC announced in the *Fairness Report* its decision to remove standard product commercials from the doctrine's coverage. The FCC based this decision on its conclusion that these commercials "make no meaningful contribution toward informing the public on any side of any issue." The Commission noted, however, that some product commercials might discuss public issues in an obvious and meaningful way and would therefore be subject to the fairness doctrine as editorial advertisements.

The *Fairness Report* brought both constitutional and statutory objections from the public. The National Citizens Committee for Broadcasting (NCCB), Friends of the Earth, and the Council of Economic Priorities sought judicial review of the FCC's decision not to apply the fairness doctrine to ordinary product advertisements. These petitioners argued that the public's first amendment right to receive commercial information gives rise to a duty on the broadcaster to broadcast counter-advertisements. The petitioners further contended that the FCC's decision was contrary to the public interest standard imposed on broadcasters by the Communications Act, and was arbitrary, capricious, and an abuse of the Commission's discretion.

These petitions and other petitions objecting to various parts of the FCC's decision were consolidated for review by the United States Court of Appeals for the District of Columbia Circuit. [I]n *National Citizens Committee for Broadcasting v. FCC, . . .* the circuit court [held that] neither the first amendment nor the Communications Act requires application of the fairness doctrine to ordinary product commercials which do not obviously and meaningfully address a controversial issue of public importance.[7] The court upheld the FCC's decision not to apply the fairness doctrine to ordinary product commercials as both proper and supported by substantial evidence.

National Citizens is significant because it denies any constitutional or statutory basis for requiring application of the fairness doctrine to product advertisements. By refusing to base a public right of access to the broadcast media for counter-advertising on the recent extension of first amendment protection to commercial speech,[8] the court has diminished the hope for a constitutionally-based public right of access on any issue. Additionally, by finding that the Communications Act's public interest standard only broadly guides the FCC, the court has granted the Commission wide discretion to administer the fairness doctrine and balance the

    7. 567 F.2d 1095 (D.C. Cir. 1977).
    8. *See* Virginia State Bd. of Pharmacy v. Virginia Citizens Consumer Council, 425 U.S. 748, 761–62 (1976).

many competing interests in broadcasting. In the future, unless obvious or compelling circumstances demand implementation of a different policy, the court will accept the agency's determination of how best to serve the public interest through the fairness doctrine.

This casenote will first examine the reasoning employed by the *National Citizens* court. It will then analyze the court's rejection of petitioners' arguments that the first amendment and the Communications Act require application of the fairness doctrine to standard product advertisements. It will be suggested that two factors made inevitable the court's holding that application of the fairness doctrine to product advertisements is neither constitutionally nor statutorily required. The first factor is the historical basis of the fairness doctrine; it is an administrative compromise, not a constitutionally required balance between broadcasters' and listeners' rights. The second factor is the courts' traditional deference to administrative agencies, including the FCC.

I. THE *National Citizens* DECISION

In *National Citizens,* the court considered separately the constitutional and statutory issues presented. Turning initially to the constitutional issues, the court rejected two arguments advanced by petitioners asserting that there is a constitutional basis for requiring the FCC to apply the fairness doctrine to standard product advertisements. First, the court dismissed the contention that statements which oppose views presented in commercial advertisements must be broadcast under the fairness doctrine simply because such statements are a form of commercial speech protected by the first amendment. Second, the court rejected the argument that the public has a significant, constitutionally protected interest in the free flow of information provided by these counter-commercials.

In rejecting petitioners' constitutional arguments, the court stressed that no individual or group has a right to broadcast a particular point of view simply because that point of view is protected speech under the first amendment. The court further determined that the fairness doctrine and the first amendment are not coextensive, because the FCC's standard for determining whether particular programming is subject to the fairness doctrine—whether the programming advocates one side of a controversial issue of public importance—is different from the courts' standard for determining whether certain speech is protected by the first amendment— whether the speech disseminates information important to the functioning of a free enterprise system. The court stated that product advertisements do not necessarily meet the more rigorous standard for determining whether to apply the fairness doctrine even though they do meet the standard for determining whether they are constitutionally protected speech. Thus, the court indicated that it is irrelevant to the fairness doctrine inquiry that such speech is protected under the first amendment. The court effectively denied a constitutionally-based public right of access to the broadcast media by finding that the first amendment protection given to commercial speech, and, thus, counter-advertisements, neither gives the public a right to broadcast such speech nor compels applying the fairness doctrine to such speech.

Turning to petitioners' statutory challenges to the *Fairness Report,* the court first rejected petitioners' argument that the 1959 amendments to the Communications Act codified the FCC's policy of applying the fairness doctrine to product advertisements. The court noted that there is no conclusive evidence that counter-advertising was part of the FCC's fairness doctrine policy prior to 1959. Even assuming that counter-advertising was part of pre-1959 policy, the court held that the 1959 amendments did not incorporate that policy into the Act. The court based its conclusion on an earlier case in which the Supreme Court found that "[w]hen the Congress ratified the . . . fairness doctrine in 1959 it did not, of course, approve every past decision or pronouncement by the [FCC] on the subject. . . ."[9] Thus, the court in *National Citizens* concluded that a policy of applying the fairness doctrine to product advertisements was not incorporated in the Communications Act.

The court next considered petitioners' second statutory argument— that the public interest standard of the Communications Act requires the FCC to allow counter-advertising. The court noted that the fairness doctrine stems from the Communications Act's requirement that broadcasters operate in the "public interest." The court stressed, however, that operating in the public interest does not necessarily entail application of the fairness doctrine to product advertisements. Instead, the FCC has discretion to decide what the public interest demands of broadcasting, and courts accord great deference to the FCC's judgment of what the public interest entails.[10] Accordingly, the *National Citizens* court found that the public interest is served as long as the FCC enforces the fairness doctrine's requirement that broadcasters "present opposing points of view whenever there is direct, obvious or explicit advocacy of one side of a controversial issue of public importance." When, as in product advertisements, indirect advocacy of one side of an issue is broadcast, opposing views need not be presented. Thus, the court concluded that the FCC's decision not to apply the fairness doctrine to standard product advertisements is within the Commission's discretion and consistent with the public interest standard in the Communications Act.

Finally, the court examined petitioners' argument that the FCC acted arbitrarily and abused its discretion in withdrawing standard product commercials from the ambit of the fairness doctrine. Petitioners acknowledged that the fairness doctrine applies only to advertisements presenting meaningful discussion on controversial issues of public importance. They argued, however, that standard product advertisements implicitly discuss the controversial issue of product desirability and, therefore, that the FCC acted arbitrarily in concluding that product desirability is not an im-

9. Red Lion Broadcasting Co. v. FCC, 395 U.S. 367, 385 (1969).
10. Columbia Broadcasting Sys., Inc. v. Democratic Nat'l Comm., 412 U.S. 94, 102 (1973).

portant, controversial issue within the meaning of the fairness doctrine. The court rejected petitioners' contention, pointing to the logic of the FCC's reasoning as evidence that it did not act arbitrarily. As the court noted, the FCC found that product desirability itself is not a controversial issue of public importance, but rather, the important, controversial issues are those underlying the issue of product desirability. Standard product advertisements, with their emphasis on product desirability, do not meaningfully address these underlying issues. On the basis of this reasoning, the court held that the FCC was warranted in concluding that standard product commercials are not subject to the fairness doctrine.

II. ANALYSIS OF THE FIRST AMENDMENT ISSUES

As noted earlier, *National Citizens* is significant because it denies any constitutional basis for the fairness doctrine. It is submitted that this conclusion is inevitable because of the courts' long held view of the fairness doctrine as an administrative, rather than a constitutional, compromise between the public's right to receive information and the broadcasters' right to exercise free speech. An examination of the Supreme Court cases addressing the relationship between the fairness doctrine and the first amendment illustrates this view.

Courts have long recognized that the primary purpose of the first amendment is to foster a well-informed citizenry by prohibiting governmental restraints upon speech and by permitting every speaker to express his ideas, so that the public may adopt those that are valuable and correct. As applied to the broadcast industry, however, this goal must be modified since the scarcity of broadcasting frequencies limits the number of speakers who can "speak" through the broadcast medium and, therefore, requires an allocation of broadcast time between competing voices.[11] Thus, although the Supreme Court recognizes that both the public's right and the broadcasters' rights are protected to some extent by the first amendment, it refuses to accord either right full constitutional protection to the exclusion of the other.

Broadcasters once claimed that the first amendment grants them, as members of the press, absolute autonomy over what is broadcast and when. They argued that the fairness doctrine's intrusion on their autonomy was a violation of their first amendment rights since it forced them to broadcast particular points of view. The Supreme Court rejected this claim, however, in *Red Lion Broadcasting Co. v. FCC.*[12] In that case,

---

11. While the FCC argues that the problem of scarcity is acute and will continue for the near future, *Fairness Report, supra* note 2, at 6, it has been suggested that the great capacity of cable television, when it becomes fully operative, may render obsolete the scarcity rationale. Brandywine-Main Line Radio, Inc. v. FCC, 473 F.2d 16, 75–76 (D.C. Cir. 1972) (Bazelon, C.J., dissenting), *cert. denied*, 412 U.S. 922 (1973). It has been argued, therefore, that scarcity is an invalid basis for a constitutional distinction between the broadcast and print media. Columbia Broadcasting Sys., Inc. v. Democratic Nat'l Comm., 412 U.S. 94, 144–45 (1973) (Stewart, J., concurring); Bazelon, *FCC Regulation of the Telecommunications Press*, 1975 DUKE L. J. 213, 223–29.
12. 395 U.S. 367 (1969).

the Court held that the first amendment does not prevent the government from requiring a broadcast licensee to share its frequency with others under the terms of the fairness doctrine. In reaching this conclusion, the Court stressed the public nature of the airwaves and pointed out that the public has a right to suitable access to ideas and information from the broadcast media. The Court found that the fairness doctrine, rather than impermissibly infringing the first amendment rights of broadcasters, adequately balances the broadcasters' rights with the public's right of access to information. Thus, the *Red Lion* Court did not find the fairness doctrine to be a constitutionally required remedy for balancing the competing interests in broadcasting. Rather, the Court upheld the doctrine as an administrative compromise of the broadcasters' and the public's interests which does not unconstitutionally infringe the broadcasters' first amendment rights.

The Supreme Court affirmed the adequacy of the fairness doctrine's balance of competing constitutional interests in *Columbia Broadcasting System, Inc. v. Democratic National Committee (CBS)*.[13] In *CBS,* the Court determined that the public's "right to be informed" by the broadcast media, albeit protected by the first amendment, does not require broadcasters to accept editorial advertisements from whoever wishes to pay for them. In reaching this conclusion, the Court noted that the FCC promulgated the fairness doctrine to ensure that broadcast licensees provide balanced presentations of important public issues. To read the first amendment as granting individuals the unfettered right to have editorial advertisements broadcast as long as they are paid for, the Court noted, would upset the delicate balance the FCC has found for serving the interests of both broadcasters and the public. The Court decided that the FCC must retain the flexibility to balance these interests, and refused to create its own balance based on first amendment values.

Red Lion and *CBS* demonstrate the Supreme Court's recognition of the inherent conflict between listeners' and broadcasters' first amendment rights. However, the Court has concluded that the fairness doctrine adequately balances these competing interests and, therefore, has found it unnecessary to develop a constitutionally-based balance. Because the Court refused to find that the public has a constitutional right to media access, persons could obtain access after *Red Lion* and *CBS* only if they could argue successfully that the issue which they wanted to address was subject to the fairness doctrine.

When the Supreme Court recently extended first amendment protection to commercial speech,[14] counter-advertising proponents believed their argument that the public has a constitutional right to broadcast media access was renewed. Commercial speech traditionally was not included under the umbrella of first amendment protection. However, in *Virginia State Board of Pharmacy v. Virginia Citizens Consumer Council,*

---

13. 412 U.S. 94 (1973).
14. Valentine v. Chrestensen, 316 U.S. 52, 54 (1942).

Inc.,[15] the Supreme Court held that speech does not lose its first amendment protection merely because it is in the form of a paid commercial announcement, or because the advertiser's interest is purely economic, and that no lines can be drawn between publicly "interesting" and "important" commercial speech and "the opposite kind." *Virginia State Board* also held that there is a reciprocal right to receive advertising.

Petitioners in *National Citizens* used *Virginia State Board* to argue that since product advertisements are protected by the first amendment, opposing information is also protected by the first amendment. Therefore, the petitioners argued, the first amendment demands that such opposing information be provided via application of the fairness doctrine to standard product advertisements. As the court in *National Citizens* recognized, acceptance of this argument would mean that the fairness doctrine is coextensive with the first amendment. Acceptance of this argument also would mean that the fairness doctrine is a constitutionally-based remedy for the conflict between the first amendment rights of broadcasters and listeners. The court in *National Citizens* rejected petitioners' contention on the basis of the Supreme Court's previous refusal to establish a constitutional basis for the fairness doctrine.

It is submitted that petitioners' argument in *National Citizens* was nothing more than an assertion that the relatively recent identification of the listener's right to receive information, and the recent extension of first amendment protection to commercial speech, tip the compromise balance in favor of the listener on the product advertisement issue. The circuit court declined to go that far and, instead, followed the Supreme Court in deferring to the FCC's opinion of the proper balance. Thus, *National Citizens* strongly reinforces the courts' characterization of the fairness doctrine as an administrative compromise which determines who has access to the broadcast medium, and forecloses arguments that the public has a constitutionally-based right of access to the medium for counter-advertising or any other type of speech. Consequently, individuals seeking access after *National Citizens* have only two hopes for obtaining it. First, they can argue that current fairness doctrine requirements demand the broadcast of their point of view. Second, they can seek changes in the fairness doctrine through lobbying directed at either Congress or the FCC with a view toward obtaining greater media access for the public. The latter method is more promising since it has greater potential to increase access. Thus, the importance of *National Citizens* is that the debate over access now will occur in legislative or administrative bodies, not in the courts.

---

15. 425 U.S. 748 (1976). . . . At issue in *Virginia State Board* was a Virginia statute which prohibited licensed pharmacists from advertising the prices of prescription drugs. A consumer group challenged the statute's constitutionality under the first amendment. Justice Blackmun, speaking for the majority, concluded that any first amendment protection enjoyed by advertisers may be asserted by the public as recipients of information, that commercial speech is not wholly outside first amendment protection, and, therefore, that the ban on drug price advertisements is invalid.

III. ANALYSIS OF THE STATUTORY ISSUES

The court's resolution of the statutory issues in *National Citizens* is important for what it says about the FCC's discretion in administering the fairness doctrine. In effect, the court stated that the determination of who should have access to the broadcast media is an administrative, not a judicial, decision. This was evident in the court's rejection of petitioners' arguments that applying the fairness doctrine to product advertisements was required by the Communications Act. The court accepted the FCC decision to the contrary in the absence of explicit statutory language supporting the petitioners' arguments.

Although the court granted the FCC wide discretion to administer the fairness doctrine, judicial review does play an important role after *National Citizens* in ensuring that the FCC follows proper decisionmaking standards. By concentrating on the FCC's decisional criteria rather than on its actual decision, *National Citizens* is a good illustration of how the District of Columbia Circuit will approach challenges to the FCC's administrative decisions. This approach is exemplified by the court's rejection of the argument that the FCC acted arbitrarily and capriciously, and abused its discretion in finding that standard product advertisements do not present meaningful discussion on controversial issues of public importance. The Commission argued that counter-commercials present only one side of a controversial issue, since commercials typically only exhort consumers to buy, while counter-commercials discuss the underlying issues regarding the desirability of buying. It also contended that applying the fairness doctrine to standard product commercials would decrease the attention given by broadcasters to more important issues covered by the doctrine and, therefore, would not contribute efficiently to informed public opinion. Furthermore, application of the doctrine to commercial advertising could undermine the economic base of commercial broadcasting. Thus, the FCC argued, product advertisements do not meaningfully discuss controversial issues of public importance and, accordingly, do not come within the scope of the fairness doctrine.

While the FCC's arguments are plausible, they are not self-evident and are subject to vigorous counter-argument. Nevertheless, given the FCC's discretion to administer the fairness doctrine and the courts' deference to the Commission's decisions, the plausibility of these arguments was sufficient for the court in *National Citizens* to refuse to reverse the FCC decision based on them. The *National Citizens* court properly concluded that the FCC had not acted arbitrarily and capriciously, or abused its discretion, in excluding product advertisements from fairness doctrine coverage. The flexibility and discretion accorded to the FCC stems in part from the courts' recognition that application of the fairness doctrine encompasses the problem of conflicting first amendment rights between broadcaster and listener, and the broader problem of public access to the broadcast media in general. The complexity of these problems is one reason the courts have not given the fairness doctrine a constitutional or statutory foundation. Instead, the courts have allowed the FCC to resolve these problems. Courts will intervene only to ensure that the FCC's administrative decisionmaking conforms with the public interest.

The issue remains whether giving the FCC wide discretion in administering the fairness doctrine produces a satisfactory solution to the problem of who should have access to the broadcast media and for what reasons. In less then ten years, the FCC has traveled 360 degrees with respect to subjecting product advertisements to fairness doctrine requirements. Nevertheless, it is submitted that the FCC's policy now rests on a sturdier foundation. The basic consideration underlying both the *Fairness Report* and *National Citizens* is that standard product commercials and counter-commercials do not present enough meaningful information to justify the difficulties and cost of broadcasting them under the auspices of the fairness doctrine. As one commentator has aptly put it, "[t]he fundamental purpose of the fairness doctrine is to inform the public on important social issues, and further an open, diverse marketplace of ideas. . . . Telling people to 'Join the Dodge Rebellion' and 'Step Up' to a larger car is simply not speech on this level."[16] Thus, the FCC and courts such as the court in *National Citizens* have concluded that product advertisements are a less important type of speech than political editorials or institutional advertising. This conclusion represents progress in the correct direction. It eliminates the confusion emanating from past attempts to tie the fairness doctrine to product advertisements and rationally allocates limited broadcast time and resources between the various issues that different groups think ought to be heard.

Commentary

THE ISSUE RAISED in these articles concerns fairness. When applied to broadcasting the fairness doctrine inquires: Has the broadcaster paid sufficient attention to a controversial issue of public importance; and has the presentation included conflicting views?

The winding trail of administrative and judicial opinions in the 1960s and 1970s which determined the scope of the fairness doctrine has pretty much run its course. Except for ads that scream forth controversy, the doctrine applies exclusively to programming. And the Federal Com-

---

16. Simmons, *Commercial Advertising and the Fairness Doctrine: The New F.C.C. Policy in Perspective*, 75 COLUM. L. REV. 1083 (1975).

munications Commission will grant licensees considerable deference as to how to balance coverage of an issue in programs. Still, even this intrusion of editorial weights and measures by government would be intolerable in the print media.

As for trade regulation, the question exclusively concerns advertising claims but applies to all media: Does an ad include statements or pictures likely to deceive? Are product claims false? Are they "unfair" in some way that the government should worry about?

The sources of these inquiries vary. The fairness doctrine originated as an administrative concoction of the FCC. In trade law, Congress has set forth the standard in Sections 5 and 12 of the Federal Trade Act.

The fairness doctrine in broadcasting not only addresses programming provided by the licensee, but in a larger sense, provides impetus to regulations regarding political speech. These provisions appear in the Federal Communications Act of 1934 in Sections 312(a)(7) and 315. The latter statute, the "equal opportunity" rule, requires broadcasters who allow one candidate to use their stations to provide an equal opportunity to any other legally qualified candidate for the same office. A station need not give any candidate an opportunity to appear. But if one candidate gets it all others get it—at the same price.

The attempt here is to require broadcasters to be fair with all candidates and to prohibit exclusive use of a broadcast frequency by a favorite. The problem, of course, is that if *all* candidates must be included in the 315 roundup, those with no chance of prevailing in the election will be included. Congress attempted to deal with the problem in part by creating certain exempt "uses"—appearances on newscasts, news interviews, and other news programs.

The FCC nearly finished the job of exempting the problem into oblivion when it ruled that debates sponsored by such organizations as the League of Women Voters would be exempt as live coverage of a bona fide news event. A head-to-head debate sponsored by the broadcast networks remains nonexempt, however. Thus, when Kennedy and Nixon debated in 1960, Congress had to suspend section 315 for a short time.

Should Congress finish the job that the FCC has started and leave entirely to a broadcaster's judgment who should or should not be included as candidates when opportunities are doled out? As Sinak observes, the commission has considerable faith in licensee judgment in the fairness area. But perhaps the fundamentality of elections to our democracy makes it essential that a candidate who feels that the broadcaster has unfairly counted him out be able to complain to the FCC for relief.

When I was with the commission during the 1980 elections, candidates from around the country would call complaining about what they thought was unfair treatment by local radio and television. The ability of the commission staff to react quickly in those cases—before the election, not when a station's license was up for renewal—helped to assure the appearance of fairness in election coverage. Postelection sanctions against a station will not make whole a defeated candidate who has been denied equal opportunities.

It is surely a messy business. One hypothetical example should suffice. Say a committee opposed to the election of one candidate, John Jones, but not favoring any other buys a media spot. Does this entitle Jones to a reply opportunity? What if Jones has a sole opponent, Tom Smith? Would it matter if Smith's picture is used in an advertisement, even though his name isn't mentioned? (It could.) What if Jones's picture is used; would Smith be entitled to a reply opportunity, even though Jones appears in a Smith ad urging Jones's own defeat?

Things get even thornier under section 312(a)(7), the "reasonable access" requirement. Under it, broadcasters are required to provide "reasonable access" to candidates for federal office. According to the statute, failure to do so can result in loss of a license.

What then is reasonable? This was the central issue in the United States Supreme Court's 1981 *Carter-Mondale* decision (*CBS* v. *FCC*). The Carter-Mondale campaign committee wanted to launch its 1980 presidential drive with a thirty-minute program in December 1979 and asked for time from the three commercial television networks. Each declined the request. CBS countered with an offer of five minutes, ABC said sometime in January, NBC offered nothing at all, emphasizing that it was too early for campaigning.

Who is to decide when a campaign is "in full swing" and the statutory right of access applies? The candidate, who after all, can be expected to make his initial demand for access at a time he believes does him the most good? The broadcasters, who are supposed to be in control of what goes out over the stations and should not be expected to fold up program schedules whenever a candidate desires to make a media splash? The FCC, a supposedly nonpolitical body but one which is always going to have a majority of one or the other party and a chairman who serves as its head at the pleasure of the president? In *Carter-Mondale* the Court upheld the FCC's interpretation of the statute and its conclusion that the networks had acted unreasonably. Does the statute cause more problems than it solves? Note that in 1981 the FCC asked Congress to remove the fairness doctrine, equal opportunity, and reasonable access provisions from the 1934 act.

As in broadcasting, assuring fairness in trade law revolves around the same questions: What is fair? Who should decide? After years of struggling, the FTC has no easy time of it. For when does puffery end and deception begin? This question is made more complex by Kramer's inquiries about what our senses really do respond to.

Let's examine two commercials. In one, an advertiser shows its shaving lather cleanly removing the sand from a piece of sandpaper. The sand, it turns out, is not actually on paper but plexiglass; the viewer has not been told this. The advertiser has substituted plexiglass for sandpaper because it photographs better. The product can actually shave sandpaper clean, but the sandpaper must be soaked with the soap for eighty minutes. Ruling: deceptive advertising (*Colgate-Palmolive Co.* v. *FTC,* U.S. Supreme Court [1965]).

In the second, a woman is sunning poolside. A tall, dark, and handsome man suddenly appears at the other end of the pool, dives in, and emerges on her side, dripping with water and oozing with intentions. He fades from view, and a bottle of Chanel No. 5 perfume appears.

There is no blatant lie here, it is a fantasy sequence. The perfume shown is actually a perfume you can buy. But what is the overall impact? Has the product been warranted for a service that it is likely to deliver? In the shaving cream ad, the product can do what it claims it can do, but the commercial does not show it. In the latter assumably nondeceptive ad, the product is not likely to produce what is suggested.

Assuming a regulator would want to do something about the latter ad, what could be done? What kind of statute could we construct to cover this type of appeal? And who would go about interpreting it? Whose interests are we trying to protect?

Along with the issue of who should decide, we must consider at what cost. Congress has. In 1980 the FTC had to fight for its life after having attempted to go after politically powerful lobbies, such as the funeral industry. Like the perfume business, the mortuary business sells intangibles: "dignity," "peace of mind," "respect for the departed." It also, of course, sells caskets and embalmings, and at a wide range of prices. Does "fairness" require a seller in so sensitive a line of work to disclose the full range of services and prices a family can choose from? Some members of Congress felt the FTC had no business monitoring the funeral industry—it was beyond matters the federal government ought to be concerned with.

We may see this argument as a transparent excuse to protect politically powerful interests, but imagine how such disclosures could get completely out of hand. What if used car salespersons had to provide a list of a car's every defect? What if magazine publishers were required to disclose the likelihood of a subscriber's never receiving a magazine due to distribution mistakes? What if authors of anthologies had to disclose to students how likely it is that their book would be out-of-date within three years? (Ouch!)

In the end, we as a society get the kind of fairness (or lack of it) from the media that we are willing to tolerate. The fairness doctrine is premised on the assumption that knowing all significant viewpoints of a controversial matter leads to an informed choice. Trade protections rely on the proposition that, while the buyer must beware, advertisers cannot resort to deceptive or false statements to get the buyer to act. And at some point, it is unthinkable—"unfair" to use the language of the act—to allow certain practices. For instance the Supreme Court found it unlawfully "unfair" to tempt children to buy candy with the promise that a nickel might be in the candy roll, when the odds of finding a coin were slim or nonexistent.

But the slipperiness of such a term as "deception," let alone "unfairness," is also evident. And so the tension about how far is too far remains a lively one in media regulation. Do we usurp the free speech interests of broadcasters by mandating fairness in a way that is forbidden for the print media? Do we distort the marketplace by limiting some types of deception but not others? Do we miss a great deal of deception because it cannot be precisely defined? Apart from the free speech implications, how much "fairness" can the free enterprise system tolerate without excessively discouraging commerce?

DLB

11

"Unprotected" Expression: Speech That Injures Reputation or Economic Interests

THE AUTHORS

VICTOR A. KOVNER is a partner in the New York City law firm of Lankenau, Kovner, and Bickford. He was graduated from Yale University in 1958 and from the Columbia University School of Law in 1961. Kovner served as administrative assistant to Senator Herbert H. Lehman, 1962–1963, before returning to private practice. He has served since 1976 as a member of the faculty of the Practising Law Institute, a continuing education organization, and as an instructor in its annual communications law seminar.

DANIEL L. BRENNER is a coauthor of this book.

CELIA GOLDWAG wrote her article while a student editor at the Columbia University School of Law. She was graduated in 1979 and practices law in New York City.

Disturbing Trends in the Law of Defamation: A Publishing Attorney's Opinion

VICTOR A. KOVNER

IN THE TWO YEARS since *Gertz v. Robert Welch, Inc.,*[1] the press has suffered a series of judicial setbacks throughout the nation. Although no single decision constitutes a radical departure from the Warren Court expansion of press freedoms, to any attorney counseling publishers the recent trend away from the principles of *New York Times Co. v. Sullivan*[2] seems ominous indeed. The gravity of this trend was dramatically evidenced in March of this year by the conflicting opinions of a divided Supreme Court in *Time, Inc. v. Firestone.*[3] This commentary attempts to review the adverse implications of the principal defamation decisions affecting the press of the last two years.

The modern law of defamation began with *New York Times Co. v. Sullivan,*[4] which held that to recover for defamation a public official had to establish with "convincing clarity" that the allegedly defamatory material was published with "actual malice"; that is, with knowledge of its falsity, or with reckless disregard as to its truth. The definition of actual malice

From *Hastings Constitutional Law Quarterly* 3(1976):363–72.
1. 418 U.S. 323 (1974).
2. 376 U.S. 254 (1964).
3. 424 U.S. 448 (1976).
4. 376 U.S. 254 (1964).

was further clarified in *St. Amant v. Thompson*[5] to require an "awareness of probable falsity," or evidence that the defendant actually "entertained serious doubts as to the truth" of the material at the time of publication. In *Curtis Publishing Co. v. Butts,*[6] the Court extended the applicability of the *Times* standard to plaintiffs who were "public figures."

The Supreme Court in *Rosenbloom v. Metromedia, Inc.*[7] extended the *Times* standard to private plaintiffs who were involved in matters of public interest.[8] The law applicable to this category of claimants changed, however, in 1974 when *Gertz v. Robert Welch, Inc.*[9] was decided by a five to four vote. Justice Blackmun provided the swing vote, departing from the plurality opinion in *Rosenbloom,* and concurring in Justice Powell's majority opinion in *Gertz* because:

> [I]t is of profound importance for the Court to come to rest in the defamation area and to have a clearly defined majority position that eliminates the unsureness engendered by *Rosenbloom's* diversity.[10]

In brief, the Supreme Court in *Gertz*: (a) excluded from the *Times* rule statements about private persons involved in matters of public interest, leaving the states to define the standards of liability in such defamation claims so long as liability is not imposed without fault; (b) limited recovery for defamation claims to actual damages (including pain and suffering, but not presumed or punitive damages) in the absence of a showing of "actual malice"; and (c) reviewed the "public figure" characterization, placing emphasis upon voluntary activities of the plaintiff, but recognizing the concept of an involuntary public figure for limited purposes.

AFTERMATH OF *Gertz*

THE ADOPTION OF VARYING STANDARDS OF DEFAMATION LIABILITY. Most representatives of the press have found *Gertz* disturbing because of the latitude granted to the states to fix their own standards of defamation liability (short of imposing strict liability) where private individuals are involved in matters of public interest. A preliminary review of the decisions of the states reveals a wide disparity in the standard selected. For instance, at least eight states have selected a negligence standard, while three have adopted the very standard of the plurality in *Rosenbloom v. Metromedia, Inc.* Recently, the New York Court of Appeals adopted a test

---

5. 390 U.S. 727 (1968).
6. 388 U.S. 130 (1967).
7. 403 U.S. 29 (1971) (plurality opinion).
8. In *Rosenbloom,* the Court applied the *Times* standard of liability to a distributor of nudist magazines who had been arrested for distributing allegedly obscene material, and who had sued a radio station for failing to report that the material seized was only "allegedly" obscene. Though not a public figure, the plaintiff was found to have become involved in a matter of public interest. *Id.*
9. 418 U.S. 323 (1974).
10. *Id.* at 354 (Blackmun, J., concurring).

of "gross irresponsibility," which requires, in effect, a showing of a gross departure from ordinary journalistic standards where private individuals are involved in matters of public interest.

While New York's apparent middle ground may not seem too burdensome for many publishers, what is most troubling is the inherent consequences of a multiplicity of standards imposed upon any publication circulated outside its state of origin. The tendency of plaintiffs to sue in forums with the least protective standards will influence the legal advice given to publishers. Where the negligence standard is presumed applicable, the publisher at press deadline may often become unduly cautious.

INADVERTENT ERROR AS A BASIS FOR LIABILITY. The adverse implications of *Gertz* were not eased when the Supreme Court denied certiorari in several libel cases in the fall of 1975, including *Thomas H. Maloney & Sons, Inc. v. E. W. Scripps Co.*[11] In *Maloney* the Ohio Court of Appeals reversed the trial court's grant of summary judgment for the defendant newspaper which had published an article about the inadvertent demolition of a building contiguous to one scheduled for demolition. The article quoted Thomas Maloney as saying, "I guess we got carried away." There was some doubt as to whether anyone made such a statement. Thomas Maloney had retired from the plaintiff construction company, and the business was run by his son, Timothy Maloney. Although the company and its principals would appear to have become "vortex public figures,"[12] having been drawn into a matter of public interest by demolishing the wrong building, the Ohio court appears to have assumed they were private individuals and applied a negligence standard. The newspaper was forced to bear the expense of a full-fledged trial over what appears to have been at most an inadvertent error.

The potential exposure from inadvertent error was dramatized by *Time, Inc. v. Firestone.*[13] In *Firestone,* the following item in *Time* magazine was the subject of the libel action:

> DIVORCED. By Russell A. Firestone Jr., 41, heir to the tire fortune: Mary Alice Sullivan Firestone, 32, his third wife; a onetime Palm Beach schoolteacher; on grounds of extreme cruelty *and adultery*; after six years of marriage, one son; in West Palm Beach, Fla. The 17-month intermittent trial produced enough testimony of extramarital adventures on both sides, said the judge, "to make Dr. Freud's hair curl."[14]

The trial court in the divorce proceeding issued a confusing order

---

11. 43 Ohio App. 2d 105, 334 N.E.2d 494 (1974), *cert. denied,* 423 U.S. 883 (1975).

12. In *Gertz,* Justice Powell wrote: "Hypothetically, it may be possible for someone to become a public figure through no purposeful action of his own, but the instances of truly involuntary public figures must be exceedingly rare. For the most part those who attain this status have assumed roles of especial prominence in the affairs of society." 418 U.S. at 345.

13. 424 U.S. 448 (1976).

14. *Id.* at 452 (emphasis added).

granting the husband's counterclaim for divorce, which alleged extreme cruelty and adultery, and, in addition, awarding alimony to the plaintiff wife. The Florida appelate courts subsequently held that because no alimony could be granted as a matter of Florida law where there had been a finding of adultery, the divorce must have been granted on grounds of cruelty alone.

Mary Firestone contended that *Time* should have been aware of the applicable Florida law and that no finding of adultery was actually made by the trial court, notwithstanding its reference to "extra-marital adventures on both sides . . . [sufficient] to make Dr. Freud's hair curl."

At least six Supreme Court justices apparently assumed that the *Time* publication was substantially false, notwithstanding Justice Marshall's persuasive dissent in which he concluded that *Time* had accurately reported the trial court's erroneous action. Significantly, after conducting an investigation, *Time* had refused a request for retraction, insisting that the item was accurate. Although the concurrence of Justices Powell and Stewart made clear that insufficient evidence of fault on the part of *Time* had been offered to sustain liability under *Gertz,* their tacit agreement that the material was, in fact, false raises a serious question as to the extent to which liability may be imposed in the presence of substantial truth, as opposed to literal truth.[15]

The Supreme Court's open and acknowledged change in defamation standards governing publication of material about private individuals involved in matters of public interest, as well as the Court's more subtle shift to a requirement of literal truth, will have a practical effect on the daily workings of the press. New questions are now being asked: How much may a publisher rely on a reporter, even one who is known and trusted, when an inadvertent error may subject the publisher to liability? How much independent and corroborative investigation need be done? What constitutes the standard against which a charge of negligence will be measured? The lack of clear answers to these new questions will necessarily inhibit publication.

Apart from the enhanced risk of liability,[16] the cost alone of defending defamation claims can have a chilling effect. At one time (but apparently no longer) this was recognized by the Supreme Court:

> Fear of large verdicts in damage suits for innocent or merely negligent misstatement, *even fear of the expense involved in their defense,* must inevitably cause publishers to "steer . . . wider of the unlawful zone," and thus "create the danger that the legitimate utterance will be penalized."[17]

---

15. In contrast, the New York Court of Appeals in Chapadeau v. Utica Observer-Dispatch, Inc., 38 N.Y.2d 196, 200, 341 N.E.2d 569, 572, 379 N.Y.S.2d 61, 65 (1975), found that a serious and acknowledged but inadvertent error should not give rise to liability since "a limited number of typographical errors . . . are inevitable."

16. *See e.g.,* Time, Inc. v. Firestone, 424 U.S. 448 (1976) ($100,000); Montandon v. Triangle Publications, Inc., 45 Cal. App. 3d 938, 120 Cal. Rptr. 186 (1975) ($150,000).

17. Time, Inc. v. Hill, 385 U.S. 374, 389 (1967) (emphasis added). The claim was for invasion of privacy for casting the Hill family in a "false light"—a claim akin to defamation.

The expenses begin at the very early stages of litigation. Discovery proceedings are time-consuming, costly, and often subject a reporter to various levels of intimidation. While these costs always have had a deterring effect, the costs—and hence the chill—are greatly enhanced when the claim is not dismissed by a motion for summary judgment and the publisher has to bear the expense of a trial.

Under the *New York Times* test, a case can be dismissed if, upon motion, the plaintiff does not come forward with "clear and convincing" evidence of "actual malice." Under a lesser standard a plaintiff frequently will be given the right to go to the jury for determination of a question of fact, e.g., did the reporter or publisher follow proper standards of care or did he act negligently?

Both the negligence standard and any departure from the defense of substantial truth offer the unscrupulous claimant or his attorney leverage to force unreasonable settlements. Such demands are especially threatening when the publisher is too small to absorb the full costs of asserting the First Amendment interests. As a result of *Gertz* and *Firestone,* fear of litigation may force small newspapers and local radio stations to withhold newsworthy material. The sacrifices will be shared by their audiences in small communities throughout the country.

THE NOT-SO-PRIVATE LIVES OF ELMER GERTZ AND MARY ALICE FIRESTONE. The stature of Elmer Gertz and his reputation in the Chicago metropolitan area, as well as his role in the litigation against the Chicago police, pose what many press representatives believe to be a potentially more serious problem—deciding who is a "public figure." Although Justice Powell said that he did not intend to alter the definition of "public figure," which had been developed in *Curtis Publishing Co. v. Butts,* his opinion contained a footnote which cited the court of appeals' questionable assumption that Gertz was not a public figure.[18]

The fears generated by *Gertz* were borne out in *Time, Inc. v. Firestone.* While Elmer Gertz was known in limited circles in Chicago, Mary Alice Firestone was widely known throughout Florida and elsewhere, even to the point of notoriety. Mrs. Firestone had been prominent in Palm Beach society for many years and her frequent appearances in the press prompted her to subscribe to a press clipping service. Her seventeen-month divorce trial elicited forty-three articles in the *Miami Herald* and forty-five articles in the Palm Beach newspapers. Clearly, she was involved in a controversy of interest to the public. Moreover, during the trial she held several press conferences. Because "access to the media" was considered a principal factor in *Gertz* in determining public figure status, many assumed Mary Firestone was a public figure and that her defamation claim would require evidence of "actual malice." Yet six justices of the Supreme Court concluded that she was not a public figure,

---

18. Gertz v. Robert Welch, Inc., 418 U.S. 323, 330 n.3 (1974). As Judge Brieant noted in Hotchner v. Castillo-Puche, 404 F. Supp. 1041 (S.D.N.Y. 1975), "[p]erhaps if attorney Gertz was not a public figure, nobody is." 404 F. Supp. at 1044.

because not all controversies of interest to the public were "public controversies" within the meaning of *Gertz*.

The plurality opinion argued that dissolution of a marriage through judicial proceedings

> is not the sort of "public controversy" referred to in *Gertz,* even though the marital difficulties of extremely wealthy individuals may be of interest to some portion of the reading public.

The Court downplayed her press conferences because they "should have had no effect upon the merits of the legal dispute" with her husband and there was "no indication that she sought to use the press conferences as a vehicle by which to thrust herself to the forefront of some unrelated controversy in order to influence its resolution."

In his dissent, Justice Marshall argued that the plurality, by making the test for public figure status be its own subjective evaluation of the importance of the "public controversy," had placed itself in the very dilemma *Gertz* sought to avoid—deciding which matters constituted a "public controversy" and which did not. The uncertainty left by *Firestone* will undoubtedly deter countless editors throughout the nation as they struggle to apply the latest interpretation of public figure or public controversy.

Both *Gertz* and *Firestone* will infringe upon the publisher's decision-making process, since a higher standard of care must be applied to private individuals. Inevitably, the names of some private individuals will be stricken from newsworthy stories, leaving the public figures and public officials as the only persons identified. Often these deletions will tend to distort the news or the role of the public persons named.

The Use of Defamation Claims to Compel Disclosure of Confidential Sources: Choice of Law and Preclusion Problems

Most publishers' counsel will acknowledge that many defamation claimants are not seeking monetary damages. Claims are typically asserted for some sort of vindication, such as retraction or the publication of an appropriate reply by the aggrieved party or his designee. Another large portion of claimants simply serve a summons and complaint (sometimes merely a summons) and leave the action unpursued so that they may say publicly that they are "suing the liars."

In recent years, however, some publishers have been confronted with the defamation suit designed to force disclosure of confidential sources. Such a suit is often brought by a public official or other person who feels damaged by leaks, or "not-for-attribution" statements made by persons with knowledge of the facts. Their objective is often neither damages nor vindication, for the underlying material may well be substantially true, but rather disclosure and punishment of the confidential source who may have performed a substantial public service at risk to his employment or career.

The First Amendment protection available to a journalist accused of defamation was thoroughly discussed in the 1958 case of *Garland v. Torre,*[19] in an opinion written by then Circuit Judge Potter Stewart. Marie Torre, a *New York Herald Tribune* correspondent, had described Judy Garland as overweight and attributed the description to an unnamed CBS executive. During discovery, defendant Torre declined to identify her source. The court decided that the reporter would have to answer if (a) the question was relevant, (b) alternative sources had been exhausted, and (c) the inquiry went to the heart of the litigation. Because the Court found that the plaintiff's questions satisfied these tests, the defendant was directed to answer, and upon her continued refusal, was jailed for contempt.

In *Carey v. Hume,*[20] the Court of Appeals for the District of Columbia required disclosure of a source used by Jack Anderson in a column which had stated that the plaintiff, an attorney, and his client, the United Mine Workers, had improperly taken records from the UMW office. The court found that the identity of the appellant's source was critical to the plaintiff's claim and compelled disclosure. A contrary conclusion by the Eighth Circuit in *Cervantes v. Time, Inc.*[21] was distinguished on the ground that in *Cervantes* the court found that there was no probability that the plaintiff would succeed in the defamation action in view of the extensive research conducted by the defendant publisher prior to the publication of the alleged defamatory material. While *Cervantes* offers comfort to a defamation defendant where the applicable standard of care has been satisfied, the Eighth Circuit unfortunately found the question of privilege to be procedural and thus declined to apply the New York "newsman's shield" statute, which had presumably been relied upon by the New York reporter who prepared the article while in New York.

The traditional law of the forum approach, when applied to defamation cases, poses the same kind of problems for the national press as those posed by the Supreme Court's abandonment of *Rosenbloom,* i.e., the claimant may choose the forum least protective of the journalist, however small the circulation in that state. Thus a private plaintiff involved in a matter of public interest might well seek to assert his claim in a state such as Kansas and presumably would avoid Indiana or Colorado. Similarly, a defamation plaintiff whose objective is the disclosure of confidential sources would make every effort to avoid instituting the action in New York where the "newsman's shield" statute is the broadest, or in any other state that has adopted a strong "newsman's shield" statute.

The choice of law alternatives was discussed recently in *Apicella v. McNeil Laboratories, Inc.,*[22] a medical malpractice action in which the plaintiff sought the sources of a medical newsletter article which had con-

19. 259 F.2d 545 (2d Cir.), *cert. denied,* 358 U.S. 910 (1958).
20. 492 F.2d 631 (D.C. Cir.), *petition for cert. dismissed,* 417 U.S. 938 (1974).
21. 464 F.2d 986 (8th Cir. 1972), *cert. denied,* 409 U.S. 1125 (1973).
22. 66 F.R.D. 78 (E.D.N.Y. 1975). *See also* Kaminsky, *State Evidentiary Privileges in Federal Civil Litigation,* 43 FORDHAM L. REV. 923 (1975).

cluded that the drug "Innovar" was extremely dangerous. The court indicated that the "center of gravity" approach for the choice of law problem was appropriate, since all the contacts in *Apicella* were in New York and the application of New York law was not contested.

Significantly, Judge Weinstein in *Apicella* decided that the First Amendment interest in protecting the source outweighed the state's interest in that information for the purposes of the malpractice litigation. In view of his decision not to compel disclosure, the judge precluded the use by either party during the course of the litigation of the entire newsletter which had been published some two years after the alleged malpractice.

A similar question of preclusion also arose in two defamation lawsuits instituted by Brooklyn's Judge Rinaldi against *The Village Voice, Inc.* and other defendants. The first suit[23] was based on an advertisement by *The Village Voice* in the *New York Times,* and the second[24] was based upon the republication of certain articles that originally appeared in *The Village Voice* by Holt, Rinehart and Winston, Inc. During the course of discovery in both proceedings, the plaintiff sought to obtain the names of the reporter's informants. The reporter refused to disclose his sources, citing the New York "newsman's shield" statute. In both actions the plaintiff moved to preclude the defendants from introducing not only the names of witnesses whose identities were kept confidential during discovery proceedings, but also any evidence obtained from informants, notwithstanding the fact that much of the material in question referred to interviews with unnamed judges, prosecutors, and lawyers critical of the plaintiff. Significantly, both motions were, in effect, denied, except that the defendant was barred from calling the unidentified confidential sources as witnesses or introducing their names at trial. Both courts explicitly declined to preclude the introduction of evidence obtained from those confidential sources.

CONCLUSION

While one is reluctant to reach dire conclusions from one or two surprising decisions, the press must recognize the unfortunate trend of increased hostility. Occasional judicial hostility to the press is apparent in related areas, such as the increasing issuance of gag orders, the rigorous enforcement of subpoenas in criminal proceedings, and even in the ever broader recognition of privacy claims. As a matter of economics, however, it is the law of defamation that is most critical to the survival of numerous newspapers and radio stations. The defamation questions of the next few years will test the very essence of the First Amendment.

23. Rinaldi v. Village Voice, Inc., No. 8824/73 (Sup. Ct., New York County, N.Y., filed April 13, 1973).
24. Rinaldi v. Holt, Rinehart and Winston, Inc., No. 12477/74 (Sup. Ct., New York County, N.Y., filed Aug. 14, 1974).

What's in a Name and Who Owns It?

DANIEL L. BRENNER

THE SCENE: a man and a woman step out of their Bill Blass-signature Continental *Mark V*, once modeled by Catherine Deneuve. He is dressed in a Johnny Carson leisure suit, Joe Namath action shirt, and Arthur Ashe shoes. His companion sparkles in gaucho pants by Pucci, halter by Gucci, lighter by Cartier, and, having forgotten to wash her hair with Farrah Fawcett shampoo, has donned an Eva Gabor wig that simply cries out for cosmetics endorsed by Polly Bergen and a fragrance from the Faberge collection sanctioned by Cary Grant.

The problem: how many exploited rights of publicity do you spot in this picture? The answer may be harder to arrive at than you think.

The right to exploit one's celebrity status is growing in importance, at least from a financial standpoint. Estimated annual royalties for licensing—the business of using famous names, titles, slogans, logos or cartoon characters to sell dolls, T-shirts, and virtually anything imprintable—are over $35 million.

The merchandising arm of MCA (television producers) expects to gross $150 million in sales of toys and games this year if their *Battlestar Galactica* program remains a public favorite. And 1977 sales of the 370 different items bearing the googly-shaped signature of Pierre Cardin—a celebrity who started as a designer— reached $250 million in 60 nations, including the Soviet Union.

Today, no motion picture of "blockbuster" status is released without due consideration of its merchandising rights, from belt buckles to cereal-box premiums. *Superman, Star Wars* and the "new" musical motion pictures like *Saturday Night Fever* and *Grease* may tell more memorable (financial) stories off the screen than on, as the movies become launching pads for the real monetary action behind a film project: tie-in sales of records, posters, clothes and gimcracks of every conceivable stripe.

The reasons for heightened interest in publicity rights are varied. It stems in part from the public's desire for tangible mementos of intangible experiences: an individual's adulation of a star memorialized in a statuette, button, or pennant. And then there is the "I was there" syndrome. Because most people miss out on many celebrated events— whether one's tastes lean to Woodstock, the arrival of the Bicentennial Tall Ships in New York Harbor or the launching of Apollo 11—a good part of our lives seems to be spent on documenting participation in more convenient, if less significant, social moments: T-shirts to memorialize a Led Zeppelin concert; bumper stickers noting a visit to the Movieland

Wax Museum or "The Thing?" (Tucson, Ariz.); limited edition medallions of celebrated and uncelebrated inaugurals, pageants and parades.

Celebrities have responded to these merchandising opportunities by carefully selecting among various options, a process made all the more urgent by the fleeting quality of fame. The need for quick, effective, and extensive merchandising of celebrity status can be explained by Andy Warhol's apt prediction that someday everyone in the world will be famous for exactly fifteen minutes. To put it another way, what *do* you do with one million unsold David Cassidy T-shirts?

Whatever the causes of the increasing interest in the right of publicity, its legal significance remains an enigma. Decisions spawned by conflicting attempts to exploit this right have been issuing from state and federal courts in recent years, leaving the meaning of the right of publicity in some confusion.

This confusion owes its origins in part to the evolution of the "right of publicity" from the "right of privacy"—legal doctrine first articulated in an 1890 *Harvard Law Review* article co-authored by Louis Brandeis. The privacy doctrine allows individuals "to be let alone." Although the right of privacy was initially directed to the kind of harm to one's reputation that could be inflicted by newspaper gossips, it has been extended to protection against appropriation of the value of one's name and likeness. Indeed, Dean Prosser's celebrated torts treatise includes that protection as part of the privacy right.

Dean Prosser was right as far as he went, but he assumed that the plaintiff would not be a celebrity, and would eschew publicity as a general course, or at least as to that part of his life that the defendant had made public. In most right-of-publicity cases today, however, the plaintiff does not object to exposure. To the contrary, exposure fuels his career and celebrity status. What he objects to is public exposure for which he was not paid, or tasteless exposure that could injure his public image.

Nonetheless, the notion of a legal wrong inherent in the right of publicity owes its philosophical origins to the right of privacy, "the right to be let alone,"—long enough, anyway, for the plaintiff to exploit for himself the value of his personality.

It is important to bear in mind that once the publicity (whether in the form of licensed merchandise or a caricature of the celebrity used for a cartoon series) is conceded to be desirable provided the price is right, the character of the legal issues changes. The interest to be protected is no longer freedom from intrusion upon the personal space of a private plaintiff. Instead, the concern is with grabbing back the proceeds of the unauthorized exploitation of one's celebrity status. In this sense, the right of publicity protects a proprietary interest of the individual, or, put more directly, a property right.

But what property right? Consider the plight of the high-flying plaintiff in *Zacchini v. Scripps-Howard Broadcasting Co.* In that 1976 opinion, rejecting a defense under the First Amendment, the United States

Supreme Court allowed Hugo Zacchini to recover under a state-created right of publicity when his 15-second "human cannonball" act was photographed in its entirety (over his objection) by a television station.

Or consider *Haelan Laboratories, Inc. v. Topps Chewing Gum, Inc.*, the 1953 case in which Judge Jerome Frank judicially coined the term "right of publicity." There, Haelan Labs had acquired, from over 500 leading baseball players of the day, the exclusive right to use their photos to produce chewing gum trading cards. Apparently, some players had thereafter granted the same right to Topps Chewing Gum. Topps contended that there was no legal interest in publication of the players' pictures that was separate and distinct from their non-assignable right of privacy. The court found otherwise.

PROPERTY IS THAT WHICH ONE CAN SELL

And then there was Cary Grant's suit against *Esquire* magazine. *Esquire* republished his picture (from one of their 1946 fashion spreads) in a 1971 photo article that superimposed (over everything below his collar line) a model clothed in an Orlon double-knit navy, rust and buff sweatercoat. Grant claimed, and the court agreed, that he was entitled to recover to prevent and deter *Esquire* from securing the monetary benefits of this sort of publicity, which Grant found offensive.

These cases present us with a mishmash of legal interests, but it seems not wholly inappropriate to call them property rights. After all, in each instance the plaintiff could have sold the appropriated rights for a fixed sum, and under our legal system we tend to call that which one can sell (or prevent others from selling), "property."

There are trade-off qualities to the right of publicity. For instance, on talk shows, authors or actors are not usually paid much for appearing. No matter; free publicity acquired through the appearance is payment enough for most guests.

But there are other rights of this sort for which the property label seems odd. Consider, for example, payment for the right to interview a political figure with an important story to tell—the much-criticized practice of "checkbook journalism." (Television interviews of Nixon and Haldeman were in this category.) And what of books containing the personal accounts of Patty Hearst's jailhouse matron or the reminiscences of a U.S. Senate doorkeeper? In such circumstances, the courts may be reluctant to grant an exclusive right to tell the story, in part because it is or ought to be in the public domain.

Then, too, if publicity is such a valuable property right, why do many people give it away for nothing? Winners of million-dollar state lotteries become instant celebrities, yet they can be found handing out free interviews, interviews that might fetch a good price if put on the open market. So, too, do those who witness falling comets and factory explosions. And (putting aside the morbidness of such a thought) imagine the value of the first interview with someone released from a tense plane-hijacking or the lone survivor of a train crash.

Such individuals have risen for a moment by dint of circumstances to the heights of celebritydom. If the use of their "personas" had no value a week before, it does now. And if such an easy come-easy go approach to the right of publicity seems appropriate, does it not also suggest that "property" is too unrefined a label for this fleeting status?

One reason for remaining hesitant to accord a well-defined property status to the right of publicity stems from the conflict between that right and the interest in free dissemination of information embodied in the First Amendment. The contributions to society made by news journalists would be jeopardized if every newsworthy action by the rich or powerful were reduced to an information bit, publishable only upon payment for its use and in any event totally under the newsmaker's control. Less Olympian in stature, if nonetheless better circulated, are the hundreds of stories turned out about the famous that would be less accessible if disclosure carried a price tag.

Perhaps this is why courts have recognized the legality of nonconsensual use of a celebrity's name and likeness in written or film biographies, even when the profit motive for such information dissemination is transparent and the subject of the biography contributes little to the advancement of civilization. In *Maritote v. DesiLu Productions, Inc.* (1964), for example, the son and widow of Al Capone were denied recovery for pain and suffering caused by the defendant's film about Capone, which they claimed invaded the deceased's right of privacy.

Then, too, in *James v. Screen Gems, Inc.,* the widow of Jesse James Jr. was denied recovery on an invasion-of-privacy claim arising from the defendant's motion picture. The great-grandchildren of composer Robert Schumann recovered nothing in a 1954 action for what they contended to be a taking of a descendible property right by the defendant, Loews, Inc., in producing a film depicting his life. And [in 1978], the heirs of Agatha Christie were denied recovery against the distributors of a novel and film based on a true incident in Mrs. Christie's life, an 11-day disappearance in 1926 that was never explained by Mrs. Christie.

ONE CANNOT DEFAME THE DEAD

Ironically, whether the right of publicity is closer to a privacy or a property interest sometimes becomes a live question only after the holder of the right has died. Logic says that if the right is more akin to the right "to be let alone," then it should expire at the same time its celebrity holder does. The law is clear that one cannot defame those who are deceased, and by analogy, publicizing the doings (presumably past) of deceased celebrities cannot be assumed to interfere with a now-extinct privacy right.

Extinguishing the right of publicity simultaneously with its holder's life is consistent with the view of those states that analyze the issue in terms of the doctrine of misappropriation (i.e., the wrongful taking of an intangible business asset such as a name like Colonel Sanders or an architectural style like the Golden Arches). If an intangible asset not otherwise protected has no value once a business is kaput—so that, for example, accidentally using a business's name does not amount to deliberately trading off that name—then the publicity asset of every individual ought to disappear upon death.

The trend, however, at least when the right of publicity takes tangible shape in statuettes or posters, has been in the direction of labeling publicity an inheritable property right.

Consider these recent cases:

• In *Factors, Etc., Inc. v. Creative Card Co.* (1977), a New York federal district court was presented with the first of what doubtless promises to be the continuing story of the merchandising of the late Elvis Presley. Presley had assigned his merchandising rights to a corporation called Boxcar Enterprises, Inc., of which he was the principal stockholder. The plaintiff Factors, Etc., Inc. and Boxcar entered into an agreement two days after Presley's demise that assigned Factors the exclusive right to use the singer's likeness in connection with all souvenir merchandise.

Meanwhile, the defendant had begun to sell Presley posters. The court granted plaintiff's motion for injunction, finding that a "right of publicity" inhered in Elvis during his lifetime, that he had exploited and had properly assigned it to Boxcar, that the right survived his death, and finally that Boxcar could assign that right.

• Another 1977 Presley case, *Memphis Development Foundation v. Factors, Etc., Inc.* before a Tennessee federal district court, involved a "not-for-profit" corporation that had promoted a statue of the King to be cast in bronze and erected in Presley's home city, Memphis (albeit without the approval of Memphis officials). To finance the $200,000 monument, the corporation announced its intention to give 8-inch pewter replicas of the statue to contributors of $25 and up. Not a bad idea, except these tokens of thanks would have directly competed with pewter statuettes of Elvis that had been expressly approved by Presley's friend and manager, "Colonel" Tom Parker, and the late singer's father.

Noting that Presley had exploited his right of publicity during his lifetime, the court said that the right to be the exclusive purveyor of Presley pewter statuettes was protected under Tennessee law and could be inherited by Elvis' heirs and assigns, and therefore enjoined the corporation from distributing the replicas.

• In *Price v. Hal Roach Studios, Inc.* (1975), the widows of Stan Laurel and Oliver Hardy and a corporation to which Hardy's widow and Laurel had granted an exclusive right to exploit the actors' names and likenesses sued the producer of the comedians' films for assigning these rights. A New York federal district court found for the plaintiffs, concluding that their assigned interests survived Laurel's and Hardy's deaths.

ACTORS'S RIGHTS NOT SERVED BY DESCENT

Finally, the surviving son and widow of Bela Lugosi sued Universal Pictures for appropriating the commercial image created by their father and husband in his role as Count Dracula. They alleged that they had inherited an exclusive right to exploit the Lugosi version of the vampire, and that Universal's issuance of licenses to produce merchandise containing Lugosi's Dracula infringed that inherited right.

The trial court held that Lugosi's right of publicity was descendible, but [the California Supreme Court] reversed on the ground that Lugosi had never personally exercised his right to exploit the commercial value of his likeness as the blood Count. Holding that the right of publicity was a form of privacy rather than a property right, the court concluded that "neither society's interest in the free dissemination of ideas nor the artist's rights to the fruits of his own labor would be served" by descent.

The foregoing distinctions may lead some to want to drive wooden stakes through their hearts. In essence, the divergence in these cases amounts to nothing more than a restatement of the question: privacy right or property right? As we have seen, the right of publicity is in many ways a mixture of the two.

Perhaps a useful way to arrive at a fixed meaning of, and a permissible duration for, the right of publicity is to step back from the privacy/property rhubarb for a moment and look at the right of publicity from the perspective of copyright law.

A copyright grants a monopoly to its holder to copy (and make other uses) of original expression that has been fixed in tangible form. The purpose of federal copyright protection is to furnish a competitive spur to inventive expression. As the Supreme Court noted in 1954 in *Mazer v. Stein*: "Sacrificial days devoted to such creative activities deserve rewards commensurate with the services rendered." The Copyright Revision Act of 1976 grants a broad federal right to authors, extending usually for the life of the creator plus 50 years.

What differentiates the right of publicity from copyright is that the celebrity does not create anything tangible; the "creation" is the personal style, the personas of the individual. Nevertheless, there is a basic creative similarity. Just as originality is the touchstone of copyright, so, too, is it the prerequisite to creation of a valuable right of publicity.

We may snicker at the origins of fame. After all, a right of publicity awards its holder just for being famous, whether because he won the Olympic decathlon (one mouthful of Wheaties at a time, to be sure) or possesses a head of hair (and a role on *Charlie's Angels*) that can be parlayed into the coiffure of the decade. Still, becoming famous *is* a talent that society chooses to reward. And that talent virtually always draws upon human inventiveness.

By comparison, copyright law has been known to grant its share of protection to objects of dubious value. As Justice Douglas noted in *Mazer v. Stein,* copyrighted works have included door knockers, piggy banks, salt and pepper shakers, fish bowls, casseroles and ash trays; indeed, *Mazer* held that "statuettes of male and female dancing figures made of semivitreous china" used in table lamps were works of art, protected under the copyright laws.

Still, it may be argued that the originality inherent in a copyrighted work is vastly different from the originality involved in creating a right of publicity. The invention of a copyrighted work steps from a conscious undertaking by the creator; by contrast, the holder of a publicity right may be benefitting from wholly fortuitous circumstances, not owing to any conscious activity. While this is not a frivolous objection, the breadth of a protected publicity right can surely be determined by the facts of each case. For instance, a teller photographed by a security camera during a bank heist could not expect much protection should the photograph later become a cult piece. On the other hand, a rock music group that had cultivated a particular pose as part of its act would be protected against T-shirt piracy of that depiction. In short, just as "copying" in copyright depends on the specific facts of the alleged infringement, so too, should interference with the publicity right be judged both by the extent of appropriation and the creative contribution made to the appropriated property. Allowances for "fair use" would be more freely granted in a right-of-publicity case. But a core of protected property would remain.

IS THE RIGHT OF PUBLICITY ASSIGNABLE?

It seems reasonable to consider the right of publicity as an interest much like a copyright but which, because it inheres in the being of the creator and not a fixed form, does not come under that legal doctrine. The right of publicity would protect the assignable interest in authorizing the manufacture of tangible goods in one's name and likeness and in granting product endorsements. Of course, once exploitation of the right of publicity produces a tangible object, that object would be protected by copyright or perhaps trademark law, depending on the character of the materialization.

Comparing the right of publicity to copyright points up two considerations. First, states would thus be free to create a right of publicity without upsetting the federal scheme of copyright, either by statute or through a judicially-interpreted common law right, as the Tennessee court did in the Elvis case.

Second, since the right of publicity operates as a spur to development of original personas and creation of extraordinary public personalities, we can use copyright law to fix the duration of the publicity right. Accordingly, while it has no place under copyright, the right of publicity could borrow the duration standard of copyright—the celebrity's life plus 50 years—as a standard measure of the extent of the right. Doing so would provide uniformity to rights that, while not identical, are akin, because society generally wishes to encourage creativity, in tangible form or as intangible personas. [This was the approach of the dissent in the *Lugosi* case. (Ed.)]

This is not to suggest that all questions regarding the right of publicity will be answered by reference to copyright principles. For instance, will impersonators of rock musicians be liable to the original performers (or, as in the case of Elvis impersonators, their heirs) under the right of publicity? How about impressionists or look-alikes who may wind up to be as popular as the originals? Then, too, what about artists who create paintings or sculptures of famous people? While the one-of-a-kind work of art may be considered a fair use, what do we do about copies of the original work, especially if they compete with "less" artistic statues or posters produced by the celebrity?

The existence of these unanswered questions should not undermine the basic point that the right of publicity is entitled to protection in the course of its orderly exploitation and should be descendible for a period of time. Invoking the principle of fair use from the copyright context will help courts to shape the contours of the right to accord with the significance of, or the sweat involved in generating, the public personas. By limiting descendibility to the standard used by copyright law, we can be fairly sure that history will not become the subdivided satrapy of descendants of once-famous people.

Doubtless, critics of a right of publicity will contend that comparison to copyright law greatly trivializes the latter, while exalting the somewhat dubious distinction of being a celebrity to ridiculous heights. Yet, for better or for worse, we are a nation of *People* and *US,* the *National Enquirer* and *Midnight*—a society that wants and needs celebrities. It seems fair to allow those who play the game whose name is fame to collect their financial rewards when they finally win. After all, isn't the right answer to the question "would you rather be rich or famous" simple? "Both."

Copyright Infringement and the First Amendment

CELIA GOLDWAG

THE COPYRIGHT ACT[1] seeks to "promote the Progress of Science and useful Arts"[2] by encouraging the creation and dissemination of ideas and information to the public. This encouragement takes the form of an economic incentive: on the premise that individuals will not produce

From *Columbia Law Review* 79 (1979):273–83.
1. 17 U.S.C. §§ 101–108 (1976).
2. U.S. CONST. art. I, § 8, cl. 8.

creative works without some prospect of pecuniary reward, the Act offers authors exclusive rights in their works.[3] Because the ultimate purpose of copyright is to advance the public welfare, the copyright privilege is limited in several important respects. Even so limited, however, copyright protection results in a partial monopoly over expression, and to the extent that it does, it conflicts with the first amendment interest in free speech. Whether this conflict can ever result in an unconstitutional abridgement of first amendment rights[4] is a question which has received considerable attention from courts and commentators in recent years.

This Note first discusses those limitations on the copyright monopoly that ameliorate much of the potential conflict with the first amendment. It then identifies one narrow situation in which the Copyright Act may clash with the first amendment. Finally, it considers whether the first amendment requires that a privilege to copyright infringement be established.

I.

The premise that copyright protection is justified only to the extent that it advances the public welfare has given rise to four major qualifications on the copyright holder's privilege. Two of these qualifications, limited duration and the authorship requirement, are important in a negative sense—their absence would pose a significant threat to speech interests. The two other limitations—the distinction drawn between ideas and the expression of ideas, and the fair use defense—play a more active role in the operation of the copyright system. As a result, these two

---

3. 17 U.S.C. § 106 (1976) grants exclusive rights in copyrighted works as follows:
> Subject to sections 107 through 118, the owner of copyright under this title has the exclusive rights to do and to authorize any of the following:
> (1) to reproduce the copyrighted work in copies or phonorecords;
> (2) to prepare derivative works based upon the copyrighted work;
> (3) to distribute copies or phonorecords of the copyrighted work to the public by sale or other transfer of ownership, or by rental, lease, or lending;
> (4) in the case of literary, musical, dramatic, and choreographic works, pantomimes, and motion pictures and other audiovisual works, to perform the copyrighted work publicly; and
> (5) in the case of literary, musical, dramatic, and choreographic works, pantomimes, and pictorial, graphic, or sculptural works, including the individual images of a motion picture or other audiovisual work, to display the copyrighted work publicly.

It is important to recognize that copyright only protects the copyright holder against unauthorized *copying*. Thus, there would be no copyright infringement if an author were independently to produce a work identical to a prior, copyrighted work. Similarly, unauthorized *use* of a copyrighted work does not constitute copyright infringement.

4. If copyright does abridge the first amendment, then it should be held unconstitutional, even though both appear in the Constitution. . . . Since the Constitution's guarantee of free speech is contained in an amendment, it supersedes any prior inconsistent material. Moreover, a constitutional grant of authority to Congress does not give Congress the right to act in a manner inconsistent with other provisions of the Constitution. *See* 1 M. NIMMER, COPYRIGHT § 1.10 [A] (1978). Of course, the longstanding nature of copyright is not a basis for refusing to hold it unconstitutional. . . . However, it should be noted that the first Copyright Act and the first amendment are roughly contemporaneous, thus indicating that the framers did not perceive any conflict between the two. . . .

limitations have the effect of accommodating most of the potential for conflict between copyright and the first amendment. The balance of this section examines the scope and effect of these four qualifications.

A copyright lasts for the author's life plus fifty years;[5] once this period has expired, the work falls into the public domain and may be freely copied. The duration limitation is closely tied to the goal of copyright, for the incentive that copyright provides necessarily diminishes over time. The duration limitation also serves first amendment values. Since the speech interest in an author's work can grow, a copyright which lasted for an unreasonable period of time would abridge first amendment interests without providing a corresponding incentive to the author. The current copyright period is so long, however, that the duration limitation is not an especially potent device for accommodating first amendment interests.

Copyright is further limited to authors. To qualify as an author, the applicant must show that he is the creator of an original work.[6] This qualification is also essential to the goal of copyright, since the development of science and the arts would be inhibited if phrases in ordinary usage could be copyrighted. However, the standard of originality is minimal, requiring independent creation rather than novelty. Consequently, the authorship requirement does not significantly restrict what can be copyrighted and is therefore not a major avenue for accommodating speech interests with copyright.

The distinction that copyright draws between ideas and the expression of ideas is a more useful device for accommodating first amendment interests. A basic premise of copyright is that only the expressions of ideas are copyrightable; the ideas themselves, however original, remain in the public domain.[7] Thus, any number of copyrights may be obtained for material that expresses the same idea, as long as each piece qualifies as an original work.

Although the notion that ideas are uncopyrightable is an old one, courts have found it difficult to articulate a formula for distinguishing between ideas and expressions. The most famous attempt is Learned Hand's abstractions test:

> Upon any work . . . a great number of patterns of increasing generality will fit equally well, as more and more of the incident is left out. The last may perhaps be no more than the most general statement of what the [work] is about, and at times might consist only of its title; but there is a point in this series of abstractions where they

---

5. 17 U.S.C. § 302 (1976) establishes the basic copyright term which begins at the creation of the work and subsists for author's life plus fifty years. In the case of anonymous works, pseudonymous works, and works made for hire, the term is 75 years from publication or 100 years from creation, whichever is shorter.

6. 17 U.S.C. § 102 (1976) ("Copyright protection subsists . . . in original works of authorship fixed in any tangible medium of expression. . . .").

7. 17 U.S.C. § 102(b) (1976) provides that: "In no case does copyright protection for an original work of authorship extend to any idea, procedure, process, system, method of operation, concept, principle, or discovery, regardless of the form in which it is described, explained, illustrated, or embodied in such work."

are no longer protected, since otherwise the [author] could prevent the use of his "ideas," to which, apart from their expression, his property is never extended.[8]

While Hand's test is a useful conceptual framework, it does not indicate where, in a series of abstractions, the line should be drawn between idea and expression.[9] Indeed, Hand eventually abandoned the abstractions test for this reason, stating that since there could be no rule for when an imitator has appropriated expression as well as ideas, decisions must "inevitably be *ad hoc*."[10] The difficulty courts have experienced in formulating a precise rule, however, does not undercut the validity of the distinction. The question is essentially one of fact, and courts have been able to apply the distinction on a case-by-case basis.[11]

Despite its difficulty of application, the idea-expression distinction is nevertheless an important device for accommodating speech interests. While there is clearly a first amendment interest in ideas, there does not appear to be a strong first amendment interest in expressions. Viewed most broadly, the first amendment's guarantee is an end in itself—essential to individual dignity and self-fulfillment. Others have attributed a narrower purpose to the first amendment, valuing free speech as necessary to a system of democratic government.[12] Under either view,

---

8. Nichols v. Universal Pictures Corp., 45 F.2d 119, 121 (2d Cir. 1930). In *Nichols,* the author of the play "Abie's Irish Rose" brought an action for copyright infringement against the producer of a motion picture entitled "The Cohens and the Kellys." Both stories involved an acrimonious relationship between an Irish father and a Jewish father and the complications which ensued when their children secretly married. The primary issue was whether defendant's film appropriated plaintiff's expressions, or merely her ideas. The court held that defendant took only plaintiff's theme, a "generalized . . . abstraction from what she wrote," and hence had not infringed plaintiff's copyright.

9. Many courts and commentators have attempted to refine further the distinction between ideas and expressions. Of these, Professor Chafee's "pattern test" has been most widely cited. Using the facts of the *Nichols* case as an illustration, *see* note [8] *supra,* he delineated copyright protection as covering the "pattern" of the work. Thus, when the idea of an Irish-Jewish marriage is borrowed, some similarity in characters and events is inevitable and hence does not constitute copyright infringement. However, the second author may not appropriate the pattern of the play, *i.e.,* "the sequence of events and the development of the interplay of the characters," without infringing the first author's copyright, even if every word of the dialogue is changed. Chafee, *Reflections on the Law of Copyright* (pt. 1), 45 COLUM. L. REV. 503, 513–14 (1945).

A corollary of the pattern test is Judge Yankwich's concept of "scènes à faire." When an author deals with a general, non-copyrightable theme that calls for "certain sequences in the methods of treatment, which cannot be avoided . . . because they are . . . in the very nature of the development of the theme," these scenes are "scènes à faire" and are therefore not copyrightable. *See* Schwarz v. Universal Pictures Co., 85 F. Supp. 270, 276–76 (S.D. Cal. 1945).

10. Peter Pan Fabrics, Inc. v. Martin Weiner Corp. 274 F.2d 487, 489 (2d Cir. 1960).

11. *See, e.g.,* Herbert Rosenthal Jewelry Corp. v. Honora Jewelry Co., 378 F. Supp. 485 (S.D.N.Y.), *aff'd,* 509 F.2d 64 (2d Cir. 1974), which involved two gold pins shaped like turtles. Since the similarities between the pins arose because both copied nature, there could be no copyright infringement. The plaintiff could not, by copyrighting a pin in the shape of a turtle, preclude others from manufacturing jewelry shaped like turtles.

12. Alexander Meiklejohn was the leading exponent of this position. Meiklejohn viewed the first amendment as an essential of self-government under a democratic system. Accordingly, he would have allowed an absolute right to speak on matters of public interest but would not have recognized first amendment protection for private speech. *See* A. MEIKLEJOHN, FREE SPEECH AND ITS RELATION TO SELF-GOVERNMENT (1972).

however, the first amendment is satisfied by access to ideas. One who appropriates the expression of another is not engaging in self-fulfillment; rather, he is appropriating another's labor without exerting any effort. There is no first amendment value in this sort of expression. Similarly, the "unfettered interchange of ideas for . . . bringing about . . . political and social changes desired by the people"[13] does not require access to expression. Thus, the idea-expression distinction is a demarcation between the first amendment and copyright: the first amendment protects the dissemination of ideas, which are not copyrightable, and copyright protects expression, in which there is generally not a strong first amendment interest.

Several courts have used the idea-expression distinction to deny first amendment claims, reasoning that an infringer's speech interests are not impaired as long as he is free to draw upon the ideas contained in the copyrighted work. For example, in *Sid & Marty Krofft Television Productions, Inc. v. McDonald's Corp.*,[14] defendants argued that the first amendment privileged their unauthorized use of plaintiff's characters in their "McDonaldland" advertising campaign. The Ninth Circuit rejected defendants' claim, finding that "the defendants . . . had many ways to express the idea of a fantasyland with characters, but chose to copy the expression of plaintiffs'. The first amendment will not protect such imitation." Similarly, in *Wainwright Securities Inc. v. Wall Street Transcript Corp.*,[15] a newspaper sued for publishing abstracts of plaintiff's copyrighted financial reports argued that the publication was privileged as an exercise of freedom of the press. The Second Circuit rejected defendant's claim, noting that while a news event is an idea, and thus not copyrightable, the particular arrangement of words used to describe that event can be copyrighted. The court found that defendant had not made a legitimate attempt to report a news event, but had instead copied the form of expression used by the plaintiff. Thus, defendant's first amendment interests were not damaged as it was still free to report the event itself.

There are, however, situations in which an individual cannot express himself fully without access to another's expression. A critic or reviewer, for example, would often have difficulty writing pungent and effective analysis without abstracting some material from his subject's work.[16] Similarly, a teacher or researcher might find it necessary to copy portions of copyrighted material. The first amendment might well be abridged if

---

13. New York Times Co. v. Sullivan, 376 U.S. 254, 269 (1964) (citing Roth v. United States, 354 U.S. 476, 484 (1954)).
14. 562 F.2d 1157, 1169–71 (9th Cir. 1977).
15. 558 F.2d 91 (2d Cir. 1977), *cert. denied,* 434 U.S. 1014 (1978).
16. The privilege of "fair quotation," *i.e.,* the unauthorized use of copyrighted material by a reviewer, is the oldest form of fair use. *See, e.g.,* Folsom v. Marsh, 9 F. Cas. 342, 344 (C.C.D. Mass. 1841) (No. 4,901) ("no one can doubt that a reviewer may fairly cite largely from the original work, if his design be really and truly to use the passages for the purpose of fair and reasonable criticism").

the Copyright Act denied the public this sort of access to copyrighted works.

The fair use defense, which comprises a final limitation on the copyright holder's monopoly, avoids this potential problem. Although courts have long recognized the need for a fair use exemption, determining what constitutes fair use has been a troublesome question. The 1976 Act, which contains the first statutory recognition of fair use, directs courts to consider four factors: (1) the purpose and character of the use; (2) the nature of the copyrighted work; (3) the amount and substantiality of the use in relation to the copyrighted work as a whole; and (4) the effect of the use upon the potential market for or value of the copyrighted work.[17] While the statute does not specify how much weight should be accorded to each of these factors, the Senate and House reports state that the statutory formulation was intended simply as a restatement of the judicial doctrine of fair use. Since the case law placed heaviest stress on the effect that the unauthorized use could have on the demand for the copyrighted work, the fourth factor should still be decisive of the fair use issue. Thus, a court should consider the remaining three factors only after it has concluded that the unauthorized use cannot affect the market value of the copyrighted work by serving as a substitute for it.

Several courts have relied upon fair use to avoid otherwise difficult first amendment problems. Indeed, the only case to date in which a court has expressly held that a copyright claim was defeated by a first amendment defense—*Triangle Publications, Inc. v. Knight-Ridder Newspapers, Inc.*[18]—could have been resolved on the basis of fair use.

Defendant in *Triangle* was a newspaper publisher who had developed a television booklet similar to plaintiff's *TV Guide.* In one advertisement for the new booklet, an actor holding a copy of *TV Guide*[19] stressed that a purchaser of defendant's booklet would receive a newspaper as well as a listing of television programs. The *Triangle* court first stated that where the first amendment and copyright conflict, the first amendment must prevail. The court found that defendant's interest in being able to speak freely and the public's interest in being informed about new products outweighed the plaintiff's copyright interest, and thus rejected plaintiff's claim. The court concluded its analysis by observing that its refusal to grant an injunction would not impair the goals of copyright since it would not inhibit the independent creation of products.

The *Triangle* case should not be viewed as establishing a first amendment privilege to copyright infringement, as it could have been resolved under the Copyright Act itself. The use in question was at most an "incidental one," and hence encompassed within the fair use doctrine. The fact that the parties were in competition with each other is irrelevant, since the use of the magazine cover—even if it were plaintiff's entire

---

17. 17 U.S.C. § 107 (1976).
18. 445 F. Supp. 875 (S.D. Fla. 1978).
19. Magazine covers are copyrightable. Conde Nast Publications v. Vogue School of Fashion Modelling, 105 F. Supp. 325, 332 (S.D.N.Y. 1952).

work—could not serve as a substitute for plaintiff's product. Thus, there was no economic detriment to the plaintiff, and defendant's fair use defense should have prevailed.[20]

Although a first amendment claim was not made in *Berlin v. E. C. Publications, Inc.,*[21] it illustrates how fair use can accommodate first amendment interests. In *Berlin,* the owners of the copyrights to a number of popular songs challenged their use in a *Mad* magazine parody. *Mad* used neither the lyrics nor the music of the copyrighted songs but only their meter and the notation "sung to the tune of . . ." Plaintiff was unable to show economic injury, and the court found that the *Mad* parody neither would, not was intended to, satisfy the demand for the original songs. Therefore, the court accepted defendant's fair use defense and refused to find infringement. *Berlin* avoided a potentially difficult first amendment issue, for as the court observed, parody is among the "independent forms of creative effort possessing distinctive literary qualities worthy of judicial protection in the public interest." Thus, as *Berlin* illustrates, by allowing the unauthorized use of copyrighted materials where a first amendment right might otherwise be claimed, fair use is a significant device for mediating conflicts between copyright and the first amendment.

The four limitations on the copyright holder's monopoly—duration, authorship, the idea-expression distinction, and fair use—effectively accommodate many first amendment claims that might otherwise arise in actions for copyright infringement. Most importantly, the idea-expression distinction will often justify a finding of infringement when an infringer's first amendment rights are not damaged, and the fair use doctrine will often sanction an unauthorized use when a first amendment right might otherwise be claimed. However, when the idea-expression distinction is not applicable because the idea sought to be expressed is "wedded" to the copyright holder's expression of it (as in the case of a graphic work), and unauthorized use cannot be sanctioned as fair use because of damage to the copyright holder's economic interests, there is a narrow, but nevertheless real conflict between copyright and the first amendment that cannot be resolved by the internal structure of the Copyright Act. The following section of the Note considers how various courts and commentators have treated this tension between the first amendment and copyright.

II.

Any analysis of the tension between the first amendment and copyright must begin with *Rosemont Enterprises, Inc. v. Random House, Inc.*[22] *Rosemont* involved a series of *Look* magazine articles entitled "The

20. Alternatively, *Triangle* might have been treated under the rubric of comparative advertising and unfair competition.
21. 329 F.2d 541 (2d Cir.), *cert. denied,* 379 U.S. 822 (1964).
22. 366 F.2d 303 (2d Cir. 1966), *cert. denied,* 385 U.S. 1009 (1967).

Howard Hughes Story." When Hughes learned that defendant Random House intended to publish a biography of Hughes that drew heavily on the *Look* articles, he had Rosemont purchase *Look*'s copyrights to the articles. Rosemont then sued to enjoin publication of the biography on the basis of copyright infringement. Defendants argued that its use of the copyrighted material was privileged under the fair use doctrine.

The court weighed three factors in considering the merits of defendants' fair use defense. It found the public's interest in free dissemination of information about Hughes to be significant, noting that an injunction would deprive the public of "an opportunity to become acquainted with the life of a person endowed with extraordinary talents who . . . made substantial contribution in the fields to which he chose to devote his unique abilities." Next, the court found that the *Look* articles were necessary to defendants' book. Finally, the court assessed plaintiff's economic injury and concluded that it was minimal. Rosemont did not claim to be receiving royalties on the *Look* articles and its own plans for publishing a biography of Hughes were deemed "speculative." The court also argued that the *Look* articles and defendants' biography were not in competition with each other. Accordingly, the court found defendants' use a fair one, and declined to enjoin publication of the biography.

Damage to the plaintiff's economic interests should have precluded a finding of fair use in *Rosemont*,[23] since the market value of the *Look* articles was clearly diminished by the publication of the Random House biography. Although a fair use defense should not have been available in *Rosemont*, however, the case did not present a real conflict between copyright and the first amendment. Since the facts of Hughes's life were in the public domain, the court's belief that defendants could not have expressed themselves without appropriating plaintiff's expression of those facts was clearly unfounded. Viewed in light of the idea-expression distinction, a finding of infringement in *Rosemont* would have been constitutional.

Time, Inc. v. Bernard Geis Associates[24] subsequently applied the *Rosemont* approach to a slightly different set of facts. *Geis* involved the Zapruder film, generally considered to be the best filmed record of President Kennedy's assassination, which *Time* had purchased and copyrighted. Several years after the assassination defendants published *Six Seconds in Dallas*, a serious examination of the Warren Commission's investigation into the assassination. Because the Warren Commission had relied heavily on the Zapruder film, defendants, after an unsuccessful attempt to secure plaintiff's consent, included several sketches of key frames in the book. Defendants conceded that these sketches were direct copies. Representing that it had further plans for the film which had been harmed by defendants' unauthorized use, plaintiff sought damages for copyright infringement.

---

23. Commentators have extensively criticized the *Rosemont* decision for this reason.
24. 293 F. Supp. 130 (S.D.N.Y. 1968).

The court first determined that the film was a sufficiently creative expression of a news event to be copyrightable, and that Time therefore held a valid copyright. Turning to the fair use defense, the court laid particular stress on society's interest in defendants' book and in the events it discussed. The court noted that although the Zapruder film was not absolutely essential to defendants' work, it was very important to the clarity of their presentation and the force of their thesis. When measured against the public's interest and the defendants' need, the court did not perceive the plaintiff's interest to be especially compelling. The parties were not in competition; therefore, defendants' use could not affect the demand for plaintiff's magazine. In addition, the damage to plaintiff's future plans for the film was deemed speculative. The court concluded that "[i]t seems more reasonable to speculate that the Book would, if anything, enhance the value of the copyrighted work; it is difficult to see any decrease in its value." Accordingly the court, citing *Rosemont,* found defendants' unauthorized use privileged as fair use.

Although the *Geis* court minimized the extent to which defendants' unauthorized use damaged the plaintiff, it is clear that defendants' book would lessen the market value of the Zapruder film since potential users of the film could refer to *Six Seconds in Dallas* instead of a *Time* publication. Nevertheless, first amendment interests were implicated in *Geis:* as in *Rosemont,* fair use was inapplicable, but in contrast to *Rosemont,* the idea sought to be expressed in *Geis* could not be divorced from the author's expression of it. Although it would have been theoretically possible for defendant to have described key frames of the film, in practice, such an approach would have merely been awkward and unsatisfactory. Since *Geis* involved speech interests which could not be accommodated by the Copyright Act itself, the court's refusal to find infringement, when infringement should have been found under traditional doctrine, can most logically be explained as based on an implicit first amendment privilege to copyright infringement.

Commentators have read *Rosemont* and *Geis* as establishing a public interest-based first amendment privilege to copyright infringement. Most have suggested that *Rosemont* and *Geis* illustrate the need for some such privilege. Drawing upon *Geis,* Professor Nimmer has concluded that the problem of the idea "wedded" to its expression will generally occur in graphic works. Therefore, he reasons that a first amendment privilege ought to be recognized for graphic works which are imbued with the public interest, most typically news photographs.[25] Nimmer suggests that a scheme of compulsory licensing, akin to that used for phonorecords, be adopted. However, if there is a need for a first amendment privilege to copyright infringement, Nimmer's proposal is clearly insufficient. An idea need not be expressed in a graphic work to be inseparable from its expression. Contemporary historical documents, such as letters, may be

25. M. NIMMER, *supra* note [4], § 1.10[C][2]. According to Professor Nimmer, the test of public interest is that the event depicted, rather than the fact that the photograph was made, be a topic in newspapers throughout the country.

characterized as ideas wedded to their expression, especially if the infringer is attempting to capture the mood of the period. On a broader level
many studies originally written as secondary works may later become
valuable as primary source materials. These will also be inaccessible to an
author attempting to assess the mood of the period.

Other commentators have urged that an even broader privilege be established, one that would, in effect, make explicit the first amendment
basis of *Rosemont* and *Geis*. A major stumbling block to this type of first
amendment privilege is that it turns on the extent of public interest, while
the first amendment value in expression has never been judged in those
terms. Although certain types of speech are entirely excluded from the
first amendment's guarantee because they are inimical to the public
welfare,[26] the first amendment generally applies without regard to "the
truth, popularity, or social utility of the ideas and beliefs which are offered."[27]

The danger, of course, is that courts will not agree on what constitutes a matter of significant public interest. Judicial applications of
Rosemont do not allay this fear. For example, a recent case involving the
unauthorized use of the silent film "The Son of the Sheik" rejected a
Rosemont fair use defense on the basis of insufficient public interest.
Rosemont was distinguished on the ground that neither "the enduring
fame of Rudolph Valentino [n]or the intrinsic literary and historical merit
of 'The Son of the Sheik' (whatever it may be) serves any public interest
sufficient to endow these defendants with the privilege of fair use."[28] It is
not the merits of the court's assessment, but rather the subjective nature
of its calculation, that is disturbing.[29]

---

26. *See, e.g.,* Miller v. California, 413 U.S. 15 (1973) (obscenity); Chaplinsky v. New
Hampshire, 315 U.S. 568 (1942) (fighting words).

27. NAACP v. Button, 371 U.S. 415, 445 (1963). Copyright adopts a similar position.
See, e.g., Bleinstein v. Donaldson Lithographing Co., 188 U.S. 239, 251–52 (1903), in which
Justice Holmes refused to hold that a circus poster was not, for that reason, a pictorial il-
lustration within the meaning of the Copyright Act, stating:

> It would be a dangerous undertaking for persons trained only to the law to constitute
> themselves final judges of the worth of pictorial illustrations, outside of the narrowest
> and most obvious limits. At the one extreme some works of genius would be sure to miss
> appreciation. . . . At the other end, copyright would be denied to pictures which appealed
> to a public less educated than the judge. Yet if they command the interest of any public,
> they have a commercial value . . . and the taste of any public is not to be treated with con-
> tempt. . . . That these pictures had their worth and their success is sufficiently shown by
> the desire to reproduce them without regard to the plaintiff's rights.

28. Rohauer v. Killiam Shows, Inc., 379 F. Supp. 723, 733 (S.D.N.Y. 1974), *rev'd on
other grounds,* 551 F.2d 484 (2d Cir.), *cert. denied,* 431 U.S. 949 (1977).

29. *See also* Meeropol v. Nizer, 417 F. Supp. 1201 (S.D.N.Y. 1976), *rev'd in relevant part
and remanded,* 560 F.2d 1061 (2d Cir. 1977), *cert. denied,* 434 U.S. 1013 (1978), in which a
Rosemont-type fair use defense was raised to plaintiffs' claim that defendant's book contained portions of copyrighted letters written by their parents, Julius and Ethel Rosenberg.
The Second Circuit reversed the district court's grant of summary judgment, stating that
where plaintiffs' damages and defendant's need were both in dispute, it would not be possible to find fair use as a matter of law. The court of appeals did not specifically counter the
district judge's assessment of the historical importance of the Rosenbergs' letters. However,
its decision to accord more weight to plaintiffs' economic interest might well have been
based on the perception that the mood of the period as established by the Rosenbergs' exact
words was not sufficiently important to outweigh the plaintiffs' copyright interest.

Moreover, it is not possible to transform this type of first amendment privilege into an objective rule by limiting it to noncommercial uses. Although such an approach would solve the inevitable problem of exploitation, the dissemination of varied ideas which the first amendment seeks to foster is not limited to ideas contained in noncommercial works. By the same token, material of significant public interest may be found in commercial publications. The infringing material in *Rosemont* and *Geis* was contained in commercial works. Indeed, the Copyright Act rests upon the assumption that authors will not expend the effort necessary to publish a work unless there is some prospect of a reasonable commercial return. Whether the infringing work is noncommercial is relevant to a finding of fair use,[30] but it is too narrow a consideration to be the basis of a first amendment privilege.

Ad hoc balancing could also be avoided if the very fact of infringement were considered to be conclusive evidence of public interest. This sort of approach, however, would totally undermine the value of copyright protection. Indeed, its effect would be to limit copyright protection to the least interesting literary, historical, and scientific works.

Thus, the effect of a public interest-based first amendment privilege is potentially devastating from the standpoint of copyright protection. Everything is imbued with public interest to some degree; any privilege, therefore, would be either totally dependent on the subjective values of the judiciary, or so broad in scope that the mere fact of infringement would be proof of public interest. This Note will next consider whether the first amendment in fact requires such a far-reaching privilege.

III.

Drawing heavily on *Geis,* many commentators have concluded that the first amendment automatically requires that there be some sort of privilege to copyright infringement. This would arguably be the correct approach if copyright regulated speech directly. In fact, however, copyright results in abridgement of speech interests only incidentally, and even then, only in one narrow situation. Therefore, the conflict between copyright and the first amendment is properly resolved by balancing

---

30. The Copyright Act directs courts to consider this factor in determining whether fair use is applicable. For example, in Keep Thomson Governor Comm. v. Citizens for Gallen Comm., 457 F. Supp. 957 (D.N.H. 1978), plaintiff, a gubernatorial candidate, held the copyright to a song entitled "Live Free or Die" (coincidentally the New Hampshire state motto) which he played during two minutes of a three-minute campaign advertisement. When plaintiff's opponent made a 60 second political advertisement in which plaintiff's song was played for 15 seconds, plaintiff brought suit for copyright infringement. The court noted that first amendment values were at stake, but observed that the fair use defense resolves such conflicts between the first amendment and copyright. It found that defendants qualified for the fair use defense: the use was noncommercial, insubstantial, and would not have an adverse effct on the market value of the copyrighted work. Although plaintiff argued that defendant's use injured him insofar as it could cause him to lose the campaign, this is not the kind of injury that the Copyright Act seeks to prevent. Copyright protects only the pecuniary injury of the copyright holder as reflected in the market value of the work.

society's interest in unencumbered expression against its general interest in the copyright laws. Society's interest in free expression encompasses both the public's interest in receiving the infringer's ideas and the infringer's interest in expressing himself. Similarly, society's general interest in fostering creative endeavors through the copyright scheme is closely tied to the interests of the particular copyright holder.

Copyright and the first amendment share essentially the same goal: both seek to create a "market-place of ideas." To a limited extent, copyright does prevent the broadest possible dissemination of information. However, if copyright protection is unduly restricted, the production of ideas for the first amendment's marketplace may be seriously hampered. Thus, the crucial question is whether the short-run harm that copyright poses to first amendment values outweighs the long-run benefits of copyright protection.

The consequences of the *Rosemont-Geis* approach to copyright are clear: it encourages ad hoc judicial decisionmaking that undercuts the value of copyright protection, creates uncertainty, and, by infusing an additional factor into the cause of action for copyright infringement, increases the likelihood of erroneous decisions. By contrast, the ramifications of disallowing a first amendment privilege to copyright infringement do not appear to be overwhelming. There will be very few situations in which idea and expression are wedded so that an author would have a real need for another's expression. In cases like *Geis,* where that need exists, imposing liability for copyright infringement—at least when that liability is limited to compensatory damages, defined by the Copyright Act as actual damages plus those profits attributable to the infringement[31]—is consistent with first amendment concerns.

If the author can recover compensatory damages for infringement, the would-be infringer has two options: he can either refer to the copyrighted work without copying it (thus placing the burden of obtaining the copyrighted work on the interested public) or he can reproduce the copyrighted material and pay for the unauthorized use in a subsequent action for infringement.[32] In either case, the public's first amendment interest in obtaining the author's ideas is satisfied. Moreover, forcing the infringer to make this choice does not abridge his first amendment rights. The infringer who demands that his use be held privileged is, in effect, demanding that his exercise of first amendment rights be subsidized in the short run by the particular copyright holder, and in the long run by the public who suffers as the efficacy of the copyright system decreases. The first amendment, however, was designed to prevent governmental re-

---

31. 17 U.S.C. § 504(b) (1976). The copyright holder is not awarded both damages and profits where they amount to the same thing.

32. 17 U.S.C. § 504(b) (1976) permits the copyright holder to recover only those profits which are attributable to the infringement and thereby allows the infringer to be charged with the exact measure of compensation. The burden of proof, however, is on the infringer. The copyright holder is only required to present proof of the infringer's gross revenue; the infringer has the burden of showing deductible expenses or elements of profit due to factors other than the infringement.

straints on expression, not to create an affirmative duty on the part of government to foster expression. Thus, where an independent and substantial governmental policy has an indirect effect on speech interests, the first amendment is satisfied as long as the speaker is left with effective alternatives. Here, the would-be infringer can either incorporate the copyrighted work by reference, or use it and pay for that use. Since being required to compensate the copyright holder for the use of his property is eminently reasonable, mere liability for copyright infringement does not burden speech interests unduly.

Certain aspects of copyright's remedial scheme are more troublesome from a first amendment standpoint. To the extent that the Copyright Act entitles the author to recover actual damages plus those profits of the infringer attributable to the infringement, there is no first amendment problem. The 1976 Act, however, allows the copyright holder to take statutory damages in lieu of actual damages.[33] These statutory damages, which were intended to avoid difficulties of proof in the copyright context, range from $250 to $10,000, in accordance with what the court considers just. When statutory damages exceed what would be necessary to compensate the copyright holder, they have the effect of penalizing the infringer's speech. The Act also provides for a maximum sum of $50,000 to be awarded in cases of willful infringement, and establishes criminal penalties where the willful infringement is for private commercial gain.[34] Where copyright and the first amendment overlap, however, the concept of willful infringement is meaningless. In this situation, it is assumed that infringement is willful, but necessary. Penalizing infringement in this context—either by statutory damages that exceed the amount needed to compensate the copyright holder or by criminal penalties—restrains free expression and is therefore unconstitutional.

Similar problems arise when the copyright holder seeks to enjoin publication of the infringing material.[35] Injunctive relief may abridge first amendment rights by preventing public access to the infringer's work. An injunction has an especially harmful effect if the copyrighted work is out of print, or otherwise inaccessible to the public, because the would-be infringer is then also precluded from incorporating the copyrighted work by reference. The same danger is present when the copyright holder brings suit in order to suppress dissemination of the copyrighted work. Thus, while the monetary relief for copyright infringement is constitutional, in the one situation where copyright intersects with speech interests, the first amendment requires that injunctive relief be severely limited.

This view of the problem—that compensatory damages are proper in an action for copyright infringement when first amendment interests are involved, but that greater damages or injunctive relief are not—is sup-

---

33. *Id.* § 504(c).
34. *Id.* § 506.
35. *Id.* § 502(a) (1976) allows courts to grant temporary and final injunctions. To the extent that injunctive relief is limited, impoundment and destruction under *id.* § 503 ought to be correspondingly limited.

ported by a recent Supreme Court decision concerning the right of publicity. In *Zacchini v. Scripps-Howard Broadcasting Co.,*[36] the entire performance of plaintiff's fifteen-second human cannonball act was filmed and broadcast by a local television station, over his expressly stated objections. The Supreme Court of Ohio found that Zacchini had a protectable interest under the state's right of publicity tort, but refused to allow recovery on the ground that the television broadcast was immunized by the first amendment.

The United States Supreme Court, drawing heavily on an analogy to copyright, distinguished its prior decisions in defamation and privacy cases and reversed. Two crucial distinctions were drawn between defamation and privacy on the one hand, and the right of publicity on the other. The former protect an individual from impairment of reputation and mental distress. By contrast, the right of publicity protects only an individual's commercial interests. More importantly, these torts differ in terms of their effect on dissemination of information. A finding of defamation or invasion of privacy requires that the tortious material be suppressed. Publication is not hindered, however, in right of publicity cases. Since the plaintiff aims only to protect his commercial interests, the sole question is whether the defendant will be allowed to profit from the plaintiff's name. In this regard, the Court stressed that Zacchini had not sought an injunction, but only monetary damages.

The Court then proceeded to examine the interests involved. Since the entire act had been broadcast, defendant's use posed a "substantial threat" to the commercial value of plaintiff's act. The Court emphasized that defendant's appropriation was not incidental, but went to the heart of plaintiff's ability to earn a living. Moreover, the Court was unwilling to attribute social utility to defendant's broadcast, refusing to find a protectable interest in obtaining "for free" that which has market value and for which one would normally pay. Finally, the Court held that to protect plaintiff's right to publicity would ultimately best serve society. Analogizing to copyright and patent law, the Court noted that the right of publicity provided the "economic incentive for [plaintiff] . . . to make the investment required to produce a performance of interest to the public." Accordingly, the Court dismissed defendant's claim of first amendment privilege, holding that:

> The Constitution no more prevents a State from requiring respondent to compensate petitioner for broadcasting his act on television than it would privilege respondent to film and broadcast a copyrighted dramatic work without liability to the copyright owner. . . . There is no doubt that entertainment, as well as news, enjoys First Amendment protection. . . . But it is important to note that neither the public nor respondent will be deprived of the benefit of petitioner's performance as long as his commercial stake in his act is appropriately recognized.

---

36. 433 U.S. 562 (1977).

Petitioner does not seek to enjoin the broadcast of his performance; he simply wants to be paid for it.

Zacchini suggests that monetary damages for copyright infringement are permissible, but that the copyright holder's economic interest can prevail only when the public has access to the material involved. Thus, a first amendment privilege to copyright liability is not required as long as injunctive relief is not allowed. Of course, the first amendment should bar injunctive relief only in those limited situations in which the infringer would not be able to express himself without using the copyrighted work.

This view of the copyright-first amendment problem requires abandonment of the traditional notion that the copyright monopoly gives the author the right to keep his material off the market as well as the right to decide how it will be used.[37] In effect, disallowing injunctive relief would establish a system of compulsory licensing for copyrighted materials that implicate first amendment interests. However, by allowing the copyright holder exact compensation for the use,[38] it preserves first amendment values without unduly abridging the economic incentive which the copyright laws are designed to provide. Finally, it allows the first amendment interests to be gauged in objective terms—since the test should only be genuine need, it can operate without regard to the public interest in the particular material infringed.

CONCLUSION

Although courts and commentators have recently paid much attention to the possibility of conflict between copyright and the first amendment, most of the potential for conflict is resolved by the Copyright Act itself. In cases of true conflict, the first amendment requires only that the infringer be allowed to print his material. Thus, when an author has a legitimate need for another's expression, the balance between the first amendment and copyright is adequately maintained if the copyright holder is allowed to recover compensatory damages, but not allowed to obtain punitive damages or injunctive relief.

---

37. 17 U.S.C. § 106 (1976) grants authors certain exclusive rights, and therefore implicitly includes the right to refrain from exercising these rights. *See* Fox Film Corp. v. Doyal, 286 U.S. 123, 127 (1932) ("The owner of the copyright, if he pleases, may refrain from vending or licensing and content himself with simply exercising the right to exclude others from using his property.").

Although the author's exclusive rights have been treated as implicitly including the right not to exercise these exclusive rights, this notion is not consistent with the American system of copyright, which is premised on encouraging the dissemination of ideas and information. Indeed, Congress has for this reason consistently refused to adopt the European concept of moral rights which allows the author certain perpetual rights, including the right to destroy the work or withdraw it from circulation, and the right to prevent mutilation or alteration of the work.

38. 17 U.S.C. § 115 (1976) establishes a compulsory licensing system for phonorecords. However, it employs a set royalty. *See id.* § 115(c)(2)(1976).

Commentary

THE ARTICLES in this chapter relate to limitations on mass media expression born from a desire to protect interests of individuals ranging from the purely economic to the purely personal, but usually a mixture of both. Copyright protection concerns the right to merchandise individual expression in the marketplace, both in terms of timing as well as price. Defamation centers on protecting individual reputation, an injury that sometimes can be liquidated in dollar terms, other times righted only by public apology, or by a publicized court victory. The right of publicity is somewhere between the two: like copyright, an interest exploitable in the marketplace; like defamation protection, a right that safeguards an interest inalienable from an individual's identity.

Let us look at the oldest of these protected rights, defamation. Kovner discusses the constitutional defense to defamation enjoyed by media, but a court does not reach the defense until the basic case against a defendant has been proved. And the defense is irrelevant from cases where the press is not the defendant.

There are two categories of defamation: slander, spoken defamation; and libel, generally written, and historically considered more harmful to reputation. Initially the First Amendment was viewed as preventing the federal government from providing a right of action sounding in libel, but the states did not impose the same limitation. The consequence is that the elements of proof that go toward proving defamation have developed state to state.

Dean Prosser in his treatise, *Law of Torts,* observed that defamation is defined by that which injures "reputation" in the popular sense and must necessarily involve the idea of disgrace. Libel began in England as a criminal offense; while states have adopted criminal libel statutes, they are no longer much used. The preferred action for someone who thinks he has been libeled is a civil suit for damages. Even though a winning defamation plaintiff may not always receive huge awards, the costs of litigating the action (recall that in the American system, each party pays the costs of the suit, not the losing party) act as an incentive to the press and others to avoid getting close to the point of falsely destroying reputation.

Besides the First Amendment defense discussed by Kovner, two defenses that generally avoid all liability once established are privilege and truth.

Two categories of privilege exist. Absolute privilege negates liability for otherwise defamatory speech regardless of the manner or purpose behind the communication. Examples include a judge's utterances in his judicial capacity; a legislator's comments in debates or reports; and an executive's statements in the course of certain official functions. Qualified privilege obtains for other defamatory speech. Immunity depends on whether publication occurred in a reasonable manner and for a proper purpose. Most significant of the qualified privileges is "fair comment on matters of public concern."

What makes the media's privilege qualified rather than absolute is that the report must be a fair and accurate report of what transpired in order to secure the privilege. Journalists lose the protection if the report fails to meet those qualifications.

How can a jury judge whether an opinion is true or false? It cannot. Because it cannot, the privilege of fair comment and criticism developed as a defense for the media. It was meant to protect criticism of and comments on the public acts of public persons and institutions.

A requirement of this defense was that the comment had to be based on facts and that the opinion be fair and delivered without malice. The courts seem to have interpreted fairness very loosely. This review of the vaudeville act of the Cherry sisters was held protected by the defense of fair comment and criticism back in 1901:

> Effie is an old jade of 50 summers, Jessie a frisky filly of 40, and Addie, the flower of the family, a capering monstrosity of 35. Their long skinny arms, equipped with talons at the extremities, swung mechanically, and anon waved frantically at the suffering audience. The mouths of their rancid features opened like caverns, and sounds like the wailings of damned souls issue therefrom. They pranced around the stage with a motion that suggested a cross between the danse du ventre and fox trot—strange creatures with painted faces and hideous mien. Effie is spavined, Addie is stringhalt, and Jessie, the only one who showed her stockings, has legs with calves as classic in their outlines as the curves of a broom handle.

The true key to this defense is that the opinion or the commentary must be directed toward public acts. The law would have been less generous if the reviewer had criticized the private lives of the Cherry sisters with the same enthusiasm.

In many ways this historical qualified privilege is incorporated in the constitutional protection established in *Sullivan.* For the idea of providing First Amendment protection to the press in defamation actions was to assure that reporters would be free to do their job with adequate breathing space, and surely fair comment on public issues falls within that category

Proof that a defamation was not simply part of fair comment but done with malice is a vexing part of the constitutional defense for plaintiffs. One tool to show malice is disclosure of confidential sources in defamation suits. As a publisher's lawyer, Kovner regrets this trend. He would be no less upset with *Herbert* v. *Lando,* a 1979 United States Supreme Court case decided after publication of his article. Anthony Herbert, a retired army officer, sued Barry Lando, reporter Mike Wallace, CBS, and the *Atlantic Monthly* over a CBS news program produced by Lando and a subsequent magazine article by him which allegedly portrayed Herbert as a liar who had made war crimes charges to explain his relief from Vietnam war command.

The issue: in order to pursue his defamation charges did Herbert have the right to inquire into Lando's thoughts, opinions, and conclusions about him, gathered while preparing the program? The Court ruled that Herbert had this pretrial right, especially in light of the plaintiff's substantive burden under the malice test requiring proof of knowing or reckless error.

Aside from privilege and the constitutional defense, there is a second major defense: truth. For the defense to work, the alleged defamation must be true in all essential points. It is not enough for a journalist to point to notes and a tape recorder and claim the story accurately reproduced the words of the source. Journalists have to be prepared to prove the truth of their source's words, not the accuracy of their own renditions of the words. Of course, if the truth of the charges were easily proved, the journalist probably wouldn't be in court.

If we analyze the relation between the tort of defamation and the other two interests discussed in this chapter—copyright and the right of publicity—it becomes clear that all three are tied to economic interests, but defamation is a passive interest, triggered by an outsider, while the other two are active interests. Persons holding a valuable copyright or an exploitable interest in personas will want to activate those interests in the marketplace. This explains why Brenner aligns the publicity interest with copyright in establishing outer bounds. Defamation, on the other hand, is an economic interest no one actively seeks to harvest. For this reason it is closer to the mental pain and distress injuries recoverable under the right of privacy.

Technological changes in mass media are likely to increase the potential to abuse each of these interests. The more outlets the more the demand for information and the more likely it is for the press to injure reputation. The more outlets the more ways originators of work can have their work improperly copied. The more outlets the more ways reporters can use and misuse the likenesses of celebrities. Consider these:

• A cable channel in New York City ran a "Who's Sexier?" contest between Cheryl Ladd and Farrah Fawcett by having callers phone one number to vote for Cheryl, another for Farrah. Was a publicity right violated?

• The ABC-TV network had exclusive rights to the 1981 world figure-skating championships. A CBS affiliate wanted to show two minutes of the championships in its local sports. ABC objected. What liability for the affiliate for running the two minutes of highlights?

• The Reagan-Bush Presidential Inaugural Committee had for sale many official souvenirs of the inauguration. Proceeds were to cover the cost of public and private inaugural festivities. An independent company sold similar goods in competition with the official items bearing the likenesses of Reagan and Bush. Can Reagan or Bush object? Can the committee? Can they object to a vendor of "Bedtime for Bonzo" posters bearing the President-elect holding the chimp?

The myriad economic interests here are complicated. The personal interests range from the poignant to the picayune. But how the law defines the rights does affect the way the media can and should cover the famous and not-so-famous.

WLR

12

Especially Protected Speech: Rights of Access to the Media

PHIL JACKLIN founded a public interest group to assure citizen access to the broadcast airwaves: the Committee for Open Media. During the 1970s Jacklin and the committee pioneered innovations in public service announcements by convincing broadcasters in the San Francisco Bay area to air "free speech messages." Controversial spot announcements are run throughout the day. A Yale graduate in philosophy, Jacklin has taught philosophy at San Jose State University and at Stanford.

JEREMY WEIR ALDERSON is a free-lance writer based in upstate New York.

JOSEPH MATHEWS is the third and final "student author" in this book. His article, written in 1979 while he was in the New York Law School, appeared in the American Bar Association publication, *Human Rights.*

Access to the Media: A New Fairness Doctrine

PHIL JACKLIN

GOVERNMENT REGULATION of broadcasting is under attack. This is nothing new. Like all industries, the broadcast industry resists regulation. Unfortunately, only the industry point of view is heard and good people are persuaded by it. Thus, in the May, 1973, issue of *Civil Liberties,* Nat Hentoff argues against the Federal Communication Commission's fairness doctrine. He understands the fairness doctrine in the conventional way as the obligation imposed on broadcasters to balance their presentation of controversial issues. More generally, the broadcaster faces an obligation to present programming in the public interest; this general obligation is particularized by the fairness doctrine which requires the broadcaster to balance discussion of controversial issues *and* to cover and present issues of public importance.

The standard argument against regulation of broadcast programming goes as follows:

• There is an asymmetry in the regulation of radio and television on the one hand and the print media on the other. We have government regulation of radio and television under the fairness doctrine; but the First

From the *Center Magazine,* May/June 1975. Courtesy Phil Jacklin.

Amendment is understood to prohibit government regulation of newspapers under any comparable fairness doctrine.
• There is no longer a justification for this asymmetry. The rationale of the fairness doctrine (and of all regulation of broadcast content) is the scarcity of usable broadcast frequencies. But there are now far fewer daily newspapers than there are radio and television stations (1,749 to 7,458). Few cities (five per cent) have competitive daily newspapers, but most are served by several television stations and plenty of radio.
• Therefore, in order to be consistent, we should defend freedom of the electronic press and oppose the fairness doctrine.

Hentoff does not affirm this conclusion. He offers it for discussion. As he says, it is "new ground" for him. His argument is all too familiar to those who read *Broadcasting* magazine and follow industry attempts to expropriate the First Amendment. On the strength of it, Senator William Proxmire has recently filed a bill to end regulation of broadcast programming.

The two premises of the above argument are correct. There is an asymmetry and there is no basis for it. Still, the conclusion of the argument is a *non sequitur*. We need not achieve consistency by changing broadcast law and giving up the fairness doctrine. We can also achieve it by extending the fairness doctrine from broadcasting to the print media. We can do this using the media-scarcity rationale as in broadcasting. If daily newspapers are more scarce than broadcast frequencies, it does not follow that frequencies are not scarce. There is scarcity when demand exceeds supply; in the media case there is scarcity when more people want access to the public than can have it.

We have a choice. Should we extend the fairness doctrine to newspapers which have no competitors and risk further government involvement? Or should we adopt the same laissez-faire policy for broadcasting that is traditional in the print media? I submit that there is a third and better alternative. If we believe in an open society and political equality, if we want to avoid the domination of mass communications by a few big corporations, then we must regulate any preponderant message-source in any medium. But, there is available to us a regulatory strategy which is fundamentally different from that involved in the fairness doctrine as presently understood and is wholly consistent with the First Amendment. We can choose to regulate access rather than content, to insure fairness about who is heard rather than fairness in what is said.

When, if ever, is there a need (justification or rationale) for government regulation of media? If there is media scarcity, does that justify regulation? Is there a way to regulate media without abridging freedom of the press? Answers to these questions are suggested by a model well known to political economy. Consider the following principles—all applicable to the problems of media law:

• That a free (unregulated) and competitive marketplace is preferable to a government-regulated or planned economy.

• That when there exists an economic monopoly or a concentration of economic power, the government must regulate that power to prevent abuses and protect the public interest. As Adam Smith explained, laissez-faire or the absence of regulation is desirable only in a condition of natural competition. When merchants must compete for their customers, the competition insures that people will be well served. But when economic power is monopolized or concentrated in a few hands, then competition ends and the government must protect the public interest. This takes us to a third and less familiar principle.

• That, in the absence of natural competition, it is better to regulate so as to guarantee a competitive marketplace by limiting the extent to which power can be concentrated (e.g., to establish antitrust laws) than to attempt to regulate the behavior of monopoly powers (e.g., by setting production quotas and standards of quality, and administering prices and wages).

I take the traditional view that democracy absolutely requires the kind of communications generated in a competitive marketplace of ideas.

The problem is that in a society of millions dependent on the technology of mass communications, most messages that reach any substantial number of people are transmitted by means of a very limited number of media. In general, the scarcity of access to substantial audiences exists, not because there is a physical scarcity of communication channels, but for economic and sociological reasons. There is no shortage of "channels" in the print media, no shortage of presses or paper; but most dailies enjoy absolute monopolies. And, although there are weekly papers and periodicals, the publisher of the daily newspaper controls eighty per cent of all print communications on local and state issues.

In most big cities, there are at the present time fifteen to twenty usable television frequencies (VHF and UHF)—the same number as will be provided in a standard cable system. But the three network-associated stations control the programming viewed by eighty-five per cent of the total television audience. (Cable television and future technology will not solve our problem.)

Each of the channels with a substantial audience—print or broadcast—is wholly controlled by a single large message-source. Thus, in a typical city, control of mass communications is concentrated in the hands of a single daily newspaper and three television stations, with the addition in some places of an all-news radio station. The power of a message-source is a function both of the number of messages produced (as counted roughly by measuring the space and time they fill) and of the number of people actually reached by those messages.

It is at this point that the battle is joined by the newspaper and broadcasting industries, which argue thus: "Suppose, as is claimed, that media regulation *is* necessary when a concentration of the power to communicate reduces competition in a marketplace of ideas. There is indeed a limited number of important communicators, but there has been no showing at all that these communicators have abused their powers or refrained from a competition of ideas. The press is doing its job. Our Watergate experience proves that the system works. It is unnecessary and foolish to run the risk of government regulation of communications."

What, then, is the performance of the media? What, if anything, is left out? National media coverage is issue-oriented and admirable in that way. But "Presidential television" and dominance of the media generally led us in the late nineteen-sixties to the brink of disaster and over. Denied regular television exposure, neither congressional leaders not the opposition party could check Presidential power. The Chief Executive dominates national attention. He is the only one with enough continuity of access to exercise national leadership. On state issues, and especially on local issues, there is virtually no one with the access appropriate to leadership except perhaps the press itself.

What ideas are left out? Ask those moved by a conception of the public interest, those who would seek access to their brothers and sisters in the media marketplace of ideas. Ask elected officials, consumer advocates, reformers, ecologists, socialists, the would be vocal poor, church people, feminists, *et al.*

On both the national and local levels, the restraints on the competition of ideas are most apparent in the absence of day-to-day political competition. Political competition is the competition of leaders and their programs for public support as expressed in the formation of public opinion. No one except the President has long-term visibility or the concomitant ability to engage in the long-term communications essential to leadership.

Why? Part of the answer lies in the fact that the most powerful media are commercial and business-oriented. There is competition, but it is a competition for the advertiser's dollar and not a competition of ideas. We ignore this because we have been taught to identify the media with the press and to understand the press on the old model of precommercial, crusading journalism. In the good old days, the newspaper publisher wrote and edited his own stories and even ran the press himself. He was a political activist, a Sentinel, an Observer vigilant in behalf of his subscribers, an Advocate with the courage to set himself and his paper against the powerful few. Things have changed. The publisher's source of revenues has shifted from subscribers to advertisers and this has changed the newspaper business in two ways. Advertisers are more interested in circulation than in editorial policy. As a result, in almost every city the largest daily has slowly achieved a monopoly position, not because of the superiority of its editorial policy but because it is the first choice of advertisers. Second, the shift of revenues has changed editorial policy. It has shifted the editor's attention from the problems of the many to the ambitions of a few. As a monopoly message-source on local issues, the paper becomes, in a technical sense, propaganda. On one hand there is the propaganda of boosterism and Chamber of Commerce public relations (e.g., in San Jose, a new sports arena before new schools, airport expansion before noise abatement). On the other hand, with respect to the problems of ordinary people, and especially the poor, there is silence, the propaganda of the *status quo*. Most big city dailies do not by themselves sustain a marketplace of ideas on local issues.

What, then, is added by the multiplicity of broadcasters? Broadcasters are typically large corporations, not crusading journalists, not people at all. Corporate broadcasters program so as to generate the largest possible audiences. Then they rent these audiences to advertisers at the rate of four dollars per thousand per minute. The lawyers and public-relations men who represent them try to identify the electronic medium with the electronic press. But does the corporation have a First Amendment right to program exclusively for profit? (The fairness doctrine prohibits it.) In fact, only about five per cent of the electronic medium is occupied with the traditional journalistic function—news, documentaries, and public affairs—the rest is electronic theater. Audience-profit maximization leaves very little place for authentic journalism. Television journalists go unprotected while the First Amendment is interpreted as the right of the broadcasting corporation to edit in order to maximize profits, and even to make the local news a form of entertainment, to make of the news itself just another format for stories of sex and violence. What these corporations seek is not freedom for journalism but freedom from journalism. (They have succeeded very well. In point of fact, the F.C.C.'s fairness obligation to cover issues has been enforced in only one case.)

There is nothing wrong with an electronic circus as long as the medium also delivers the kind of communications required for democracy. We owe very much to the journalism of the last five years. Still, even the best journalism is no substitute for free speech. There is a profound reason why this is so. Journalists are supposed to be objective and nonpartisan. They themselves are not supposed to participate in the competition of ideas, or to lead people to action. The press sustains a competition of ideas only to the extent that it provides access to spokesmen who are not themselves journalists.

The question then arises: How can a journalist decide in a disinterested way what issues and spokesmen to present? There is no solution to this problem. Indeed, the question is unintelligible. Message-choice, like all choice, presupposes the chooser's interests and needs. Journalists usually avoid the problem by reporting new events relative to something that is already in the news. But in a mass society, the news is identical with what is reported; and what has not been reported is not yet news.

How, then, can the journalist decide what *new* issues and spokesmen should gain access to the public? He can decide only because he does have values and interests; hopefully only by making a judgment about what people want and need to know. Authentic journalism is public-interest journalism. But when businessmen-publishers and corporations do the hiring and the firing, there is no guarantee that we will have authentic journalism. Spiro Agnew's concern was not misplaced: "A small group of men decide what forty to fifty million Americans will learn of the day's events. . . . We would never trust such power in the hands of an elected government; it is time we questioned it in the hands of a small and unelected elite."

There is another consideration here which is decisive all by itself. Even if there were a competition of ideas between five or ten powerful sources, that would not be good enough for democracy. A society is democratic to the extent that all its citizens have an equal opportunity to influence the decision-making process. Clearly, communication is essential to this process—just as essential as voting itself. (Imagine a society of one thousand in which everyone votes, and all are free to say what they please, but only five people have the technology and power to reach *all* the others. Each of the other 995, except at overwhelming expense, can communicate only with a small circle of friends. Suppose the "five" are wealthy businessmen.)

The media must be regulated, not only to insure a competition of ideas, but so that all citizens have an equal opportunity to influence and shape this competition. "Fine, but is democracy possible in a society of two hundred million people?" Representative democracy is possible. As voters, we are represented in city hall, at the state capitol, and in the Congress by people who, to some extent at least, vote on our behalf and answer to us. These people are supported at public expense and use public facilities. All right, we need to establish parallel institutions which give us representation in public debate, i.e., representation in the media marketplace.

There are many possibilities. Our elected representatives and their ballot opponents and/or prospective opponents—leaders all—might be provided free media time and space on a regular basis. But we should not limit representation in the media marketplace to elected officials and party leaders. There are other ways in which spokesmen representative of whole groups can be identified. Formally organized nonprofit groups like the Sierra Club and the Methodist Church can select spokesmen, and membership rolls will demonstrate that these spokesmen are representatives. Small, informally organized groups of the type characteristic of much citizen activity could achieve short-term access by demonstrating by petition that a substantial number of people supported their efforts (as in the access-by-petition procedure in Holland). A plan for a system of representative access recognizing these four kinds of access has been drawn up by the Committee for Open Media. The details establish the feasibility of the general proposal. The F.C.C. could establish some such system of access in broadcasting under its present authority, or Congress could do it. But what about the monopolistic daily newspapers?

It is useful to imagine what a new Communications Act would be like if we sought to develop a new strategy for media regulation oriented to regulation of access. We could regulate monopolistic or dominant message-sources in order to protect a competition of ideas in which all have some opportunity to participate or be represented. We could create a system of representative access of the sort sketched above or, alternatively, a new Communications Act might have the four following provisions:

THE ONE-TENTH CONCENTRATION RULE. Any dominant message-source (one which controls over one-tenth of the messages reaching any population of over one hundred thousand) in any medium—be it print or broadcast—shall recognize an affirmative obligation to provide access to the public.

THE TITHE IN THE PUBLIC INTEREST. Each dominant message-source shall make available ten per cent of all message capacity (time and/or space) for citizen access. Message capacity shall be defined in terms of time and space and also audience-availability to that time and space. Since in broadcasting there is a fundamental difference between the function of full-length programs and spot messages, ten per cent of each would be made available. (Perhaps there should also be a tithe or tax of ten per cent on all profits to pay for production of citizen messages.)

THE ALLOCATION OF ACCESS BY LOT. Access to time and space shall be allocated by lot among registered citizens. Every registered voter is, in virtue of this act, a registered communicator.

THE ACCESS-CONTRIBUTION MECHANISM. It shall be permissible for individuals to make access-contributions to designated representative persons or groups. It will be permissible for the citizen to designate a representative person or group to use his or her access spot. Individual organizations will be permitted and encouraged to solicit contributions of access time and space.

The access-contribution mechanism makes possible effective grassroots support for various organizations at low cost (in time and money) and may lead to individual identification with the groups supported. It is a communications institution which generates community and community organization.

Access designations will, in effect, be votes—expressions of concerns and priorities—with respect to what is communicated. Everyone will participate in message-selection. Communication will reflect the needs, values, and priorities of all citizens.

The great advantage of the access approach is that it provides a strategy for media regulation which is in the spirit of the First Amendment and wholly consistent with it. The decisive difference between the regulatory strategy of the old law and the proposed new law is the distinction between the regulation of message content and the regulation of access. Or, to put the difference another way, it is the difference between the prohibition of certain message-content and the prohibition of monopolization of access by any message-source or groups of sources.

The First Amendment prohibits government censorship; it prohibits laws regulating message content. But regulation of access does not entail regulation of content. Whatever source gains access is free to express any message whatever in the sole discretion of that source. While it is arguable that total denial of access is a form of censorship, surely it is not censorship to tell someone who talks all the time to stop talking for a bit so that others may speak. In contrast, the present law requires a regulation of content (broadcast programming). It requires "government censorship" in order to protect "the public interest" and especially to prevent an imbalance of programming that is not "fair" to some points of view. The tension between the Communications Act of 1934 and the First Amendment generates a choice between finding a way to regulate program content which does not risk government control of mass communications, and not regulating broadcast programming out of respect for the First Amendment. Given the preferences and power of the broadcast industry, the government has usually opted for no regulation. The fairness doctrine is rarely enforced. Unfortunately laissez-faire—*de jure* or *de facto*—is morally unacceptable in any context in which power is concentrated.

This returns us to the three principles of political economy and the general theory of regulation. Consider the third principle once more: that, in the absence of natural competition, it is better to limit the size and power of large entities, so as to protect competition, than it is to regulate the behavior of these powers. Thus, it is better for the government to use antitrust laws to force, say, Standard Oil to divest than for the government to mandate production quotas, set product standards, and administer prices. Surely, in such a sensitive field as communication, it is better to regulate access than to rely on government paternalism in the regulation of message-content. As always, free speech in a marketplace of ideas is our best hope.

Everyman TV

JEREMY WEIR ALDERSON

HOW CAN ANYONE DEFEND Public Access Television? Critics point out that "Access" (as it's called) has presented some of the worst conceived, worst produced programs in television's history, punctuated by sensational features like a transsexual's striptease, cock tattooing, and even a

From *Columbia Journalism Review* 19(1981):39–42.

horrifying repeating loop of a puppy being shot to death. Nonetheless, Access has not only defenders but vigorous proponents who see in it vitality, honesty, variety, relevance, and television's brightest hope. At the root of these conflicting views is one central fact: Public Access Television is the world's only form of television in which no authority decides what can or cannot be televised. For better or worse, Access is the one place where people can televise almost anything they want.

Access arose from circumstances so prosaic that no one foresaw what they would produce. Those circumstances included the exasperating tendency of TV signals to bounce off Manhattan's skyscrapers, creating so many ghosts that the multiple images on many home screens could be cleaned up by no method short of exorcism. In 1965, two exorcists arrived in the guise of cable companies convinced that New York was ripe to become the first metropolis with cable television.

Because there were no appropriate precedents, the city moved cautiously, granting, at first, only temporary operating authority, so as to have time to study alternatives. The city felt it had the right to demand something from the cable companies in return for the city services and rights of way the companies would require. In 1970, after considering recommendations from almost every conceivable community source, the city and the cable companies settled on franchise contracts that included landmark provisions for Public Access.

In 1972, the FCC imposed modified Access requirements on all cable' companies with 3,500 or more subscribers. Today, dozens of cable systems (no exact count is available) offer some form of Public Access. It flourishes in such diverse locations as San Diego, East Lansing, Michigan, and Ohio's Miami Valley, but in terms of the sheer quantity and variety of programming produced, New York City remains the leader.

Under New York's rules, transmission time on either of two Public Access channels (there are twenty-six cable channels in all) is available on a first-come-first-served basis for up to an hour per person per week. Regular time slots can be reserved, and there is no charge for use of the channels, but programs cannot carry advertising. On a third, so-called Leased Access channel, there is a nominal transmission fee (fifty dollars per hour per cable company), and commercial programs are permitted.

Though in some locales cable companies are required to provide production assistance, in New York they are required only to transmit, without interference, whatever programs the Access producers provide, either on tape or via live feed. There is just one exception to the noninterference rule: cable companies are not required to transmit material so obscene that they themselves might be prosecuted. Some producers fear the companies will use this loophole to get control of Public Access channels.

Access was a radical departure from the policy of previous eras in which no one had dreamed of demanding free public access to the printing press, telegraph, radio, or telephone. In theory, Access was to be a sort of televised Hyde Park in the center of the "Global Village," returning to the individual the opportunity to be heard that mass society had taken away. In practice, Access was greeted with more enthusiasm than anyone anticipated, as scores of would-be producers lined up to reserve time for their shows.

By 1974, the nonprofit Experimental Television Cooperative (ETC) had opened in a cramped lower-Manhattan loft. By relying on volunteers for labor, and by using undersized industrial or homemade equipment, ETC brought the cost of television production down to as little as twenty dollars per black-and-white half hour. Though the technical inferiority of ETC-produced programming often turns off network-nurtured viewers (without capital, Access producers can only lament that if God Himself were to appear on Access most people would pass Him by as a low-budget production), ETC's opening was a tremendous spur to Access's development in Manhattan, where most producers must pay production costs out of their own pockets.

Today, Manhattan's three Access channels present more than 300 programs each week, including almost as much original prime-time programming as the three networks combined. Most of these programs can't be seen beyond Manhattan, and, of course, many of them are awful, but, as one hardly need point out, many network programs are awful too.

Through Access, countless new writers, performers, and technicians have gained their first television experience. So many women, blacks, Hispanics, and members of other minorities have their own programs as to put network tokenism to shame. But Access is more than the sum of its opportunities or the "Vanity Video" for which it is sometimes mistaken. The viewing public, too, has benefited from Access. Despite its rampant amateurism, Access has redefined television's potential by creating new kinds of programming and a new television aesthetic.

"I think broadcasting is over," declares "Coca Crystal," whose popular program "If I Can't Dance You Can Keep Your Revolution" mixes drugs (she often smokes marijuana on camera), radical politics (no nukes, no draft, etc.), and black humor (e.g. an "ad" for "Sado-Maspirin"—increases your sensitivity to the lash), to form what she calls "an eighties version of an underground paper." "Making pabulum for the masses is finished," she continues with the charactristic fervor of an Access partisan. "I believe in *narrow*casting."

"Narrowcasting"—gearing programs to a limited target audience—is possible on Access because of its small expense, and because a program doesn't have to be popular, or even potentially popular, to be on Access. As a result, weekly programs are devoted to a seemingly endless list of topics seldom treated seriously by the networks, including astrology, consumerism, feminism, haute couture, salsa music, comic books, radio serials, gospel singing, sports handicapping, hypnotherapy, parapsychology, and even a little known theology called "Absolute Relativity."

Some of the better examples of New York's Access narrowcasts would be: *Impact on Hunger,* which each week deals with a different facet of world malnutrition, including starvation in New York City itself; *The*

Irish Freedom Show, which regularly presents such features as an interview with an Irish socialist giving his party's platform for peace in Northern Ireland; and *Towards Aquarius,* hosted by ghetto activist "Kanya,"
who addresses such topics as Harlem hospital closings, which he asserts
are intended to drive blacks from the inner city to make way for white
real estate development. Many Access advocates believe that programs
like Kanya's, which tackle tough community issues, represent one of Access's greatest strengths.

Not all Access programs are narrowcasts. Many shows are intended
for a mass audience and some of these, taking advantage of cable's less
restrictive regulatory framework, present material that could never be
broadcast. The best known examples of this genre are the sex shows, including: *Midnight Blue,* television's first "erotic variety show," whose executive producer is Al Goldstein of *Screw* magazine; *The Ugly George
Hour of Truth, Sex, and Violence,* which consists in part of interviews with
women whom George has lured off the street and talked into undressing
on camera; and *Maria At Midnight,* hosted by stripper Maria Darvi, who
hopes her Access exposure will one day land her a lucrative movie contract.

Not surprisingly, the sex shows have aroused a lot of censorious ire.
At one point, Manhattan Cable Television threw *Midnight Blue* off its
system for several weeks, and an outraged New York congressman
played tapes of it for the House Communications subcommittee, demanding that this immorality be stopped. (At the moment, a fragile compromise has Access producers voluntarily sticking within the limits of an
"R" rating.) But morality isn't the only issue. The Access sex shows are
moving into a lucrative market that broadcasters can't directly enter.
Midnight Blue is already being syndicated around the country, and Ugly
George is seeking European distribution. Certainly the networks can have
no enthusiasm for one day seeing Leased Access programs compete for
audiences and advertising.

Even if one is not enthralled by the Access sex shows, one may see in
them the price that must be paid for the salutary freedom that Access producers enjoy—a freedom that has been put to many nonpornographic
uses. At a time when the networks still sought ways to "treat" the topic
of homosexuality, Leased Access was regularly transmitting *Emerald
City,* a well-crafted program which "started out to show anything gay,"
one producer said, and included scenes of men kissing, reviews of gay
bathhouses, and anti-homophobia editorials. Though *Emerald City* caught
on in New York and San Francisco, it died because it couldn't expand into
enough markets to command the ad rates it needed to survive. Where
Leased Access rights were not legally guaranteed, *Emerald City* could not
secure a regular time slot.

Waste Meat News is another now-defunct program which benefited
from Access's free environment. It consisted entirely of skits satirizing a
"typical" day of network television. One continuing skit was a supposed

weather report entitled "Leather Weather," in which a bound, reclining woman in a kinky leather costume was used as a weather map, getting doused with water where it rained, covered with shaving cream where it snowed, etc. Some other skits featured:

- A consumer report on a "Foreign Language Cursing Detector," a must item for traveling xenophobes afraid that a foreigner might curse them out without their knowledge.
- An advertisement for a self-improvement school teaching the quality most necessary for success: meanness.
- A David Susskindian interview with the latest group to come out of the closet demanding recognition and respect; people who have murdered their spouses.
- An adventure series, "Suicide Emergency Squad," in which three Charlie's Angelish women who (according to the intro) "really know how to stop a suicide and still turn on a TV audience" try to prevent a man from killing himself by eating a Burger King Whopper.
- A late-night movie, "Frightened At Sea," in which two World War Two submarine commanders track each other until they realize they're on the same ship.
- An "Incredible Hulk" type series entitled "Sewerman," about a child abandoned for safekeeping in Manhattan's sewers during the Cuban Missile Crisis, now grown up and prowling the city.
- An advertisement for a new phone company service, "Dial-A-Thrill," which offers callers pre-recorded messages appealing to every possible sexual appetite.

At least *Waste Meat News* came to a better end than *Emerald City.* Its creator, Ferris Butler, voluntarily withdrew it from circulation last fall when he was hired to write for the revamped *Saturday Night Live.* Butler is quick to credit Access for his success: "The freedom to discuss things, to write on a wide variety of subject matter, enabled me to open up my creativity and use my talents better, and as a result, that helped me to move on to something else."

Taken together, the Access shows define a new television aesthetic—an aesthetic of reality, as opposed to the network aesthetic of illusion. On Access, people appear more natural, talk more freely, and address more issues of real concern than on any other form of television. To this may be added the spontaneity of the live transmissions preferred by many Access producers. Access is the true progenitor of programs like *Saturday Night Live* and *Real People,* but unlike the subjects of *Real People* the real people on Access don't need glib Hollywood types to introduce them and thus distance their own real lives from the real lives of their audience.

How many people are watching? Nobody knows for sure, because no rating service includes Access programs. There are, however, some interesting indications. A survey conducted in East Lansing showed that some people there subscribe to cable just to receive the Access programs. A

Manhattan Cable Television survey profiled Access viewers as younger, better educated, and more upwardly mobile than average. Evidence that Access is finding a growing audience may be found in the rapidly over-loading switchboards of some Access phone-in shows and the recognition that Access stars like Coca Crystal and Ugly George receive as they walk down the street.

Leonard Cohen, the coordinator of New York City's Office of Tele-communications, has dubbed the city's experiment with Access "an ab-solutely great success," but, despite its many achievements, the Access concept is in deep trouble. Cable companies, many of which are owned by giant conglomerates that also own pay-TV syndicates, were not happy when the FCC promulgated its Access requirements. They saw in Access the nuisance of dealing with dozens of local producers, and a large poten-tial for pressure group complaints about controversial Access shows. Most importantly, they were reluctant to give up channels which, they hoped, would prove more lucrative carrying pay television services (often from their own parent companies) or free services (old movies, sports, news, etc.) that might be more effective than Access in attracting new subscribers.

In 1976, Midwest Video, a small cable company chain, sued the FCC to be freed fom Public Access obligations. It won in the Supreme Court, which ruled that the FCC had exceeded its statutory authority in ordering Access, but the case had an unintended boomerang effect. Mike Botein, a New York Law School professor who fought on the losing side, says the decision "turned out to be one of the best things that ever happened to Access," because, after the Court ruled, local governments which had previously relied on the FCC started following New York's lead in in-sisting on Access as a franchise condition. As competition for cable fran-chises has heated up, local governments have frequently gotten more Ac-cess channels (and even Access studios) through negotiation than they would have under the FCC rules. Still, the battle is far from over.

For one thing, what's passing for Access in many places has little or nothing to do with the experiment started in New York. According to Sue Buske, the executive director of the National Federation of Local Cable Programmers (NFLCP), a pro-Access umbrella group, "The cable com-panies are trying to blur the distinction between Local Origination [cable company controlled] and Access by introducing the concept of 'Communi-ty Programming,' in which the topic is community oriented but is ultimately chosen and presented by the cable operator, not by the com-munity." Access has also been subverted by the imposition of rules that make Access time difficult to obtain or subject to the discretion of the cable operator.

In their determination not to be forced into giving up channels, even for limited Access, the cable companies have taken their fight to Con-gress. Last summer, with the before-the-fact advice and after-the-fact support of two cable company organizations—The National Cable Televi-sion Association and the Community Antenna Television Association—

Senators Hollings, Cannon, Packwood, Stevens, Goldwater, and Schmitt introduced a bill (S.2827) that would have forbidden any level of government to "require or prohibit any program origination by a telecommunications carrier . . . or obligations affecting the content or amount of such program originations."

The NFLCP, the National Citizens Committee for Broadcasting (currently chaired by Ralph Nader), the National League of Cities, and a host of other nonprofit organizations rushed to oppose S.2827, which was scheduled to come to a vote without a hearing. The bill's sponsors insisted that its provisions had been misread and that it had never been intended as an attempt to eliminate Access, but the bill's opponents simply did not believe that claim. Although S.2827 eventually stalled, many are still worried that the 97th Congress will produce its own brand of anti-Access legislation—a possibility that appears all the more likely in the light of Reagan's election and the conservative shift in Congress.

If Access survives, technological innovations may greatly expand its horizons. The increasing availability of satellite time would permit linked Access channels across the country to form an alternative distribution network, and the continued development of interactive (two-way) television could make Access an ideal medium for electronic town meetings. (Promising experiments in both of these directions have already been made.) Ironically, Access's dreams won't be fulfilled until the viewing public wakes up to what it has been missing. If that doesn't happen soon, television's brightest hope may be buried in the wasteland.

Should Children Be Protected from TV Commercials?

Joseph Mathews

EVER SINCE TELEVISION has evolved as a fixture in American homes, its value as one of the most powerful marketing tools has been recognized by those interested in reaching the subscribing public. They include businessmen, politicians and even religious preachers. Business has utilized this medium to the fullest extent and in fact, the very existence of commercial broadcasting depends on the financial resources of its sponsors. Nowhere is commercial persuasion more effective than with children. This raises the question of fairness—especially when it is directed toward children who cannot even distinguish program from message.[1]

From *Human Rights* 8(1979): 24–27; 48–54, published by the Section of Individual Rights and Responsibilities of the American Bar Association, copyright © 1979, American Bar Association.
1. See Children's Television Programs, Report and Policy Statement, 39 Fed. Reg. 39396.

Parents and concerned citizens have long been apprehensive about the inherent dangers of unchecked commercial exploitation of young minds and have instituted actions for the regulation of both the quantity and quality of children's programs. Recently, concern has been voiced over the effect of advertisements geared toward children.

At the root of the antagonism toward broadcast advertisements is their inherent intrusive and persuasive elements. Peggy Charren, the president of Action for Children's Television (ACT), an organization which epitomizes the concern of responsible parents, says: "Few parents would allow a salesperson to enter their home and place an electronic device on their children designed to transmit periodic messages to the children hawking the seller's wares. That practice would certainly be considered unethical or unscrupulous, if not evil."

Attention has been focused mainly on children under 13, because teenagers are considered to have developed the cognitive skills required to evaluate commercial messages. Whatever the effect produced by commercial messages, it is far from negligible because children watch television three to four hours a day until the age of 11. It is estimated that these children will be exposed to more than 20,000 advertisements each year. The effect is substantial, especially upon preschool children who cannot read.

Empirical studies unanimously report that very young children lack the capacity of differentiating commercial messages from programming. Because they are not aware of the nature of advertisements, younger children show increased acceptance of advertisements and thus more often request that their parents purchase the products advertised. Children six through twelve view commercials with increased skepticism as they advance in age and develop a more critical attitude toward what they see.

But even older children could be deceived by the false impression created by an advertisement or its implied deceptive nature. The controversy over a Wonder Bread commercial is a case in point. In the advertisement, while a child was shown to rapidly grow bigger in successive images, the announcer said, "Wonder Bread builds strong bodies 12 ways."[2] Children might be led to think that Wonder Bread does possess qualities to make them grow strong overnight. Even adults might be misled in that they would think that this brand of bread contains important nutritional elements that are lacking in others. The Federal Trade Commission (FTC) ordered that particular advertisement halted.

So far, the Commission has been reluctant to declare all advertisements toward children to be unfair or deceptive per se. In particular instances, the FTC has dealt with demonstrated unfair or deceptive trade practices. In the case of the Wonder Bread commercial, the FTC held that the impression created that Wonder Bread has extraordinary quali-

---

2. *In re* ITT Continental Baking Co., 83 F.T.C. 865 (1974), <u>modified and enforced</u>, 532, 2d 207 (2d Cir. 1976).

ties was misleading and therefore false advertising. The Commission did not uphold the charge of unfairness. The Commission did, however, observe that certain truthful messages could be termed unfair if they capitalize on the vulnerabilities of their audience.

In the matter of vitamin or over-the-counter drug advertisements to children, the Commission also showed belated awareness of the question of unfairness. Originally, a complaint against the advertisers was overruled, but the companies involved in the manufacture of drugs voluntarily withdrew from advertising their products when children formed a majority of the audience. Recently the Commission issued a consent decree forcing Hudson Pharmaceutical Corporation not to show the Spiderman Vitamins advertisement to audiences of children. The company also agreed to discontinue advertisements featuring super hero figures such as Spiderman.[3]

Although the Commission recognized that children are immature and unqualified to make intelligent choices of vitamin supplements or other drugs, it did not issue any broad ruling covering all manufacturers.

Public interest groups like ACT have waged a relentless campaign for a total ban on advertisements to children, when children form a sizeable portion of audience, charging unscrupulous exploitation of children's naivete. TV-host selling or hero-figure selling presents such a problem. When television characters like Spiderman or Fred Flintstone exhort children to do something or extoll the quality of a product, children tend to accept what such characters say. Therefore, if one character praises the richness of a certain type of candy and another exhorts the children to obey traffic safety rules, children quite naturally assume that both messages are of equal import.

Moreover, excessive use of products such as candy can cause undesirable health problems, too. Activist groups have attacked such advertising as unfair and have petitioned authorities to ban them. Two such petitions[4] have prompted an FTC study and, based on the FTC staff recommendation, the Commission has embarked upon extensive rulemaking which might even lead to a total ban on certain types of advertisements. The concern here is on advertising candies or other between-meal snacks which contain excessive amounts of sugar. The petitions cite the dangers to dental health and other nutrition-related problems, arguing that when these products are advertised to children who are unaware of the selling intent, it is both deceptive and unfair within the meaning of Sections 5 and 12 of the FTC Act.

The FTC considered the following choices: 1) that of banning all televised advertisements for any product that is directed to, or seen by a sizeable

---

3. *In re* Hudson Pharmaceutical Corp., 89 F.T.C. 82 (1977).

4. ACT filed a petition requesting the Commission to promulgate trade regulation prohibiting the advertising of candy products on television when children form a substantial audience. The Center for Science for the Public Interest also petitioned similarly concerning snack foods which contained added sugar. FTC Proposed Trade Regulation Rulemaking and Public Hearing, 43 Fed. Reg. 17967 (1978).

portion of children who are too young to understand the selling purpose or to evaluate the advertisements, 2) that of banning advertisements for candies and other sugared products to such child audiences and 3) that of requiring that the advertising of sugared products to older children be balanced by nutritional or health disclosures, to be funded by the advertisers.

This approach is certain to provoke constitutional challenges. It is one thing to crack down on what is unfair or deceptive but quite another to employ a total ban on advertisements. This involves the fundamental rights of various parties: the right of children to be free from exploitation, businessmen's right to pursue their trade through advertising, and the First Amendment rights of broadcasters and viewers. The Federal Trade Commission has expressed First Amendment implications in its Notice of Proposed Rulemaking.

In the past, most of the FTC's crusades against unfair trade practices involved only the showing of unfairness or deceptiveness; the court would usually grant the FTC's request. This was because earlier Supreme Court decisions accorded no protection for purely commercial speech. This trend continued until the Court decided *Bigelow* v. *Virginia.*[5] In *Bigelow,* the Court reversed a conviction for violation of a Virginia statute that made advertising of abortion information a misdemeanor. The Court rejected the contention that the publication was unprotected because it was commercial. The decision was based on a fundamental right (right to abortion) as well, and the question whether purely commercial speech is protected was left open.

In *Virginia Pharmacy,*[6] the Court for the first time, dealt with the question of pure commercial speech and its protection. A Virginia statute made advertising of prescription drug price information by licensed pharmacists an unprofessional conduct. The challenge was not made by a pharmacist, but by prescription drug consumers. The Court recognized that dissemination of commercial information is vital to the American public:

> As to the particular consumer's interest in the free flow of commercial information, that interest may be as keen, if not keener by far, than his interest in the day's most urgent political debate. . . . So long as we preserve a predominantly free enterprise economy, the allocation of our resources in large measure will be made through numerous private decisions . . . even if the First Amendment were thought to be primarily an instrument to enlighten public decision making in a democracy, we could not say that the free flow of information does not serve that goal.

Even though commercial speech was given protection, the Court indicated that it is still subject to regulation. Time, place and manner restric-

---

5. Bigelow v. Virginia, 421 U.S. 809 (1975).
6. Virginia State Board of Pharmacy v. Virginia Citizens Consumer Council, 425 U.S. 748 (1976).

tions were allowed, even in traditional First Amendment cases when important Governmental interests were involved. Untruthful speech, commercial or otherwise, has never been protected for its own sake. With regard to deceptive or misleading commercial speech, the Court made it clear that "the First Amendment, as we construe it today, does not prohibit the State from insuring that the stream of commercial information flows cleanly as well as freely."

How this new development will affect the FTC's effort to regulate advertisements is an open question. The difference between truthful commercial speech and untruthful commercial speech may not be readily apparent in many situations. Judicial scrutiny will be invoked with increasing frequency in the Commission's decisions.

Truthful commercial speech cannot be regulated without weighing First Amendment interests against governmental interests. Proponents of the ban point to the special protection accorded to children in all fields of law. Reliance on different fields in child protection laws may be misplaced. These laws were made to deal with specific and immediate threats to the welfare of children. Obscenity was never a protected form of speech.

The problems involved in a total ban on advertisements to children are much more complicated. The rationality of a total ban is questionable when it is directed to children of all ages. Older children are supposed to have developed the understanding to distinguish program from message. Preschoolers, however, lack the skills to make such a distinction. But even there, all concerned are not in agreement as to the effect of advertisements. Proponents of the ban cite low level parent-child conflicts and development of psychological imbalances. But others argue that the parent-child conflicts in this respect are seldom intense or persistent. Moreover, they point out, positive learning experiences can result from this parent-child interaction. It is highly unlikely that courts would buy this argument and allow all messages to go unchecked.

Professor Thain recommends that the FTC should ban advertisements to children, based on the criteria the Commission developed when it dealt with rulemaking in cigarette advertising—whether it offends established concepts of fairness, whether it is immoral, unethical, oppressive or unscrupulous, and whether it injures competitors or consumers.[7]

Unfairness is at the root of the issue because children cannot be considered "miniature" adults. According to Piaget's widely accepted theory on children, childhood can be divided into three stages. The first stage is from birth of the child to two years of age, during which the child is primarily dependent on sensory-motor activity. The second stage lasts roughly from two to six years of age where the child cannot reason deductively or inductively and may heavily rely on intuition. From age six to

---

7. Thain, *Suffer the Hucksters to Come unto the Children?* 56 BOSTON U.L. REV. 651 (1976).

eleven, the child develops ability to extract abstract principles from specific experiences and the ability to reason deductively. When the child achieves this ability, childhood ends.

The major concern of activists has been the effect of advertisements on children aged two to six, commonly termed "preschoolers." Is it fair to direct sophisticated advertising technique to win over these preschoolers?

Perhaps this queston should be considered along with an additional question: What are the financial implications of such advertisements? Commercials for programs where children form the majority of the audience are mostly advertisements of breakfast cereals, snack foods, candy and toys. A study, based on 1970 data, showed that the three leading advertisers on children's television programs accounted for nearly 30 percent of the total revenues from such shows—nearly $24 million.

It should be noted that *Virginia Pharmacy* accords protection to commercial speech on the premise that such publication is necessary for the informed exercise of economic decisions. But here, advertisements are imposed upon children who are incapable of any such reasoned decison. Preschoolers do not even differentiate between program and nonprogram material. This might well take advertisements directed at younger children out of the scope of *Virginia Pharmacy.*

At least in the case of preschool children, any form of advertisements to them can thus be termed unfair within the meaning of Sections 5 and 12 of the FTC Act. An argument for such unfairness when dealing with children of all ages might lose its force. Older children do understand the persuasive nature of commercial messages.

Apart from all other considerations, one should consider the economic repercussions of a total ban on advertising as proposed by ACT and other groups. According to Gail E. Lees, it will have a deleterious effect on both the quantity and quality of children's programs. If the stations reduce the commercials from the present level of 9.5 minutes per hour to 6 minutes per hour, they could function profitably. A total ban probably would eliminate children's programs altogether.[8]

According to Professor Thain, the networks can weather such a ban just like they survived the ban on cigarette advertising. Most stations are highly profitable and therefore can accommodate loss of revenue. Moreover, stations do operate under license from the FCC and that requires them to air programs of public interest without regard to their funding.

There is another problem that cannot be ignored when a total ban on child-oriented advertising is contemplated. Regulatory efforts have to contend with the situation that children do nearly all their television viewing (84 percent) at times when adults make up a majority of viewers. Therefore, most of the advertisements aimed at children are directed to adults as well. A total ban on commercials with children in mind may be

---

8. Lees, *Unsafe for Little Ears? The Regulation of Broadcast Advertising to Children,* 25 U.C.L.A. LAW REV. 1131 (1978).

overbroad, and fall prey to constitutional attacks. Hence, any regulation of speech has to be narrowly tailored to proscribe only that speech with which it purports to deal.

In spite of the First Amendment developments regarding commercial speech, Reich is of the opinion that it should not affect the FTC's fencing in of violators.[9] The spirit of *Virginia Pharmacy* is to afford the buying public an unfettered flow of commercial information so that it can make informed choices. According to Reich, the Commission's rationale of proscribing unfair or deceptive business practices accomplishes the same objective. Deceptive commercial speech or lack of commercial speech might affect the economic decisions of the public. For example, a claim that a particular medicine will cure colds and other ailments, when it only stops bad breath, would certainly induce the public to buy it unnecessarily.

In this regard, the FTC has quite an arsenal of measures to proscribe deceptive practices. Moreover, compared to the buying public, the Commission has the expertise to investigate claims made in commercials. If the FTC staff determines a certain practice to be deceptive, it issues a complaint against the offender.[10] If the offender agrees to discontinue the practice, the FTC can negotiate a consent decree which becomes a cease and desist order binding on the offender, subject to civil penalties. If the complaint does not result in a consent decree, the staff can ask for an adjudicated cease and desist order. The Commission's decisions can be appealed to federal courts.

A drawback of this approach is that, in an adjudicated cease and desist order proceeding, the commercial in question can be proscribed only *after* the final order. This could be a long process and in that time the commercial would have run its normal course. Nevertheless, the specter of a concerted effort by the FTC to fence in several violators could persuade potential offenders into self-regulation.

The FTC could issue trade regulations to be complied with by the industry. These rules or industry guides should be very specific and narrowly stated. This approach would set a policy that would be uniform for everyone concerned. That the FTC has authority to issue such rules has been judicially determined. Through these rules, the FTC could set certain advertising standards. Where an advertised product has an undesirable side effect, the Commission could require affirmative disclosure of such possibilities. At least with regard to older children, these measures might prove to be effective and Constitutionally viable.

Any "fairness" approach to children's advertisements would invoke judicial challenges and yet this avenue is worth pursuing. The FCC did not consider product advertisement as a topic of grave public interest. Lees suggests that in light of *Virginia Pharmacy*, the FCC should reconsider that decision and cites the example of the effectiveness of anti-

---

9. Reich, *Consumer Protection and the First Amendment: A Dilemma for the FTC?*, 61 MINN. L. REV. 705, 722 (1977).
   10. 15 U.S.C. § 45(b) (1976).

smoking commercials on the level of smoking. The cure for bad speech may not be a ban but more speech. In view of the limited broadcast frequency spectrum and the government's licensing of it for public interest, the FCC can require the airing of opposing views on children's product advertisements.

No one can tell for certain what repercussions *Virginia Pharmacy* will have on the field of children's television. Perhaps there is no reason to be alarmed about the sudden protection accorded to commercial speech. Meaningful regulation is not ruled out, and as Reich has assessed, the FTC's efforts also lead to the same result. But the FTC can no longer act as the arbiter of what is good and what is not. Deceptiveness and unfairness have been hazy concepts to which the FTC gave meaning as the situation arose. There are signs that that era has come to an end.

Commentary

WITHIN A FEW LIMITS, such as defamation and obscenity, publishers can do what they like with their publications. If they oppose the democratic candidate for mayor, that candidate's name can be eliminated from the publication. If they hate golf, they can instruct their sports editor to forget the game exists. If they visualize thousands of little circles of family readers being offended by photos revealing the sex of naked animals, they can have their art department use an airbrush to render the animals sexless. The democrats, golfers, and artists on their staffs may rebel; readers may protest; a rival magazine may compete more successfully as a result; but the publishers' power in such cases is unmistakable.

This power existed at the time that the First Amendment was adopted. The ability of individuals to become part of the press then may have had more to do with whether they could read and write than whether they could compete with established newspapers.

But as time passes—as the United States grows in population to more than 225 million at present—many people believe they speak with the puniest of voices. How can the individual citizen compete with a publication or a broadcast station? The answer seems clear to Jacklin: access to the media for anyone who has a voice worth hearing.

Jacklin's position was supported earlier by Jerome Barron, a law professor who published in the June 1967 issue of the *Harvard Law Review* an article in which he argued that the press stifles unpopular and unorthodox views by closing them out. Barron called for "an interpretation of the First Amendment which focuses on the idea that restraining the hand of government is quite useless in assuring free speech if a restraint on access is effectively secured by private groups." In effect, Barron was proposing that anyone who has something to say should have the right to say it in the press. Failure of that right he considered an abridgment of free expression. Considering the concentration of mass communication in relatively few hands, and considering also the high cost of establishing a new medium of mass communication, Barron argued persuasively. It *is* a denial of effective expression if a spokesperson for a cause hopes to speak to an audience larger than a street corner crowd and finds the media closed.

However, when Barron argued before the United States Supreme Court that the *Miami Herald* should have printed a letter from a candidate for the Florida House of Representatives under a state statute creating a right of reply to press criticism for candidates, the Court found the statute to be an unconstitutional intrusion on the editorial process, *Miami Herald Publishing Co. v. Tornillo* (1974). Note that a year earlier, the Court had decided that individuals and groups had no right to purchase advertising time on radio and television stations to comment on public issues, *CBS, Inc. v. Democratic National Committee.* A paid right of access in broadcasting was therefore rejected by the Court in 1973, and a state-created access right for candidates was nullified in *Tornillo.* While a right of "reasonable access" was created by Congress in radio and television in Section 312(a)(7) of the Federal Communications Act of 1934 (see the Commentary in Chapter 10), access as a mandatory right for all seems to be a dead issue.

What happened to Jacklin's argument? Although published in 1975—after several years of work by Jacklin and his committee—only one station in the San Francisco Bay area still carries "free speech messages," although the concept has appeared in varied forms in other markets.

We can agree in principle with Jacklin, and yet wonder how a policy that conforms to Jacklin's guidelines could operate. The problem is much like the ancient one: we should be ruled by philosopher kings, but who is to choose them? Until such questions can be answered, we must limp along with the system we have.

Not everyone is as sanguine about the performance of cable access television as is Alderson. Consider the review by Brian Winston, staff writer, in the *Soho News* in 1981.

> Everybody in the wacky world of Public Access seems to know the ideological implications of the normal rules of television production. They are designed to prevent anybody but a few licensed professionals from expressing themselves on the box. Therefore, misaligned cameras taking out-of-kilter shots, reversing eyelines and actions are nothing so much as blows for freedom. This attitude, which seems to govern [Manhattan Cable] Channels C and D, is a bit like complaining of the sexist cast of the English language and proceeding to talk gibberish to overcome it. . . . None of this has anything to do with what Public Access could really mean and what for a number of years various people have been struggling to make it mean. The possibility of using cable television to reintegrate our scattered lives in some way

requires a cable system sensitive to that sort of work . . . that a majority of homes be wired . . . and some . . . real sense of community. Without these factors Public Access is likely to reduce itself to the endless, boring parade of manic egos . . . that we currently have before us on C and D.

Because it generally is uncensored, access programming can be robust and racy. It thus joins the sex and violence channels that have, according to some cable operators, attracted more interest than any other type of specialized programming.

It may be that adult programming will filter into a community more by means of access than by offering adult pay television services such as those described in Chapter 9. Why? Because as cities set forth requirements for cable systems they may insist on an uncensored access channel as part of the system but also insist that the operator not program an adult channel. So, while access in broadcasting is no longer an especially active idea, access may be the tail that wags the body of material ultimately to be found on the cable.

Conceptually, access comprehends an especially protected category of speech. Unlike obscene or defamatory speech, which generally is left unprotected by the First Amendment, access speech gets a boost by the First Amendment. It is especially protected, at least under the Barron theory, because it is a justified way to make good on the guarantees of the First Amendment in a world of social communications dominated by the mass media.

A similar claim of "special protection" can be made with respect to children's television. In 1980 the Federal Communication Commission's Special Task Force on Children's Television concluded that a "market failure" has occurred in commercial support of programs for young children. Advertisers do not support sufficient levels of programs for young viewers: then, only one weekday network program, CBS's "Captain Kangaroo," existed; today that program is only aired on weekends.

Because children are an important and sizable portion of the audience, programming to serve their needs should increase, according to the task force. Among the options considered was for the Federal Communication Commission to prescribe a set number of hours of children's programming per week a television station must carry.

Most people agree that if children are going to watch a lot of television—and they are—they should have at least some programs designed for their level of maturity. National public television's "Sesame Street" is the most celebrated children's program. But is there a quantifiable obligation as well on commercial broadcasters to meet daily needs of the child audience, even if there are no advertisers to pay for the programs? Like access speech, children's television would then become an especially protected type of expression.

Mathews's article focuses on a different part of the children's television controversy: even if some advertisers want to sponsor kid shows, and they always have, do the effects of this advertising on young children justify limiting or banning it? The Federal Trade Commission's childrens' advertising rulemaking, begun in 1978 to consider limiting or banning children's advertising, ended in a defeat for the original staff's theory: by 1981 a reconstituted staff had concluded that the difficulty of trying to ban certain commercials outweighed whatever unfairness was visited upon young viewers by such advertising.

What is significant here is that the 1974 FCC Children's Television Report had concluded that commercial sponsorship was an acceptable price to pay for children's programming. Broadcasters could not be expected to upgrade the amount and quality of this programming if they could not attempt to find sponsors for the programs.

But a different result might have been reached. Suppose the FTC had found that advertising to young children was deceptive and unfair and suppose that judgment had been sustained by the courts. Suppose the FCC then concluded that broadcasters had a duty to carry children's programs, and if the FTC said no ads, then too bad for broadcasters. Can a concept like especially protected speech—such as children's programming—ignore the marketplace realities this obligation entails?

With children's programs, we can again look to the new technologies to provide a fresh perspective. Of the various options considered by the FCC task force, one was to provide children's programs by new market players. Today at least one cable network provides a daily children's channel—Warner Amex's Nickelodeon.

Inclusion of this channel is a must for any new cable franchise proposal. Like Cable News Network, it is precisely the type of new service that a broadband technology like cable can offer without having to bump more profitable programming to meet a community's television needs. In the long run, as channel capacity expands through cable, we will be able to look to Nickelodeon and its competitors to meet the needs of kids. In the short term, lawyers and broadcasters will be faced with the knotty problem of how much programming for children is enough to satisfy the public interest criteria by which we grant use of broadcast spectrum.

WLR

13

Toward a True Marketplace for the Marketplace of Ideas

DANIEL L. BRENNER

IT HAS BEEN ESTIMATED that nearly one-half the productive labor in this country is dedicated to the related activities of gathering, processing, and interpreting information. The mass media are major players in the information industry. Take the newspaper business. According to the United States Department of Labor, it ranks first among large manufacturers, with 432,000 employees. It ranks ahead of steel, cars, and car products.

Large, perhaps, but in the architecture of the "Information Age" any newspaper is a pygmy when compared to the powerful American Telephone & Telegraph. In the coming years the newspaper and phone companies may find themselves locked in competition to provide information that consumers and businesses want. The controversy will not be fought out in newsprint or over phone lines, but on the video screen.

There, these information providers will be joined by industries that have long used video to deliver their products. Consider cable television, which uses wire, not broadcast spectrum, to deliver programming. By 1990 it is estimated that 50 percent of television homes will be wired with cable. Historically, cable has provided better reception of local stations and signals from distant locations. Satellite distribution has made it possible for cable systems to provide additional distant signals and specialized program services, such as all-movie, all-sports, or all-news channels not available over broadcast channels.

Cable's biggest competitive advantage is that it provides many more channels than other video delivery systems. Almost all cable systems have capacity for at least twelve channels; new and upgraded systems offer as many as fifty or more channels. And cable systems can provide for two-way services beyond video programming: shopping and bill-paying, access to computerized data banks, burglar alarm systems, and viewer polls.

Another new source of video signals in Multipoint Distribution Service (MDS). Multipoint Distribution Service signals are transmitted on microwave frequencies that require a special receiving antenna to convert the signal to frequencies used by conventional television sets. Originally intended for hotels and multiple dwellings, MDS has increasingly been used in private homes to deliver pay video services. A forthcoming service, Direct Broadcast Satellites (DBS), will deliver program signals directly from a satellite orbiting the earth to small dish antennas on home roofs or relay points. Additionally, lower-powered television stations could be added to urban areas where new full-power stations would cause unacceptable interference with existing stations.

And prerecorded programming, with its advantage of leaving the scheduling entirely up to the viewer, will grow in importance. Both video recorders and video disc players let consumers play prerecorded tapes or discs, recorders also allowing for off-the-air program viewing at a later time. This feature creates a "time diversity" for off-the-air shows not offered by other delivery systems. In addition, videotapes and discs allow individuals to view programs that might not be broadcast over the air or by cable systems because of their narrow or prurient appeal.

In this new environment the marketplace lies in the living room, bedroom, and kitchen, wherever a video display screen is found. Industries that once served vastly different needs will become head-to-head competitors for the eyes and ears of home audiences.

The prizes in the video sweepstakes are enormous. Up for grabs potentially is the mammoth national audience of television, newspaper and cable subscription fees, revenues from yellow-page and newspaper classified ads, even some of the United States Postal Service's business. How to frame a regulatory scheme that offers the best range of information services at the lowest prices poses an enormous challenge.

Some persons think that allowing the marketplace to determine the winners and losers as we do in other economic sectors is the best approach. Certainly there is precedent for this, both in economic and First Amendment terms. Some information providers have heretofore led lives relatively free of regulation. Such media as newspapers, video discs, and yellow-page publishers do not have to come to a Federal Communications Commission for the right to be in business. Others, such as broadcasters, have benefited from a policy of government protection through licensing, at least until the 1970s, based on the belief that the service they provided justified an economic vigilantism toward new video entrants. Still others, such as DBS and the locally franchised cable systems, do not yet have a developed regulatory expectation.

Do some generalized principles arise in a First Amendment analysis of this area? Professor Monroe Price, of the University of California School of Law, suggests in "Taming *Red Lion:* The First Amendment and Structural Approaches to Media Regulation," *Federal Communications Law Journal,* Spring 1979, that the twin general goals of diversity and access, with a minimum of contingent government intrusion, be included in any regulatory scheme. Consider these other principles, suggested by Price and others, to create a media structure more sensitive to First Amendment issues:

• Do not restrict the choice of video delivery system by how programs are funded: by direct payment, through advertising, or by other means. There should be no regulatory preference for advertiser- or distributor-supported programming over the programming consumers pay for directly.

- Encourage program access for independent producers and individuals on such broadband systems as cable by treating the service as a common carrier for certain purposes.
- Abandon policies that protect existing media over new competitors.
- Reduce restrictions on cross-ownership of new media by existing media owners where the effect is to inhibit the development of those new media.
- Require rate-regulated entrants (such as AT & T) to participate in new media industries only if they establish separate subsidiaries for nonrate-regulated activities or entirely divest rate-regulated from nonrate-regulated activities.

These principles are hotly contested by the industries that might suffer under their enforcement, but they constitute policy considerations that top the communications agenda in the 1980s.

To be specific for a moment, consider the goal of "access." It is unlikely that a commercial broadcaster will become regulated as a "common carrier" (like AT & T); the law says access to a telephone company's communications facilities must be offered to all on a nondiscriminatory basis. Expanding, if not full, First Amendment protection for radio and television, especially in light of deregulation at the FCC, makes a compulsory access scheme unlikely. A fee for use of spectrum might someday be imposed on broadcasters. But content regulations over commercial broadcasters designed to accomplish First Amendment ends are most unlikely, and so, too, a right of access.

As to local cable systems, as we saw in Chapter 12 the results of access are mixed. But the legal question is clear: Should cable systems like newspapers have no right of access guaranteed? Or should they work more like common carriers? Should cable systems be completely allowed, as is the case in broadcasting, to produce programs for any channel it distributes? So long as there is extra channel capacity to carry programs produced by others, there is no problem. Newcomers in programming can climb aboard. But saturated systems are already upon us, even among systems with dozens of channels. Will a cable system be entitled not merely to compete with a specialized cable channel but to replace it with its own more profitable service? Would local governments, as the principal franchising authorities, be wise to categorize systems as partly common carriers before the program rights of the cable system operator are established? More generally, why does it make sense to include a system operator within the fold of the First Amendment's protected press?

The issues are more than philosophical. A ferocious fight has already erupted among information providers and carriers to get their services into homes. Some will want to be conveyers, like the first cable companies that desired nothing more than to retransmit by wire off-the-air broadcast signals. Others will want to create programming. Some already do both: the two largest pay cable programming services, Home Box Office and Showtime Entertainment, are also subsidiaries of large multiple system operators.

There are other issues besides deciding who gets what slice of the video delivery market. As noted earlier, individual broadcasters have sought to protect themselves against new competitors, either from new entry within the industry or from new services like cable, claiming that their ability to serve the public would be jeopardized. Consider, then, an editorial in the *New York Times,* May 4, 1981, concerning AT & T's proposed electronic yellow pages to be sold to the home video market:

> What newspapers most want now is not a guarantee of survival in their present form but a public policy that recognizes two vital public interests: that the information business remain open to the largest possible number of practitioners and that the advertising revenues so essential to independent news-gathering not be siphoned off by other enterprises.

As I interpret this, it means: let anyone enter the "Information Age." But don't let new entrants, particularly the phone companies, dip into the classified advertising or display advertising revenues of newspapers to finance the ventures.

It is not as crass an argument as I have made it seem. What if the advertising revenues of newspapers shifted to electronic yellow-pages so that the revenues were no longer used to support the worldwide news bureaus of the *Washington Post* or the *New York Times* but to underwrite free electronic games and trivia contests carried on a home video terminal system supplied by telephone companies? The papers could increase the cost of subscriptions to offset advertising losses, but would they be able to cover the entire loss? Should the government nip a telephone company's ambitions to get into the home video field because if it fails to, the printed press—the one medium we know existed when the First Amendment was adopted—might be annihilated?

What will emerge in the next ten years is a world of competing systems offered by existing television entrepreneurs and newcomers to videolike newspapers. No doubt the importance of home based media will grow. Will this new power justify greater content regulation? Recall that the *Pacifica* Court decision (Chapter 9) justified content control based on the "intrusive" power of the media. That intrusiveness will surely intensify as the functions performed by home video service expand.

Speaking in 1981 to the Telecommunications Policy Research Conference—an annual law/economics meeting held for the benefit of communications policymakers—Senior Judge David L. Bazelon reminded listeners to distinguish between market power used to gain an oligopoly in the production of news and entertainment and the *Pacifica*-like power inherent in a medium. He urged policymakers to confront economic power on its own turf, not chase the issue into "the hoary swamps of government regulation of speech."

I believe that the marketplace ambitions of, say, a Gannett Corporation or AT & T should be reviewed under traditional antitrust theory—

guarding against wrongly acquired market shares or predatory trade practices—and not labeled as detrimental simply because of the power that results to the company in terms of larger speech opportunities. Collaterally, we should develop policies that induce more competitors, not policies that try to regulate the speech of existing competitors.

In the debate over who should be allowed to provide information services, a company's "power" will sometimes be cast in economic terms, other times in free speech terms. There is an important difference. As you consider who should be allowed to do what with our technological plenty, bear in mind the distinction of these two approaches.

Still, for some the issue cannot be cast in economic terms exclusively. Freedom of expression is an essential part of our form of government, and concentration of media interests can pose special problems to this freedom. Does freedom of expression change when the number of independent voices shrinks because of concentrated ownership?

Freedom of speech and a competitive marketplace seem to go hand in hand. If the market becomes more concentrated, should the government intervene to assure opportunities for more voices? Or is intervention, even in the name of assuring diversity, a well-intentioned abridgment of media freedom condemned absolutely by the First Amendment?

This conundrum is reflected as well as anywhere by Judge Learned Hand's observation in *United States* v. *Associated Press* (1943) that the interest in disseminating news from different sources

> is closely akin to, if indeed it is not the same as, the interest protected by the First Amendment; it presupposes that right conclusions are more likely to be gathered out of a multitude of tongues, than through any kind of authoritative selection. To many this is, and always will be folly, but we have staked upon it our all.

INDEX

ABC News, 130
Abrams, Floyd, 145–46
ABSCAM tapes, 187–88
Absolutist view of First Amendment, 103,
    105. *See also* First Amendment
Access to common carriers, 274
Access to media. *See* Right of access to
    media
"Actual malice" (required for press
    liability), 98, 214, 245–46
Adams, John, 16
Administrative agency discretion, 208–9
Advertising, 191–200
    children's, 262–68
    cigarette, 201, 266
    claims by advertisers, 196–97
    disclosures, 267–68
    effects, 198
    and First Amendment, 193–96
    market approach, 198–99
    message of copy, 192–93, 196–97
    typography, 192
Agnew, Spiro, 252–53
Alberts v. *California*, 172
Alcorn v. *Mitchell*, 84
Alderson, Jeremy Weir, 248
Alien and Sedition Acts, 14, 125
Allocation scheme of 1952, 61
All the President's Men, 76–77
Alpert, Hollis, 157, 163
Aman, Reinhold, 190
American Bar Association
    Canons of Ethics, 147
    *Standards Relating to Fair Trial and Free
        Press*, 135, 140
Anderson, Jack, 220
Antitrust law and the media, 275–76
Apicella v. *McNeil Laboratories, Inc.*,
    220–21
Associated Press, 130
AT & T, 149, 272, 274, 275
Atlantic Monthly, 245–46
Atomic Energy Act, 132

Bailey, F. Lee, 149
Banzhaf v. *FCC*, 194, 201, 202
Barber v. *Time, Inc.*, 105
Barron, Jerome, 268
Barrow Report, 61
"Battlestar Galactica," 222
Bazelon, David L., 35, 186, 194, 205, 275
Bazemore v. *Savannah Hospital*, 91
"Bedtime for Bonzo," 247

Bell, James F., 183
Bender, Paul, definition of privacy, 100
Beneficial Corp. v. *FTC*, 192–93
Berlin v. *E. C. Publications, Inc.*, 235
Bernius, Robert C., 144
Bernstein, Carl, 76
Bickel, Alexander, 124, 142
Bigelow v. *Virginia*, 264
Bigler, Tom, 188
Black, Justice Hugo, 4, 32, 122, 125, 137,
    153
Blackmun, Justice Harry, 128–29, 178,
    215
Blackstone, Sir William, 125
Bleinstein v. *Donaldson Lithographing Co.*,
    238
Bloustein, Edward J., 82, 94
    definition of privacy, 100, 103–6
    role of privacy and the individual
        100–101
Bogart, Joe, 33
Book of Daniel, The, 104
Botein, Mike, 260
Bradlee, Benjamin, 189
Brandeis, Justice Louis, 16, 27–28, 29,
    115, 159, 223
Brandywine-Main Line Radio, Inc. v. *FCC*,
    200, 205
Branzburg, Paul, 69, 72
Branzburg v. *Hayes*, 15, 20, 21, 26, 77, 95
Brennan, Justice William, 122, 127, 135,
    145, 153, 159, 172, 178
Brenner, Daniel L., 175, 214
Bridges v. *California*, 137
Briscoe v. *Reader's Digest Association*, 106
Bristol-Meyers Co., 196
British licensing laws, 124–25
Broadcasters as corporations, 252
Bryan, J. Stewart III, 144
Burger, Chief Justice Warren, 128, 143,
    152, 156, 161, 173
Burnside, Ambrose, 125

Cable television, 272
    access channels, 255–61
    and FCC, 55–56, 59
    R-rated channels, 187
    specialized channels, 61, 271, 274
Caldwell, Earl, 69
Cantrell v. *Forest City Publishing Co.*, 98,
    105
Cardin, Pierre, 222
Cardozo, Justice Benjamin, 172

DANIEL L. BRENNER is legal assistant to the chairman, Federal Communications Commission. Prior to holding this position he was an attorney with the law firm of Wilmer, Cutler & Pickering, Washington, D.C., where he specialized in communications law. He participated, on behalf of one of the three commercial television networks, in the Federal Trade Commission children's television advertising rulemaking and he has participated in numerous Federal Communications Commission proceedings. He attended Dartmouth College and holds the B.A., M.A., and J.D. degrees from Stanford University. He has been lecturer in mass media law at Stanford, and lecturer in jurisprudence as well as lecturer for the Program for Advanced Studies in Federal Regulation for the Washington School of Law, American University, Washington, D.C.

WILLIAM L. RIVERS is Paul C. Edwards professor of communication, Stanford University, where he was given the Walter J. Gores Faculty Achievement Award for Excellence in Teaching. He is a noted author of many books and articles in educational and political journals, and was given in 1966 the Sigma Delta Chi Distinguished Research Award for the influential *The Opinionmakers*. His career includes service as columnist and correspondent for several major publications; he has been consultant and adviser to private corporations and public agencies. He holds the B.A. and M.A. degrees from Louisiana State University and the Ph.D. degree in political science from American University, Washington, D.C.